3/7

ALSO BY DAVID A. NICHOLS

Eisenhower 1956: The President's Year of Crisis—
Suez and the Brink of War

Lincoln and the Indians: Civil War Policy and Politics

A Matter of Justice: Eisenhower and
the Beginning of the Civil Rights Revolution

IKE AND McCARTHY

*Dwight Eisenhower's Secret Campaign
Against Joseph McCarthy*

David A. Nichols

SIMON & SCHUSTER
New York   London   Toronto   Sydney   New Delhi

Simon & Schuster
1230 Avenue of the Americas
New York, NY 10020

First Simon & Schuster hardcover edition March 2017

SIMON & SCHUSTER and colophon are registered trademarks
of Simon & Schuster, Inc.

For information about special discounts for bulk purchases,
please contact Simon & Schuster Special Sales at 1-866-506-1949
or business@simonandschuster.com.

The Simon & Schuster Speakers Bureau can bring authors to
your live event. For more information or to book an event, contact
the Simon & Schuster Speakers Bureau at 1-866-248-3049 or visit
our website at www.simonspeakers.com.

Interior design by Lewelin Polanco

Manufactured in the United States of America

10 9 8 7 6 5 4 3 2 1

Library of Congress Cataloging-in-Publication Data

Names: Nichols, David A. (David Allen), 1939– author.
Title: Ike and McCarthy : Dwight Eisenhower's secret campaign against Joseph
    McCarthy / David A. Nichols.
Description: First Simon & Schuster hardcover edition. | New York : Simon &
    Schuster, 2017. | Includes bibliographical references and index.
Identifiers: LCCN 2016037570| ISBN 9781451686609 | ISBN 1451686609
Subjects: LCSH: Eisenhower, Dwight D. (Dwight David), 1890–1969. |
    McCarthy, Joseph, 1908–1957. | United States—Politics and government—
    1953–1961. | Anti-communist movements—United States—History—
    20th century. | Cold War—Social aspects—United States. | Eisenhower,
    Dwight D. (Dwight David), 1890–1969—Influence. | Presidents—United
    States—Biography.
Classification: LCC E836 .N5295 2017 | DDC 973.921092—dc23 LC record
    available at https://lccn.loc.gov/2016037570

ISBN 978-1-4516-8660-9
ISBN 978-1-4516-8662-3 (ebook)

To William Bragg Ewald, Jr., and Fred I. Greenstein,
pioneers a generation ago in the study of Eisenhower and McCarthy

CONTENTS

PREFACE

Beginning in 1950, Wisconsin's junior senator, Joseph R. McCarthy, threw the United States into turmoil with his reckless, unsubstantiated charges that a variety of citizens, especially government employees, were Soviet agents. McCarthy's disregard for the truth, his insatiable appetite for headlines, and his willingness to damage reputations turned "McCarthyism" into an enduring epithet in our political language.

Yet by the end of 1954, McCarthy's political influence had been essentially destroyed. How did that happen? The answer—fully told for the first time in this book—is that Dwight D. Eisenhower made it happen.

Ironically, in 1953, due to Eisenhower's election, McCarthy acquired a new platform for his crusade. The Republicans held a one-vote majority in the Senate. As a result McCarthy was appointed chair of the Government Operations Committee and its permanent investigative subcommittee. In that capacity, the senator subpoenaed witnesses, conducted one-senator hearings, accused witnesses of guilt by association and labeled as "obviously communist" anyone who dared to invoke constitutional protections against self-incrimination.

In 1953, the nation was still at war in Korea and recovering from the traumas of depression and World War II. The Cold War with the Soviet Union created a climate of fear that was the lifeblood of McCarthyism, especially the fear of subversion. But in January 1954, that began to change. McCarthy's prestige was at its zenith, with a Gallup Poll approval rating of 50 percent favorable, 29 percent unfavorable. But Eisenhower had concluded that the senator was more than a nuisance; he was a threat to the president's foreign policy goals, to his legislative program, and to his party's and his own electoral prospects.[1]

So Eisenhower did something breathtaking and dangerous; he launched a clandestine operation designed to wrap a scandal around the neck of a prestigious US senator in the president's own party in an election year. That is what the 1954 Army-McCarthy hearings, lasting almost two months, were really about.[2]

THE CONVENTIONAL WISDOM

The standard explanations for McCarthy's political demise are well known: McCarthy, an alcoholic, did himself in; he was damaged by Edward R. Murrow's legendary *See It Now* television program; his reputation was tarnished by the unsympathetic glare of the television cameras and by his confrontation with the wily Boston attorney Joseph Nye Welch at the Army-McCarthy hearings. In this conventional version, the final nail in McCarthy's political coffin was the censure vote by the US Senate on December 2, 1954, which McCarthy lost 67 to 22.

In recent years, pro-McCarthy revisionists have attempted to repair the senator's reputation by arguing that his political enemies destroyed him to cover up Soviet espionage in the US government. Eisenhower took the possibility of subversion seriously but firmly believed that his methods would be more effective and equitable than McCarthy's demagogic tactics.[3]

In 1984, William Ewald published a book called *Who Killed Joe McCarthy?* Ewald drew on an immense cache of documents that Fred Seaton, the assistant secretary of defense, had collected on President Eisenhower's orders during the 1954 Army-McCarthy hearings. Seaton possessed thousands of pages of letters, phone transcripts, memoranda, and documents that he had taken with him when he became secretary of the interior and—when he left the government—had hauled home to Nebraska. Ewald, who worked for Seaton at the Interior Department, recalled Seaton pointing to a locked file and saying "I'll never open that until you-know-who tells me to," referring to Eisenhower. When Seaton died, his "Eyes Only" file was donated to the Dwight D. Eisenhower Presidential Library in Abilene, Kansas, where I have reviewed virtually every page. In addition, I have had access to documents declassified since Ewald and other leading authors on McCarthy published their books in the 1980s.[4]

Joseph McCarthy's senatorial correspondence has been sealed for the lifetime of his daughter. But my objective is to tell the Eisenhower story that has been so long neglected by historians.[5]

This is a book about a particular era in US history—a time when power brokers embraced attitudes and behaviors unacceptable today. Attitudes regarding race, gender, and homosexuality have changed but, in the 1950s, gays and their relationships were not just denigrated, they were openly persecuted. Just the rumor—not the fact—that a government official was homosexual could cost that person a job. Homosexuals were widely perceived to be security risks, subject to blackmail by communists. As the reader will discover, the Eisenhower administration reflected the prejudice and discriminatory practices of the era.

This is a story about strategic deception, a realm in which Dwight Eisenhower was demonstrably expert. In 1944, the Allies under Supreme Commander Dwight Eisenhower successfully fooled the German leadership about when and where the largest military expeditionary force in human history would land in Europe. Operation Fortitude involved fake armies, dummy landing craft and airfields, fraudulent radio transmissions, and misleading leaks through diplomatic channels and double agents. Eisenhower understood that carefully planned, rigorously implemented deception could confuse an enemy until he makes a mistake; then he can be ambushed. That, politically, is what Eisenhower did to McCarthy. Only a half-dozen trusted aides knew what was really happening. Others—including most of the era's great reporters—missed the story.[6]

Much of the conventional wisdom includes the enduring myth about the Eisenhower presidency—that Ike was a disengaged, grandfatherly president more interested in playing golf than in the effective exercise of leadership. That legend—now thoroughly discredited by two decades of intensive research—was initially generated by historians who never forgave the popular general for defeating Adlai Stevenson in 1952. But in part, Ike was the author of his own myth. He was obsessive about protecting the Oval Office from anything controversial.

In particular, critics grumble that Eisenhower failed to speak out about the great domestic issues of his time: civil rights and McCarthyism. His detractors depict him as downright cowardly in his response to the Red-baiting senator. Many would agree with the columnist Joseph Alsop, who, in 1954, after listening to an Eisenhower news conference statement intended to counter McCarthy, exclaimed, "Why, the yellow son of a bitch!"[7]

Ike had not won the war in Europe by making speeches. He did not believe that presidential rhetoric would damage McCarthy. History shows that presidential oratory rarely results in historic change; transformative progress is most possible when a president, faced with a crisis, seizes the opportunity to exercise leadership; consider Abraham Lincoln and the Civil War or Franklin D. Roosevelt and the Great Depression. However, pundits persist in rating presidents for their skillful use of the "bully pulpit."[8]

Complaints that Eisenhower took too long to act against McCarthy are contrary to the facts. Any effort to destroy McCarthy during 1953 would probably have failed. There were eight to twelve senators who frequently supported McCarthy's positions on communist subversion; therefore, the president lacked an anti-McCarthy majority. Though Democrats supported the president on most foreign policy issues, leaders such as Lyndon B. Johnson delighted in treating McCarthy as "a Republican problem."[9]

President Harry Truman had openly denounced McCarthy for three years, but his attacks had only enhanced the senator's prestige; Ike ruined him in half that time. The Eisenhower operation against McCarthy in 1954 was not without its glitches. The general understood that in war or political conflict, a commander must constantly adjust a strategic mission to new realities. He often repeated the maxim "Plans are worthless, but planning is everything." [10]

In this case, the planning involved Eisenhower's rigorous delegation of operations to a half-dozen trusted subordinates. Those men were expected, like foot soldiers in a war, to put their lives and reputations on the line to protect the president and extinguish McCarthy's influence. Dwight Eisenhower's deceptive operation, mediated through his trusted lieutenants, "killed" Joe McCarthy.

PROLOGUE

Friday, October 3, 1952, Milwaukee, Wisconsin. The Eisenhower-for-President motorcade was preparing to drive to the Milwaukee Arena, where General Eisenhower would climax a long day of campaigning with a 9:00 p.m. speech.

The candidate had decreed that no candidate running for office would ride with him and Mrs. Eisenhower. Douglas Price, an aide to Eisenhower who had organized the motorcade, recalled that the decision reflected "Eisenhower's disdain" for Wisconsin Senator Joseph R. McCarthy. The senator from Wisconsin had not been just banned from the general's car; he had been assigned to car number six, behind lower-ranking Wisconsin Republican officials—a transparent snub. Price was alarmed when he saw McCarthy "bolt out of car number six," walking briskly toward Eisenhower's car. But Price was relieved when he saw the senator "shoulder his way into a car behind Ike's car."[1]

It had been a difficult day for the candidate. Because of his dislike of McCarthy, he had tried to avoid campaigning in Wisconsin. But he had been pressured to do so by the Republican National Committee, which was concerned about winning Wisconsin's electoral votes. Ike was forced to campaign with the senator all day long. His brother Milton said that Ike "loathed McCarthy as much as any human being could loath another." Eisenhower deemed McCarthy to be "a curse on the American scene, both domestically and in the world."[2]

THE RISE OF JOE MCCARTHY

While he was president of Columbia University and, later, as commander of the North Atlantic Treaty Organization (NATO) in Paris, Eisenhower had observed McCarthy's rise. The Soviet occupation of Eastern Europe, the communist takeover of China in 1949, and the North Korean invasion of South Korea in 1950 had reinforced the public's fear of a global communist conspiracy.

For voters, the specter of spies in their midst was especially frightening. In August 1948, Whittaker Chambers, a former communist, had alleged that Alger Hiss, a former adviser to President Roosevelt, had spied for the Soviets. Hiss was eventually convicted of perjury, due in part to efforts by California senator Richard M. Nixon, Ike's subsequent vice presidential running mate. On February 3, 1950, British authorities arrested Dr. Klaus Fuchs, who had worked on the atom bomb in the United States, for channeling nuclear secrets to the Soviet Union.

Six days after Fuchs's arrest, McCarthy delivered a speech at the Republican Women's Club in Wheeling, West Virginia. The senator announced that he had "here in my hand" the names of 205 communists in the State Department. That he did not actually have those names did not trouble him. When repeatedly asked for them, he dissembled, finally reducing the number to 57. William Ewald wrote that, from Wheeling onward, McCarthy presided over "a permanent floating press conference. Lights, cameras, microphones followed him everywhere."[3]

In 1951, McCarthy attacked George C. Marshall, Eisenhower's wartime boss and military mentor, who had served President Truman as secretary of state and defense. On June 14, on the floor of the Senate, McCarthy effectively charged Marshall with treason. "It was Marshall," the senator intoned repeatedly, who had supported

Josef Stalin's demands at the postwar conferences, delivered China to the communists, and drawn the dividing line at the 38th parallel in Korea, setting the stage for the North Korean invasion. McCarthy accused Marshall of spearheading "a conspiracy of infamy so black that, when it is finally exposed, its principals shall be forever deserving of the maledictions of all honest men." McCarthy converted that speech into a book entitled *America's Retreat from Victory: The Story of George Catlett Marshall.*[4]

Eisenhower was incensed about McCarthy's assault on his colleague. On August 22, 1952, at a news conference in Denver, the general was asked about charges that George Marshall was a traitor. He rose from his chair, marched to the center of the room and declared, "There was nothing of disloyalty in General Marshall's soul. . . . If he was not a perfect example of patriotism and loyal servant of the United States, I never saw one." He concluded, "I have no patience with anyone who can find in his record of service for this country anything to criticize."[5]

On October 2, Eisenhower campaigned across Illinois, arriving in Peoria that afternoon, preparing to campaign in Wisconsin. Earlier that day, a plane carrying Governor Walter Kohler of Wisconsin and Senator McCarthy touched down in Peoria. That evening, Ike reluctantly agreed to meet with McCarthy in his hotel room. He chose not to reveal what was said in that meeting. Two aides, Tom Stephens and Kevin McCann, sat nearby. Stephens recalled hearing nothing, but McCann, years later, near death, thought he remembered that "the air turned blue" and that he had never heard the general "so cold bloodedly skin a man." That account is open to question. Wisconsin was a pivotal state in the campaign, with twelve electoral votes. However much Ike detested McCarthy, he was unlikely to have confronted the senator so harshly prior to campaigning with him the next day. When McCarthy emerged from the meeting, a *New York Times* reporter, William Lawrence, asked him what had happened. "We had a very, very pleasant conversation," McCarthy responded, noting that he planned to introduce the general the next day in Appleton, the senator's hometown. However, in

Appleton, following McCarthy's introduction, Eisenhower made no mention of McCarthy or support for the senator's reelection campaign. That foreshadowed his strategy as president: he would refuse to use McCarthy's name in public.[6]

A REGRETTABLE DECISION

As his car moved through the streets the night of October 3, Eisenhower was still smarting from a painful experience on the campaign train that afternoon. Aware of his animosity toward McCarthy, Governor Kohler had asked to see an advance copy of his speech. Reading it, he discovered a paragraph—seventy-four words long—praising the patriotism of George C. Marshall.

Eisenhower was looking forward to sticking a rhetorical thumb in the senator's eye as McCarthy sat on stage in Milwaukee. The paragraph was simple and straightforward, noting that there had been "charges of disloyalty" against Marshall and concluding "I know him, as a man and a soldier, to be dedicated with singular selflessness and the profoundest patriotism to the service of America." Kohler feared that offending the senator could cost Eisenhower the state's electoral votes. He quickly enlisted allies, including Sherman Adams, Ike's chief aide on the campaign train, and convinced Adams that including the paragraph would reap more trouble than it was worth.

Adams arranged a meeting with Eisenhower. After listening to the argument, Ike interrupted, "Are you telling me this paragraph should come out?" "Yes," responded Adams. "Take it out," Eisenhower snapped. When Gabriel Hauge, a speechwriter, accosted the candidate to confirm the news, Ike growled an angry "Yes!" Eisenhower, Hauge recalled, "was purple down to the root of his neck, and glowering."[7]

An experienced world leader but an inexperienced party politician, Eisenhower capitulated, failing to express support for the man who had made him a wartime leader. Fred Seaton, the Nebraska publisher handling the press for the campaign, had been unaware of Ike's decision to drop the seventy-four words. He had already hinted

to *New York Times* reporter William Lawrence that a paragraph praising Marshall would be in the address.[8]

That night, Eisenhower delivered a fervent cold warrior's speech,
sounding much like McCarthy. He deplored how communism had
"insinuated itself into our schools, our public forums, some of our
news channels, some of our labor unions, and—most terrifyingly—
into our Government itself." He decried subversion in "virtually
every department, every agency, every bureau, every section of our
Government." He castigated a government run by men who "con-
doned the surrender of whole nations to an implacable enemy," with
that enemy "infiltrating our most secret counsels." Those who had
allowed this to happen, he declared, were guilty of "treason itself."
After the speech, Eisenhower tried to avoid McCarthy but McCarthy aggressively pushed into the general's presence and forced him
to shake hands.[9]

The next morning, William Lawrence's report in *The New York
Times* stated that although Ike had been unenthusiastic about campaigning with McCarthy, "General Eisenhower did bow to the Wisconsin Senator's urging and eliminate from his Milwaukee speech
tonight a defense of his old friend and chief, General of the Army
George C. Marshall." According to Lawrence, Eisenhower had informed McCarthy at their Peoria meeting of his intent to praise
Marshall. McCarthy had allegedly told Eisenhower that "he had no
particular objection to General Eisenhower's saying anything he
wished to say, but he believed a defense of General Marshall could
be made better before another audience."[10]

McCarthy himself was undoubtedly the source of that false report. The implication was devastating: that McCarthy had personally
persuaded Eisenhower to betray his former mentor and superior.
Ike never forgot that humiliation. For decades, historians assumed
that this episode proved Eisenhower's cowardice in the face of Mc-
Carthyism, when the cause was actually Ike's political naiveté.

On November 4, Eisenhower won the Electoral College 442
to 89, carrying thirty-nine of the forty-eight states, including Wisconsin.

STAFFING IKE'S POLITICAL ARMY

Eisenhower knew that at some point he would have to deal with McCarthy; initially, he had other priorities. His longtime practice of selecting a small group of trusted subordinates to carry out special, often confidential, assignments would eventually pay off. Those men, important operatives during the campaign, would become Eisenhower's political foot soldiers during his presidency. They included Sherman Adams, a former New Hampshire governor who became Ike's chief of staff; Attorney General Herbert Brownell, Jr., a New York attorney who had played a large role in engineering Eisenhower's nomination; Brownell's deputy, William Rogers, another New York attorney; John Foster Dulles ("Foster" to Ike), secretary of state and a former policy adviser to New York Governor Thomas E. Dewey; and former Massachusetts Senator Henry Cabot Lodge, Jr. ("Cabot" to Ike), a major organizer of the Eisenhower for President movement. Lodge was appointed US representative to the United Nations and would serve as a confidential political adviser. James Hagerty, Dewey's former press secretary, became Eisenhower's spokesman and confidant in dealing with McCarthy. Eventually, Ike would recruit Fred Seaton to serve in the Pentagon. Those men shared Eisenhower's negative view of Joe McCarthy.

Ike also brought onboard General Wilton B. Persons ("Jerry" to Ike). He had served on Eisenhower's staff during the war and then on the general's NATO staff. Persons would be the White House's chief congressional liaison, accountable to Sherman Adams but often working directly with the president. A conservative Alabaman respected by the Republican right wing, including McCarthy, Persons would serve as the protector of the fragile one-vote Republican majority in the Senate.

Eisenhower was ready to govern. But he would never live down the egregious decision he had made to eliminate seventy-four words of praise for George Marshall from his speech on October 3, 1952.

PART 1
1953: PRIORITIES

CHAPTER 1

THE FIRST CONFRONTATION

"Nothing else mattered half as much as Joe McCarthy." That was Sherman Adams's recollection of the mood of the Eisenhower White House staff in 1953 and 1954. In that climate, numerous historians have blithely assumed that Eisenhower dithered while McCarthy's victims suffered and that Ike's inaction constituted cowardice in response to the demagogue's assault on civil liberties.[1]

EISENHOWER'S PRIORITIES

The reality was more complex. Though the White House staff soon split into factions over how to deal with McCarthy, the new president was not so conflicted. Eisenhower believed in setting priorities, and his paramount priority was preventing another world war. That meant ending the Korean War as quickly as possible. He sought to blend a political party rusty at the art of governing with a determined effort to calm the fears of internal subversion.

Ike saw Joe McCarthy as a symptom, not a cause. The public's fears could not be defused by attacking the senator himself, only by addressing underlying realities. The new president sought credibility with the American people as their premier defender against enemies, both foreign and domestic. That task would consume most of his first year in office. Once done, if need be, the issue of Joe McCarthy could be more directly addressed.

Ike knew he was vulnerable to McCarthy's "guilt-by-association" demagoguery. Following the war, as military governor of the US occupation zone in Germany, Eisenhower had necessarily cultivated warm relationships with communists and Soviet leaders. His friends fretted constantly about whether McCarthy might exploit those associations. However, Eisenhower believed that prematurely addressing the McCarthy threat would probably backfire.[2]

Eisenhower devised a simple prescription for dealing with Joe McCarthy in 1953: *ignore him*—at least in public. The senator, he wrote in his diary, "is, of course, so anxious for the headlines that he is prepared to go to any extremes in order to secure some mention of his name in the public press." He concluded, "Nothing will be so effective in combating his particular kind of trouble-making as to ignore him. This he cannot stand."[3]

Hence, Eisenhower refused to use McCarthy's name in public. He steadfastly maintained that commitment, to the consternation of friends and critics who implored him to denounce the senator. His approach was not as passive as it appeared; it was designed to get under McCarthy's skin. To Ike, the most insulting stance he could take toward McCarthy was to say, in effect, "You don't really matter."

Ike believed that McCarthy wanted to run for president in 1956. He did not intend to let that happen. There would be time in 1954, once the new administration was well established, to more directly address McCarthy's threat to any plans Eisenhower had to run for a second term.[4]

MCCARTHY'S CONGRESS

Eisenhower, who knew the British system intimately, understood that he was not a prime minister. He could not shape or even marginally influence the organization of the 83rd Congress. The Republicans settled their leadership issues by January 2, 1953, nearly three weeks before Eisenhower's inauguration. None of the top leaders in the Senate—Majority Leader Robert Taft of Ohio, President Pro Tempore Styles Bridges of New Hampshire, and Republican Policy Committee Chairman William F. Knowland of California—was an Eisenhower loyalist. Taft was the man Eisenhower had defeated for the Republican presidential nomination, the man regarded as the likely nominee until Ike declared his candidacy. The conventional wisdom is that Ike and Taft became good friends in 1953; however, like most political rivals, they papered over their differences with a superficial civility. Most important, Taft, as majority leader, controlled appointments to Senate committees and therefore could define McCarthy's role in the new Congress.[5]

Joe McCarthy rode into Washington, DC, in January 1953, committed to weeding out communist villains in every corner of government. Taft granted McCarthy precisely what he wanted; the chairmanship of the Government Operations Committee and therefore control of its Permanent Subcommittee on Investigations. McCarthy exploited his new status immediately. He announced that Roy M. Cohn, an assistant US attorney for the Southern District of New York, would serve as chief counsel for the investigative subcommittee. Cohn, a twenty-five-year-old legal prodigy, had received his law degree from Columbia University at the age of nineteen, too young to take the bar examination. By 1953, he was an experienced investigator and had assisted in the prosecution of Julius and Ethel Rosenberg, who had been sentenced to death for espionage. At Cohn's insistence, McCarthy added G. David Schine, the handsome son of a wealthy New York family, as an unpaid "chief consultant." Schine's only credential was a superficially written six-page pamphlet, "Definition of Communism," that had been placed in the rooms of his family's hotels. Attorney General Herbert Brownell recalled that the two men were quickly observed to be "inseparable."[6]

Dwight Eisenhower could control none of this. Furthermore, the Republican Party had only a one-vote majority—48 to 47 with 1 independent—in the Senate. That was not a real majority because the conservative wing of the party numbered eight to twelve senators, depending upon the issue. The Republican margin in the

House was also fragile—221 to 211. If he wanted to get anything important through Congress, Eisenhower would have to placate the anticommunist stalwarts in both houses.[7]

The Senate Rules Committee approved a fund of $200,000 for McCarthy's subcommittee—double the previous year's budget. The *New York Times* editors opined that the Senate had delivered "what amounts to a vote of confidence in Senator McCarthy."[8]

THE EISENHOWER ERA BEGINS

For Eisenhower, preparing the inaugural address was a tense experience. The speech endured nine drafts—really more, given Ike's penchant for penciled editing. He wanted "a high-level talk" that would neither attack the Democrats nor saber rattle toward the Soviets, focused on the "question of free men" more than "the current world situation." He wrestled with "how to do it without becoming too sermon-like."[9]

At his inauguration on January 20, Eisenhower recited the difficulties the nation had endured; depression, world war, and conflict in Korea. Missing, except by allusion, was any mention of communism or the Soviet Union. Nor did he say anything about the threat of internal subversion—Senator McCarthy's agenda. His address was a call not to arms but, in a favorite phrase he used on other occasions, to "waging peace."[10]

The next day Eisenhower arrived at the Oval Office. He recorded in his diary, "Plenty of worries and difficult problems. But such has been my portion for a long time." This day felt "like a continuation of all I've been doing since July '41." Not quite; Ike was not experienced in party politics. True, he had demonstrated the capacity to cope with powerful, sometimes difficult personalities, including Douglas MacArthur, Franklin Roosevelt, Winston Churchill, and George Patton; but he had never dealt with a politician like Joe McCarthy.[11]

There were already signs of trouble for Eisenhower's Pentagon appointments. Eisenhower's nominee for secretary of defense,

Charles "Engine Charlie" Wilson, the former president of General Motors, had run into trouble in the confirmation process. He had agreed to sever his ties with the company but retained stock that, if sold, would result in significant capital gains taxes. The catch was that General Motors provided equipment to the US military. At a hearing the previous week, Wilson had insisted that he perceived no conflict of interest "because for years I thought what was good for our country was good for General Motors and vice versa." [12]

UN Ambassador Henry Cabot Lodge, Jr., complained to Attorney General Herbert Brownell that Wilson "seems to be a very arrogant man and a man with no understanding of government." A former senator, Lodge was offended that Wilson, sitting in the president's box at the inaugural parade, with "a loud voice and a great deal of laughter," had compared members of Congress to "hoot owls." Wilson, he grumbled, needed "a complete change of heart and mind; otherwise he will be unable to get any results in Congress." The evening of January 22, Eisenhower held a contentious off-the-record meeting with Wilson, Brownell, and Secretary of the Treasury George Humphrey. At 7:21 p.m., Jim Hagerty announced; "Mr. Wilson visited the President this evening and volunteered his intention to dispose of all his stock in General Motors." [13]

Robert Ten Broeck Stevens, the nominee for secretary of the army, was similarly reluctant to sever his relationship with J. P. Stevens and Company, his family firm. Arthur Krock, in *The New York Times*, characterized all this as "a bad start" for the new administration, contradicting Eisenhower's campaign pledge to "clean up the mess" in Washington. [14]

MCCARTHY'S SEARCH FOR TARGETS

With his investigative subcommittee staffed and funded, McCarthy was ready to intensify his hunt for communists. The senator was impulsive, jumping erratically from one target to another. Deputy Attorney General William Rogers's private assessment of McCarthy was critical: "Joe never plans a damn thing, he doesn't know from one week to the next, not even from one day to the next, what he's going to be doing. . . . He just hits out in any direction, no plan, no forethought." McCarthy typically searched for subversion among people low on the food chain with an agenda more designed to generate headlines than to uncover genuinely subversive activity.[15]

McCarthy had begun his rise to prominence with attacks on the State Department, so he initially harassed John Foster Dulles's department with small-scale accusations and investigations. However, Eisenhower urged that, for the time being, cabinet members adopt "a sympathetic attitude" toward such investigations and inform committee chairs of "constructive plans" to address their concerns. "A negative approach," the president ordered, "was to be avoided."[16]

McCarthy quickly served notice that he had no respect for the president or his loyal subordinates. General Walter Bedell Smith had been Eisenhower's chief of staff during the European campaign and a planner of the details of the Normandy landing. Most recently, he had served as CIA director under Truman. Eisenhower nominated Smith to be Dulles's undersecretary of state. On Eisenhower's second day in office, McCarthy and his allies put a hold on Smith's confirmation, delaying it for most of a month.[17]

McCarthy found an even juicier target in Eisenhower's nomination of Harvard President James B. Conant for US high commissioner in Germany. *The New York Times* called Conant "a splendid appointment" and stated that "as president of a great American university and as a distinguished scholar, scientist and educator, he can count on commanding the respect of the Germans" and "the support of the whole American people." However, three weeks later, Sherman Adams's deputy, Bernard Shanley, confided to his diary that, due to McCarthy's opposition, Conant's confirmation was "in jeopardy." On February 3, McCarthy wrote the president that he was "strongly opposed" to Conant's confirmation and that the educator's assertion that there were no communists teaching at Harvard showed "a woeful lack of knowledge of the vicious and intricate

Communist conspiracy." On February 4, Eisenhower called McCarthy and apparently succeeded in backing the senator off; that day, the Senate Foreign Relations Committee unanimously recommended confirmation for both Smith and Conant, who were confirmed on February 6.[18]

THE BOHLEN BATTLE BEGINS

Those skirmishes were McCarthy's warmups for his first big conflict with Eisenhower. The United States had been without an ambassador in Moscow since September 1952, when George Kennan had offended the Kremlin by publicly comparing the Soviet Union's repressive policies to those of Nazi Germany. Eisenhower selected Charles E. "Chip" Bohlen, a State Department Soviet expert who spoke fluent Russian. He had served in the Soviet Union and had been an interpreter and adviser at international conferences with Soviet leaders during and following World War II. The president knew Bohlen; in 1951, as commander of NATO, he had held numerous conversations with him about how to deal with the Soviets. He had found Bohlen's attitude "tough, firm but fair." Ike recalled in his memoirs, "I came to look upon him as one of the ablest Foreign Policy officers I had ever met."[19]

However, Bohlen's nomination confronted a conservative backlash on his role at the Yalta Conference in February 1945. Yalta, a resort city on the Crimean Peninsula in the Soviet Union, had hosted face-to-face discussions among President Roosevelt, British Prime Minister Winston Churchill, and Soviet Premier Josef Stalin. The meeting had addressed both the reorganization of postwar Europe and the perceived need to persuade the Soviet Union to join the ongoing war against Japan. Republican conservatives, led by Senate Majority Leader Robert Taft, believed that the physically frail Roosevelt, counseled by men such as Bohlen, had signed off on the Soviet occupation of Eastern Europe. Nevertheless, Eisenhower secured Taft's agreement to lead the fight for Bohlen's nomination; one enticement may have been Eisenhower's appointment of his son, William Howard Taft III, as ambassador to Ireland, a choice, Ike told him, that "was based solely upon merit." On February 27, Eisenhower sent the Senate his formal nomination of Charles Bohlen as ambassador to the Soviet Union. The stage was set for Ike's first major confrontation with McCarthy.[20]

On March 2, Bohlen told the Senate Foreign Relations Committee that he would not condemn the Yalta Agreements. He asserted that the accords themselves had been reasonable but the Russians had violated them, especially in Poland. Though some senators on the committee deplored the Allied desertion of Poland to the Soviets, Bohlen pointed out that Soviet military forces had already occupied that country by the date of the Yalta conference and could not be dislodged.[21]

"A SICK FRIEND"

Suddenly an unexpected event transformed the international situation. About two in the morning on March 4, 1953, the phone rang in National Security Advisor Robert Cutler's bedroom. Cutler picked up the receiver to hear the voice of Allen Dulles, the CIA director: "I've just learned that Uncle Joe [Stalin] has had a stroke and is either dead or dying. Do you think I ought to wake up the Boss?" They agreed to wait until the president's normal rising time and meet in the Oval Office at 7:30. On that cool, rainy day, Dwight Eisenhower entered the Oval Office wearing a brown suit and tie, his choice of color when it was going to be a "hard day." His first words: "What do you think we can do about this?" They discussed drafts of a statement and settled on one, thoroughly edited by the president himself.[22]

In his statement, without mentioning Stalin by name, the president affirmed that "the thoughts of America go out to all the peoples of the U.S.S.R.—the men and women, the boys and girls—in the villages, cities, farms and factories of their homeland. They are the children of the same God who is the Father of all peoples everywhere." Eisenhower invoked the almighty again "to watch over the people of that vast land" and allow them to live "in a world where all men and women and children dwell in peace and comradeship." [23]

Stalin died on March 5. The president issued a one-sentence statement offering "official condolences to the Government of the U.S.S.R. on the death of Generalissimo Joseph Stalin, Prime Minister of the Soviet Union." That afternoon, Under Secretary of State Smith told committee that he and Bohlen had been "sitting up with a sick friend" and that Stalin's illness had cost them "a lot of sleep the last two nights." [24]

Stalin's death did not alter the situation with respect to Bohlen's nomination. On March 10, the Senate Foreign Relations Committee—after approving six other diplomatic appointments—rejected Secretary Dulles's plea for quick action on the Bohlen nomination. Expecting to testify, Bohlen was kept waiting for an hour and a half outside the hearing room. Nevertheless, Eisenhower resolved to "fight it out." [25]

RUMORS

Chip Bohlen had never undergone an FBI investigation. Rumors bubbled up about his personal life that reflected the homophobia of the period. When the rumors surfaced—eagerly disseminated by Joe McCarthy—FBI Director J. Edgar Hoover ordered an inquiry. The columnist Drew Pearson recorded in his diary that, on March 5, FBI agents visited him and "asked whether Bohlen was a homo and then quoted me as having once said he was." Pearson, who did not particularly like Bohlen, told the agents that he had "never had the slightest suspicion or thought along this line." [26]

However, a week later Dulles fretted to Sherman Adams that the Bohlen nomination was "on very shaky grounds" due to "moral" allegations. Alexander Wiley, the senior Republican senator from Wisconsin and chairman of the Foreign Relations Committee, stated that the nomination hinged on efforts "to cut through rumor and get at the facts." [27]

On Monday, March 16, Dulles engaged in a flurry of phone calls, trying to assess the status of the Bohlen nomination. Dulles told Eisenhower about "certain rumors afloat," and the president urged him to check with State Department counselor Douglas MacArthur II, who had worked closely with Bohlen. MacArthur found the allegations "incredible" and was confident that Bohlen, a married man, had "a normal family life." Eisenhower never wavered; he "had not the slightest intention of withdrawing Bohlen's name," and he ordered that the secretary should so inform Senator Taft. Dulles called Taft and informed him that the president "was determined to stand behind the Bohlen nomination."[28]

Finally, Dulles called Bohlen, who was quarantined at home with the measles, to assure him that there was "no weakening of the President's determination to stand by his nomination." He wanted to be certain that Bohlen would not withdraw, "because that would leave the President in an embarrassing position." Bohlen assured Dulles that he had no such intention, "none whatever."[29]

Dulles did not address the issue that had caused him and the president to pin down Bohlen on staying the course: Bohlen's brother-in-law, Charles Thayer, was about to be dismissed from the State Department. Thayer, the US consul general in Munich, had been repeatedly investigated concerning unproven accusations of communist leanings and homosexuality. Nevertheless, J. Edgar Hoover and McCarthy had targeted him for removal as a security risk. The case was putting serious strains on the Bohlen family. It was evident that the price of Bohlen's confirmation would be the resignation of Thayer. Dulles ultimately admitted to Bohlen that the Thayer situation had been the reason for his phone call.[30]

McCarthy, sensing a loss of momentum in his effort to keep the Bohlen rumor mill going, escalated his attack on Dulles. In a speech on the Senate floor, he declared that "our Secretary of State is completely misinformed on Bohlen's usefulness as an expert on Communism." The containment policy, supported by Bohlen, had "delivered millions of free men and women to serfdom and death." The senator thundered, "We want no part of this 'Chip' off the old block of Yalta." He asserted that Eisenhower would surely withdraw the nomination if he saw the "entire file" the FBI had on Bohlen—implying again that he himself had reviewed its contents.[31]

On March 18, Dulles called Bohlen into his office to plan their hearing strategy before the Foreign Relations Committee. He suggested that Bohlen downplay his advisory role at Yalta and depict himself as primarily an interpreter; Bohlen retorted that he was unwilling to play the "village idiot." Dulles asked once more, "Is there anything in your past that might be damaging?" Bohlen replied, "No." Dulles called Sherman Adams and, in effect, communicated to the president that he had become convinced beyond any doubt that "there was nothing to the [homosexuality] story after discussing it with Bohlen."[32]

Later that day, Dulles and Bohlen departed for Capitol Hill. Dulles decreed that they go in separate cars, leading Bohlen to wonder if he "would have the courage to stand up to the McCarthyites." Bohlen's fears were unfounded; Dulles was brilliantly persuasive. In a three-hour closed-door session, he discredited the rumors about Bohlen's personal life and effectively made the case for his experience and expertise. He still argued that the ambassador to Moscow was not in a policy-making position, whereas Bohlen, in his present position as a State Department counselor, was. Though that assertion bordered on absurdity, it provided protective cover for pro-Bohlen senators. The next day Arthur Krock endorsed the fiction that the Soviet ambassador "is not by function a policy maker." Foreign policy, he wrote, was the province "of the President and two or three of his ministers."[33]

Based on the secretary of state's virtuoso performance, the Foreign Relations Committee voted unanimously that day—15 to 0—to approve Charles Bohlen as the next ambassador to the Soviet Union. At Eisenhower's news conference on March 19, the momentum for Bohlen's nomination was evident; still, reporters asked the president to comment on McCarthy's assertion that "it was a serious mistake for you not to withdraw the Bohlen nomination." Eisenhower responded that he had "a full report" from the secretary of state. He continued, "I have considered Mr. Bohlen a man to be thoroughly trained in State Department functions and practices, familiar with Russia . . . and he seemed to me to be a very fine appointment."[34]

Once the Senate committee approved Bohlen, the State Department accepted Charles Thayer's resignation. Thayer's cover story was that he was resigning to resume his writing career. On March 21, Secretary Dulles called his brother, Allen, the CIA director, to tell him that Bohlen understood "about the Charlie [Thayer] situation and that it is no longer a real difficulty as far as he is concerned."[35]

THE MCLEOD PROBLEM

Back in February, in an attempt to appease McCarthy, Dulles had appointed a new security officer. His choice was Scott McLeod, a former FBI agent and aide to Republican Senator Styles Bridges of New Hampshire, a known McCarthy admirer. McLeod quickly fulfilled his role; in his first three weeks on the job, he dismissed twenty-one State Department employees who were alleged to be homosexual.[36]

However, just when the Eisenhower team thought they had the obstacles to Charles Bohlen's nomination under control, rumors surfaced—almost certainly spread by the McCarthy camp—that McLeod had doubts about Bohlen's fitness for office. Dulles, based on his own review of the FBI summary report on Bohlen, had overruled McLeod's doubts. In response, McLeod committed two major indiscretions. First, he went over Dulles's head to White House congressional liaison Jerry Persons. Sherman Adams discussed that contact with Eisenhower and called Dulles, who angrily declared that McLeod "needed straightening out." However, if his aide resigned now, Dulles feared it "would probably cause a floor fight on Friday when the nomination comes before the full Senate." Adams responded that he and the president did "not propose to let that happen" and urged Dulles to reach an accommodation with his security officer. However, in conversation, Dulles found McLeod, "very stubborn" and, to his further discomfort, he learned that McCarthy had threatened to subpoena the security officer for a televised hearing.[37]

On March 20, McLeod's second indiscretion surfaced. Reading his morning paper, Dulles felt as if he had been slapped in the face; McLeod had apparently leaked his dissent over Bohlen to McCarthy and the press. Dulles angrily grumbled to Adams and Jim Hagerty that McLeod "is obviously in close touch with McCarthy." Adams urged Dulles to talk once more with McLeod; Eisenhower personally called the secretary to say he would back whatever he decided to do. However, after more discussion with Ike, Adams called Dulles back, warning him to "remember relations on the Hill [and] the explosion that could come." Nevertheless, he stated that if McLeod "does not come clean you cannot keep him." [38]

By the time Dulles confronted the wayward aide, his anger had abated. McLeod was embarrassed and repentant. As Dulles later explained to Adams, McLeod had unwittingly intersected McCarthy's grapevine. He had discussed his doubts with his former boss, Senator Bridges, who mentioned the concern on a ride to the airport with Senator Herman Welker of Idaho, who spent the evening with McCarthy. McCarthy then gave the story to the papers, once again leaving the clear impression that he had seen the full FBI file on Bohlen.[39]

Dulles informed McLeod that the president had authorized him to demand his resignation, but he offered him "a fresh start"—in effect, probation. McLeod provided a written apology, thanking the secretary for his "patience and understanding." Dulles warned McLeod that, as security officer, he could not "testify before a Congressional Committee" without authorization from the president or the secretary. Then he spirited his troublesome aide out of the city to an undisclosed location, leaving McCarthy's staff frustrated over attempts to deliver a subpoena.[40]

At his March 20 news conference, Secretary Dulles, with Senator Wiley at his side, denied that he had "summarily overridden" McLeod's judgment—McCarthy's charge—on Bohlen's security clearance, nor had he misrepresented the facts in his testimony before the

Senate Foreign Relations Committee. "I did not find in the Federal Bureau of Investigation reports in summary, any facts indicating that Mr. Bohlen might be a security or loyalty risk," he said. He maintained that there was "no disagreement" between him and McLeod and the aide would continue in his job. He reminded the reporters that the day before, President Eisenhower had defended the Bohlen appointment, knew about every item in the Bohlen file, and did not intend to withdraw the nomination.

McCarthy challenged Dulles, saying "From all the information we have, any statement that both Dulles and McLeod agree on Bohlen would appear to be untrue." He again proclaimed, "I know what's in Bohlen's file." The FBI file, the senator said, included sixteen closely typed pages of "what could be termed derogatory information."[41]

THE FBI REPORT MUDDLE

With the McLeod matter put to rest, the Bohlen controversy migrated to the question "Who may see the FBI report?" Senator Taft proposed that one or two senators from the Foreign Relations Committee be delegated to review the report. On March 21, Attorney General Brownell informed Dulles that he had been unable to persuade the reluctant J. Edgar Hoover "to change his mind about having some senator look at the Bohlen File." In addition, Senator Wiley was now insisting that one of the two senators be a Democrat, a proposition Brownell heatedly opposed. Brownell cautioned Eisenhower that Taft's solution would "open up Pandora's box to certain senators"—obviously McCarthy. That argument persuaded Eisenhower to delay a decision on whether to insist the senators be given access to the file.[42]

Meanwhile, on the Senate floor, the debate grew rancorous. On March 23, Republican senators led what *New York Times* columnist William S. White called "the first general and determined counterattack ever made on [McCarthy] within his own party in the Senate." The senator was accused of abusing both Secretary Dulles and the president. Taft defended his proposal to have the Foreign Relations Committee designate two members to review the FBI report on Bohlen. He maintained that more broadly exposing a file filled with gossip could damage Bohlen's reputation and "destroy the F.B.I."[43]

Eisenhower made his final decision the morning of March 24. Dulles called Taft to say that the president "would overrule Brownell if necessary, making it plain that this was a special case." The president wanted assurances that the sources of the FBI's information would not be compromised. Dulles phoned Attorney General Brownell: "We are agreed that we must do something to clear this situation up. The rumors have become so thick that unless someone on the floor of the Senate is in position to dissipate them the situation will be very serious." The attorney general acquiesced, and Dulles sent Wiley a formal letter stating that two senators had been approved to review "the summary of the FBI report regarding Mr. Bohlen." The committee then selected Taft and Democratic Senator John Sparkman of Alabama.[44]

However, Dulles's words "the summary" triggered a whole new brouhaha. What would the two senators get to see—a "summary" of the FBI report or the "raw material"? Unable to reach the attorney general, Dulles, in Taft's presence, phoned J. Edgar Hoover to inform him that the senators wanted to see the "raw files, as well as the summary." Hoover was adamant: "The raw material file is never made available to anyone." Dulles put Taft on the phone; he quoted McCarthy's claim on the Senate floor that "he had seen the entire file," an assertion the FBI director denied. Hoover said he would provide the raw file only if the attorney general ordered him to do so. Having lost the previous arguments, Brownell drew the line and supported Hoover, maintaining that it was "really a protection to the senators if they did not see the material." They should, he said, "take Hoover's word that it was a complete summary." Reluctantly, Taft accepted the decision; he and Sparkman would review only the summary.[45]

On March 24 at 5:45 p.m., after reviewing the FBI document,

Taft and Sparkman emerged from the secretary of state's office. Pressed by a flood of questions, the senators commented to reporters that they had found the summary "unusually complete." Taft described it as "25 pages, single spaced" and "very long and detailed." They confirmed that Dulles's testimony before the committee had been "a very fine statement of the summary." [46]

On March 25, McCarthy rose on the Senate floor to deliver his final tirade in opposition to Bohlen's appointment. Decrying "two black decades," he declared that "history will write large the names of those who sold out this country at the diplomatic tables at home and abroad." He called the Bohlen nomination "a grave and inexcusable mistake on the part of our Secretary of State" and accused Bohlen of playing "directly into the hands of international Communism" in a "government of, by and for Communists, crooks and cronies." He sneered at Dulles's suggestion that Bohlen, rather than being a policy maker at Yalta and Potsdam, "was only an interpreter." McCarthy let Ike off the hook; the president, he said, "burdened with work and pressed for time," had not had the chance "to study the complete record of Bohlen." [47]

The Senate debate that followed was described by *The New York Times* as "bitter." Taft sparred with McCarthy, insisting that the FBI summary had nothing in it "reflecting on the loyalty of Mr. Bohlen in any way"; he had found no evidence that Bohlen was "a bad security risk," a veiled reference to the homosexuality rumors. Sparkman confirmed that view, saying he had found no evidence of "anything wrong with the character, integrity or honesty of Mr. Bohlen." "So," Taft concluded, "I myself came to the conclusion that Mr. Bohlen was a completely good security risk in every respect, and I am glad so to report to the Senate of the United States." [48]

TOWARD CONFIRMATION

Eisenhower's March 26 press conference was sandwiched in between that final Senate debate and the confirmation vote, scheduled for the twenty-seventh. Asked again whether Mr. Bohlen was his "personal choice" for ambassador to Moscow, he delivered a ringing endorsement. "I have known Mr. Bohlen for some years," he said. "I was once, at least, a guest in his home, and with his very charming family. I have played golf with him. I have listened to his philosophy. So far as I can see, he is the best qualified man for that post that I could find. That is the reason his name was sent to the Senate and the reason it stays there, because I believe, still, that he is the best qualified man we could find today."

A reporter asked what the president thought McCarthy's "objectives have been in the Bohlen case, as affecting your appointment?" "I am not going to talk about Senator McCarthy," he snapped—a rare occasion when he mentioned the name. However, he warned that congressional investigations could be pursued "to the point that you are damaging from within what you are trying to protect from without." McCarthy commented only mildly on the president's support of Bohlen, saying "I am sure he is very serious when he says Bohlen is the best man. But it so happens that I differ with him." He admitted that he had "no remote hope of success" in derailing the nomination.[49]

The next day, the Senate voted 74 to 13 to confirm Charles Bohlen as ambassador to the Soviet Union. The negative votes included eleven Republicans, while thirty-nine Democrats supported the nomination. Secretary Dulles called Senator Taft to thank him; Taft is alleged to have grumbled in response, "No more Bohlens." McCarthy was unrepentant, mocking the president's statement about Bohlen being the "best man" for the job: "I hope that those of us who felt he was the worst man for the job will be proven wrong."[50]

Eisenhower had won an important strategic victory over McCarthy. He had not permitted the senator's fearmongering to dictate an appointment of great importance. When the outcome became apparent, Ike discussed McCarthy's motivations with Sherman Adams and his deputy, Bernard Shanley. He commented that "the only thing" McCarthy wanted "was headlines" and he did not care how he got them. Ike declared, "McCarthy has the bug to run for the presidency in 1956." Slapping his knee, Ike thundered, "The only reason I would consider running again would be to run against him." Shanley "let out a whoop," whereupon the taciturn Adams glared at his aide as if he were "completely out of order"—"which," Shanley conceded, "I was."[51]

CHAPTER 2

"DON'T JOIN THE BOOK BURNERS!"

By April 1953, the pattern of Joe McCarthy's relationship with the Eisenhower White House had been set. Still fixated on the State Department, he would test Eisenhower's will with small skirmishes, preparatory to opening up a bigger, headline-grabbing investigative target.

On March 28, the day following Charles Bohlen's confirmation by the Senate, McCarthy announced he had negotiated an agreement with the Greek owners of 242 New York–based merchant ships to end all trade with Communist China, North Korea, and eastern portions of the Soviet Union. The agreement, he boasted, would have "some of the effect of a naval blockade." Moreover, his representatives were "negotiating" with additional Greek shipowners in London.[1]

Alarm bells sounded in the White House and the State Department. The senator's bold interference with executive-branch authority over foreign affairs confirmed columnist William S. White's conclusion that although McCarthy had lost the battle over Bohlen, "his war goes on." White concluded, "Mr. McCarthy's essential power may in no sense be lessened, and may even be increased." At the height of the Bohlen debate, McCarthy had said to one reporter, "You wait, we're gonna get Dulles' head."[2]

The administration dispatched Harold E. Stassen, the director of the Mutual Security Administration (the successor agency to the Marshall Plan), to testify at McCarthy's closed-door subcommittee hearing on the Greek shippers. Stassen reported to Secretary Dulles that McCarthy had declared that "anyone who does not agree with him is trying to kill more boys in Korea." Stassen had shot back that McCarthy was "undermining" the administration's efforts to make peace.[3]

The White House moved quickly to rein in the situation. On April 1, Vice President Richard Nixon arranged a luncheon for Secretary Dulles and Senator McCarthy. Nixon had apparently warned the senator that he was wading into deep constitutional waters. The day before the luncheon, McCarthy had backpedaled in a letter to the president, carefully avoiding the word "negotiate" that he had so freely employed at his news conference. "No agreement as such was made with the Committee, nor did the Committee assume any obligation," he wrote. He asserted that the agreement had been reached among the shippers "and presented to us."[4]

McCarthy emerged from his luncheon meeting with Dulles, uncharacteristically quiet. Beseieged by reporters, the secretary, he said, would issue a statement and they would have "nothing to say" otherwise. Dulles's statement called what had happened with the Greek shippers an "informal understanding"; the shippers "had voluntarily agreed among themselves" to cease trading with communist nations. He thanked McCarthy for pledging to communicate future developments "to the proper authorities." Arthur Krock, the *New York Times* pundit, noted McCarthy's abandonment of his original assertion that he had negotiated an agreement with the shippers: "How many times can't you mean what you said?" he asked. Columnists Stewart and Joseph Alsop read higher ambitions into McCarthy's shipping gambit. "It is almost universally agreed," they wrote, "that McCarthy's objective is the Presidency and nothing less."[5]

When asked at his news conference the following day if Senator McCarthy's agreement with Greek ship owners had "undermined"—Stassen's word—administration policy, President Eisenhower suggested that "infringed" might be a more appropriate term.

"The exclusive power of negotiating such arrangements, anything that is legal, belongs to the Executive," he said. A "misguided" action by anyone else could not alter that. Reminded of McCarthy's use of the term "negotiate," at his Saturday news conference, he tersely replied, "How do you negotiate when there is nothing that you can commit?" Obtaining "promises" or "some kind of expression of opinion or intention" might take place. "But that," he said, "in my mind, is not negotiation."

When asked whether he was "unhappy" with what had happened, Eisenhower snapped, "I am not in the slightest bit unhappy. . . . The mere fact that some little incident arises is not going to disturb me. I have been scared by experts, in war and in peace, and I am not frightened about this." His subtle message to Joe McCarthy: "I am not scared of you; you, in fact, don't matter very much."[6]

THE EISENHOWER WAY

Eisenhower still refused to take on McCarthy in public. When supporters pressed him to abandon that approach, his response was unrelenting. "The President of the United States cannot afford to name names," he wrote Harry Bullis, a General Mills executive. "Nothing would probably please [McCarthy] more than to get the publicity that would be generated by public repudiation by the President." To the diplomat William Phillips, he wrote, "I deplore and deprecate the table-pounding, name-calling methods columnists so much love." Though he might relish "a good fight," he had learned that "such methods are normally futile."[7]

Eisenhower never repudiated his McCarthy strategy, even after leaving the White House. William Ewald, who assisted the former president in writing his memoirs, recalled an anecdote that Ike eventually deleted from the manuscript. His brother Milton had urged him "to announce to the world that I strongly disapproved of all that McCarthy was doing and all that he stood for." Eisenhower had responded that attacking McCarthy would only "greatly enhance his publicity value without achieving any constructive purpose." He reaffirmed his intention to publicly ignore McCarthy: "I would not demean myself or the Presidency by getting in the gutter with him." On another occasion, Milton urged Ike to make an anti-McCarthy speech that would "tear him apart." The president countered that such a strategy would "only backfire" and "probably draw down upon me the fury of the entire United States Senate because, let me tell you, it's a club. No president goes around attacking one member of the Senate without having the rest of them coalesce behind him." [8]

Eisenhower's approach to dealing with McCarthy was not nearly as passive as it appeared. He instinctively understood that treating him as inconsequential would drive the senator into self-destructive behaviors; he sensed that repeated presidential snubs over time would have a cumulative effect. There was another, pragmatic aspect to the Eisenhower strategy. Given the senator's demagogic skills, the president knew he must avoid saying or doing anything that would make himself, not McCarthy, the issue.

In spite of his dismissive public demeanor, the president was privately annoyed at McCarthy's antics. On April 3, the day after his news conference, Ike wrote his brother Edgar that "for the past couple of days I have been completely fed up and it is high time I was getting away from here for three or four days. Sometimes I think only a miracle will make it possible." [9]

THE TROUBLED VOICE

Eisenhower and Dulles had handled McCarthy's foray into negotiating shipping agreements with minimal fuss. That would not be the case with McCarthy's assault on the Voice of America (VOA). President Truman had placed most foreign information activities, including the Voice, under the umbrella of the International Information Administration (IIA), an agency of the State Department. When Eisenhower took office, that agency had a staff of about ten thousand—around 40 percent of the State Department's personnel—and a budget exceeding $100 million per year. [10]

Early on, Eisenhower and Dulles agreed that the propaganda

operation should probably have its own independent agency, outside the State Department. They had not had time to act on that perception when, on February 13—while the fight over Bohlen's confirmation was still under way—McCarthy announced that his subcommittee would hold televised hearings into "management and subversion" in Voice of America operations. At least fifty employees had been subpoenaed, and a personnel shake-up was rumored. Following his subcommittee's executive session, McCarthy told reporters that "there are people in the Voice of America who are doing a rather effective job of sabotaging Dulles' and Eisenhower's foreign policy program."[11]

McCarthy had zoned in on a particularly vulnerable agency in the State Department. On February 16, Secretary Dulles called Sherman Adams, "bothered" about the VOA, which was "not in very good condition and is now being investigated by Sen. McCarthy." Speechwriter Emmet Hughes described the agency as a "soggy, fogbound information program." Adams ordered his deputy, Bernard Shanley, to brief Eisenhower about "the barrel of rotten apples we have in the Voice."[12]

Dulles let McCarthy's agitation pressure him into a hasty decision on new VOA leadership. He recruited Dr. Robert L. Johnson, the president of Temple University, to take over the VOA and "help clean it up." Johnson turned out to be a troublesome choice. He insisted on the need to "study" the VOA for sixty to ninety days, and he wanted an ironclad pledge that the agency would be separated from the State Department. Eisenhower and Dulles urgently wanted a new boss for the agency and had intended to postpone those matters until later. Somehow, Johnson misread his conversations with both men. When Eisenhower authorized the announcement of his appointment "to head and to study the entire operation of the Foreign Information Service," Johnson threatened to back out. He did not want to "head" the agency without the preliminary study he deemed essential. The appointment was already public; if Johnson withdrew, McCarthy might subpoena the educator to testify about his misgivings.

Eisenhower bluntly wrote Johnson that their "misunderstanding" had to be cleared up. First, no firm decision had yet been made to convert the IIA into "a separate agency of government." Second, it was not acceptable for Johnson to "stay on some indefinite, indeterminate status for a matter of months." The VOA needed "firm and quick direction." Therefore, the "study function" should last "a matter of days only—not of months." Johnson finally capitulated to Eisenhower's wishes, but this rocky start indicated his tenure would be short and stormy.[13]

Meanwhile, in reaction to McCarthy's investigation, panic had set in among VOA's bureaucrats and librarians in the overseas libraries. On January 30, VOA officials instructed the libraries to avoid using "materials produced by controversial persons." On February 18, VOA headquarters sent out the first of two directives forbidding the use of any books or materials written by communists. On February 25, the VOA libraries were ordered "to destroy the July 1946 issue of the Annals of the American Academy of Political and Social Science." Two months later, the order went out to remove works by authors who had refused to testify about their communist affiliations, resulting in the removal of books by almost two dozen writers, including the mystery writer Dashiell Hammett.[14]

As if the VOA had not suffered enough adverse publicity, on March 4—two days after Robert Johnson began his new job— Raymond Kaplan, a forty-two-year-old radio engineer, threw himself in front of a truck near Massachusetts Institute of Technology. Kaplan's suicide note, leaked to the press, attributed his action to persecution by McCarthy's subcommittee. "Once the dogs are set upon you," Kaplan wrote his wife, "everything you have done since the beginning of time is suspect." Kaplan believed that suicide was the only way he could protect his wife and son from being "continuously hounded for the rest of your lives."[15]

On March 18, under Robert Johnson's new leadership, the VOA issued instructions moderating the previous Draconian rules about books in the libraries, permitting the use of "Communist material" solely to "expose Communist propaganda or refute Communist lies."

That action brought a loud protest from Senator McCarthy, resulting in a new directive from the State Department prohibiting outright the use of writings by "Communists, fellow travelers, et cetera."[16]

At that point, the White House gambled that leaking the word that the old organization's days were numbered would take some steam out of McCarthy's investigation. By March 20, "authoritative sources" disclosed that the IIA would be shut down after June 30 and replaced by an independent agency outside the State Department.[17]

"SCUMMY SNOOPERS" IN EUROPE

Once the Bohlen fight was settled, McCarthy dispatched his chief lieutenants to Europe to dig for dirt on the VOA. On April 2, Dulles informed European embassies and consulates that "Roy Cohn, Chief Counsel; David Schine, Chief Consultant, U.S. Permanent Sub-Committee on Investigations" would be visiting Paris, Frankfurt, Berlin, Bonn, Munich, and Vienna to investigate IIA programs. The two men, the secretary's missive said, were to be extended "all possible courtesies" by US diplomats.

On April 3, in an "eyes only" telegram, Dulles warned the chief US diplomats in Britain, France, Austria, and Germany that they had "no authority" to provide information to Cohn and Schine "re security matters or policy directives." In particular, no information "contained in personnel security files will be divulged to investigators." Later that day, he was infuriated to discover that Scott McLeod's secretary had been spotted at the airport showing his "eyes only" telegram to Cohn and Schine as they prepared to depart.[18]

After a brief stay in Paris, the two McCarthy aides took off for Bonn, Germany. On arrival, Cohn stated that they had already uncovered "millions of dollars' worth of waste and mismanagement" in the IIA. The spectacle of Cohn and Schine rummaging for scandals in Germany surely concerned Eisenhower's friends, who worried constantly about McCarthy exploiting Eisenhower's postwar communist associations while in command there.

Cohn and Schine's antics in Europe also generated gossip about the men's relationship, some of it salacious.[19] One day in Bonn, the two men rushed back to their hotel to retrieve a notebook Schine had left behind. In the lobby, Schine batted Cohn over the head with a rolled-up magazine and they chased each other into Schine's room. The hotel maid later found the room in a shambles. When asked about the incident, Cohn called the story "just one of many lies in this fantastic newspaper article." Cohn introduced Schine as "a management expert," saying he had "written a book about the definition of Communism," a gross exaggeration about a six-page pamphlet. The European junket underlined a new reality: the Roy Cohn–David Schine relationship would become central to the conflict between Joe McCarthy and Dwight Eisenhower.[20]

WAGING PEACE

Dwight Eisenhower, focused on his Cold War priorities, appeared to pay little attention to the escapades of what one newspaper called the "Gold Dust Twins."[21] On April 15, when they arrived in Belgrade, Ike was working on the most important speech of his new presidency. Following the death of Stalin on March 5, Eisenhower had wrestled with options for reaching out to the new Soviet leadership. He decided to use his address, scheduled for April 16 before the annual meeting of the American Society of Newspaper Editors in Washington, DC.

That was a dangerous decision. Eisenhower knew his "Chance for Peace" speech would be delivered against the backdrop of McCarthy's demagoguery on communist subversion, punctuated by headlines generated by Cohn and Schine on their European junket. On April 12, a feature-length article in *The New York Times* called Senator McCarthy "the most talked about man in the capital today," next to the president. His strong opposition to Bohlen, his alleged agreement with Greek shipowners, and the hearings of his investigative subcommittee had raised his prestige to a new level. "All in Washington agree it is risky to quarrel with him," the article concluded. In that climate, Eisenhower's April 16 address clearly risked the charge from McCarthy that he was "soft on communism."[22]

Nevertheless, Ike stuck to his peacemaking priorities. He ruminated about themes for that speech with speechwriter Emmet Hughes. "The average citizen," he told Hughes, "can't—in a whole lifetime of work—earn as much money as it takes to make the jet plane that flies above his head." He wanted to "convert all this armament spending into the things that raise living standards." "I don't feel like making any more speeches condemning the Russians," the president concluded, "until I can *offer* some peace plan."[23]

The address took at least twelve drafts, not counting the president's penciled edits, and was reviewed by the CIA, the Defense and State Departments, and key allies, including Winston Churchill. After meeting with Eisenhower on April 12, Hughes complained to his assistant, Robert Kieve, that he had "come to the point where I just think the President's hopeless" regarding speech preparation. Ike himself complained to Sherman Adams that "this speech preparation is too big a strain."[24]

The stress was such that Ike decided to get out of town. On April 13, he flew to Augusta, Georgia, to play golf, taking the speech with him. However, on the night of April 15, he suffered a painful abdominal attack. The morning of the speech, National Security Advisor Robert Cutler found the president "depleted and in general misery." That night, Eisenhower moved slowly along the side of the crowded auditorium toward the podium; Cutler saw "sweat glistening on the President's brow and cheeks." Ike's delivery was labored, Cutler recalled. "There was slackness in his robust voice; its hearty earnestness seemed mute. His big hands so tightly gripped the sides of the speaking lectern that I could see the whiteness of his knuckles." During the speech, he thought the president seemed "a little dizzy and tremulous."[25]

Nevertheless, Eisenhower delivered a stirring address. "A nation's hope of lasting peace," he stated, "cannot be firmly based upon any race in armaments but rather upon just relations and honest understanding with all other nations." He deplored "the way of life forged by eight years of fear and force. What can the world, or any nation in it, hope for if no turning is found on this dread road?"

Eisenhower eloquently recounted the human costs of the Cold War:

> Every gun that is made, every warship launched, every rocket fired signifies, in the final sense, a theft from those who hunger and are not fed, those who are cold and are not clothed. This world in arms is not spending money alone. It is spending the sweat of its laborers, the genius of its scientists, the hopes of its children. The cost of one modern heavy bomber is this: a modern brick school in more than 30 cities. It is two electric power plants, each serving a town of 60,000 population. It is two fine, fully equipped hospitals. It is some 50 miles of concrete highway. We pay for a single fighter plane with a half million bushels of wheat. We pay for a single destroyer with new homes that could have housed more than 8,000 people. This, I repeat, is the best way of life to be found on the road the world has been taking. This is not a way of life at all, in any true sense. Under the cloud of threatening war, it is humanity hanging from a cross of iron.[26]

When he finished, the president walked slowly into a small, private parlor. Cutler found him there, "pale, covered with clammy perspiration." Eisenhower said he felt "chilly" but was no longer in "misery"; the pain in his gut had subsided. The papers the next day reported that the president had been ill from "food poisoning," had had "a slight fever," and had returned immediately to Augusta, where his physician had put him to bed. The speech drew immediate praise from members of both parties and allied leaders abroad. In the wake of such effusive praise, McCarthy was silent.[27]

On the day of speech, Roy Cohn and David Schine left Belgrade for Athens. They concluded their trip on April 20 with five hours in London, where the *Financial Times* labeled them "scummy snoopers," and arrived the next morning back in Washington, DC. In an appearance on NBC's *Meet the Press,* Cohn charged that the State Department had put "a tail" on them during their trip, the purpose of which "was to feed all of sorts information and stories to the hostile press so they could smear us up a little bit." In fact, the State Department *had* carefully monitored their travels, with frequent reports to Secretary Dulles.[28]

INTERNAL SECURITY

Throughout 1953, Eisenhower shadowboxed with McCarthy on the issue of who could best protect the country against communist subversion. The president understood that McCarthy's obsession with subversion was aimed, however irresponsibly, at a genuine problem. In the midst of the Cold War, the government was legitimately concerned about Soviet spies, moles, and assets. Dramatizing that concern, Julius and Ethel Rosenberg had been convicted of espionage in March 1951 and condemned to death. On Eisenhower's first day in office, appeals for clemency for the couple were waiting on his desk, but he did not grant clemency.[29]

In his first meeting with Republican congressional leaders on January 26, Eisenhower had announced that he would employ government personnel on a "security rather than loyalty" basis, implementing the philosophy that "working for the Government is a privilege rather than a right." He intended to move "vigorously to establish an adequate security program," overseen by Attorney General Brownell.[30]

Ostensibly, the Eisenhower program sought to protect the legitimate rights of employees, creating hearing advisory boards whose members came from outside the agency under investigation. The columnist Walter Lippmann, a frequent Eisenhower critic, deemed the new policy an improvement over President Truman's approach; the former president's program had been so focused on loyalty that a negative decision in a hearing could label the employee in question, justified or not, as "a spy and a traitor." Eisenhower's program, treating employment as "a privilege" without explicit loyalty implications, seemed more even-handed.[31]

However, the program had its dark side: if an employee were deemed a security risk "by reason of personal habits or actions," as Brownell put it, that opened the door to wholesale dismissal of persons who were not necessarily spies. The frequently cited categories included alcoholics, philanderers, "blabbermouths," especially homosexuals, who were perceived as vulnerable to blackmail by communist agents. Eisenhower's program proposal was not simply a reaction to McCarthy. But Brownell recalled that, as time passed, the president would "point to his program as the best way to destroy McCarthy and McCarthyism by taking the issue of internal security away from him and dealing with it in a responsible manner."[32]

Attorney General Brownell presented the final draft of the employee security program to the cabinet on April 27. Following the meeting, the White House issued Executive Order 10450, entitled "Security Requirements for Government Employment." The opening lines of that document were vintage Eisenhower. The national security required that all persons "privileged"—the key word—"to be employed in the departments and agencies of the Government, shall be reliable, trustworthy, of good conduct and character"—i.e., not a "security risk"—"and of complete and unswerving loyalty to the United States." The order pledged "equitable treatment" for those seeking "the privilege"—that word again—of government employment.[33]

THE TAFT PROBLEM

When he began his first year in office, Eisenhower had necessarily relied on Republican Senate Majority Leader Robert Taft to manage relations with McCarthy. He had uncomfortably witnessed Taft's capitulation to McCarthy's demands for investigative powers, but he had been heartened by Taft's steadfast defense of the Bohlen nomination.

However, in his diary, Eisenhower called April 30 "one of the worst days I have experienced since January 20th." When he had taken office, he had ordered departments and agencies to comb through Truman's budget for savings. That morning, he presented Republican legislative leaders with recommended cuts of approximately $4.4 billion, an accomplishment in which he took great pride.

What blindsided the president was that suddenly—in Ike's words—"Senator Taft broke out in a violent objection to everything that had been done." The majority leader angrily called the cuts insufficient and contended that they would "insure the decisive defeat of the Republican party in 1954." He threatened "to go on public record" against the revised budget. In reaction to "the demagogic nature" of his tirade, the president's temper quickly reached the boiling point. However, before he could explode, others seized control of the argument, giving Eisenhower time to contain himself and prevent a "completely unbridgeable" rupture in his relationship with Senator Taft.[34]

Eisenhower did not know that Taft was a very sick man. Three weeks later, the senator entered Walter Reed Army Hospital for treatment for hip pain that had first erupted after a round of golf with the president in Augusta. He was diagnosed with cancer and never returned to full-time service in the Senate.[35]

The April 30 incident encouraged Eisenhower to depend increasingly on Vice President Nixon for legislative and political counsel, including coping with McCarthy. By June 1, that transition was complete. Ike observed in his diary that Taft's "irascible" personality made him "far from being a Dick Nixon, who is not only bright, quick and energetic—but loyal and cooperative." On June 11, California Senator William Knowland, a McCarthy ally whom Eisenhower distrusted, assumed the leadership of the Senate Republicans. As a result, the president would need Nixon more than ever.[36]

BURNING BOOKS

Eisenhower complained about June 1953 being one of the most demanding times in his young presidency. At a cabinet meeting on June 5, Eisenhower said he needed "help to keep his disposition."

He felt particularly misused by the months-long controversy over banning books in the VOA's overseas libraries. He was no fan of censorship, and he was thoroughly irritated at how the VOA and the State Department had handled McCarthy's effort to ban books from the shelves at the overseas libraries. On June 14, the Alsop brothers called "book-burning" in those libraries "cowardly." That day, the president, out of patience on the book censorship issue, traveled to New Hampshire to speak at Dartmouth College's commencement.[37]

Eisenhower's remarks at Dartmouth have been characterized as "off the cuff" because no speechwriter was involved. Still, he had consistently argued that a president cannot indulge in loose talk; indeed, that had been his message to friends urging him to take on McCarthy. Bernard Shanley confirmed that Ike's "off-the-cuff speeches are pretty well considered before he makes them." That day, Eisenhower's revulsion at McCarthy's call for censorship boiled over.[38]

To the students, Eisenhower quoted the maxim "The coward dies a thousand deaths, but the brave man dies but once." "It is not enough merely to say I love America," he declared, "and to salute the flag and take off your hat as it goes by, and to help sing the Star Spangled Banner." Then he delivered the provocative declaration that would be quoted the next day around the globe:

> Don't join the book burners. Don't think you are going to conceal faults by concealing evidence that they ever existed. Don't be afraid to go in your library and read every book, as long as that document does not offend our own ideas of decency. That should be the only censorship. How will we defeat communism unless we know what it is, and what it teaches, and why does it have such an appeal for men, why are so many people swearing allegiance to it?

The statement was transparently anti-McCarthy. Eisenhower defended dissenters; even if their ideas "are contrary to ours, their right to say them, their right to record them, and their right to have them at places where they are accessible to others is unquestioned, or it isn't America." White House sources characterized the president's comments at Dartmouth as "pure, premeditated and unadulterated Eisenhower." McCarthy delivered a witty retort. "He couldn't very well have been referring to me," the senator said. "I have burned no books."[39]

At the president's news conference on June 17, UPI reporter Merriman Smith asked if Eisenhower's remarks at Dartmouth had been "critical of a school of thought represented by Senator McCarthy?" "Now, Merriman," the president responded, "you have been around me long enough to know I never talk personalities." He clarified that he did not support books designed "to persuade or propagandize America into communism" and he would not "propagate Communist beliefs by using governmental money to do it." Excluding such propaganda, he stated, "I am against 'book burning' of course—which is, as you well know, an expression to mean suppression of ideas. I just do not believe in suppressing ideas. I believe in dragging them out in the open and taking a look at them. That is what I meant, and I do not intend to be talking personally and in personalities with respect to anyone."

Robert Donovan, a *New York Herald Tribune* correspondent, asked whether "a controversial book" available on American bookshelves could also "be on the bookshelf of one of our libraries abroad?" "I should think so, speaking generally," Eisenhower responded. He reminded reporters how widely it was believed that World War II had occurred "because we had failed to read *Mein Kampf* seriously." He asked, "Why shouldn't we, today, know what is going on? How many of you have read Stalin's *Problems of Leninism*? How many of you have really studied Karl Marx and looked at the evolution of the Marxian theory down to the present application?" He repeated the maxim "Know your enemy." In a veiled reprimand to McCarthy, the president concluded, "It does no good for me just to get up and shout, 'I am against communism.' What is it?"[40]

Ike's news conference comments were widely interpreted as Eisenhower reneging on his Dartmouth comments, but that analysis is too simplistic. He had repeated, "I am against 'book burning.'" The Alsop brothers characterized the president at Dartmouth as "the real Eisenhower" and the man handling the same issue at the news conference as "the public Eisenhower." The public and private Eisenhower were both on record saying, in effect, "I hate censorship."[41]

THE ROSENBERG PROBLEM

The president's other major problem that month was the execution of Julius and Ethel Rosenberg, scheduled for June 19. The couple had been convicted and sentenced to death for providing classified information to the Soviets while Julius had been employed at the Army Signal Corps at Fort Monmouth, New Jersey. From his first day in office, Eisenhower had been besieged with pleas to spare the Rosenbergs, partly because they had two children, ages six and ten. The president had assigned White House Deputy Assistant Bernard Shanley and the Attorney General's Office to review "the whole record of the conviction and appeals all the way through the courts."[42]

Given McCarthy's anticommunist crusade, any leniency toward the Rosenbergs could be political dynamite. Ike later explained to his cabinet that he had rigorously reviewed the evidence based on four criteria: whether the verdict had been unanimous, whether the country might benefit if the Rosenbergs provided evidence against other spies, whether there was "sufficient substance to the crime to warrant the death penalty," and "the psychological effect in the world at large if the Executive were to reverse the decision of the Judiciary in this case."[43]

On February 11, Eisenhower had issued a statement he had drafted himself. The Rosenbergs, he said, had been "tried and convicted" for "conspiring to share secret atomic information relating to the national defense of the United States." Their crime "could very well result in the death of many, many thousands of innocent citizens." Having uncovered no "new evidence" or "mitigating circumstances," he concluded, "I have determined that it is my duty, in the interest of the people of the United States, not to set aside the verdict of their representatives."[44]

However, Eisenhower's statement did not close the door on the possibility of clemency; he had indicated to the cabinet his willingness to reopen the case if, at any time prior to execution, new evidence or new considerations warranted. As the execution date drew near, Eisenhower was hounded by advocates for mercy. He met with four clergymen on June 15—the day after his Dartmouth speech—and responded to their plea: "If I were in the place you men are in, I would be doing the same thing you are doing, asking for clemency for these people; but I am not in your position and I can't get up and walk away as you are going to."[45]

Once again, Eisenhower's aides found no new evidence to vindicate the Rosenbergs. Ike wrote a long letter to his son John, sharing his discomfort amid "a very considerable amount of furor." Eisenhower had been intensively lobbied with pleas for mercy because one of the condemned was a woman and "because of the two children of the couple." However much he brooded as the day of execution drew near, Eisenhower embraced "the hope that it would deter others." Then, on June 17, Supreme Court Justice William O. Douglas granted a temporary stay of execution. Allen Dulles told his brother, Foster, that the justice's action put the matter "in a hell of a mess."[46]

The day of the executions—Friday, June 19, 1953—Eisenhower held a 10 a.m. cabinet meeting. Though McCarthy was not mentioned, the specter of what he might do about delay of the executions or clemency hovered over the meeting. The president said he could not "remember ever a 48-hours where he felt more in need of help from someone—more intelligent than I." Central to the discussion was the fact that other spies—including Klaus Fuchs, whom the British had sentenced to fourteen years in prison—had not been executed. Then there was David Greenglass, Ethel Rosenberg's brother, who had testified against the couple and whose life had been spared. Henry Cabot Lodge stated that he believed that the difference "can be easily explained." Eisenhower responded, "Not easily for me."[47]

After the meeting, Foster Dulles called Herbert Brownell. They had planned to attend a baseball game that night, but Dulles concluded that they "had better not go," both for their own safety and because of how it would look if they were photographed "enjoying themselves together while the execution was taking place."[48]

Later that day, the full Supreme Court declined to support Justice William O. Douglas's stay of execution. That afternoon, Bernard Shanley took the final draft of the president's statement into the Oval Office for his signature. While Eisenhower was on the phone on another matter, Sherman Adams whispered to Shanley that Ethel Rosenberg's mother was seeking to speak to the president. Without informing the president, they had her escorted to the attorney general's office.[49]

Eisenhower's statement repeated his previous conclusion that "the Rosenbergs have received the benefit of every safeguard which American justice can provide." He asserted, "By immeasurably increasing the chances of atomic war the Rosenbergs may have condemned to death tens of millions of innocent people all over the world. The execution of two human beings is a grave matter. But even graver is the thought of the millions of dead whose deaths may be directly attributable to what these spies have done." He concluded, "I will not intervene in this matter."[50]

Julius and Ethel Rosenberg were pronounced dead at 8:16 p.m. Eastern Time.[51]

CHAPTER 3

"YOU'RE IN THE ARMY NOW!"

It had been a "week of trouble," Eisenhower told his cabinet a few days after the Rosenberg executions in June. South Korean president Syngman Rhee was resisting the negotiation of an armistice in Korea; Winston Churchill had suffered a stroke; and Robert Taft was gravely ill. The president—perhaps arguing with himself—reminded the cabinet members that "long faces do not win battles." Eisenhower did not know that by the end of summer, Senator Joseph McCarthy would be hounding the US Army for communists.[1]

By mid-1953, McCarthy had honed a formidable arsenal of techniques for turning fear into headlines. Employing his subpoena power, he could compel testimony, under oath, from nearly anyone with short notice and without a vote by his subcommittee members. He repeatedly conducted one-senator hearings, ignoring the Senate's tradition of requiring a quorum of the committee's membership before holding hearings. The senator made shrewd use of senatorial privilege, which immunized him against libel when he made outrageous statements on the Senate floor, during a committee hearing, or to the press.

Finally, McCarthy stood the Fifth Amendment to the Constitution, which guarantees protection against self-incrimination, on its head. In McCarthy's world, anyone who "took the Fifth" to avoid

testimony about communist associations was obviously a communist. When Albert Einstein, a refugee from Nazi Germany, openly
urged his colleagues to refuse to speak in McCarthy's hearings, even
if it meant "jail or economic ruin," McCarthy countered that anyone handing out such counsel "is himself an enemy of America."[2]

"I HATE CENSORSHIP!"

The last week in June, McCarthy continued his demagoguery over
allegedly communist books in the overseas libraries, announcing
new hearings and subpoenas for twenty-three authors. *The New
York Times* reported that several hundred books by more than forty
authors had been removed from IIA library shelves. Democrats in
Congress complained that Eisenhower had retreated from his condemnation of "book burning" at Dartmouth College.[3]

On June 26, Eisenhower dispatched a letter to Robert Bingham
Downs, the president of the American Library Association, to be read
at the organization's annual meeting in Los Angeles. Emmet Hughes,
who had drafted the message, recalled that Ike intended it to be "another blunt warning on the ugliness of McCarthyism." Eisenhower
christened the country's librarians the protectors of "the precious
liberties of our nation: freedom of inquiry, freedom of the spoken
and the written word, freedom of exchange of ideas." "A democracy chronically fearful of new ideas," he asserted, "would be a dying
democracy." Eisenhower took direct aim at McCarthy—as always,
without mentioning his name. "There are some zealots," he wrote,
"who—with more wrath than wisdom" would censor what people
are free to read. "Freedom cannot be served by the devices of the ty-
rant," he warned, and "freedom cannot be censored into existence."[4]

Eisenhower was fed up with the book controversy and how the
State Department had handled it. At his cabinet meeting that same
day, he ordered Secretary Dulles to provide a statement at the next
meeting "on our book policy abroad." Americans could not fight
communism, he said, "by ducking our heads in sand." Though he
deplored "propagandizing for the Commies," the department should

be able "to lay down a general rule of reason." Dulles responded that the hundreds of books removed from the shelves "were not because of any directive" from the State Department; rather, librarians had acted out of "fear of or hatred for McCarthy." Besides, the law authorizing the libraries required that books "be descriptive of the U.S. or U.S. foreign policy"; strictly enforced, that requirement would exclude Shakespeare and the Bible. The president countered that such "arguments can be carried to extremes." He sighed. "I hate censorship."[5]

At the president's July 1 news conference, Raymond Brandt, a reporter with the *St. Louis Post-Dispatch*, prodded the president about "some confusion between your Dartmouth speech and your press conference speech in which you said it was perfectly all right for the State Department to burn books or to do as they pleased with them." Eisenhower bristled, "I said 'burned books'?" He said he had simply stated that the government could not legally promote the reading of books that advocated the overthrow of the US government. Brandt shot back, "I think there was a phrase there." Eisenhower barked, "What was that phrase?" "That they could do as they pleased about it," the reporter responded. Eisenhower countered, "I don't think I said they could do as they pleased." Brandt pointed out that mystery writer Dashiell Hammett's books had been "thrown out of the libraries." Ike snapped, "Who were they thrown out by?" Brandt suggested that a list had been provided to the librarians. "Here? In Washington?" the president shot back. Brandt provided the answer Ike wanted: "Oh, no; by the libraries overseas." "I think someone got frightened," Eisenhower said. "I don't know why they should. I wouldn't; I will tell you that, I wouldn't."[6]

That was not strictly accurate; Eisenhower, if not frightened, was clearly concerned that McCarthy might resurrect Ike's friendly postwar associations with communists and Soviet leaders in Germany. At a June stag dinner in the White House, Arthur Hays Sulzberger, *The New York Times'* publisher, perhaps at Ike's behest, proposed "political amnesty" for those who had ended questionable associations prior to the Berlin Airlift in 1948; such an amnesty would prevent their "automatically having a black mark." The day after his July 1 news conference, Eisenhower asked Herbert Brownell to involve J. Edgar Hoover in a review of that proposal. However, Ike eventually wrote Sulzberger that "the experts in the field"—meaning Brownell and Hoover—had declared the proposal "impractical." That was because communists, employing "lies, treachery, and deceit," often planted "sleepers" in important positions and such persons might "have merely cloaked their true feelings." Eisenhower understood that McCarthy would probably denounce such a proposal as "amnesty for traitors"—and include the president of the United States.[7]

MCCARTHY IN TROUBLE

Then McCarthy made a mistake that allowed Eisenhower to embarrass him. On June 18, he appointed a veteran Red hunter, Dr. J. B. Matthews, as executive director of his investigation subcommittee. Mathews had been chief of research for the House Committee on Un-American Activities from 1938 to 1945. Unknown to his new employer, Matthews had written an article entitled "Reds and Our Churches" for the July 1953 issue of *American Mercury.* Its opening line stirred up a hornet's nest: "The largest single group supporting the Communist apparatus in the United States today is composed of Protestant clergymen."

The Democratic members of McCarthy's subcommittee denounced the essay as "a shocking and unwarranted attack against the American clergy." Charles Potter, McCarthy's Republican subcommittee colleague from Michigan, called for Matthews's dismissal and condemned his charge that seven thousand Protestant clergy were providing "the party's subversive apparatus with its agents, stooges, dupes, front men and fellow travelers." The National Council of Churches declared that the piece reflected "a degree of stupidity and misrepresentation which can be reached only in an atmosphere of suspicion, distrust and fear." On Sunday, July 5, prestigious pulpits across the country reverberated with denunciations of Matthews.[8]

McCarthy resisted the protests. He refused to accept Matthews's resignation, insisting he had the authority to individually hire or dismiss subcommittee staff members. At a heated two-hour closed session on July 7, the subcommittee was unable to reach an agreement. However, by the next day, Republican leaders in the Senate were predicting that McCarthy would be forced to accept Matthews's resignation.[9]

The Matthews uproar was, as Bernard Shanley put it, "an opportunity which we couldn't miss." William Rogers urged a rapid response. "The reason Joe gets away with so damn much," he told Emmet Hughes, "is that he always has the other guy on the defensive before the slugging starts—and here's our chance to get Joe on the defensive." Shanley, with Eisenhower's approval, called Dr. Everett Clinchy, the Episcopal priest who headed the National Conference of Christians and Jews. Shanley urged Clinchy to send the president a telegram protesting Matthews's article and signed by the three prelates—Catholic, Jewish, and Protestant—on the NCCJ governing board. The telegram arrived at midday, calling "the sweeping attack" on the patriotism of Protestant clergymen "unjustified and deplorable."[10]

"I want you to know at once that I fully share the convictions you state," Eisenhower wrote the NCCJ leaders. He denounced "irresponsible attacks that sweepingly condemn the whole of any group of citizens," asserting that such assaults "betray contempt for the principles of freedom and decency," when directed at "such a vast portion of the churches or clergy." Once again, he preserved his "principles, not personalities" strategy, avoiding mention of either McCarthy or Matthews.[11]

The challenge was to deliver Eisenhower's letter to the press before McCarthy could announce his dismissal of Matthews. Richard Nixon and William Rogers waylaid the senator, allowing time for release of the president's statement; that left the impression that Eisenhower had forced McCarthy to accept Matthews's resignation. Emmet Hughes told Shanley that, after playing that trick on the senator, he "didn't see how Bill Rogers could ever look Joe McCarthy in the eye again."[12]

The operation had the desired effect. *The Washington Post* declared that Eisenhower's charge that such attacks on the clergy were "alien to America" was effectively saying that "McCarthyism is alien to America." *The New York Times* called the president's message "a direct shot by President Eisenhower at Senator Joseph R. McCarthy." Eisenhower had "struck, and struck hard, at the peculiar form of un-Americanism which has come to be known as McCarthyism." He had, the paper declared, "slapped Mr. McCarthy down."[13]

Shanley recorded in his diary that the Matthews episode was "the first real nail in the McCarthy coffin." Eisenhower expressed pleasure to Emmet Hughes because "that guy"—McCarthy—in defense of Matthews had talked "about not censoring anybody, when all he's been doing is trying to act like a goddam censor himself."[14]

A STRESSED PRESIDENT

Six months in the presidency had taken a toll on Eisenhower. On July 10, the day after the Matthews uproar, the president informed Nixon that as soon as Congress adjourned, he intended to vacation for five or six weeks. That very day, he hoped to skip the cabinet meeting and get out of town. However, aides persuaded their grumpy boss that they had business to bring up that would require his presence.[15]

On his way to the meeting, Shanley encountered the president "in a complete foul mood"; Ike did not even say "Good morning." He was visibly exasperated during Nixon's opening remarks. Suddenly, the vice president declared that they were all there "to congratulate the President on his leadership on the great anniversary of his nomination." The president, Nixon said, was a dedicated fisherman who had become a "fisher of votes" in the Congress. In honor of this anniversary, the staff had draped two dozen large fishing lures on a three-foot-square plaque. As Press Secretary Jim Hagerty and another staffer attempted to turn the plaque for viewing, one of the lures hooked Hagerty's pants "in an embarrassing location." The more the press secretary tried to extricate himself, the worse it got. The room shook with laughter, led by Ike, whose "tears were just streaming down his face." Finally, Agriculture Secretary Ezra Benson produced a penknife and cut Hagerty out of his problem, ruining his best blue suit. Shanley quipped to the president that this "was one fly he hadn't expected." [16]

After the cabinet meeting, the president hosted a gathering to sign a bill creating a commission on intergovernmental relations. A staffer described McCarthy as "lost in the crowd." Shanley observed that he looked "awfully queer, as though he wasn't sure he should have come." Eisenhower looked out at the group, spotted McCarthy in the back row, waved and boomed, "Hello there!" McCarthy waved back and smiled. Once again, even to his face, Ike had not used the senator's name. [17]

Despite the Matthews affair, McCarthy's subcommittee voted 4 to 3 along party lines to affirm the senator's authority to employ or discharge staff members without a vote; in response, the three Democratic members walked out. A week later, the Democrats rejected a two thousand-word letter from McCarthy urging their return. By mid-July, *The New York Times* found the senator "in the middle of a widening storm," the result of "sharp attacks on both the Senate and White House fronts." "For the first time in his career here," wrote William S. White, McCarthy "has been thrown upon the defensive and, indeed, compelled to retreat." Arthur Krock headed his July 12 column "President Gets Tough and Finds It Pays Off." He equated the president's strategy with Colonel William Prescott's order to the Minutemen in 1775: "Don't fire until you see the whites of their eyes." [18]

In response to such reports, Edward "Swede" Hazlett, a boyhood friend of Ike, congratulated the president that "at last you are ready to crack down on McCarthy." Eisenhower responded, "I disagree completely with the 'crack down' theory." To attack out of "anger or irritation," he said, would "do far more to destroy the position and authority of the attacker than it would do to damage the attacked." [19]

On July 22, the weary President Eisenhower faced the press.

Richard Wilson of Cowles Publications noted that many people were urging the president to "bring some discipline into the Republican Party by cracking down on McCarthy." Ike tersely reminded the reporter that he never dealt "in terms of personalities, and I don't now." Nevertheless, he took a shot at McCarthy's methods: "You cannot get ahead merely by indulging extremist views and listening to them. What do they bring? They don't bring majority action."[20]

PEACE IN KOREA

On the Fourth of July weekend, Eisenhower received a letter from Robert Johnson, the IIA director, saying his doctors "have given me final orders to leave my present post within thirty days." Whatever his health issues, Eisenhower was probably glad to see Johnson go. Once Johnson indicated his intention to resign, Eisenhower moved quickly to resolve the remaining issues with the IIA. On July 7, Johnson, almost certainly on Eisenhower's orders, announced that officials in the overseas libraries had been instructed to restore numerous books to their shelves. The new criteria reflected Eisenhower's view that combating communism mandated knowing what it was. While "these libraries are in business to advance American democracy, not Communist conspiracy," Johnson asserted, "it would be unwise to foreclose the opportunity of using, to serve affirmatively the ends of democracy, something that a Communist has written for an entirely different purpose." Predictably, McCarthy termed the new directive "completely ridiculous"; he argued that the sole purpose of any communist author was to bring about "the end of democracy," not its idealistic "ends," as Johnson had stated.[21]

Eisenhower had already submitted a plan to Congress to establish the United States Information Agency (USIA) outside the State Department. This time Eisenhower, rather than Dulles, selected the new director. He chose Theodore Streibert, the former head of the Mutual Broadcasting System, who was working with

High Commissioner James Conant in Germany. The new agency was scheduled to come into being on August 1.[22]

Suddenly, events in Korea seized center stage; Eisenhower's great mission since taking office had been to end that war, eclipsing all concerns with Joe McCarthy. On Friday afternoon, July 25, the president huddled with Secretary Dulles to review the status of the armistice talks. He stayed up until nearly 1:30 a.m., reminiscing with aides about the end of the war in Europe. Assistant Staff Secretary Arthur Minnich noted that, on Saturday, Eisenhower "was under considerable strain" and "stayed up long beyond his customary bedtime on Saturday night, again talking almost incessantly to his close friends." The White House expected the truce to be signed on Sunday morning; if that happened, the president wanted cabinet members to attend church with him. However, the signing ceremony was delayed until Sunday evening.

Finally, the word came. On Sunday, July 26, at 10:00 p.m. Eastern Time, the president spoke to the nation: "Tonight we greet, with prayers of thanksgiving, the official news that an armistice was signed almost an hour ago in Korea." He reminded the American people that "we have won an armistice on a single battleground— not peace in the world. We may not now relax our guard nor cease our quest." The President closed with the words from Abraham Lincoln's second inaugural address: "With malice toward none; with charity for all; with firmness in the right as God gives us to see the right, let us strive on to finish the work we are in . . . to do all which may achieve and cherish a just and a lasting peace, among ourselves, and with all nations."[23]

McCarthy recognized that the political winds were not blowing in his direction. Eisenhower's success at peacemaking could derail his own embryonic presidential ambitions. The night the armistice was announced, McCarthy, at Nixon's urging, announced that his now all-Republican investigative subcommittee would shift its emphasis from communism to corruption. The Democrats still refused to return to McCarthy's subcommittee. William S. White described the decline in McCarthy's fortunes; for the first time, he wrote, Senate

Democrats were "in almost unbroken array against Senator McCarthy," and key Republicans were demonstrably less supportive.[24]

McCarthy's commitment to a change of direction lasted less than a week. During August 1953, he sniped at several prospective investigative targets, again denouncing aid to allies shipping strategic goods to China, accusing Allen Dulles of "covering up" subversive activity in the CIA, and alleging that secret documents processed in the Government Printing Office might be accessible to communist spies.[25]

In spite of the apparent decline in McCarthy's fortunes at home, Eisenhower was plagued with the impact of the senator's investigations on US prestige abroad. At the July 9 National Security Council meeting, he expressed himself "much disturbed and concerned that so many of our allies seem frightened of what they imagine the United States Government is up to." "The name of McCarthy," he noted, "was on everyone's lips and he was constantly compared to Adolf Hitler." John Foster Dulles confirmed that some European leaders believed they were witnessing the rise of "an American fascism."[26]

McCarthy's negative impact was not confined to Europe. Francis O. Wilcox, chief of staff for the Senate Foreign Relations Committee, recalled a trip to Asia with Republican Senator Alexander Smith of New Jersey. Wherever they went, Asian leaders had made "strong representations" about McCarthy, wondering "when somebody was going to do something about it." Upon their return, the men visited with Eisenhower. For what must have felt like the hundredth time, Eisenhower said, "Gentlemen, I refuse to get down in the gutter and fight with Senator McCarthy. . . . It would only be degrading to the office of the President of the United States for me to engage in combat with a person like Senator McCarthy."[27]

On July 9, the day of that disillusioning NSC meeting, Ike wrote UN ambassador Henry Cabot Lodge "in the midst of a difficult day," recalling a statement attributed to George Washington in 1789: "My movements to the chair of the government will be accompanied by feelings not unlike those of a culprit who is going to the place of his execution."[28]

DEPLOYING IKE'S "RESERVE DIVISION"

On July 7, G. David Schine was notified that he would be drafted into the US Army. That seemingly small incident was destined to grow into the scandal that within a year would become the reason for the Army–McCarthy hearings.

Roy Cohn immediately launched a frantic effort to keep Schine with him on the McCarthy subcommittee. The day after Schine received his notice, McCarthy asked General Miles Reber, the army's legislative liaison officer, to come to his office. The senator, Reber recalled, "told me that he was very interested in securing a commission as a reserve officer in the Army of the United States for his assistant, Mr. G. David Schine." Cohn "emphasized the necessity for rapid action." Reber received "numerous phone calls" from Cohn urging "expedition in this case" plus additional pleas from McCarthy. About a week after their meeting, the adjutant general informed Reber that Schine was not eligible for a commission.[29]

Any doubt that Eisenhower was aware of the agitation on behalf of Schine is dispelled by the fact that Cohn personally pled his case with two of Ike's closest wartime associates. In August, he urged Undersecretary of State Bedell Smith to use his influence to get Schine a commission. Smith made phone calls to his army contacts and then informed Cohn that Schine was ineligible and no exception could be made. In response, Cohn went to the White House and asked the congressional liaison, General Jerry Persons—another Eisenhower comrade in arms—to inquire whether the navy could provide a commission for Schine. Persons called an admiral's aide, who, treating a call from the White House as serious business, relayed the inquiry to Admiral James L. Holloway III, the chief of naval personnel. Persons received the navy's response through the president's naval aide, probably reflecting a presidential review: the navy would not provide a direct commission to a young man eligible for the army draft.

Struve Hensel, the Pentagon's general counsel, recalled that Sherman Adams had informed him about Cohn's visit to Persons. If

Adams was involved, so was the president. After all, it was the White House, where, as Adams later recalled, "Nothing else mattered half as much as Joe McCarthy." In any event, Cohn's pleas were rejected at every turn. That rejection would have ramifications. Washington insiders knew that, with rare exceptions, Cohn selected McCarthy's investigative targets, and the US Army was now in his investigative cross hairs. By implication, so was the general in the White House.[30]

About the time Schine got his draft notice, Eisenhower made a phone call to Fred A. Seaton in Nebraska, asking him to serve in the Pentagon. Though no direct connection between the two events can be documented, their ultimate convergence is indisputable. Seaton's son Don recalls that his father hinted that Eisenhower's stated reason was to "put a muzzle" on Secretary Charles Wilson, a paramount need in coping with Joe McCarthy.

Eisenhower, the military commander, liked to put key men in position in anticipation of a battle, even when he did not know exactly how or when the clash would take place. Therefore, he asked Seaton to take a redesigned assistant secretary position in the Defense Department. Bernard Shanley called the new job "the top liaison job in the Defense Department and the Hill." That meant Seaton would often deal directly with McCarthy. Seaton went to the White House for an off-the-record discussion with the president on July 13 and returned on July 27, the day after the Korean armistice was announced.[31]

Fred Seaton was part of the Eisenhower political clan. He had grown up in Manhattan, Kansas, just down the road from Eisenhower's Abilene. The Seatons, a newspaper family, had been active in Republican politics. Fred's father had been a secretary to Senator Joseph L. Bristow, who had endorsed Ike's application to West Point. During the 1936 presidential campaign, Fred had served as secretary to Alfred M. Landon, the Republican nominee. In 1937, he had moved to Nebraska to become the publisher of the *Hastings Daily Tribune*. After the death of Nebraska Republican senator Kenneth S. Wherry in November 1951, the governor appointed Seaton to fill the seat, but Seaton agreed not to run in 1952. However, during the year he served in the Senate, Seaton developed a friendly relationship with McCarthy. He was among those who traveled to Paris to urge General Eisenhower to run for president. When Eisenhower and Seaton met, Fred's wife, Gladys, recalled that it was "love at first sight." When Eisenhower agreed to become a candidate, Seaton joined the campaign as press liaison.

William Ewald recalled that Fred Seaton was "a smoothie," politically astute and skillful in relations with a wide range of people. More important, he was, as Gladys Seaton put it, "wholly devoted to General Eisenhower"; Seaton quickly became known as "Ike's trouble shooter." The one blemish on his record was that prior to Ike's campaign appearance in Milwaukee, Wisconsin, on October 3, 1952, he had hinted to the press about the general's plan to praise George Marshall, unaware that Wisconsin politicians had persuaded Eisenhower to delete those words from his speech.[32]

Eisenhower needed Seaton and was determined, whatever the obstacles, to install him in the Pentagon. The man he had initially relied upon to manage McCarthy, Robert Taft, died on July 31. When the cabinet met that morning, Eisenhower decreed that "under no circumstances" should cabinet members or White House staff "give any indication of having any interest" in the contest over the majority leader's position between California Senator William Knowland and Illinois Senator Everett Dirksen. Later that day, he issued a statement calling the passing of Robert Taft "a tragic loss to America." Taft, he said, had served the nation "with distinction and integrity" and would be "greatly missed." The president added: "I have lost a wise counsellor and a valued friend." He ordered the flags on government buildings in Washington, DC, flown at half-staff. A few days later, Knowland was unanimously elected to succeed Taft as majority leader.[33]

VACATION!

On Saturday morning, August 8, the president and Mrs. Eisenhower departed the White House for National Airport. While Mamie visited her mother in Denver, Ike planned to go trout fishing and put to use the lures that had so embarrassed Jim Hagerty the previous month. Ike wrote a friend that day that although he expected "one of these never-ending emergencies could pop up its head," he was determined "to forget all this political yammering" and "go up in the hills, fry a fish and cook a pancake; and, when I get on the golf course, try to stay under 120." [34]

The first emergency took only a few days. On August 12, the president learned that the Soviet Union had successfully tested a thermonuclear device, ending the US monopoly on hydrogen weapons. The other major event, a week later, was a coup in Iran, engineered by British intelligence and the CIA. That covert operation overthrew Prime Minister Mohammad Mossadegh and his cabinet, restoring Mohammad Reza Pahlavi, the shah of Iran, to his throne. [35]

Though Eisenhower was immersed in those events, he carved out time to nail down Fred Seaton's new role. He confronted skepticism among White House staff about the appointment. Bernard Shanley worried that the liaison job "was a position [in] which you couldn't win and most surely [would] lose." Jerry Persons agreed, expressing the opinion that Seaton "was not really qualified for the job." Shanley called the president in Colorado to express their concerns, but Eisenhower was resolute. Shanley recorded in his diary that the president "had seen Seaton and was committed to offering him the position." [36]

Secretary Wilson was also apparently reluctant; he knew the new assistant secretary would be Ike's man, not his. By that time, neither Eisenhower nor White House staff was inclined to grant Wilson a veto. Speechwriter Robert Kieve complained that Wilson constantly "exuded General Motor-ism" and told "truly pointless" stories. He termed Wilson "not terribly articulate," a man who often gave "no real impression he's been doing any productive thinking." Eisenhower himself had become impatient with Wilson. Richard Nixon recalled Ike's annoyance when Wilson, sitting next to him in cabinet meetings, blew smoke rings into the face of the president, who had quit smoking years earlier. Sherman Adams attempted to limit Wilson's interaction with the president. Eisenhower told Adams he didn't want aides "to come in here and bother me the way Charlie Wilson does. He comes in here and sits here and asks me questions about details of his own job and if he wasn't able to do them, he shouldn't have the job."[37]

Seaton would inherit the frustrating task of dealing with the secretary of defense. The Nebraskan made a third trip to Washington, this time to discuss his new job with Wilson himself, and phoned the president in Colorado to report on the meeting. The same day, the president wrote Wilson, "This morning I had a long talk with Fred Seaton. He told me about his recent conversation with you. I am of the personal opinion that he could and would do you a very fine job as a policy man in the field of cultivating good relations for the Defense Department." He made it abundantly clear how special the new man was to him. Seaton, Ike wrote, had traveled with him "all over the United States" during the campaign. "Not only does he have many good and useful qualities, but he is, of course, well acquainted with most of the individuals now serving intimately on my staff." Therefore, in the event of "an emergency in the White House staff, I might have to call upon him to come in and help out." Eisenhower bestowed a commanding general's stamp of approval on Seaton: "I have always looked upon him as a 'reserve division,' ready to go into action."[38]

Ike's artful suggestion that he might eventually want Seaton in the White House underlined Seaton's influence with the president; Wilson was expected to take him seriously. On September 3, the White House—not Wilson's office—announced Frederick A. Seaton's recess appointment to a "new position" serving as the department's principal liaison with Congress. Seaton told reporters he would "do his best" and was "deeply moved by the confidence the President and Secretary of Defense Wilson have shown in me by this appointment."[39]

DECLARING WAR ON THE ARMY

Ike's characterization of Fred Seaton as his "reserve division" on August 24 was timely. The president's congressional staff had surely

alerted him that McCarthy planned to launch hearings the following week on communists in the US Army. The senator gave a direct
hint in a speech on August 28 in St. Louis to the American Legion
National Security Commission. A month earlier he had announced,
at Nixon's behest, that he would shift his investigative emphasis from
communism to corruption. Now he declared his determination to
pursue communist subversion even if his probes embarrassed the Eisenhower administration. The senator ridiculed colleagues—perhaps
a jab at Nixon—who were saying "Now that we're in power why
don't you lay off! Don't embarrass this Administration." Decked out
in a Legion uniform, McCarthy proclaimed, "As long as I am in the
United States Senate I'll guarantee there will be no protection for
communism, corruption or treason. I don't give a tinker's dam who
is embarrassed by it." [40]

McCarthy's first hearing in search of communists in the US
Army took place at 10:30 a.m. on Monday, August 31, in room 126
of the Federal Court House in Foley Square, New York City. It was
a one-senator hearing, with McCarthy flanked by attorney Frank
Carr (who had replaced J. B. Matthews as subcommittee executive
director), Roy Cohn, and David Schine, who would not have to
report to the army until November. Three army employees were
slated to testify; Doris Walters Powell, a clerical worker; Francesco
Palmiero, a security officer; and Albert Feldman, a warehouse employee.

McCarthy's interrogation of Doris Walters Powell provides a
microcosm of the senator's techniques for intimidating witnesses
and converting the testimony of low-level employees into headlines.
After the young woman was sworn in, McCarthy's first words were
designed to strike fear into this African American clerical worker
on maternity leave. "Let me say this, Mrs. Powell," McCarthy began.
"We have information of Communist party membership on your
part." He warned her, "A number of people have come into the
committee guilty of no crime except membership of the Communist party, which legally, you know, is not a crime unless the party
is using force or violence in the overthrowing of the government.

In the end, when they leave the committee room they are guilty of perjury. If the answer tends to incriminate you, don't answer. Tell the truth or don't answer."

The fear in Powell's voice leaps from the pages of the transcript. "I am on maternal leave from the government," she plaintively responded. During the war, Powell had worked as a clerk-typist for the New York War Production Board; since 1950, she had been employed at the New York Quartermaster Corps office, 111 East Sixteenth Street. When asked the nature of her present duties, she responded that she was a "procurement-clerk," processing invoices requiring payment by the government for food for the army.

McCarthy and Cohn barked questions so rapidly that Powell became confused. When she expressed her bewilderment, McCarthy pounced: "Be sure you answer the question. . . . We do have evidence here, strong evidence of activities on your part—of Communist activities. . . . We have no interest at all in having you guilty of perjury. Don't answer unless you know what you are answering."

Cohn delivered the jackpot question: "Have you ever been a member of the Communist party?" Powell hesitated. "I don't feel as though I have been—not to my knowledge." "Do you think you might have been without your knowing about it?" Right on cue, McCarthy jumped in to advise Mrs. Powell's attorney that he should advise his client "that we have the positive evidence—that is correct, Roy, isn't it—of Communist activities and Communist membership. I have no interest at all in having this woman be a perjury case." Cohn repeated, "Have you ever been a member of the Communist party?" Powell responded once again, "I don't feel that I have been."

McCarthy's premise for badgering this witness was that, between her two stints in government service, Powell had worked for *The People's Voice*, an African American–oriented newspaper in Harlem that Doxey Wilkerson, an alleged communist, had taken over after World War II. McCarthy stalked his prey with his patented guilt-by-association technique. "You went to this meeting, these Communist meetings?" Powell responded, "Now I realize, yes." When asked about attending a radical school, she recalled having attended lectures around 1946 or 1947 "on Negro history." Cohn asked, "Do you now realize that that was a Communistic school?" "Now I realize, yes," she confessed, but she insisted she had never attended lectures about "overthrowing the government." "But you say you weren't a Communist?" Powell retreated to her mournful answer: "I don't feel I was."

McCarthy pressed Powell on whether she had paid "any dues to the Communist party?" Intimidated, Powell said, "I am thinking." "You would remember if you paid them money, I assume?" McCarthy barked. Powell granted that she might have made "contributions" or given to "collections." "Did you give [to] collections where you knew the money was going to the Communist party?" "No, I didn't, no. Not to my knowledge that it was going to the Communists."

McCarthy asked if Powell had ever been "issued a membership card of the Communist party?" Roy Cohn added a sinister warning: "Be very careful." "I received a card—something," Powell confessed. "I had to have membership to get into a meeting where Doxey Wilkerson was attending." Cohn asked if the card had "Communist Party" printed on it. Powell, confused, thought she had not received that kind of card.

McCarthy moved in for the kill: "Isn't it correct that you said before you attended this Communist meeting with Wilkerson and that you were issued a card which showed in its face that you were being given membership in the Communist party, and it had a number on the card?" Powell eventually responded "yes" but insisted, "I never signed it. I never applied. I never signed anything." Pressed by Cohn, she confessed that Doxey Wilkerson's secretary had given her the card. Powell claimed she had only wanted to help with the paper "for the benefit of the Negro people"; it was later she learned that the leaders at the *Voice* "were found to be Communists."[41]

Afterward, McCarthy, without revealing names, informed reporters he had interrogated army civilian employees whose jobs involved handling classified information that could "tip off troop movements" but who denied their membership in the communist party. The woman, he said without identifying her, was involved with "purchasing and checking invoices" regarding shipments of food to "practically every base" around the globe. McCarthy misled reporters about the length of Powell's interrogation, stating that she had been questioned for twenty minutes when, in fact, it had been an hour.[42]

On September 3, *The New York Times* reported that McCarthy had "ordered" the army to produce the personnel files of the three army employees he had interrogated and the names of the loyalty board members who had approved their employment. That demand was contrary to President Truman's 1948 executive order barring the provision of information about federal employees' loyalty without White House clearance, later modified to require the department head's approval. Based on that directive, the army refused to disclose the names of the individuals on loyalty boards. The army's legislative liaison officer, General Miles Reber, stated that the issue "might have to be carried to President Eisenhower for a showdown." Senator McCarthy, the *Times* reported, "conceded that President Eisenhower's permission might have to be sought."[43]

Senator Joe McCarthy had launched a frontal assault on General Dwight D. Eisenhower's army.

CHAPTER 4

THE SECRETARY AND THE SENATOR

The implications of Joe McCarthy's decision to pursue communists in the United States Army were profound. Henry Cabot Lodge, a frequent Eisenhower adviser, believed it proved McCarthy was out to destroy Eisenhower. Lodge told Army Secretary Robert Stevens in early 1954 that he had "no doubt" that McCarthy had picked on the Army "because Eisenhower was in the Army."[1]

But Lodge ascribed a coherence to McCarthy's decision making that others contradicted. Deputy Attorney General William Rogers asserted, "Joe never plans a damn thing." However, the threat was implicit, if not explicit. Roy Cohn was determined to punish the army for its treatment of David Schine, and some pundits agreed with Eisenhower that McCarthy had "the bug to run for the presidency in 1956."[2]

STEVENS TAKES CENTER STAGE

This situation put Robert Stevens in the eye of the storm. He heard about McCarthy's August 31 hearing about communists in the army while on vacation at his Montana ranch and quickly wired McCarthy that, as soon as he returned to Washington, he would call the senator's office "to offer my services in trying to assist you to correct anything that may be wrong." That action was typical for Stevens;

he cherished the illusion that he could charm McCarthy into being prudent about his investigation.[3]

Eisenhower knew that Stevens would need supervision. On September 7, a week after McCarthy's first interrogation of army personnel, the president summoned Stevens to Denver. His objective was to establish a clear policy to address McCarthy's insistence on obtaining the names of the people on the "loyalty boards"—the Truman-era panels that had cleared the senator's August 31 witnesses for service. In addition, he apparently briefed Stevens about Fred Seaton's new role in the Pentagon.

After talking with the president, Stevens outlined to the press the dual strategy Eisenhower had ordained. The secretary promised "wholehearted cooperation" with McCarthy's investigation but added that existing presidential executive orders—referring to Truman's 1948 directive—might require him to withhold confidential loyalty information. "So far as Communist infiltration of the Army is concerned," he said, "I'll oppose it to the limit of my ability." Asked if he would be willing to testify, Stevens responded, "Oh, sure."[4]

That was the plan. Officials would smilingly cooperate with McCarthy—but only to a point; then, citing the Truman ruling, they would dig in their heels about the names of panel members and the release of confidential personnel records. Herbert Brownell later called Eisenhower's strategy "a turning point" in dealing with McCarthy. It would be subsequently codified in an executive order in November that laid the foundation for a future claim of executive privilege, to be used against McCarthy.[5]

However, Steven's reflex was to negotiate personally with McCarthy. Upon returning to his Washington office the next day, he set up a luncheon meeting with the senator. Afterward the secretary again invoked Eisenhower's policy of cooperation—again, only to a point. He assured the press that there would be no "cover-up" or "whitewash" but said he might have to take the issue to the White House for resolution.[6]

Immediately, a trio of Eisenhower's key operatives began checking up on Stevens, fearing he might go overboard in accommodating

McCarthy. The morning after Stevens's luncheon with McCarthy, Rogers called the secretary, ostensibly about an army personnel issue. "I feel a little like Joe McCarthy, calling you on this matter," he quipped. That was Rogers's glib lead-in to ask about the luncheon meeting and "How are you getting along with Jumping Joe?" Stevens's response was upbeat: "I would say I got along perfectly well yesterday. I am not the kind of a fellow to go around borrowing trouble." He proclaimed himself "perfectly willing" to yield on small matters but, "when it comes to major policies backed by Executive Orders of the President, we are going to stand tightly and see what happens." Rogers responded, "I think half the battle is to have a good relationship with him."[7]

Struve Hensel, the Pentagon's general counsel, was less sanguine. On September 10, he phoned Stevens to inform him that he had discussed McCarthy's demands regarding the loyalty boards with Assistant Attorney General Lee Rankin. Rankin had urged that they develop "an over-all policy" endorsed by both the attorney general and the White House and that Truman's executive order prohibiting the sharing of personnel information should be rewritten. Fred Seaton provided handwritten notes on that conversation to Sherman Adams, presumably for the president's eyes; apparently, he had been listening in on the call, five days prior to his scheduled swearing in.[8]

Then McCarthy escalated his charges against the army, announcing that he had secured a "restricted" army document entitled "Psychological and Cultural Traits of Soviet Siberia." The article had been distributed to the Army Far East Command "to develop an understanding of the Soviet people which will be militarily useful in case of war." McCarthy described the document as "the best Communist propaganda I've seen in some time"—"95 per cent Communist propaganda. Two or 3 or 5 per cent is a slap on the wrist for communism."[9]

The army struck back, accusing McCarthy of releasing a "restricted" military intelligence document—an offense that, on conviction, could result in a $10,000 fine and up to ten years in prison. McCarthy confessed that he had not known the seventy-five page document was "classified," but he was not intimidated. General Matthew Ridgway, the army chief of staff, informed Stevens that McCarthy was demanding that an officer appear before his subcommittee, "prepared to furnish details regarding this pamphlet." Stevens wondered if he should go to New York "and see Joe or the staff and see what it is they want and when they want it and get the thing back on track." [10]

As a result of Stevens's efforts to appease McCarthy, Doris Walters Powell, who had testified on August 31, was suspended. McCarthy called Powell "a 100 per cent Communist," although her attorney insisted that she had never joined the Communist Party, "nor did she ever consider herself a Communist." McCarthy called Powell's suspension "another good, strong indication that the secretary of the army was sincere in his statement that he was going to cooperate in getting rid of Communists and alleged Communists." [11]

The Pentagon was a cauldron of fevered activity in preparation for the president's return from vacation and McCarthy's mounting confrontation with the army. On September 14, Stevens met with key Pentagon and military leaders. The participants agreed that it was imperative to uphold Eisenhower's twofold strategy; the memorandum summarizing the meeting stated, "Senator McCarthy should be informed by Mr. Stevens that he (Mr. Stevens) does not intend to recommend to the President that the loyalty and security files of the employees in question nor the names of individuals who may have granted or withheld security clearances in their cases, be released." However, the secretary would "make every effort to communicate his position to the Senator in as straightforward but friendly a manner as possible." The conferees fully expected that, upon receiving such news, "Senator McCarthy will probably explode in the press." [12]

Three days later, Roy Cohn called Stevens to ask what time on Monday "would be convenient" for the secretary to testify at a hearing on communists in the army. Cohn's second agenda item was about David Schine. "We are a little pressed for time on that personal matter," Cohn said, referring to Schine. Stevens had no news to share. That was one of Cohn's numerous calls during the month, piggybacking his queries about "that personal matter" onto subcommittee business.[13]

SEATON TAKES CHARGE

On September 15, Ike's "reserve division" was officially deployed. Fred Seaton was sworn in as assistant secretary of defense and installed in an office next door to Secretary Wilson and general counsel Struve Hensel. Seaton had already surmised that Army Secretary Stevens was conducting a quixotic crusade to single-handedly manage the army's relationship with McCarthy. That evening, Stevens flew to New York with Wilson and Treasury Secretary George Humphrey for a dinner in Stevens's honor. At 9:45 the next morning, Stevens breakfasted with McCarthy at the Waldorf Towers suite of David Schine's parents.[14]

The day following Stevens's breakfast meeting with McCarthy, Seaton tried repeatedly to get a phone conversation with the secretary. Finally, at 5:39 p.m., Stevens called him back. Though he was superficially friendly, Seaton's intent was to assert his role and restrain Stevens's penchant for personal diplomacy with the dangerous McCarthy. Seaton asked the secretary for "your own appraisal" of the meeting with the senator. Stevens asserted that "so far the thing has gone along surprisingly well." He had agreed to provide McCarthy the names of the people who had reviewed one case involving an alleged homosexual, but "I refused, of course, on the loyalty files and things of that kind. Joe was definitely pleased with the conference; so I feel I had accomplished quite a bit."

It was not encouraging that Stevens had thrown McCarthy a low-level personnel bone. Mixing flattery with questions, Seaton revealed that he, too, had talked with McCarthy. "You must have done a bang-up job with him," he said to Stevens. "He complimented you highly." However, Seaton pointedly added, "The only thing I was surprised at was that he said he had established a liaison." That was a sticking point; Eisenhower's explicit assignment to Seaton was to serve as Pentagon liaison with Congress, especially McCarthy—a matter the president had surely discussed with Stevens in Colorado. However, Stevens had recruited John G. Adams, Struve Hensel's assistant general counsel, as "the Army's liaison with McCarthy and his committee." [15]

Stevens backpedaled, assuring Seaton that Adams, as his personal representative, would be "reasonably close to you." Therefore, "if McCarthy calls up, and I am not here and he calls you, you take it on and see what it is and we will talk about it later." He claimed he understood what was expected. "We will keep that"—meaning relations with McCarthy—"coordinated with you in any way you want. In other words, we will not go off here by ourselves." The secretary exuded a nervous optimism: "I think we are getting along well with Joe," although, he added, "I don't know how long it will last."

Seaton mixed more flattery with a subtle warning. "You have done such a good job," he said, "that you may find yourself a representative of everybody in the Department of Defense. Have you thought of that?" That was his smooth way of warning "Be careful what you do." When Stevens said he would be pleased to be of service, Seaton responded, "I was half-serious and half-facetious." "At the moment we are in good shape," Stevens tried to assure him, adding "I am sure glad you are there." Indeed, reinforcing that fact had been Seaton's purpose for the conversation. [16]

THE GENERAL RETURNS TO THE FRONT

About 7:40 p.m. on September 19, the president's plane, the *Columbine,* touched down at National Airport. Front-page pictures of the smiling, waving Ike supported a *New York Times* reporter's conclusion that the president "had the ruddy look of a man who had spent much time out-of-doors." [17]

At 10:30 a.m. on September 21, McCarthy held another closed-door hearing. Afterward, he charged that material written by Russian authors containing "calculated misinformation" had been used by the US Army in courses for officers. However, he noted that Robert Stevens had been present at the hearing and that the secretary "was eager as was the subcommittee" to eliminate any Soviet propaganda in those courses.[18]

On the day of that hearing, Eisenhower spoke in Boston at a Republican fund-raising dinner and addressed McCarthy's favorite issue, "making certain that every government employee is a loyal American." Once again, without using the senator's name, he denigrated McCarthy's methods. He expressed pride that "we have opposed the confusing of loyalty with conformity, and all misguided attempts to convert freedom into a privilege licensed by censors." Eisenhower warned, "We must, even in our zeal to defeat the enemies of freedom, never betray ourselves into seizing their weapons to make our own defense." He envisioned an America that "is too strong ever to acknowledge fear—and too wise ever to fear knowledge." "This," the president concluded, "is the kind of America—and the kind of Republican Party—in which I believe."[19]

On September 29, Senator Joseph McCarthy and Jean Kerr, a research assistant on his office staff, were married at the Cathedral of St. Matthew the Apostle. Vice President and Mrs. Nixon attended; so did Robert Stevens. The president and Mrs. Eisenhower sent regrets. Three White House aides, including Sherman Adams, represented the president. Ike had more pressing business. The next day, he conducted his first news conference since leaving for vacation in Colorado and began by stating "I intend to designate Governor Earl Warren as Chief Justice of the United States." Given the importance of that news, reporters did not bring up McCarthy's investigation of the army.[20]

The issue of internal security—McCarthy's issue—hovered over almost every presidential meeting. At the October 2 cabinet meeting, C. D. Jackson, Eisenhower's psychological warfare advisor, shared that Theodore Streibert, the new USIA head, "had separated 2500 people since taking charge of the new Information Agency." Eisenhower exploded: "If there are 2500 security risks in one office, I am going to quit!" Jackson hastened to explain that not all of the

2,500 were security risks, and that the number reflected a general reduction in personnel.[21]

In spite of constant urging to crack down on McCarthy, Eisenhower resolutely maintained his commitment to speak about "principles, not personalities." Still, some of the president's most fervent supporters could not comprehend his refusal to speak out. His brother Milton shared a letter with Ike from Nicholas Roosevelt, an author, diplomat, and distant cousin of Theodore and Franklin. Roosevelt implied that the president had become the captive of his party's reactionary wing, personified by Joe McCarthy, "neo-fascist, insanely ambitious and utterly unprincipled." Roosevelt lamented "the President's failure to stand up to McCarthy." Ike wrote Milton "a personal and confidential" response to Roosevelt's letter, encouraging him to write his own letter summarizing the president's thoughts.

Eisenhower's reaction to Roosevelt's critique was harsh: "The writer labors under the false but prevalent notion that bullying and leadership are synonymous; that desk-pounding is more effective than is persistent adherence to a purpose and winning to that purpose sufficient support for its achievement." "As for McCarthy," he continued, "only a short-sighted or completely inexperienced individual would urge the use of the office of the Presidency to give an opponent the publicity he so avidly desires." He said he had repeatedly spoken out, "without apology or evasion," for upholding "the right of the individual, for free expression of convictions, even though those convictions might be unpopular, and for uncensored use of our libraries, except as dictated by common decency." The president asserted, "There would be far more progress made against so-called 'McCarthy-ism' if individuals of an opposing purpose would take it upon themselves to help sustain and promote their own ideals, rather than to wait and wait for a blasting of their pet enemies by someone else."

Eisenhower wrapped up his argument: "I have no intention whatsoever of helping promote the publicity value of anyone who disagrees with me—demagogue or not!" "I have not changed," he declared. "I stand for exactly the same things that I have stood for for many years." As president, he had "never indulged in bitter personal indictment or attack. To my mind, that practice smacks more of the coward and the fool than the leader." [22]

The president's anger reflected his growing impatience with both McCarthy and those who were harassing him to crack down on the senator. Still, Roosevelt had touched a nerve; Ike passed the letter to Bryce Harlow, his congressional liaison aide, who responded, "in some respects this man is wrong, in my opinion; in some respects, he should be listened to." Harlow's counsel was not to openly confront McCarthy but instead to present a major legislative program to Congress for debate during 1954. In an election year, Congress "will weasel, procrastinate, compromise, bicker and frustrate. In the process, it will probably fail to do much that you seek to have done and will probably do quite a number of things you will find very distasteful." That, he argued, would provide the moment to confront the demagogues by appealing to the American people. "If you make the fight when the gauntlet is thrown, the Nation, I believe, will rally to you and not to the Congress." During the subsequent two months, Eisenhower largely adopted Harlow's strategic vision; he began to put together an ambitious legislative program that would be a direct challenge to the conservative wing of his party. [23]

ASSAULT ON FORT MONMOUTH

Fred Seaton had good reason to worry about Robert Stevens. On October 2, the Army secretary made a major concession to McCarthy's staff. Roy Cohn and Frank Carr, the McCarthy subcommittee's executive director, had selected Fort Monmouth in New Jersey, where Julius Rosenberg had worked, as a prime target for investigation. The two men came to Stevens's office to complain that Major General Kirk V. Lawton, the post commandant, was stonewalling their requests for personnel to testify. In their presence, Stevens phoned Lawton about his employees who were "under a cloud" and stated, "I now authorize you in my name to give permission in any cases that may be involved." Stevens was confident that "nothing but good will come out of it." Though the Truman executive order forbade sharing personnel files, Stevens emphasized that "if a properly accredited representative of one of the committees of Congress wants to call a member of your establishment to talk to them there or have him appear before a hearing, I want to make him available."[24]

Based on that conversation, Lawton decided he could suspend the personnel in question. On October 6, the army announced that Lawton had suspended several employees at the Signal Corps laboratories at Monmouth "for security reasons," citing Eisenhower's Executive Order 10450 from April embodying the principle that employment was "a privilege, not a right." On October 8, as a result of Stevens's order to Lawton, six civilian employees at Monmouth testified before Roy Cohn and twelve more were scheduled for the next day.[25]

Sensing the chance to gain more headlines, McCarthy terminated his honeymoon and rushed back to take charge of the Monmouth investigation. Once back, he rolled out sensational charges every day. He was free to emerge from closed-door hearings and tell the press anything he wished, accurate or not, knowing that reporters would report whatever he said. On October 12, McCarthy announced that his subcommittee had unearthed a trail of "extremely dangerous espionage" at the Fort Monmouth radar laboratories that "will envelop the whole Signal Corps." The espionage, the senator said, dealt "with our entire defense against atomic attack." He had examined five witnesses in executive session, one of whom had worked with Julius Rosenberg during World War II; he announced plans to seek testimony from thirty more employees.[26]

The next day, McCarthy revealed that an army officer had informed the subcommittee that "a sizeable amount" of "top secret" documents had disappeared from the Signal Corps. If those documents "got into the hands of an enemy they could be extremely dangerous to this country," the senator declared. According to John Adams, the story of the stolen documents "was entirely hot air."

He traced the story to a nineteen-year-old East German defector who had falsely claimed he knew about the theft. Adams had informed McCarthy that the story was bogus "within two days after the story first appeared." The senator ignored Adams's revelation and dispatched an aide, James Juliana, to Germany to interrogate the so-called scientist, who now worked as a stock clerk in the Army Post Exchange. "He didn't tell Juliana anything," Adams recalled, "because he didn't know anything." Nevertheless, Juliana flew back to New York and was quoted as saying "I have interviewed this scientist and I have obtained from him and now have in my possession highly classified documents" that had been transmitted to the East Germans.[27]

The pressure from McCarthy's investigations tempted the Eisenhower administration to indulge in its own violation of civil liberties. Herbert Brownell had been asked to speak at the National Press Club on October 14 on the subject of the Fifth Amendment and "people who claimed immunity before congressional committees." To assist him with that appearance, Brownell urged the president to expand Executive Order 10450, defining employment as "a privilege," so that employees invoking the Fifth Amendment would not be immune to an employment or retention investigation. In response, Eisenhower signed Executive Order 10491, amending the criteria for launching an investigation of a government employee to include "Refusal by the individual, upon the ground of constitutional privilege against self-incrimination, to testify before a congressional committee regarding charges of his alleged disloyalty or other misconduct." That action reflected the corrosive moral impact of McCarthy's witch hunts; Brownell and Eisenhower, normally inclined to be more protective of constitutional rights, were now violating the spirit, if not the letter, of the Fifth Amendment.[28]

On October 14, McCarthy announced that the army had suspended five additional civilians at Fort Monmouth for "Communist activities," bringing the number to ten. The senator had also interrogated a "top scientist" and "close personal friend of Julius Rosenberg" who confessed that, in 1946, he had taken home forty-three "secret documents." The next day McCarthy proclaimed that the wartime espionage ring Rosenberg had set up at Monmouth during 1942–43 "may still be in operation." [29]

On October 16, Stevens summoned the courage to resist this contrived panic about Fort Monmouth, saying that the army had "no evidence that any documents had been compromised or that files had been tampered with" at Signal Corps headquarters. Nevertheless, he insisted to Army Undersecretary Earl Johnson that "the Army is getting along fine with Joe. He is getting headlines and is entitled to them. Fundamentally, he has been fine with us." [30]

The day-by-day revelations continued. Following another executive session, McCarthy announced, "I have just received word" that an "important" employee at the Monmouth radar laboratories and a close friend of Julius Rosenberg "admits that he was lying . . . and now wants to tell the truth." While being cross-examined by Roy Cohn, the witness broke down, began to cry, and was taken to another room to be treated by a doctor and a nurse. [31]

THE MONMOUTH JUNKET

Robert Stevens still nourished the illusion that he could personally persuade McCarthy to back off. On October 19, he did an extraordinary thing; he invited McCarthy and Cohn to accompany him on a trip to Fort Monmouth the following day. He expressed his hope to J. Edgar Hoover that the outing might make McCarthy "willing to turn this [investigation] back to the Army with the information he has so that we can take responsibility for following it from here in." [32]

At midmorning on October 20, the secretary's plane took off; besides McCarthy and Cohn, the party included John Adams and administrative assistants to Everett Dirksen and Charles Potter, Republican senators on McCarthy's subcommittee. David Schine had planned to go, but fog delayed his flight from New York. To implement Stevens's plan to secure an agreement with McCarthy, John Adams had drafted a statement that he and Stevens hoped McCarthy might issue at the end of the day, affirming the senator's satisfaction with the progress of security operations at Monmouth. When they arrived at the Monmouth County airfield, they were met by General Kirk Lawton, New Jersey Senator Alexander Smith, and Congressman James Auchincloss and were issued badges inscribed "secret" or "confidential."

On their way to the base, General Lawton asked the secretary to inspect some secret equipment; however, only those with the "secret" badges could enter the building. Though the restriction was waived for Senators McCarthy and Smith, it was not for Cohn. Cohn flew into a rage and demanded that Adams get him a car to take him immediately to New York. "This is the end; this is war," he threatened. "We'll really start investigating this place now; they let Communists in but they keep me out." Later, over lunch, Cohn, still agitated, told Adams that there would be "no favorable press release by McCarthy that day." Cohn followed McCarthy to the men's room and urged him not to make a positive statement.[33]

At the news conference afterward, Stevens announced that twelve more Fort Monmouth employees had been suspended; McCarthy said he would conduct a hearing with six or seven more the next morning. In spite of Cohn's anger, McCarthy pronounced himself "very favorably impressed" with what Stevens and Lawton had done "to clear up this situation." He emphasized that "an extremely bad and dangerous situation has existed here over the years" but expressed confidence that "the great majority" of employees at the fort were "loyal, true and doing an outstanding job for their country." Stevens commended the "good evidence of the kind of teamwork between the Executive and Legislative Branches" and concluded, "We have made a lot of progress here today."[34]

Meanwhile, David Schine was scheduled to be inducted into the army in less than two weeks, so Roy Cohn was still pressing Robert Stevens for a special assignment for him. Schine called Secretary Stevens the day after the Monmouth trip to inquire about his status. "I have reviewed this whole situation with Mr. Wilson," Stevens said. "Neither he nor I can see an appropriate way to avoid the basic training." However, Stevens made a promise that would return to haunt him; once Schine completed basic training, "I think there is an excellent chance that we can pick you up and use you in a way that would be useful to the country and to yourself. Just what that would be, I don't know." With Schine's training completed, they could develop a plan "that would work out satisfactorily for you and for the Government and for everybody." "Everybody" clearly included Cohn. John Adams was "dumbfounded" when he learned about Stevens's pledge.[35]

However, Cohn frantically kept up the pressure. On October 27, he called Stevens from New York about "our young friend here." Cohn argued that because the subcommittee was in the midst of an investigation, "we would like him around for a while." One officer had suggested to Cohn that Schine "could be furloughed for a couple of weeks." Cohn asked about a possibility he had apparently raised previously with Stevens, "this C.I.A. thing." Cohn wondered if "the people over there pick him up right away?" Ever accommodating, Stevens offered to talk with Allen Dulles, and Cohn responded, "I would appreciate that."[36]

It is possible that Eisenhower vetoed that proposition. The next day, October 28, Stevens, after twice calling an unidentified person at the White House (not Allen Dulles), phoned Cohn with the news that the CIA could not use Schine because they "have to train people and want them for a long period." However, Stevens had decided that he was "willing to assign him, after being drafted to [the] First Army," and Schine's first mission would be "temporary duty of two weeks" to complete his committee work, not to be extended.[37]

Fred Seaton worried increasingly about Stevens's tendency to cave in to what McCarthy wanted. An hour after Stevens made his promise to Cohn about Schine's special induction privileges, Seaton called him. His purpose was once again to buck up Stevens's resistance to McCarthy's demands for loyalty board records. Standing firm against McCarthy's demands, Seaton said, was "a matter of principle," and he offered Stevens his help "in fighting that one." Stevens blithely responded, "I am working well with McCarthy; and

I will say yes to stuff that makes sense and no to what does not." He planned to tell McCarthy "no" regarding the senator's demand for those records. Though the issue might end up on the president's desk, Stevens understood that "under existing Executive Orders we cannot give this stuff out." Seaton cautioned Stevens, "If Joe gets into this situation, you play hell in getting anyone to serve on those boards." "We can order them to serve," countered Stevens. "But then," Seaton warned, "you will always have [the] inclination to settle things the way he wants them settled."

Stevens turned defensive, maintaining that there was "nothing to worry about in my relations with Joe and that committee. We have a good working relationship" and "the fact that I am going to turn him down will be nothing that will upset me or the relationship." Stevens's naiveté troubled Seaton. He resorted to flattery to soften Stevens's reaction, expressing his "complete admiration" for how he had handled the situation. Then Seaton counseled, "If Joe is sincere, then we have nothing to fear; but if he gets to be completely a demagog[ue] on this subject, then we will; but that is not your fault." He shrewdly framed his counsel to the wishy-washy secretary as an accomplished fact. "I am tickled to death you have said no, you are not going to produce them," he said, referring to the loyalty board records. "People are inclined if Bob Stevens says this is so, it is so; and you don't need confirming evidence from across the river." "Across the river" was Seaton's euphemism for the White House—a not-so-subtle hint about the source of Seaton's marching orders. His final warning oozed with manipulative flattery: "You are too smart to let [McCarthy] make a satellite out of you." Stevens promised to talk with Seaton "the minute it looks like it is getting out of hand." [38]

SKUNK HUNTING

Seaton knew that Stevens had rubber in his backbone. Two days after Seaton's phone call, John Adams wrote Stevens about an intense conversation he had held with Seaton, Struve Hensel, and Assistant Attorney General Lee Rankin about the problem of "revealing security information and names of hearing board members." Seaton and Hensel had reinforced the mandate that "you will not reveal the names of the members of screening, hearing or appeals boards" and "you will not permit members of these boards whose names are known to make revelations with reference to security hearings in which they participated." Rankin had affirmed the Justice Department's support for that position and promised to provide a draft statement in case "we find it necessary to make a public pronouncement" about the policy and the reasons for it.[39]

Eisenhower's October 30 cabinet meeting revolved around the same issue: what information could be released to congressional committees. In fulfillment of Lee Rankin's counsel, Herbert Brownell presented a draft replacement for the existing Truman executive order, to be labeled Executive Order 10510. The new order reduced the categories for classifying documents to three—"top secret," "secret," and "confidential"—and eliminated Truman's fourth category, "restricted."

Impatient with the situation, Eisenhower, walked into that cabinet meeting determined to get the issue behind them. When Dulles pleaded for delay so the State Department could draft its own regulations, Eisenhower snapped, "Now wait a minute," and insisted that such work be done following the issuance of the order. When Secretary Wilson argued for keeping the "restricted" category, the president patronized him, saying "I know a good bit about defense" and calling "restricted" a "useless classification." Besides, he grumbled, "Moscow has all our 'restricted' material" and "no one gets angrier than I when I see classified material in [the] papers." The president was wound up now. "My own feeling," he fumed, "is we've classified open things and leaked real secrets so much it's sickening." He confessed that "the proposed order is really a public relations matter and that the Administration will benefit greatly by putting it through." Ike shut off further debate: "With all we've gone through on this, let's make December 15 the effective date." The cabinet acquiesced in a decision that had clearly been made before they entered the room.[40]

After two months of McCarthy investigating the army, fear stalked the halls of the White House, the Pentagon, and army outposts. Earlier on the day of the cabinet meeting, John Adams phoned Stevens about a tragic case that resulted indirectly from McCarthy's tactics. A witness named Louis Kaplan—the same last name as Raymond Kaplan, who had committed suicide in March—had been called; a former communist by that name had testified earlier, and "this particular witness has been plagued for about 15 years by having the same name." Kaplan had been suspended at Fort Monmouth on October 22 due to "nothing but a mistake in identity."[41]

General Lawton continued to suspend Fort Monmouth employees. On October 27, *The New York Times* reported that twenty-seven persons had been suspended. By the end of the month, he had suspended thirty-three, with two others in limbo. On a Friday afternoon, Stevens shocked John Adams by handing him a stack of folders containing the dossiers of all the suspended employees. "He wanted to know how to dispose of them," Adams recalled, "by Monday." Adams was "thoroughly shaken." He wanted to reinstate all the suspended personnel but feared that if he did, "McCarthy would come crashing down demanding blood, probably mine." He was eventually able to restore twenty-five to duty, but the other eight had to wait five years before the courts cleared them.[42]

Adams's qualms were justified. McCarthy's conciliatory demeanor on the Fort Monmouth trip lasted barely twenty-four hours. Stevens's attempts to appease the senator had failed, vindicating Eisenhower's strategy that it was smarter to ignore McCarthy than to engage with him. McCarthy had converted his Fort Monmouth investigation into a seemingly authentic discovery of espionage at a critical army establishment.

The evening following his trip to Fort Monmouth, McCarthy responded to his critics in a speech in New Jersey. He roared to an appreciative audience, "You don't go skunk-hunting in striped trousers and a tall hat while waving a lace handkerchief." A few days later, he repeated that harangue in Chicago, declaring he was on "the most important skunk hunt ever" and adding that he did not "give a tinker's dam what the bleeding hearts" said about his methods. "The closer we get to the nerve center," he proclaimed, "the louder and louder will be the screams."[43]

In spite of the anguish of the employees suspended in response to McCarthy's agitation, Eisenhower steadfastly refused to "get down in the gutter" with McCarthy. He was surely acquainted with a World War II–era adage that perfectly captured his stated policy: "Don't get into a pissing contest with a skunk." Or, in this case, with a self-proclaimed "skunk hunter." Yet, that was what Dwight Eisenhower and Herbert Brownell would soon contemplate doing.

CHAPTER 5

THE TURNING POINT

Dwight Eisenhower approached the anniversary of his election to the presidency with satisfaction. He had led his party, out of office for a generation, in learning how to govern again, working carefully with the Republican leadership to manage its fragile one-vote majority in the Senate. Domestically, by executive action, he had created the Department of Health, Education, and Welfare (HEW) and had made marked progress in desegregating the District of Columbia and enforcing desegregation in the armed forces. In foreign affairs, he had successfully terminated the Korean War and implemented a "new look" in defense policy, relying more on nuclear weapons for deterrence. The president had also courageously signaled his willingness to seek peace with the Soviet Union in the wake of the death of Josef Stalin.[1]

Politically, the bleeding sore was still McCarthy. Eisenhower had tilted successfully with McCarthy over Chip Bohlen's appointment as ambassador to the Soviet Union. He had countered McCarthy's deal with the Greek shipowners, aimed at discrediting Allied trade with communist nations. Ike himself had campaigned against "book burners" and had replaced the International Information Administration, a favorite McCarthy target, with the new United States Information Agency. But he still endured McCarthy's increasingly ferocious investigation into communist infiltration into the institution to which Ike had given his life: the US Army.

"HARRY DEXTER WHITE WAS A RUSSIAN SPY"

When Herbert Brownell took office as attorney general, he had ordered the collection and review of loose paperwork found in "desktops, cubby-holes, and closets" in the Justice Department. His aides had uncovered a cache of documents concerning Harry Dexter White, a Treasury Department official in the Truman administration who had resigned in 1947 and died the following year. The FBI had suspected White of passing sensitive information to the Soviet Union. The documents Brownell's office stumbled upon revealed serious malfeasance by the Truman White House in handling the case.

Brownell took the "shocking" discoveries to the president and proposed that they be made public. His motivation was threefold: (1) to ensure that he could not be accused of a cover-up if he failed to reveal the truth; (2) to head off a movement in Congress "to tighten the laws relating to internal security" in a manner contrary to the administration's program; and finally (3) to provide "an important contrast" to Joe McCarthy's "slap-dash investigations of Communist infiltration." According to Brownell's memoirs, Ike responded to the proposal to go public by saying that "if I had the facts it was advisable to do so." Brownell was scheduled to make two speeches in Chicago on November 6. He and the president agreed that the attorney general would reveal the White story at a luncheon meeting of the Executive Club in that city.[2]

When it came to major policy statements, Eisenhower's subordinates were not independent agents, nor did they make speeches broadcasting important revelations without the president's review. Brownell did more than share the facts with the president; he recalled years later that he had read the speech "out loud" to Eisenhower. Eisenhower had wanted a means of upstaging Joe McCarthy, and the attorney general had unearthed a whopper. Ike did not mind causing Harry Truman discomfort, given the former president's partisan rhetoric during and following the 1952 campaign. The delegation framework was typical of Eisenhower: Brownell—not the president—would take any heat that the White disclosures generated.[3]

Unfortunately, no one with deep Washington political experience reviewed the plan, including the decision to deliver the indictment in a political rather than judicial or legislative setting. Richard Nixon, an increasingly important political adviser, was in the Far East. As Henry Cabot Lodge argued to Ike months later, there was no staff member in the Eisenhower White House "whose primary responsibility is political strategy for you." That was an invitation to disaster, especially when dealing with McCarthy. Eisenhower and Brownell did not know it yet, but they had made a major miscalculation.[4]

Two days prior to the speech, Ike suffered a moment of apprehension; he knew he and Brownell were playing with fire. Once again, he contemplated the possibility that McCarthy might target for investigation his close associations with communists during and after the war in Europe. On November 4, he resurrected Arthur Hays Sulzberger's June proposal for granting amnesty to those who had repudiated their communist associations prior to the Soviet blockade of Berlin in 1948. He asked that the Justice Department restudy the issue because he thought that, in the previous review, J. Edgar Hoover had assumed Ike was asking about amnesty for genuine communists, not innocent people. Eisenhower recalled that during and after the war, "many prominent officials of the Allied Governments were at that time talking in terms of support of the Soviets." "In Washington," he added, "there was much of the same." Starting in 1941, he recalled, "it was a policy of our government to foster friendship with the Soviets."

Ostensibly, Eisenhower was writing about a younger, unnamed person, not himself, but his memorandum was analogous to an alcoholic who tells a counselor, "I have a friend with a drinking problem." That person, Eisenhower continued, "could *very easily and very honestly* have said many things that today would indicate or imply an unjustified support of Communism." In spite of Brownell's previous rejection of the proposition, the president still wanted "some formula that could be applied to cases of individuals who have *never* been Communists, but who had spoken favorably of the Soviets." Apparently, Brownell responded negatively once again and Ike was persuaded not to pursue the issue.[5]

Despite these qualms, the president and the attorney general plowed ahead with their plans for the speech in Chicago. Brownell launched the day at the White House by releasing presidential Executive Order 10501, voiding Truman's previous directive on how defense information was to be protected. That was the directive that had generated hot discussion at the October 30 cabinet meeting. The new order eliminated the "restricted" category the president had scorned and that, Brownell asserted, the Truman administration had used to impose "a form of censorship, unwarranted in peacetime" that could be used to cover up "derelictions." "Derelictions" were precisely what Brownell planned to describe that day regarding the Harry Dexter White case.[6]

That noon, Attorney General Brownell declared, "Harry Dexter White was a Russian spy." That fact, Brownell asserted, had been known "by the very people who appointed him to the most sensitive and important position he ever held in Government service." White's spying activities had been "reported in detail by the F.B.I. to the White House by means of a report delivered to President Truman." Nevertheless, on January 23, 1946, Truman nominated White, then assistant secretary of the Treasury, "for the even more important position of the executive director for the United States in the International Monetary Fund." The president received an updated FBI report in February 1946 and failed to inform the Senate Banking and Currency Committee in time to derail White's nomination to the new post. On April 30, Truman had written a letter commending him for his "distinguished career" with Treasury. White died in 1948, Brownell disclosed, "without the prior Administration ever having acted on the F.B.I. report."

That case, he concluded, "is illustrative of why the present Administration is faced with the problem of disloyalty in Government." One of Eisenhower's first acts in January had been to order each agency "to weed out" security risks, including "those whose personal habits and activities made them prey for subversive elements." The attorney general asserted that "fourteen hundred fifty-six persons have been ejected from Government service because they were found to be security risks." "President Eisenhower," he proudly proclaimed, "is cleaning up the mess in Washington." [7]

A war of words had been launched; White House Press Secretary Jim Hagerty confirmed that Eisenhower had approved the speech in advance, saying "The President told the Attorney General it was his duty to report it to the American people."

Truman's initial response was to call Brownell's charges "purely political" and claim that, as soon as his administration had learned about White, "we fired him." Hagerty retorted that "Mr. White was not fired, he resigned" and Truman's statement was "not true." Truman countered that "White was fired by resignation." Then Hagerty read aloud Truman's letter of April 30, 1946, in which Brownell had quoted praising White for serving with "distinction" in his Treasury post. Next, South Carolina governor James F. Byrnes, who had been Truman's secretary of state at the time, confirmed that Truman had seen the FBI report while White was in the midst of the confirmation process for the IMF position. [8]

Almost overnight, Brownell's speech ignited what the attorney general called "a storm of controversy." Eisenhower's personal secretary, Ann Whitman, noted in her diary that the "H. D. White bombshell exploded in full fury. A sorry mess. Personally I am convinced the boss did not have any inkling of [the] tempest to be aroused." Neither did the attorney general; his daughter Ann recalls that, years later, Brownell stated that "the only thing he regretted in public life was delivering the Harry Dexter White speech." The columnist Marquis Childs called the speech "a two-edged sword," and the columnist Arthur Krock branded it a "bombshell with a tendency to kick back." [9]

However authentic Brownell's charges were, he and Eisenhower quickly lost control of the story. Truman's combative denials, even when false, made such a sharp-edged attack on a former president appear unseemly. As the *New York Times'* editors opined, "Attorney

General Brownell has made a poor choice of timing and of method in reopening the case" in a fashion that might provoke a "reckless renewal of McCarthyism."[10]

On Tuesday, November 10, the House Un-American Activities Committee (HUAC) subpoenaed former President Truman. In a speech that night, he defended his record on anticommunism and condemned the administration for "yielding to hysteria rather than resisting it." He castigated "fake crusaders who dig up and distort records of the past to distract the attention of the people from political failures of the present."[11]

By the morning of Wednesday, November 11, the backlash had spread to the Republican ranks. The HUAC chair, Republican representative Harold H. Velde of Illinois, backpedaled on his subpoenas in response to pressure from House Republican leaders and White House staff. Brownell softened his stance with a statement citing "laxity" by the Truman administration rather than any hint of treason. The attorney general asserted that he had "no intention of impugning the loyalty of any high official of the prior Administration."[12]

A FRACTIOUS NEWS CONFERENCE

The Harry Dexter White case dominated the president's November 11 news conference. Brownell had accused the former Democratic president of harboring a communist spy. Eisenhower was determined to distance himself from the issue, even if it left his attorney general out on what Brownell called "the proverbial limb." Ironically, Brownell was present to witness what *New York Times* columnist James Reston called "one of the stormiest White House news conferences of recent years." Merriman Smith asked for the president's reaction to "ex-President Truman having been subpoenaed by the House Un-American Affairs Committee." That gave the president an opening to deliver his prepared statement.

"I can't say a great deal about this," he began, giving the impression that he had not been deeply involved, a 180-degree shift from Jim Hagerty's assertion that the president had approved the speech.

The attorney general, he said, "reported to me that there were certain facts that had been coming to light in his Department that he felt should be made available to the public, and that he felt moreover it was his duty to do so. He told me that they involved a man named White, a man whom I had never met, didn't know anything about. I told him that he had, as a responsible head of Government, to make the decision, if he felt it was his duty to make these things public to do it on a purely factual basis. He did tell me that the information had gotten to the White House, and that was all. So that was my last connection with it until this incident occurred of which you speak."

Having painted a picture of personal ignorance, Eisenhower asserted that he did not want to criticize Congress "for carrying out what it conceives to be its duty." Regarding the Truman subpoena, he stated, "I would not issue such a subpoena." A reporter asked if Eisenhower believed that "former President Truman knowingly appointed a Communist spy to high office?" Ike called that "inconceivable."

Raymond Brandt from the *St. Louis Post-Dispatch* asked, "Were you consulted while plans were being laid to bring the White story out?" Ike responded with a brusque "No." A report had been made to him about "certain information that the Attorney General considered it his duty to make public, and he did mention the word 'White,' although as I say, I didn't know who White was." Later, regarding the FBI report on White, Eisenhower insisted that Brownell had "never told me" that President Truman actually had seen the FBI papers, only that "they went to the White House. Now, that is all he ever told me." Brownell sat and listened in discomfort; he later recalled, "That wasn't so." [13]

When pressed as to why Brownell had presented the evidence before a group rather than a grand jury or a committee of Congress, Ike responded, "The Attorney General is here to answer it himself. Let him answer it." A reporter shot back, "He has refused to answer questions, you see." The room erupted with laughter. Another reporter chimed in, "It is true that Mr. Brownell is here, but he won't see reporters. I wonder if we can ask you to exert your influence to get him to see us"; that spawned another round of laughter.

The president pushed his attorney general as far away as possible. "I am not going to give him orders as to methods in which he handles responsibilities of his own office," he said. Brownell's revelations had "aroused tremendous interest. Now we will see how he handles it, and I am not going to color his case or to prejudice his case in advance in what I say about it." Brownell was out on a limb, truly alone.

Finally, when a reporter asked if Brownell had told the president that the FBI report had called Harry Dexter White a spy, Ike, clearly irritated, reprised his opening statement, almost verbatim, concluding "You have to follow your own conscience as to your duty. Now that is exactly what I knew about it." Merriman Smith mercifully ended the session: "Thank you, Mr. President." [14]

"Some of the roughest minutes of the Eisenhower Administration were over," James Reston reported. A little later on the day of the news conference, the president went to Arlington National Cemetery for an Armistice Day ceremony. When the smiling Eisenhower exited, he noted that he had just come from a press conference where "all they wanted to ask me about was the White case." The president added with a grin, "That Brownell can sure stir things up." [15]

Rumors of a rift between Eisenhower and his attorney general became inevitable. The next day at his cabinet meeting, with Brownell in attendance, Ike attempted to put that allegation to rest. "I called him before the Press Conference to consult on what I would say," he said. Brownell, the loyal soldier, stated that the president had "helped greatly" with his press conference comments and had put the issue "back on track." Ike confessed to the attorney general, "I committed you to putting out facts." Brownell responded that they had managed "to make [the] point it got to the White House," a fact "pretty well accepted now." Ike expressed amazement at the press's "unanimity" in defending the past administration and White. [16]

James Reston headed his next column, "All Lose in White Case." Reston's losers included Brownell, Truman, Congress, US prestige abroad, and—above all—Eisenhower. Remarkably, the experienced reporter swallowed Eisenhower's deceptive scenario: "Mr. Brownell knew the implications of his speech but he did not explain them to the President. He asked for the green light and the President gave it to him without inquiring into what was happening."[17]

Years later, in his memoirs, Eisenhower further narrowed his personal involvement with the White case, confining his role to a "phone conversation" about Brownell's plan to make the speech. Indeed, there had been a phone call—more than one—plus extensive personal interaction that Ike chose to ignore. No other single episode reflects more vividly how Dwight Eisenhower authored his own myth as a not-in-charge president, so widely accepted by historians for decades.[18]

"THE ADMINISTRATION HAS FULLY EMBRACED ... MCCARTHYISM"

It was Harry Truman's turn to take the stage. On November 12, the former president declined to comply with the HUAC subpoena, citing "universally recognized constitutional doctrine." He was scheduled to speak on radio and television on November 16. The day of the Truman speech, the White House issued two statements, in the words of The New York Times, "disassociating President Eisenhower further from the political free-for-all started by his Attorney General's charges." The first maintained that the president had not seen or approved an advance copy of the speech, a pointless distinction since the attorney general recalled having read the speech to Eisenhower. Jim Hagerty stated that he had received a copy but had not shown his copy to the president; that appeared to contradict the press secretary's November 7 statement that the president had "approved" the speech in advance. The second statement cited Ike's memoir, Crusade in Europe, to prove—reports to the contrary—that he had not met Harry Dexter White when discussing the future of Germany in 1944 with Treasury Secretary Henry Morgenthau, Jr.[19]

That night, Truman demonstrated that he had not lost his political touch. Herbert Brownell, not Ike, was the villain, he claimed. The attorney general had "lied to the American people," making "false" and "phony" charges in asserting that Truman had purposely promoted a spy. He had "degraded" the administration of justice with "cheap political trickery," and "deceived his chief as to what he proposed to do." The former president claimed he had learned about White's possible treason too late to derail his confirmation to the IMF, but he had downgraded the appointment from a managerial position to simple membership on the board of directors. Truman's defense was that he had permitted White to take the position in order to camouflage a continuing FBI investigation. "It is now evident," the former president concluded, "that the present Administration has fully embraced, for political advantage, McCarthyism."[20]

In spite of testimony by J. Edgar Hoover contradicting Truman's account of an ongoing FBI investigation, Truman had won the public argument. James Reston concluded, "Personalities have overwhelmed principles. The primary issues of Communist infiltration in the Government and the Attorney General's use of the F.B.I. files in a public luncheon club speech have been smothered in yards and yards of cotton-wool."[21]

Watching the furor from New York, Henry Cabot Lodge was dismayed. He wrote a "Dear General" letter to Eisenhower, critical of the fact that Leonard Hall, the Republican National Committee chairman, had publicly stated that communist subversion would still be an issue in the 1954 election, "a virtual admission that we've accomplished nothing constructive of our own." He was incensed that the RNC had provided "a publicity build-up for the Harry Dexter White Speech." Lodge argued that Brownell should have turned the issue over to the courts instead of making a speech. A court decision would have produced "the maximum of political benefit, minimizing the complaints about 'McCarthyism.'" He hoped the president would treat his observations as "suggestive for you to use in a press conference."[22]

The morning of November 18, armed with Lodge's sage advice, Ike set out at his news conference to put the White hullabaloo behind him. When Merriman Smith brought it up, the president responded, "I should like to make [cl]ear, ladies and gentlemen, that so far as this case itself is concerned, I haven't another single word to say about it, certainly not at this time, and don't intend to open my mouth about it."

Another reporter brought up Len Hall's assertion that communism in government would be the big issue in the 1954 elections. Eisenhower followed Lodge's counsel to the letter. Thanks to his administration's internal security program, he said that he believed that "this whole thing will be a matter of history and of memory by the time the next election comes around." A reporter noted Truman's charge "that your administration has now embraced McCarthyism. Do you have any comment on that?" Ike snapped, "I am ready to take the verdict of this body on that."[23]

A PRIVILEGED PRIVATE

Robert Stevens was still trying to placate McCarthy. The day Brownell delivered his controversial speech, he invited McCarthy, Cohn, subcommittee director Frank Carr, and John Adams to lunch at the Pentagon. His purpose was to reassure the senator that the army was already rigorously investigating subversives. The discussion inevitably migrated back to Cohn's relationship with David Schine. McCarthy pressed for a New York assignment for Private Schine, suggesting he be assigned to West Point to look for procommunist influences in textbooks.[24]

However, the next day, McCarthy shocked Stevens with a phone call asking, as a "personal favor," that the secretary not assign Schine back to his committee. In that conversation, McCarthy called Schine "a good boy" but said there was "nothing indispensable about him." The call reflected the strange hold Cohn had over the senator. Cohn was "on the verge of quitting the committee" because he was so angry over Schine's treatment. Cohn, McCarthy said, "was completely unreasonable about the situation" and "thought Schine should be a general and work from the penthouse of the Waldorf." Stevens informed McCarthy that he had agreed with Cohn to let

Schine use the first two weeks after induction to complete his work in New York and then he could obtain passes on weekends or week-nights as needed. McCarthy endorsed that plan.[25]

Schine had been formally inducted into the army on November 3 and had been assigned to New York, as Stevens had agreed. Stevens had also agreed to approve passes for Schine the first four weekends he was at Fort Dix and frequent night passes—privileges rarely granted to new draftees. In addition, Schine obtained other privileges, thanks to Stevens. The secretary ordered the post commander to provide Schine with an office for committee work. However, Schine and Cohn decided that they could conduct "committee business" more effectively fifteen miles away at the Stacy Trent Hotel in Trenton.[26]

But Stevens's hopes for peace with McCarthy were soon dashed. On November 13, Stevens announced that he had discovered "no evidence of espionage" at Fort Monmouth. In response, McCarthy angrily declared that Stevens's failure to uncover espionage "makes it necessary to open public hearings almost immediately." Hearings were set to begin on November 24. As John Adams put it, "The siege was on again."[27]

Stevens decided to try again to placate McCarthy. On November 17, he entertained McCarthy, his aides, and George Sokolsky, a pro-McCarthy commentator, in high style at the Merchants Club in Lower Manhattan. McCarthy ordered a double Manhattan and the most expensive steak on the menu—as payback, he told Stevens, for "what you did to us." He complained, as he ordered another double Manhattan, that Stevens had "called me a liar before the whole country." After that two-hour lunch, as John Adams recalled, Stevens "walked into another trap." McCarthy suddenly proclaimed that he wanted them all to fly to Fort Dix to "see Dave."

It was one of those wild Joe McCarthy afternoons; the senator pressured Schine's chauffeur into letting him drive the specially equipped Cadillac limousine to the airport. To the group's discomfort, he swept through the Holland Tunnel, siren howling and red lights flashing, giggling all the way. Later, when the secretary's DC-3 landed at McGuire Air Force Base in New Jersey, all, including Schine, posed for pictures in front of the plane.[28]

"A DECLARATION OF WAR AGAINST THE PRESIDENT"

Meanwhile, McCarthy demanded equal time to respond to Harry Truman's attack on "McCarthyism." The networks capitulated and scheduled McCarthy's address for the evening of November 24.

The night prior to McCarthy's speech, Eisenhower accepted the America's Democratic Legacy Award at a B'nai B'rith dinner in honor of the fortieth anniversary of the Anti-Defamation League, the Jewish organization famed for combating anti-Semitism. Chastened by how badly the Harry Dexter White affair had gone, Ike returned to core principles. He invoked the frontier values of his hometown, Abilene, where justice was defined "by the right to meet your accuser face to face . . . by your right to go to the church or the synagogue or even the mosque of your own choosing; by your right to speak your mind and be protected in it." His invocation of "the right to meet your accuser face to face" was widely perceived as an anti-McCarthy statement. In the Harry Dexter White episode, perhaps Eisenhower had relearned a lesson from his war experiences: If you imitate your enemy, you risk becoming like him. And if that is not who you really are, you will be supremely incompetent in carrying it out.[29]

McCarthy presented a stark contrast to those values in his televised address the evening of November 24. He asserted that Truman had "made a completely untruthful attack upon me." Instead of "McCarthyism," he offered "Trumanism," "the placing of your political party above the interest of the country." Truman, the senator declared, had made five false statements about the Harry Dexter White case. The sixth, he said—the "granddaddy of them all"—was "Oh, it's all McCarthy's fault" and "Isn't that nasty McCarthy an awful man."

Then McCarthy turned his guns on Eisenhower. "A few days ago," he said, "I read that President Eisenhower expressed the hope that by election time in 1954 the subject of communism would be a dead and forgotten issue. The raw, harsh, unpleasant fact is that communism is an issue and will be an issue in 1954." He patronized the president, citing "those very well-meaning people who speak about communism not being an issue" when, to the senator, communism was paramount among "the other great evils which beset us today." To prove his point, McCarthy cited the case of Harry Dexter White and asserted that the Republican Party's "batting average has not been too good."

McCarthy waded into foreign policy, lamenting that American prisoners of war were still being held and "brainwashed" by the Chinese. The government run by his party was guilty of "whining, whimpering appeasement." He attacked the policy of providing "billions of dollars each year to help our allies build up their military strength"—funds that then "pay for the shipment of the sinews of war to Red China." In protest, the administration had sent only "perfumed notes." The United States could end this pernicious trade, McCarthy asserted, "without firing a shot" by blockading the coast of China and telling the allies: "If you continue to ship to Red China while they are imprisoning and torturing American men, you will not get one cent of American money. If we do that, my good friends, this trading in blood-money will cease." [30]

Neither Eisenhower nor Truman listened to the speech. Special Assistant to the President C. D. Jackson, Ike's easily agitated adviser on psychological warfare, did—and was appalled. He wrote Sherman Adams the next morning that listening to McCarthy had been "an exceptionally horrible experience." Jackson called McCarthy's speech "an open declaration of war on the Republican President of the United States by a Republican senator." Two days later, he was still fuming and shared his unvarnished opinion with James Reston. Reston reported that White House staff members were "hopping mad" about the speech and one had described the address as "a declaration of war against the President." Stewart Alsop called McCarthy's speech "a blunt warning to President Eisenhower" to "play the game my way—or else." Roscoe Drummond, a favorite columnist of Eisenhower's, asserted, "Senator McCarthy, in effect, launched his campaign for the 1956 Republican presidential nomination."[31]

A WHITE HOUSE IN TURMOIL

Jackson believed that Eisenhower had been consistently wrong in his approach to McCarthy. Ike's "disastrous appeasement" had begun in 1952, when the general had deleted words of praise for General Marshall from his Milwaukee campaign speech. "I am very frightened," he wrote in his diary three days after the McCarthy speech. Jackson lobbied John Foster Dulles to intercede with the president. On November 27, Eisenhower—in Augusta, Georgia, for the Thanksgiving break—learned from Dulles that Jackson wanted a high-level discussion on Monday to deal with McCarthy's diatribe; Ike, irritated, responded that "their only answer would be to do nothing," but Dulles suggested that the president read McCarthy's speech. "Why?" Ike asked. The secretary replied that the senator had called for a blockade of trade with China. Eisenhower grumbled that McCarthy "was never interested in facts, just something to shoot at." Ann Whitman recorded Ike's exasperated question: "Does he want to declare war today?"[32]

In Eisenhower's absence, Jackson continued to stew. He confessed to Jim Hagerty that he had leaked his "declaration of war" assessment of the McCarthy speech to the newspapers and extracted a pledge from the press secretary to discuss the speech at Monday's staff meeting. On Sunday, Jackson saw Dulles, who shared "two terrifying facts": that "the President had not read the McCarthy speech or been briefed on it" and that, as of Sunday afternoon, Brownell had not read it either. Jackson despaired, "This place is really falling apart."[33]

At Monday's staff meeting—"Black Monday," Jackson called it—Hagerty discussed the problem of leaks to reporters. "After [a] moment of dead silence," Jackson confessed to telling James Reston that McCarthy had "declared war on the President" and lectured the staff on the evils of appeasement; he warned that that the "three Little Monkeys act" would not work.

The discussion degenerated into what Jackson called a "big

rhubarb" between two factions. The legislative liaison staffers opposed taking on McCarthy, while the Jackson group argued for responding in order to retain Democratic support of the president's
legislative program. Bryce Harlow eventually convinced the group
that a carefully crafted statement at the president's press conference
would give the matter "just the right amount of importance." However, another round of squabbling erupted over the content of the
statement. Finally, they agreed to take drafts to a meeting with the
president.[34]

Unknown to the staff, Eisenhower and Dulles had been meeting
on the same issue: how to respond to McCarthy. By then Ike had
apparently read the speech. They decided that Dulles should hold a
news conference focused on the issue of support for allies. The next
morning, he would return for Eisenhower's final approval of his
statement before facing reporters.[35]

CROSSING THE RUBICON

At 8:30 a.m. on December 1, Dulles met with reporters to respond
to McCarthy's criticisms of Eisenhower's foreign policy. Reporters
were informed that his statement had been approved by Eisenhower
and would be publicly supported by the president at his news conference the following day. As Ike preferred, Dulles never mentioned
McCarthy's name. He addressed "a widely publicized criticism of this
Administration's foreign policy" that the United States had sent its
allies "perfumed notes" rather than use "threats and intimidation to
compel them to do our bidding." The secretary labeled that charge
an attack on "the very heart of United States foreign policy." It was,
he asserted, in American interests "to assist certain countries but that
does not give us the right to try to take them over, to dictate their
trade policies and to make them our satellites." Dulles extolled the
foundations of Allied assistance by means of "well-located bases," participation in the "early warning system," and reliance on their "large
industrial strength to keep the balance of world power" in favor of
the West. "We do not," he stressed, "propose to throw away those

precious assets by blustering and domineering methods." His final words left no doubt of the president's support: "These fundamentals of our foreign policy were agreed on by President Eisenhower and me before I took my present office. These principles still stand."[36]

C. D. Jackson called Dulles to praise his statement and inform him that there had been "quite a flap" over the president's upcoming press conference. Dulles concurred that "if the President starts to twist and turn tomorrow, it will be pretty bad." Jackson pleaded with him to "have a word" with Eisenhower to ensure that he took a strong stance. Dulles responded that "if he doesn't I am finished, I might as well quit."[37]

The next morning, the White House staff staged a bureaucratic soap opera. Jackson, frozen out of the staff meeting, finally located the group in Assistant Press Secretary Murray Snyder's office, and, as he put it, "we went at it again." Speechwriter Robert Kieve, like Jackson, was worried; he called a draft statement "a truly sad document: a defensive, cringing, cowardly page-and-a half of purely negative prose."[38]

Finally, at 9:00 a.m.—with the president's press conference scheduled for 10:30—the key advocates were ushered into the Oval Office to present the president two versions of a statement supporting Dulles's remarks. One was C. D. Jackson's, the other apparently Bryce Harlow's. What followed was what Jackson called a "battle royal."[39]

The president first read Harlow's draft, Jackson noted, "with visible irritation." Then he started to read Jackson's version—and exhibited "great irritation." He choked on the words in the opening sentence: "I do not consider that the President of the United States should indulge in name calling, even the name of the junior Senator from Wisconsin." The second sentence specified "the senator in his television appearance last week." Those statements violated Ike's cardinal rule of refusing to mention McCarthy. Eisenhower, Jackson recalled, "slammed it back at me and said he would not refer to McCarthy personally." Jackson's account in his diary repeated Ike's favorite declaration about McCarthy: "I will not get down in the gutter with that guy."

However, once the issue of personalizing the statement was settled, Eisenhower, the master editor, went into action. Jackson was amazed as Ike "himself began very ably to firm up the text as he re-read it again, this time very carefully." The mood shifted from "divided snarling into united helping him along" until the president "dictated the last paragraph exactly as it finally appeared." "The group almost cheered," Jackson recalled, and "what started as a ghastly mess turned out fine." Jackson exaggerated; Eisenhower had used almost nothing from Jackson's draft.[40]

At the news conference, Eisenhower turned to the subject that had been "getting a lot of headlines" and launched into his prepared statement. He was now resolute; he was not going to abandon Dulles as he had Brownell. "I am in full accord with the statements made yesterday by Secretary Dulles in his press conference," he said. "The easiest thing to do with great power," he continued, "is to abuse it— to use it to excess." The United States, he said, must not "grow weary of the processes of negotiation and adjustment that are fundamental to freedom" and slide into "coercion of other free nations." To do so "would be a mark of the imperialist rather than of the leader."

Eisenhower repeated his previous assertion "that fear of Communists actively undermining our government will not be an issue in the 1954 elections." He further challenged McCarthy, saying, "It is imperative that we protect the basic rights of loyal American citizens. I am determined to protect those rights to the limit of the powers of the office with which I have been entrusted by the American people." He pivoted toward the strategy Bryce Harlow had recommended in October in response to the letter from Nicholas Roosevelt, calling for "a progressive, dynamic program enhancing the welfare of the American people. . . . In any event, unless the Republican Party can develop and enact such a program for the American people, it does not deserve to remain in power."

He ended his formal statement with "Now, that is what I am going to say about these late headlines, and on that and any closely related subjects, there is not another word to say. With that one proviso, I will mount the usual weekly cross and let you drive the nails."

It had been a bravura performance; Eisenhower's flawlessly modulated statement, though not mentioning the senator, had come off as confident, principled, and fully in charge. The statement was so effective that no reporter asked a question about McCarthy or his speech.[41]

James Reston opined that "President Eisenhower today took personal charge of his Administration's counter-attack on Senator Joseph R. McCarthy of Wisconsin." William Lawrence quoted close associates of the president as saying that Ike "had crossed a political Rubicon." The turning point in the Eisenhower-McCarthy conflict had arrived.[42]

McCarthy got the message. Later that day, he issued a statement backing away from confrontation and expressing "a great deal of admiration for the President." He labeled as "ridiculous and untrue" suggestions "that I am challenging President Eisenhower's party leadership." However, he reiterated his contention that "the question of communism will be an important issue in 1954" because the Democrats were still "soft on communism." He told reporters he had "no intention or desire" to seek the presidency. Uncharacteristically, McCarthy took no questions.[43]

"ATOMS FOR PEACE"

"Waging peace," a favorite Eisenhower concept, could be a hazardous activity in the McCarthy era. Nevertheless, on December 8, after returning from meeting with the Allies in Bermuda, Eisenhower delivered a visionary speech before the United Nations, proposing to "move out of the dark chamber of horrors into the light" by making atomic energy available for peaceful purposes throughout the entire world. "It is not enough," he declared, "to take this weapon out of the hands of the soldiers. It must be put into the hands of those who will know how to strip its military casing and adapt it to the arts of peace. The United States knows that if the fearful trend of atomic military buildup can be reversed, this greatest of destructive forces can be developed into a great boon, for the benefit of all mankind."[44]

Eisenhower's "Atoms for Peace" speech was warmly received at home and abroad. *New York Times* columnist William S. White asserted that the president's talk had "greatly strengthened his hand in world affairs against critics in his own party. At his December 16 news conference, the last of the year, the reporters' questions were focused mostly on the president's proposal to share nuclear energy with the world.[45]

For the moment, McCarthy had been pushed to the sidelines by Dulles's and Eisenhower's strong responses to his televised address and the president's dramatic proposal to share atomic secrets. That did not mean he had given up his crusade against the army, a cause Roy Cohn continued to press with his boss. Cohn, John Adams recalled, was "hounding me relentlessly to get David Schine assigned to New York." Adams continued to insist that, except for the concessions Secretary Stevens had already made, Schine be treated like any other soldier. Cohn's response: "The Army is making Dave eat shit because he works for Joe."[46]

In fact, the privileges Stevens had approved for Schine were generating morale problems among Schine's peers at Fort Dix. Adams solicited a letter from McCarthy recommending normal treatment for the soldier. Two hours later, Cohn was on the phone, screaming at Adams "The Army is going to find out what it means to go over my head." "Is that a threat?" Adams asked. "No, that's not a threat," Cohn said. "It's a promise, and I always deliver on my promises." Adams informed Stevens about Cohn's threat—that "the Army has double-crossed me for the last time" and "the Army is going to pay for this." Then, to add fuel to the fire, Cohn learned that Schine's basic training schedule had been expanded to include Saturday mornings. He raged to Adams that the army had "double-crossed" him four times by (1) denying Schine a promised commission, (2) not assigning him to New York immediately, (3) canceling some weeknight passes, and now, (4) extending basic training to Saturday mornings.[47]

Stevens was still trying to be a peacemaker; he scheduled lunches with McCarthy in New York on December 10 and 17. On December 17, Adams brought up the Schine situation, hoping to encourage McCarthy to express the doubts he had expressed privately. In response, Cohn became even "more violent" about Schine, intimidating McCarthy. He had previously agreed to give Adams a ride to the train station in Schine's Cadillac. Cohn was seething, spouting vulgarities all the way; suddenly—in the middle of the block on Park Avenue near Forty-sixth Street—he slammed on the brakes and screamed at Adams, "Get out and get to the station however you can!" As Adams exited, he recalled, "McCarthy asked me again to ask Secretary Stevens if he could not find a way to arrange for Schine to be assigned to New York."[48]

PEACE WITH MCCARTHY?

On Christmas Eve 1953, Dwight Eisenhower wrote his old friend Swede Hazlett that the month had been had been "one of the busiest in my life." Ike had weathered the storm over Harry Dexter White and, in partnership with Dulles, had put McCarthy into his place on foreign policy—at least for the time being. He had conducted important meetings with allies in Bermuda and returned to deliver a triumphant proposal at the United Nations on the peaceful uses of atomic energy. Now he was preparing for three grueling days of meetings with Republican congressional leaders to hammer out a bold legislative program. In that long letter to his friend, Ike did not mention McCarthy.[49]

The people Reston called "the political gladiators," including Eisenhower and McCarthy, were present on Saturday, December 12, at the Gridiron dinner, a traditional Washington event where political figures poke fun at one another. A highlight of the evening was "the Eisenhower Waltz," featuring "one step forward, hesitate . . . one step sideways, glide; one step back, stop." Harry Truman was satirized for "running against the wrong Hoover" (J. Edgar) in the Harry Dexter White case. A Joe McCarthy impersonator sang a song that ended with the line "Look over your shoulder; I'm walking behind."[50]

Eisenhower ran three days of meetings with Republican congressional leaders on December 17, 18, and 19 with near-military precision. McCarthy was present, a rare occurrence. Eisenhower outlined ambitious proposals regarding foreign aid, his Atoms for

Peace program, taxes, a farm aid program, enhancement of Social Security benefits, and an increase in the minimum wage. It would be, without question, the most sweeping legislative program proposed by a Republican president since Franklin Roosevelt.[51]

Reporters interpreted Eisenhower's closing statement on the nineteenth as pledging even more vigorous actions against subversives. Attorney General Brownell had proposed seeking enhanced authority for wiretapping in espionage cases and authority to compel a witness to testify in spite of the Fifth Amendment privilege. McCarthy issued a statement praising the president's leadership in the meetings; "I was not displeased at anything I heard." By December 19, Eisenhower had seized control of both the national agenda and the news spotlight. He had survived a tumultuous first year in the White House and was still held in high esteem by the American people. The Gallup Poll at the end of the year reported that if the American public were to name a "Man of the Year," that man would be Dwight D. Eisenhower.[52]

The old soldier understood that the moment to negotiate an armistice is when you are in a position of strength. So he may have sanctioned one last effort to reach an accommodation with Joe McCarthy. Prior to the 1954 elections, there was usually someone, either in or out of the White House, trying to mediate and head off a rupture in the Republican Party. Roy Cohn cited two efforts, both of which he assumed—probably erroneously—had originated in the White House. In his book *McCarthy*, he reported that Milton Eisenhower had lunched with George Sokolsky and asked, "What can be done to work things out?" McCarthy had responded negatively to that olive branch. Cohn also stated that the same month, probably sometime late in the year, White House congressional liaison Jack Martin secured a private meeting with McCarthy. Martin's proposition was that the senator end all public hearings, hold only executive sessions, and share the minutes of those hearings confidentially with the president so he could act on their implications. Cohn recalled that McCarthy "rejected the proposal flatly." He came to believe that McCarthy's rebuff of the Martin proposal "triggered a high-level decision to destroy the Senator."[53]

Neither of those peace initiatives fits Eisenhower's mode of operation. It is unlikely that he would have dispatched his brother to lobby a biased news commentator such as Sokolsky. The Martin mission was probably initiated by the congressional liaison aides, headed by Jerry Persons. The proposal, as reported by Cohn, so violated the separation of powers doctrine that Eisenhower, a zealous defender of that constitutional principle, probably neither initiated nor approved the effort.

The third effort at peacemaking cannot be linked directly to Eisenhower, although it was more his style. Vice President Richard Nixon had returned from his trip to the Far East on December 14, in time to participate in the Republican leadership meetings. It is conceivable that he and McCarthy found time to plan a get-together at Key Biscayne, Florida, during the Christmas break.[54]

Whether planned or accidental, Nixon and William Rogers seized the chance to spend significant time in Key Biscayne with McCarthy, gently encouraging him to support the administration and diversify his investigations. According to a leading Nixon scholar, "They did not try to get any commitments from him, nor did the senator make any promises." Whether this episode bore Ike's fingerprints is immaterial; Nixon and Rogers both knew what the president wanted.

William Ewald describes the scene: "Sitting there in the sunshine, a drink in his hand, Joe seemed to agree with them—seemed to give them reason to hope that in the New Year he would play on the team; be a good boy." That description fits McCarthy's comments to reporters on December 30, following the meetings. He said his subcommittee was considering broadening its investigations to include tax cases, "compromised at ridiculously low figures" during the Truman administration.[55]

Despite the apparent comradery, Nixon and Rogers had delivered an implicit warning: If Joe McCarthy failed to modify his behavior, especially toward Ike's army, the old warrior in the White House might deal very differently with him in 1954.

PART 2

1954: MOBILIZATION

CHAPTER 6

"EISENHOWER'S FIRST MOVE"

By the second week in January 1954, the peace policy toward Joe McCarthy was all but dead. For a year, Dwight Eisenhower had endured the tyranny of the Republican one-vote majority that dictated conciliation with McCarthy. In Florida, Richard Nixon and William Rogers, two trusted presidential surrogates, had delivered a velvet-gloved warning. On Monday, January 4, the vice president gave reporters the hopeful impression that McCarthy had decided to "soft-pedal" his Communist-hunting activities.[1]

The next day, McCarthy labeled the report that he was changing directions "a lie." "No administration official," he told attendees at a news conference, "from Eisenhower on down the line, and no Republican Senator has ever remotely suggested how our committee should operate or what our field of investigation should be." "Whoever originated those stories," he declared, "was either lied to or he was deliberately lying."[2]

On January 4, John Adams received another signal from the McCarthy camp that there would be no peace. Roy Cohn called to demand information on "a captain or a major, a doctor or a dentist, who is on duty at Camp Kilmer, and who is a Communist." Irving Peress, a New York dentist, had been drafted into service under the 1950 Doctor Draft Law to address an acute shortage of medical personnel during the Korean War. Assigned the rank of captain, Peress had been promoted to major because of a congressional grade adjustment act for which McCarthy had voted. Peress, when asked about any relationships to "subversive organizations," had written "Federal Constitutional Privilege" instead of "yes" or "no"—He had effectively "taken the Fifth." When that was discovered, the army initiated steps to separate him from the service and on December 30, 1953—five days before Cohn's phone call to Adams—the army vice chief of staff approved Peress's discharge. He was granted the standard option for an officer facing involuntary separation: he could select any departure date up to ninety days thereafter. He chose March 31, 1954.[3]

The Peress investigation heralded a more intensive phase in McCarthy's campaign against the army. And with that, the peace policy toward McCarthy would end. When McCarthy escalated his army inquiry, Eisenhower would accept C. D. Jackson's contention in December that McCarthy had "declared war on the president." Characteristically, Eisenhower would "wage peace" for as long as possible, but once he decided an enemy was implacable, his response could be lethal.[4]

BATTLE PLAN

In early 1954, Eisenhower implemented phase two of the strategic vision he had conceived for his presidency when he took office. His first year had been dominated by the inevitable problems of organizing a new administration, plus ending the war in Korea and responding to Stalin's death. His focus in 1954 would be persuading the Congress to pass "a list of legislation of wide scope." Persistent voices in the White House still argued that McCarthy's vote and support were essential to that end.

The third rail of the Eisenhower plan would be running for a second term. He camouflaged that intent by stating that the third and fourth years of his presidency would be the time to "get out and swing for [the] program." Ike often maintained that he had not sought the presidency, nor did he covet a second term. The hard-driving soldier behind the smile consistently cloaked his ambition in a call to duty. In the shadow of Franklin Roosevelt, he could not hope to be ranked as a great president without a second term. In his memoirs, Eisenhower characterized 1954 as "the history of the resolution of a host of problems," crowning his inventory of that year's challenges with "McCarthy riding high." A Gallup Poll published in January reported that 50 percent of the American public held a favorable opinion of the senator, with 29 percent negative.[5]

To mobilize for phase two and prepare for the 1954 congressional elections, Eisenhower temporarily brought Henry Cabot Lodge, the UN ambassador, into the White House as a political adviser. On arrival, Lodge quickly concluded that "the McCarthy problem was the most imperative issue facing the President." He repeatedly whispered in Eisenhower's ear that McCarthy wanted to be president. When asked in his first news conference of 1954 whether an allusion to "the next three years" implied he would not run again, Eisenhower was coy, responding that political friends—surely including Lodge—had advised him to make that "one thing I should never talk about."[6]

Eisenhower's golfing vacations often constituted a presidential calm before the storm. As the New Year began, Ike was in Augusta, Georgia, planning a legislative whirlwind once he returned to Washington. He arrived at the White House on Sunday, January 3. On Monday at 8:30 a.m., he chaired a cabinet meeting in preparation for launching his program. That night Ike stole a page from Franklin Roosevelt's playbook with a "fireside chat"—he did not call it that—with the American people on radio and television. Eisenhower reviewed in simple language the themes in his upcoming State of the Union message, scheduled for Thursday. The talk was short on specifics and long on appeals to "individuals and American families—deeply concerned with the realities of living."

Eisenhower sought to reassure Americans traumatized by depression, war, and Cold War tensions that he did not intend to dismantle basic New Deal programs. "This administration," he said, "believes that no American—no one group of Americans—can truly prosper unless all Americans prosper." He called for action to eliminate "the slum, the out-dated highway, the poor school system, deficiencies in health protection, the loss of a job, and the fear of poverty in old age"—in short, "any real injustice in the business of living." The president expressed his "strong belief that the Federal Government should be prepared at all times—ready, at a moment's notice—to use every proper means to sustain the basic prosperity of the people."

Predictably, Joe McCarthy's name did not appear in the president's remarks. Neither did he mention communism, only a veiled allusion to "security standards" for government employees.[7]

That was all a carefully planned prelude to the State of the Union message on January 7. At noon, Eisenhower made a grand entrance into the House of Representatives, shook hands as he proceeded down the aisle, ascended the platform, and flashed his famous grin at the assembled crowd. He bowed toward the visitors' gallery, where Mamie and her parents were sitting, but that put McCarthy in his line of sight. At that moment, McCarthy, William S. White reported, "caught his eye with a wave of the hand from a seat near the front. Eisenhower smiled and waved back" and then turned the other way to respond to the clapping, cheering crowd.[8]

In the speech, Eisenhower touted his administration's accomplishments during "the most prosperous year" in the nation's history. Racial desegregation had been advanced in the armed forces and the District of Columbia. Fighting had ceased in Korea. He proclaimed "a great strategic change" during 1953; that "precious intangible, the initiative," he said, "is becoming ours." He would use that initiative to reach three goals: protect the freedom of the American people, maintain "a strong, growing economy," and "concern ourselves with the human problems of the individual citizen." The remainder of the speech was a recitation of the program proposals he had hammered out with his legislative leadership in December.

The president indirectly addressed the McCarthy challenge in a section of the speech entitled "Internal Security." He boasted that, under his employee security program, "more than 2,200 employees have been separated from the Federal Government." In a blatant appeal to McCarthy's base, the president, who was still learning the political game in Washington, had waded into the Washington numbers game.

Eisenhower's other rhetorical gambit aimed at McCarthyites was to suggest that membership in the Communist Party was "akin to treason." He proposed that Congress deprive such persons of their US citizenship, subject to their being convicted in the courts of conspiring to overthrow the government. According to *The New York Times*, that pronouncement produced "by far the noisiest demonstration" of the night.[9]

WARNING SHOTS

The tone was unmistakable; in the second year of his presidency, the general had seized political command. That week, he quietly instigated warning shots over McCarthy's head, including a flurry of proposals for circumscribing the senator's investigative authority. Senate Majority Leader William Knowland urged an end to "one-man rule" in investigative committees. South Dakota senator Karl Mundt proposed enhancing the status of the Senate Internal Security Subcommittee, chaired by Senator William Jenner of Indiana. Some Democrats, including John McClellan, the Arkansas senator who had led the Democrats' July walkout from McCarthy's subcommittee, suggested establishing a joint Senate-House committee on internal security.[10]

The administration's hand in this agitation was thinly disguised. In a rare interview, Sherman Adams, the president's front man, endorsed "a relatively permanent system for dealing with Communists." He added, in language typical of Eisenhower, that this suggestion was not intended to "limit the latitude" of committees such as that headed by Senator McCarthy. It is unlikely Adams would have agreed to such an interview without his boss's approval.[11]

The New York Times described the proposals as "a carrot and a stick" strategy, designed by the administration to push McCarthy to investigate "fields other than subversion." The carrot would be the "juicy tax files of the Truman Administration," a strategy Nixon and Rogers had probably previewed in Key Biscayne. The stick was "a warning that the Administration would cooperate only with the Jenner Committee in aiding inquiries on subversion." [12]

The objective was to isolate McCarthy and position the president as the Republican Party's leader on communist issues in the 1954 campaign. The Democratic leadership looked on with amusement. Lyndon Johnson, for example, stood serenely above the fray, stating that he had "nothing to say" and that McCarthy was "a Republican problem." [13]

It would all come to naught. On the January 10 broadcast of *Meet the Press*, Knowland expressed doubt that the Senate would strip McCarthy of his authority "to investigate communism and confine himself to corruption in Government." Eisenhower and his congressional aides had nurtured no illusions about what could be expected from the proposals to clip McCarthy's legislative wings. The fight with McCarthy would not be won in the byzantine world of Senate committee structures, where the Wisconsin senator still held great sway. [14]

Unlike the president, Robert Stevens clung naively to the hope that he could make peace with McCarthy. New Jersey's Republican senator Alexander Smith called Stevens on January 12 and asked, "Is Joe behaving?" Stevens responded, "I would say so. I have never had any trouble myself at all with Joe." Roy Cohn, on the other hand, was "not the easiest fellow to deal with." Stevens chose to ignore McCarthy's continued persecution of army personnel. That very day, the papers reported that Aaron Coleman, a Fort Monmouth engineer who had worked for five years on an early-warning system against Soviet attack, had been suspended. McCarthy had threatened him with both perjury and espionage charges because of Coleman's association with Julius Rosenberg when the convicted spy had served at Fort Monmouth. [15]

The Coleman situation exemplified McCarthy's ruthless use of the subpoena. A continuing threat to the Eisenhower administration was that the senator might subpoena personnel records. On January 12, Deputy Attorney General William Rogers instructed Philip Young, the chairman of the Civil Service Commission, to refuse to honor such subpoenas on the grounds that the files contained "the result of investigations by the FBI and other investigative agencies and such disclosure might impair the work of those agencies." That was, Herbert Brownell wrote in his memoirs, "a decisive blow" by the president to "cut off access of McCarthy's committee to records of the executive branch."

The more serious threat was that McCarthy might subpoena key personnel to testify, including advisers to the president. Eisenhower had assigned Brownell to address that danger, too. By early 1954, the Justice Department had sketched out the constitutional foundations of an executive order, subsequently labeled "executive privilege," to protect the president, his advisers, and classified information. On January 7, the day of the president's State of the Union address, John Adams wrote Rogers that he believed the time had come to use the executive privilege tool to thwart McCarthy's agitation for testimony by members of the army's loyalty panels that had cleared new employees during the Truman years. "Fred Seaton indicated to me yesterday," he commented, "that he was going to talk about it in the White House because he feels that it would be better to attempt to get something done now, rather than when the pressure is on."[16]

THE QUEST FOR AMMUNITION

Fred Seaton was now center stage on such issues. John Adams called him "a White House pet" or "the White House man at the Pentagon." He recalled, "I have never been precisely sure of the White House role. I never was told exactly what went on 'over there.'" "Over there" and "across the river" were Seaton's euphemisms for the White House. Adams came to understand that he had been enlisted as a foot soldier in a political war, to be sacrificed, if necessary, for the greater good. As he watched the president from "across the river," he observed, "Eisenhower's indifference was deceptive; he could be in control while appearing to loaf."[17]

The president needed more than defensive weapons, though; the situation demanded ammunition to use against McCarthy. By January 7, Seaton had apparently concluded that the silver bullet might be the relationship between Roy Cohn and David Schine. That night, he discussed Schine's status at length with John Adams.[18]

The next day, January 8, Seaton called Stevens; based on his talk with Adams, he wanted to know whether the army was coddling Schine, who was scheduled to leave for Camp Gordon in Georgia once he completed basic training at Fort Dix. Seaton said he "was afraid that we would get our neck in the noose if that Schine boy was sent to a special training course for investigation." Columnists were speculating that Schine had been granted a special deal, although the primitive IBM program for sorting out candidates listed Schine as technically qualified. "I told John [Adams]," he said, "that I didn't believe that Schine should be kicked around." But, he inquired, was Stevens certain that "somebody did not slip a gear on those cards?"

Stevens was indignant at the implication; the decision had been properly made, and he was prepared to let "the chips fall the way they may." He continued, "I know the winds are going to blow, Fred, and I don't relish it, and I don't know what I am going to do about it." The frustrated army secretary sighed, "You're damned if you do, and damned if you don't."

Seaton reminded the secretary for whom he spoke; he worried aloud that a special status for Schine "will turn out to be an unfortunate assignment" for McCarthy and the White House "because of what has taken place between the President and the Senator." He suggested that the secretary pull rank by "looking into this thing yourself" and confirm that "you are sure of the facts." Seaton grimly added, "I am not sure of them."[19]

That same day, John Adams, in Massachusetts for a speaking engagement, was packing to check out of his hotel room. The phone rang. It was Frank Carr, Roy Cohn's colleague on McCarthy's staff.

Carr shared news that instantly gave the army counsel a knot in the pit of his stomach: David Schine had been assigned KP duty at Fort Dix that weekend. Adams declined to intervene and asked Carr not to tell Cohn how to reach him, but Carr insisted that he had no choice. Adams called the hotel switchboard, asked the operator not to transmit any calls from New York, and hurriedly finished packing. The phone rang before he could get out the door. He picked up the receiver and said, "Hello." Roy Cohn said, "Hello, John." Adams hung up.[20]

SPARRING WITH THE PRESS

Eisenhower's first news conference of 1954 was scheduled for January 13 at 10:30 a.m. The president normally reserved time prior to a news conference for a briefing by Jim Hagerty. However, at 9:00 a.m. that day, Seaton arrived in the Oval Office, followed a half hour later by Stevens. Though both meetings were off the record, Seaton undoubtedly addressed the agenda he had discussed with some urgency on January 7–8 with Adams and Stevens, including G. David Schine's service in the army.

As a result of those two conferences, the president got only a few minutes with Hagerty before confronting reporters. His exasperation with the schedule—and perhaps with what he had discussed with Seaton and Stevens—was evident. He complained to Hagerty that "having a press conference in [the] middle of getting up [the] legislative session is damn silly."[21]

That day Eisenhower emphasized to reporters his mission since January 4: pushing the administration's program. When asked how he expected Congress to react, he responded, "Look: I want to make this very clear. I am not making recommendations to Congress just to pass the time away or to look good or for anything else. Everything I send to Congress I believe to be, and the mass of my associates believe to be, for the good of this country; therefore I am going to work for their enactment. Make no mistake about that. That is exactly what I am here for and what I intend to do."

For a president notorious for scrambling his syntax, those care-fully rehearsed lines were incisive and emphatic. Then *New York Post* reporter Robert Spivack asked a question that moved Ike to resort to his characteristic fog of words; he requested a breakdown of the 2,200 persons the president had stated the administration's security program had separated from government employment. Ike danced around the question. "No detailed report has yet been made to me," he said and shifted the responsibility to the Civil Service Commission. That agency, he explained, had dropped more than 180,000 people, "so this 2200 is not a great number." He granted that some of the 2,200 had resigned without knowing they were targeted for dismissal, but, he concluded, "Those 2200 have gone in one form or another."[22]

Eisenhower had underestimated the fallout from his foray into the numbers game. The day after the president's news conference, White House counsel Bernard Shanley complained in his diary about a late-in-the-day, contentious two-and-a-half-hour meeting, held "because there was much carping and criticizing by the Demo-crats that we could not substantiate our figure of 2200 security risks among people who had been separated from the Government." He noted that "this statement was in the Union message." Democrats had charged that the 2,200 number included alcoholics and "per-verts." Eisenhower acquired an unwanted ally in the controversy when McCarthy insisted that "practically all" of the 2,200 had been removed "because of Communist connections and activities of per-version."[23]

Ike did not intend to abandon the other plank of the anticom-munist program he had staked out in his State of the Union ad-dress. On January 12, the day before his news conference, he sent Brownell a legislative proposal "to create a commission to study the question of outlawing the Communist Party." Brownell would subsequently oppose outlawing the party on grounds that such a law could be "construed as an arbitrary exercise of legislative power, violating the due process protections in the Constitution." He also feared that such a law would drive the movement underground and "increase the already difficult investigatory job of the FBI."[24]

At the time, Eisenhower was indulging in crass political calculation. He wanted to exploit the issue in the 1954 congressional elections. As stated in his State of the Union address, he intended that loss of citizenship would apply only to any citizen "who is convicted in the courts of hereafter conspiring to advocate overthrow of this government by force or violence." [25]

TIGHTENING THE STRATEGIC CIRCLE

Inexplicably, the day after he met with the president on January 13, Stevens called McCarthy. The secretary said, "I would like to have a little visit" and wondered if "it would be in or out of order to buy you a cocktail?" McCarthy responded, "I would favor that very much." They agreed to meet at 5 p.m. Why that meeting—especially the day after Stevens had met with the president? It is doubtful that Eisenhower asked Stevens to do it; he knew how naive the secretary was about McCarthy. In any event, Stevens had realized that the administration's approach to McCarthy, personified in Fred Seaton, had changed. The secretary liked to cast himself as the man on the white horse, riding in to salvage the situation. He had apparently decided to make another stab at peacemaking. [26]

That day, John Adams stopped by the Capitol to see the man he had hung up on a week earlier: Roy Cohn. David Schine would end his duty at Fort Dix the next day. Following a two-week leave, he would be assigned to Camp Gordon, Georgia, for possible training as a military police officer. Adams reluctantly informed Cohn that Schine might be assigned overseas after he finished his training. Cohn's response was heated. "Stevens is through as secretary of the Army," he snarled. Adams asked, "Really, what's going to happen if Schine gets an overseas assignment?" "We'll wreck the Army," Cohn shot back. McCarthy, he said, had "enough stuff on the Army" to run an indefinite investigation. They would smear the army in every way possible. Cohn angrily denounced that "lousy, double-crossing Stevens."

The situation escalated from bad to worse. Just before Stevens left for a trip to the Far East on the seventeenth, he and Adams learned that Schine's tour in Georgia would last five months, not the eight weeks they had mistakenly anticipated. When Frank Carr called on another matter, Adams asked how Cohn was taking that news, only to learn that Cohn did not know. Adams recalled that Carr's delivery of that information to Cohn, who was vacationing at a Schine-owned hotel in Boca Raton, Florida, "was a declaration of war to Roy Cohn." Within ten minutes, the enraged counsel called Adams demanding to know if the news was accurate. Seven hours later, he was back in Washington.[27]

As the anniversary of his inauguration approached, Eisenhower took time in his diary to contemplate his first year in office. The conflict with McCarthy hovered over his comments. He found the press corps in constant violation of the adage "Always take your job seriously, never yourself." Reporters, he noted, were "concerned primarily with personalities" and infatuated with gossip. Though his relationships with congressional leaders "have been on the whole better than I anticipated," Ike regretted that, following Taft's death, "no one of real strength has shown up on the Senate side." He found Majority Leader William Knowland "helpful and loyal, but he is cumbersome."

Eisenhower acknowledged, in almost clinical fashion, the hostilities he had encountered from the Republican Party's reactionary wing. He had been aware, even before running for office, "of some of the deep-seated differences that would separate me, in the event of a successful election, from some of the House and Senate leaders." He recalled that Democrats seeking to recruit him to run for the presidency had argued "that I would be further separated in political philosophy from such people as Senators Jenner, McCarthy, Millikin, Bridges, Langer and others than I would the Democratic leaders."[28]

MCCARTHY MAKES A MOVE

On January 19, McCarthy launched a new phase in his investigation of communists in the army. Frank Carr called John Adams to inform him that by two o'clock that day, five members of army loyalty boards would be expected to appear before Senator McCarthy to testify. If the board members did not show up voluntarily, McCarthy would subpoena them. Adams believed it was no accident that this action took place the morning after Cohn, angry over the status of Schine, had returned from Florida. "The McCarthyites planned to use the Loyalty Boards," he concluded, "as a weapon to punish the Army for mistreating Schine." Stevens was out of the country, so the army's counsel was responsible for a decision. Adams's reaction: "I was damned if I would send them into McCarthy's star chamber." An hour later, Carr called to ask if the board members were coming. Adams's response was "no," that only he would appear. "Joe doesn't like to be surprised," Carr warned Adams. "You better go see him first."

Adams hurried over to the Senate, where he buttonholed McCarthy before the senator's 2:00 p.m. hearing. When Adams pleaded for withdrawal of the demand that the loyalty board members appear, McCarthy growled that he was through negotiating with the army. He "issued an ultimatum to me in front of the press, which was duly printed in newspapers throughout the country," Adams recalled. McCarthy gave Adams until Friday, January 22, to produce the individuals he wanted; if he did not, McCarthy would issue subpoenas for five members, requiring them to testify at 10:00 a.m. on Monday, January 25.

Then McCarthy added a sly wrinkle: he would interrogate the board members not only about the loyalty program but about graft and misconduct in their ranks, a more legitimate role for his subcommittee. He would not permit them to be accompanied by counsel representing the army, nor would he accept their refusal to speak based on "a blanket reference to Presidential directives"; if they tried that, they would be required to cite specific sections of the law. If not satisfied with their answers, McCarthy said, he would cite them for contempt as he would any board members who declined to appear.

Adams rushed back to the Pentagon and gathered all the army employees he could reach who had ever served on a loyalty board. He instructed them not to respond to any subpoenas from the

McCarthy committee and to bring them to him. Then he reached out for help, calling Deputy Attorney General Rogers. In a memorandum, Adams told Rogers "unequivocally" that he intended "to direct them not to answer the subpoenas," but he would need "assistance outside the Pentagon." He asked for a meeting with the attorney general, and Rogers agreed to arrange it. Adams later claimed that he had told Rogers, "Either stand up now, or the press will say that the Eisenhower administration had backed down before McCarthy. The Army can't do it alone." [29]

Meanwhile, at 4:30 that afternoon, Eisenhower sat down to discuss politics with Henry Cabot Lodge. There is no record of the meeting, but Lodge's memorandum to the president the following day reflected the discussion. The agenda had been what Eisenhower had brought Lodge into the White House to do: advise him on the politics of the 1954 congressional elections. However, Lodge was not thinking just about 1954; he wanted the president to exploit the congressional campaign to set the stage for running for a second term in 1956.

Lodge headed the memorandum "Basic Position of the President Concerning Congressional Elections." His message was replete with implications for dealing with McCarthy and other fringe elements in the party. Lodge urged Ike to avoid being sullied by the partisan wars. He attached a draft statement for use with the press, stating the president's belief in the two-party system, his obligations "as titular leader of his Party," his commitment to his program, and his belief in the separation of powers in the government. He recommended an above-the-fray posture that would underline "the dual responsibility of the President" to serve as both "party leader and constitutional President."

In a confidential note, Lodge concluded, "If you are asked whether you will campaign in the 1954 congressional elections, you can say that you expect to take part in the spirit of the above statement." That would mean "no *wholesale* presidential support of *all* GOP nominees"—a recommendation with implications for McCarthy's allies. Though the Republicans might not win in the fall,

Lodge advised, "if you stay within the spirit of the above, it should be possible for you to come through the campaign with unimpaired prestige, *regardless of the outcome*, and at the same time, discharge your full duty as titular head of the Republican Party." Lodge implied that such a strategy would set the stage for 1956.[30]

The mood at the White House that morning was upbeat. At the January 20 cabinet meeting, the president commented on the GOP senators who opposed the administration's program. Perhaps recalling Lodge's advice the previous afternoon, he said he saw "no reason getting anyone elected who is trying to double-cross us." He would treat any of those double-crossers "as a prodigal son and kill [the] fatted calf for him if he changes—if not I have need for my own beef." By that time, Eisenhower almost certainly knew about McCarthy's threat the previous day to subpoena members of the army loyalty boards.[31]

A COUNCIL OF WAR

At 4:00 p.m. on January 21, Herbert Brownell convened a meeting in his office. A Who's Who of presidential advisers was present: Sherman Adams, Eisenhower's chief of staff; William Rogers, the deputy attorney general; Henry Cabot Lodge, Jr., the UN ambassador and presidential political adviser; Gerald Morgan, a presidential assistant and congressional liaison; and John Adams, the army counsel. Missing were Jerry Persons and Fred Seaton, the latter perhaps to keep his role under the radar. The most notable absences were army secretary Stevens, still traveling in the Far East, and defense secretary Wilson, who, despite his position, was not a close Eisenhower confidant. The gathering would be a seminal moment in the conflict between President Eisenhower and Senator McCarthy.[32]

Who really caused the meeting to take place? Arguably, it was Joe McCarthy, by virtue of his deadline the next day for the issuance of subpoenas for loyalty board members. Herbert Brownell chaired the meeting. That was no accident. His subsequent account puts Eisenhower front and center in the origins of this gathering. He revealed that "the ostensible purpose of the meeting was to discuss Senator McCarthy's request to subpoena members of the army's loyalty and security board regarding their actions in the case of one of the individuals under investigation at Fort Monmouth." The subpoena issue transcended what Eisenhower and Brownell had addressed in Executive Order 10501 in November protecting confidential records. Brownell disclosed that he had discussed the projected get-together with the president, saying that Eisenhower had "asked my advice as to his constitutional powers to order the army personnel to honor the subpoenas." Eisenhower felt strongly, he wrote, that McCarthy could not violate the constitutional "separation of powers between the two branches of government" or deny the president's "implicit right" to invoke executive privilege. He had shared a lengthy memorandum with Eisenhower, tracing that privilege back to George Washington.[33]

So this was Dwight Eisenhower's meeting, although he was not present. As was his practice, he had talked with the key members in advance. By meeting in the Justice Department, not the White House, the participants maintained the appearance that the Oval Office was not involved.

The memorandum Brownell had shared with the president was the first item on the agenda on January 21, spawning an in-depth discussion of McCarthy's threat to subpoena loyalty board members. Brownell recalled, "We decided that it would be improper to respond to McCarthy's subpoena." The discussion of executive privilege spilled over into a discussion of Roy Cohn and G. David Schine. John Adams noted that "in each instance where McCarthy made a demand on us for loyalty board members, it was almost immediately preceded by a flare-up between us and Roy Cohn over the New York assignment requests for David Schine." Brownell later called the news a "bombshell." Sherman Adams remembered the account as "strange and incredible" and traced it back to Cohn's agitation for a special commission for Schine in July 1953. In retaliation for denial of that request, Cohn had apparently pressured McCarthy into investigating the army.[34]

Without a doubt, Eisenhower already knew about the privileges sought for David Schine. Fred Seaton had almost certainly discussed them in his January 13 off-the-record meeting with the president. Ike had known that, in July 1953, the agitation on Schine's behalf had invaded the White House, with Roy Cohn pressuring Jerry Persons into calling naval personnel. Therefore, the expressions of shock were a bit contrived; the real "bombshell" was the realization that, just possibly, the scandal could be used against Joe McCarthy.

On January 21, in response to John Adams's narrative, Sherman Adams asked the army counsel, "Have you a record of this?" Adams did not. The chief of staff snapped, "Don't you think you ought to start one?" He confirmed in his memoirs that he had ordered the army counsel to "draw up a detailed chronological account of the whole affair."[35]

The meeting ended about 5:30 p.m. As the men left the attorney general's office, they knew that their political world had changed. Brownell recalled, "Following the meeting, I gave my opinion to the president that he was justified under the Constitution in resisting McCarthy's demand."[36]

Herbert Brownell characterized the meeting as "the first time the administration mobilized its forces on a broad front." Years later, Henry Cabot Lodge stated that the January 21 meeting "marked President Eisenhower's first move against McCarthy and led to McCarthy's ultimate downfall." Brownell concluded that, thereafter, "the executive branch was prepared to fight."[37] In other words—so was Dwight Eisenhower.

CHAPTER 7

"NOT FIT TO WEAR THAT UNIFORM"

On the evening of January 21, Joseph McCarthy addressed the annual National Association of Manufacturers dinner in Chicago. When reporters asked, "Will you be a Presidential candidate in 1956?," McCarthy responded, "Ike is my candidate. Under no circumstances would I be a candidate in 1956." Eisenhower's key advisers in the White House, especially Henry Cabot Lodge, thought otherwise. The men at the meeting on January 21 in Herbert Brownell's office now believed they were engaged in a battle with McCarthy for the integrity—and possibly the future—of the Eisenhower presidency.[1]

Roy Cohn had no doubt how momentous that meeting had been. Years later, he stated in *McCarthy* that "the men who met in the Justice Department that day were among the masterminds behind the movement to stop Senator McCarthy." He charged that they had eventually resorted to "successive degrees of coercion which did not stop at outright blackmail."[2]

"CROSSFIRE"

Near the end of their discussion, the Brownell group had wrestled with what steps to take in preparation for the looming confrontation with the Wisconsin senator. The attorney general conceded that McCarthy, by announcing his intention to interrogate loyalty board members about misconduct and corruption—not just communism—"had effectively cornered us." If the senator issued subpoenas, the administration would be forced to produce the board members but instruct them "to refuse to answer any questions directed at their participation in the loyalty program." That was a fearful prospect; once the board members confronted the predatory senator, they might be badgered into revealing security secrets. The issue was how—both short and long term—to deal with this situation.

The group settled on three options. The long-term tool was embodied in the memorandum that Brownell had carried into the meeting. That document reflected months of Justice Department study regarding "executive privilege" that would bar testimony by presidential advisers. However, that was a weapon guaranteed, once employed, to provoke a major confrontation with McCarthy, something they were not quite ready to consider.

A second alternative was a draft letter John Adams had brought to the meeting, declining to provide the loyalty board members for testimony. Brownell suggested that the Justice Department edit that letter to be more of a "state document," citing historic precedents and justifying a "blank refusal" to obey McCarthy's subpoenas. The problem was that McCarthy had threatened to issue subpoenas the next day, January 22. The revised letter could not be available in time. With the subpoena deadline tomorrow, what could they do today?

What they could do, even so late on January 21, was to fan out and personally lobby the other Republican members of McCarthy's subcommittee. The emissaries would explain the situation to those senators and—especially important, according to John Adams—"emphasizing the abuses we had received in the matter of Private Schine." Adams's handwritten note on a copy of his memorandum for the record captured the verdict: "We should surround McCarthy."

Meetings were arranged immediately. John Adams and congressional liaison Gerald Morgan saw Everett Dirksen a half hour later. Adams recalled that Dirksen had pledged to try "to put a stop to McCarthy's abuse of the Army," seek to end the agitation for privileges for

Schine, and retract "the improper threat of subpoenaing Loyalty Board members in retaliation." Dirksen talked openly about the possibility of firing Cohn. Later that evening, Adams's deputy, Lewis Berry, saw Senator Potter and set up a noon meeting the next day for William Rogers to brief Potter in greater detail. About that time on the twenty-second, Adams spent thirty minutes with Senator Karl Mundt.[3]

Those conversations had the desired effect. At two that afternoon, McCarthy and his Republican subcommittee members convened a hurriedly called meeting. Following two hours of heated discussion, McCarthy made twin decisions designed to extricate himself, for the moment, from a direct confrontation with the White House. First, he announced that it "was not urgent" that he interview loyalty board members until Secretary Stevens returned from the Far East. Second, to appease the boycotting Democrats, he announced his willingness "to concede that any member of the subcommittee, at any time, had the right to ask for a subcommittee vote on the discharge of any staff member." That concession had obvious implications for Roy Cohn. When reporters asked whether Cohn might resign, McCarthy responded, "Roy is one of the most brilliant young men I have ever met. He is extremely valuable to the committee. I would be very disappointed if he left."[4]

Nevertheless, Cohn soon felt the political landscape shudder beneath his feet. Senator Stuart Symington, a Missouri Democrat who had been boycotting McCarthy's subcommittee, had apparently heard that trouble was brewing. He asked Cohn to come to his office. When the young attorney arrived, Symington motioned him to a chair, closed the door, and sat down. He leaned forward, looked Cohn in the eye, and spat out a single word: "Crossfire." Then he slowly repeated the word. Cohn did not understand. Symington elaborated slightly. "You," the senator said as he walked Cohn to the door, "have to worry about crossfire."

Cohn reflected on that strange conversation a few days later when the phone rang in his hotel room; it was Symington. The senator had another one-word message: "Resign." Cohn asked why he should do that. Symington snapped: "Crossfire. Resign." Years later, Cohn could not recall "a moment in my life when I was more thoroughly bewildered and uneasy." Nevertheless, he was not about to permit an insinuation about his relationship with David Schine to determine what he did.[5]

JOHN ADAMS IN THE LION'S DEN

Given the fallout from the January 21 meeting in Herbert Brownell's office, McCarthy wanted more precise information on what had transpired. Following the meeting with his Republican colleagues on January 22, he called John Adams and asked him to come to his home that night. Remarkably, Adams agreed to go.

It was cold, with snow on the ground, when Adams knocked on the door of the McCarthy residence at 8:30 p.m. Once inside the door, the senator plied the army counsel with food and liquor (which Adams declined) and gave him a big package of Wisconsin cheeses to take home. Adams later summarized the subjects discussed in the three-hour meeting as "twofold": the never-ending issue of assigning Private Schine to New York City and the senator's request that loyalty board members be made available for interrogation.

That night, McCarthy aggressively pursued the issue of Schine's army assignment. Adams recalled that the senator "on at least ten occasions during the evening stated that he didn't see why it wouldn't be possible for the Army to give Schine some obscure assignment in New York and forget about it." McCarthy warned that Cohn, upset over Schine, might launch a venomous "vendetta" against the army. Yet McCarthy characterized Schine as "useless, no good, just a miserable little Jew, who will never be of any help to [the] Army wherever assigned." However, Cohn had "very powerful connections" with the right-wing press and could cause the army great grief.

Although he had delayed issuing subpoenas, McCarthy had not given up on interrogating the loyalty board members. He told Adams he needed to "find a means of saving his face"; that made it "absolutely necessary" for him to interrogate the board members, without grilling them about the loyalty-security program. Exhausted, Adams responded that the matter should wait until Secretary Stevens returned from the Far East. About 11:15 p.m., Adams went home, sat down at his dining room table, and composed a memorandum to add to the stack of documents he was compiling for Sherman Adams.

Adams had exercised atrocious judgment in spending three hours alone with the cunning senator. McCarthy's motive was obvious; he was pumping Adams for information. The unanswered question in the situation is what Roy Cohn had on the senator that would impel him to continue to demand a special assignment for Schine, whom he clearly didn't care about. At one point in the conversation with Adams, McCarthy had dropped his voice and said, "The walls have ears, and maybe my room is tapped." The senator fretted that if Cohn resigned, he might accuse McCarthy of anti-Semitism. Cohn was in Florida that night. Afterward, McCarthy phoned him to report that he was "disturbed" because Adams apparently "had backing higher up." In his autobiography, Cohn quoted McCarthy: "This has got to be coming from the top."[6]

In the next few days, McCarthy formalized the concessions he had granted to lure the Democrats back to his subcommittee. According to *The New York Times*, McCarthy "surrendered today much of his one-man authority over the Senate Permanent Subcommittee on Investigations." The Democrats could now hire their own counsel and, if they unanimously opposed a public hearing, the question would be taken to the parent Government Operations Committee for a majority vote. Above all, McCarthy capitulated on the linchpin of the walkout: his exclusive authority to hire and dismiss staff members without a subcommittee vote. Senator McClellan announced the Democrats' acceptance of the agreement. McCarthy, reporter William Lawrence concluded, had "carefully avoided any new showdown with the Eisenhower Administration on the constitutional right of the Executive Branch to keep secret its Government personnel loyalty procedures."[7]

THE NUMBERS GAME

Demands continued for Eisenhower to explain the makeup of the 2,200 dismissed persons he had cited in his State of the Union address.

At his January 27 news conference, independent reporter Sarah Mc-Clendon suggested that the president's revelation made it appear "that if you are employed by the Federal Government and you suddenly leave or quit, your friends may think you have been fired for security reasons." Ike danced around an answer, calling it "a very confused business" when there are "so many hundreds of thousands, millions of people employed by the Government, unusual and cloudy cases arise." But, he concluded, "As I have told you before, our idea is here that we should not charge anyone with disloyalty or subversive activities unless that is proved in a court of law." Another reporter noted that, according to the director of the Civil Service Commission, the authority to explain the 2,200 rested with the White House. "We are going around in circles, are we not, sir?" Eisenhower returned to ambiguity and dumped responsibility on a subordinate. He noted that "the Attorney General drew up this security order" and "was more intimately aware of the circumstances than I was."[8]

On February 3, much to the president's annoyance, reporters again asked if there was "any more information about the 2200?" Ike joked that he had "found out some little time ago that you people have a very widespread interest in this thing." He had "several groups" studying the question, and the information would eventually be made available. Eisenhower rejected guilt by association but was also determined to deny people "the privilege of government employment if they are security risks." When asked if he would personally provide the report or defer to his subordinates, Ike quipped, to laughter, "Well, it could be both."[9]

The president's irritation over this distracting issue was evident at the cabinet meeting two days later. Secretary of Defense Charlie Wilson complained of "the near impossibility of collecting data on reasons for personnel dismissals" and estimated it would cost $100,000 to develop the statistics requested by the Civil Service Commission. Ike snapped that the military had "plenty of red tape around personnel records" and "there would be notations as to the reason for the dismissal of each employee." "Don't tell me you can't do it in defense," he growled. "I invented the system. You can ask for fat, bald-headed majors and they'll come tumbling out of the IBM machines." The President declared, with finality, that once a report was issued on the breakdown of the 2,200, they should say, "That's all there is, boys, there isn't any more."[10]

THE PERESS PROBLEM

The morning after Adams's extraordinary visit to the McCarthy home, George Anastos, a subordinate of Roy Cohn, called General Ralph W. Zwicker, the commandant at Camp Kilmer, New Jersey. Anastos demanded the name of the "Communist captain-major-dentist-doctor" hiding at his base, resurrecting the issue Cohn had called about on January 4. When Zwicker called McCarthy's office to validate the request, he unwittingly violated regulations by revealing Irving Peress's name.[11]

On January 27, Cohn phoned John Adams and demanded that Major Peress testify in New York on January 30. "We warned you about this fellow," Cohn growled, "and you've done nothing about it, and now we want him." When Peress appeared at a closed-door McCarthy subcommittee hearing, he promptly invoked his constitutional rights. Afterward, McCarthy announced he would demand that the army court-martial an unnamed army dentist who had invoked the Fifth Amendment in a hearing. In response, Peress decided to advance the date of his request for separation to February 2. His request was granted effective that day.[12]

When McCarthy heard that Peress had asked to be discharged, he rushed a letter to Secretary Stevens's office demanding that the dentist be retained for court-martial. Because Stevens was in Asia, the letter landed on John Adams's desk. Adams investigated and determined that Peress could not be court-martialed for exercising his constitutional rights. He considered holding Peress for a few days and telling McCarthy that they were "reviewing" the situation. Then he decided "To hell with McCarthy."[13]

Robert Stevens landed at Washington National Airport on February 3. Stevens had not been informed about the Peress situation.

When quizzed about Peress's discharge, Stevens said that "if this man is either a Communist or invoked the Fifth Amendment, he is not entitled to an honorable discharge."[14]

The next day, Adams briefed Stevens about a contentious conversation with Frank Carr about "our Communist Major." McCarthy, Carr had said, "is still hot under the collar" and "wanted all sorts of investigations on it." Again, Adams demonstrated abysmal judgment, stating "I thought I would go to his house." He was saved from that fate when Stevens apprised him that the senator had left the city on a nationwide speaking tour.[15]

"TWENTY YEARS OF TREASON"

Joe McCarthy was still, in Eisenhower's words, "riding high." The first week in February, the senator announced a nine-speech, eight-day tour, arranged and financed by the Republican National Committee. While billed as a series of Lincoln Day dinners, it resembled the sort of trip a future presidential candidate might take to test the political waters. McCarthy's nationwide tour reflected the RNC's judgment that, in William Lawrence's phrase, McCarthy would be "a big gun in the Republican Arsenal" in the fall elections. The *New York Times* reporter concluded that the senator continued to be "one of the most powerful and feared men in the United States Senate." By an 85-to-1 vote, McCarthy had just won $214,000 in funding for his subcommittee's investigations. Lawrence noted that "recent public opinion polls indicate that Senator McCarthy's political strength is increasing."[16]

On tour, McCarthy repeatedly charged that the Roosevelt and Truman eras had constituted "twenty years of treason." Richard Nixon recalled years later that the administration's leaders waited apprehensively for the moment when McCarthy would denounce "twenty-one years of treason." On February 5, McCarthy paraphrased Abraham Lincoln to proclaim that the Democratic Party "stands for government of, by and for Communists, crooks, and cronies." RNC chairman Leonard Hall, appearing on NBC's *Meet the Press*, called McCarthy an "asset" to the party in this election year. When asked whether the party, by paying McCarthy's expenses, was endorsing the senator's treason theme, Hall responded, "That's right."[17]

Enraged Democratic leaders challenged Eisenhower to halt the attacks on their loyalty to the country. In particular, they reacted to a speech by Sherman Adams alleging that Democrats were "political sadists," attempting to press a "fear deal" on the country by forecasting a new depression. Jim Hagerty responded for the White House that the president's chief of staff had been "just giving the people the facts." Stuart Symington asserted, "There is one man in the United States who can stop that kind of talk." The Missouri senator charged that the president's own "false" claims about weeding out 2,200 security risks in the government was another slap at the patriotism of Democrats.[18]

THE PERILS OF MIMICKING MCCARTHY

Given Sherman Adams's relationship with the president, Ike had likely approved that highly partisan speech. In any event, Henry Cabot Lodge deemed it a mistake. On February 9, he wrote Eisenhower that partisan remarks "were better made by Republican Senators and Governors rather than by those close to you." He called it "out of character for bitterly partisan remarks to be associated with you." When close subordinates talk about "their work or jobs, no fault can be found." But if they want to talk politics, they should "talk *pro-Eisenhower* and not anti-Democrat." Lodge attached a statement he suggested the president use at his news conference the following day, stating that the president "never enters into personalities" and was not and never had been "a narrow partisan."[19]

Ike knew that Lodge was right; every time he was tempted to imitate McCarthyist tactics, it backfired. At his February 10 news conference, he followed Lodge's prescription to the letter. Asked about members of his administration charging that Democrats were "soft toward subversives in the Government," Ike responded, "Well, I think, first of all, it is quite apparent that I am not very much of a partisan." He joked about the split in his own party, noting that Senator Knowland described himself "as a majority leader without a majority in the Senate." He expressed appreciation for Democratic support for aspects of his program and concluded, "I have my own doubts that any great partisanship displayed by members of the executive department is really appropriate in this day and time." He repeated the point: "I don't believe in bitter partisanship. I never believe that all wisdom is confined to one of the great parties."

Another reporter edged closer to a question about McCarthy, asking about Republican leaders who charged that all Democrats "are tinged with treason or that they are all security risks, without distinction." Eisenhower resorted to a favorite tactic, pleading ignorance: "I have seen no such statement." If so, it was "not only untrue, but very unwise." Democrats, he noted, after all, had "fought for America." Asked if that meant he would advise officials in the administration to avoid extreme partisanship, Ike responded, "That is correct."

Robert Spivack of the *New York Post* zeroed in on Leonard Hall's statement that McCarthy was "an asset" and that the RNC supported the senator's charge of "twenty years of treason." "Do you," he asked, "approve of underwriting the tour or agree with Mr. Hall?" The president, James Reston reported, "was visibly impatient" at the question and the reporter's quote of McCarthy's slogan. Ike responded "with a light edge to his voice": "I am not going to comment any further on that. Particularly, I have said many, many times that I am not going to talk about anything where personalities are involved. I will not do it."[20]

On their way back from the news conference, Eisenhower, thoroughly annoyed, told Jim Hagerty, "Press conferences are really a waste of time. All these reporters are interested in is some cheap political fight. It's too serious a time to have that sort of stuff as the major problem of our times." He sighed. "What a life." Nevertheless, Henry Cabot Lodge read the papers the next day with satisfaction. He praised the president for demonstrating that "the Presidential press conference is an educational force, because you got precisely the ideas you wanted into the opening paragraphs of the news stories." That night, McCarthy responded to the president's statements, saying he had "no plans for a major change in my line of speeches."

Asked if this meant he was defying the president, he insisted he was not and that Eisenhower was "doing a good job."[21]

However, earlier that day in California, the senator had charged that President Eisenhower was "grossly in error" for not cutting off aid to allies, notably Great Britain, for trading with Communist China. George Sokolsky, the pro-McCarthy radio commentator, warned John Adams that McCarthy, so enthusiastically received in San Francisco, would become increasingly difficult "because he's got California." A few days later, Sokolsky advised Adams that "Joe's got Texas now." That sounded like a politician's campaign manager counting big states for a presidential run.[22]

However much he avoided mentioning McCarthy in public, Eisenhower was active behind the scenes. After his February 10 news conference, he met alone with Robert Stevens. Ostensibly Stevens was reporting on his Far East trip, but the president spent most of the time coaching Stevens on how he should respond to the Peress matter in a McCarthy subcommittee hearing. The secretary, Eisenhower said, should admit any error, give the committee "every pertinent fact, leaving nothing more to be uncovered," explain how the mistake had occurred, take "full responsibility," and, finally, express his confidence "in the efficiency and loyalty of the Army and stand on that." Following those obligatory statements, Stevens "was *not* to placate or appease anyone or degrade himself in any way." If any "browbeating" occurred, Ike said, Stevens "should leave the hearing and inform the chairman that he would return only when he could be assured of courteous treatment." After that grilling in the Oval Office, Stevens could have nurtured no doubts as to who was in command of the response to McCarthy's charges.[23]

EISENHOWER AND LINCOLN

February 12 was Abraham Lincoln's birthday, a time to invoke the sixteenth president's eloquent call for "malice toward none and charity for all." In spite of Eisenhower's counsel to avoid extreme partisanship, *The New York Times* headlined a news article "Attacks

Continue." Still, his closest lieutenants were being more careful. Vice President Nixon urged the Republican Party to "avoid indiscriminate attacks on Democrats as a group."

McCarthy was not listening. Early in the week, he charged that the "Democratic Administration over the past twenty years has deliberately and knowingly allowed Communists to take any position in Government they desired." He called again for a blockade of the coast of China and demanded that the allies stop the "blood trade" with the communists.[24]

In the February 14 *New York Times*, James Reston contemplated "the Lincoln Spirit in 1954," contrasting Eisenhower and McCarthy. Given the Democratic dominance in the country, the Republicans could win in the fall only by identifying an "additional element" that would draw voters to their cause. Reston gave Eisenhower credit: "He has ended the bloodshed in Korea. He is trying to reduce tensions with the Soviet Union. He has not put class against class or party against party, or tried to destroy the social and economic gains of the last twenty years. In short, he believes that peace and unity, which the nation did not have in the last years of the Truman Administration, are that 'other element' that will provide the margin of Republican victory."

On the other hand, Reston wrote, McCarthy "believes that the best defense in politics is a good offense" and that "by attacking and attacking" on the issue of Communist subversion, the GOP could win. His conclusion: "Unable to get the President to come down to Senator McCarthy's level, or to get the Senator to go up to the President's, the political strategists in the party have decided to travel both roads at the same time."

Reston succinctly summarized the situation: "As it is now, the President is trying to produce confidence in the face of the Soviet menace, and McCarthy is stirring up fear; Eisenhower is trying to draw the parties together, and McCarthy is setting them apart; Eisenhower is urging cooperation with the allies, and McCarthy is attacking their policies and purposes; Eisenhower is trying to bury the past and McCarthy is trying to resurrect it." What Reston called "the Eisenhower Faith" was closest to Lincoln's "spirit of moderation and generosity" and could potentially provide "the decisive political element." McCarthy was arguing that "the Lincoln spirit is not enough. And the ironic aspect of it is that many of the politicians, Democrat as well as Republican, seem to agree with the Senator."[25]

The issues that burdened the president did not diminish. At a February 15 meeting with Republican congressional leaders, Ike grumbled that Senator William Langer of North Dakota was "dragging his feet" on the nomination of Earl Warren to be chief justice of the Supreme Court. He fretted about the deteriorating situation in Indochina, where an anticolonial war was under way, noting that the French wanted twenty-five planes and four hundred technicians. Eisenhower had sent ten planes and two hundred mechanics whom he had ordered be withdrawn by June 15. At the previous meeting, he had stated that he was "frightened about getting ground forces tied up in Indochina." Still, he lamented, "We can't get anywhere in Asia by just sitting here in Washington and doing nothing—My God, we must not lose Asia." But Ike's deadline for withdrawing the technicians underlined his unspoken judgment; if the French had not turned the tide of battle by then, the war would soon be over.[26]

LEAKING THE SCHINE STORY

G. David Schine had completed his basic training at Fort Dix, New Jersey, on January 16; his two-week posttraining furlough ended on the thirtieth. The army announced that Schine was being transferred to Camp Gordon, Georgia, "for evaluation and disposition." When asked, McCarthy stated that he did not know of any special treatment for Schine.[27]

Meanwhile, since the January 21 meeting in Brownell's office, John Adams had been responding to Sherman Adams's instruction—it felt like an order—to develop a full record of the privileges sought for Schine. On February 3, he completed his first edition of the Schine records. Not quite trusting the White House, he sent the documents first to William Rogers, not Sherman Adams, telling him it was "the only copy which is leaving my possession." He included the memorandum "which reports on an evening meeting I had with McCarthy about 10 days ago." [28]

Rogers apparently alerted the White House. Sherman Adams called the army counsel the afternoon of February 16 to find out why the White House had not yet received the report. John Adams immediately dispatched a copy to the chief of staff. The president was leaving for the West Coast the next day, and Sherman Adams's call may have reflected Ike's desire to see the report before he departed. [29]

About that time, Joseph Alsop, the *Washington Post* journalist, visited John Adams's office seeking information about the army's conflict with McCarthy. Alsop claimed he had been "sent" by Henry Cabot Lodge. That was significant, given how closely Lodge was advising Eisenhower about the politics of the situation. Given that stamp of approval, John Adams reached into his desk drawer, took out the summary he had compiled on Sherman Adams's orders— forty-one pages long—and handed it to Alsop. "It would be quicker and more accurate if you just read this," he said. He insisted that the information be kept off the record, a condition Alsop accepted and honored. Alsop read the documents right there, "snickering from time to time." After he departed, Adams had a momentary qualm of conscience; what had he done? He decided that there was "no use being just a little bit pregnant" and called in three other reporters, showing them the documents "under the same conditions I had established with Alsop."

Adams thereafter gave himself credit for putting "a bomb out there, ready to explode." In any event, the word was spreading. Senator Potter told Senator Symington about "a document" he had seen in the Pentagon. Adams learned that Alsop had told Fred Seaton about seeing the documents, saying "there are lots of them floating around." [30]

By February 17, Eisenhower was desperate to escape from Washington. He startled the assembled reporters by strolling into his 2:00 p.m. news conference two minutes early. He apologized for "trying to compress my schedule today. I hope, the Lord willing, in about an hour to be on my way to Southern California." Eisenhower was in no mood for serious discussion. He touched on two frothy subjects, the plan of England's queen mother to visit the United States and the price of coffee. CBS News correspondent Daniel Schorr asked if the president was satisfied with his remarks at the last news conference on "extreme partisanship." Ike refused to bite: "Well, I have no particular profound comment to make on that question." He had presented his views "about extremism of any kind in this political world, and I didn't particularly offer advice to anyone." The reporters got the message and did not return to that subject.

To Ike's irritation, the fuss over the 2,200 government dismissals was still on their minds. When asked if he wished to comment on the Civil Service Commission's projected report, he tersely responded, "Well, no." Then Eisenhower turned to Jim Hagerty, feigning a lack of knowledge about a matter about which he was fully informed: "Didn't you tell me that the Civil Service Commission, I think, is going to have a preliminary statement on this thing sometime— today is it?" Hagerty replied, "Yes, four o'clock." The president repeated, as if that were news to his ears: "Four o'clock." He added that "their final answer," not the preliminary report, "will take a little bit of time to compile." The news conference ended after only twenty-two minutes. Ike was out the door, heading to California to play golf and clear his head after a tumultuous six weeks.[31]

After Ike left town, Philip Young, the civil service director, released his preliminary report, showing that the president had overstated the situation. Only 430 of the 2,200 had been separated due to security concerns, and the loyalty of just 29 had been questioned. The main body of discharges and resignations had arisen from "sexual deviation," drinking, falsification of employment applications, and related traits that made access to classified materials unsafe. Two days earlier, at the Republican congressional leaders' meeting, Massachusetts senator Leverett Saltonstall, the Armed Services Committee chairman, had called the fuss about the 2,200 "a funny thing." "I never expected," he quipped, "to have sex perversion as a topic of conversation at the dinner table until I came to Washington."[32]

HUMILIATING A HERO

The day that John Adams dispatched his report to Sherman Adams, February 16, Frank Carr called the army counsel. He instructed Adams to bring General Ralph Zwicker, the commandant at Camp Kilmer, where Irving Peress had served, to a February 18 hearing on subversives in the army. Carr held out the usual Roy Cohn olive branch regarding David Schine: "We might get Joe to back off on this if you fellows [would] be a little reasonable." He referred to Schine as a "hostage" and wisecracked, "All the Army has to do is capitulate and all its problems will be over." Adams later phoned Secretary Stevens about the summons for Zwicker. Adams believed it would be "a first-class go-round" and that they had no choice but to make the general available.[33]

On the seventeenth, Adams flew to Camp Kilmer to talk with General Zwicker, cautioning him not to reveal either names or security information to McCarthy, based on President Truman's 1948 executive order protecting personnel information.* That night, in New York City, the taxi carrying Joe and Jean McCarthy had an accident. Joe was knocked temporarily unconscious, and Jean ended up in the hospital with a broken ankle. McCarthy went to his hearing the next day sleep deprived and, according to John Adams, in need of a belt of whiskey to get himself going.[34]

---

* Truman's 1948 executive order restricted the release of personnel information to a congressional committee. That differed from Eisenhower's April 1953 Executive Order 10450, which focused on the criteria for hiring personnel, proclaiming that government employment was "a privilege, not a right." The Truman order was modified by Eisenhower's October 1953 Executive Order 10501 that eliminated "restricted" from the Truman information classifications that included "top secret," "secret," and "confidential." The Truman order would be fully replaced by Eisenhower's sweeping May 17, 1954 "executive privilege" order prohibiting the subpoena of executive branch personal advisers (including presidential advisers) to testify; see chapter 14.

That day, February 18, bearing copies of Stevens's four-page letter to the senator about Peress, Adams accosted McCarthy outside his hearing room. The document precisely followed Eisenhower's February 10 instructions to Stevens. The secretary admitted to "defects in the Army's procedures" and took full responsibility, provided all the relevant facts (including Peress's automatic promotion as a result of congressional action and his legal right to request separation), outlined the corrective measures he had instituted, and dissected false rumors to the contrary. The letter informed the senator that reversing Peress's discharge was not legally possible and the law would not permit a reversal based on the officer's invocation of his constitutional rights. Finally, Stevens made sure, in Eisenhower's terms, to effectively express his confidence "in the efficiency and loyalty" of the army officials involved.[35]

McCarthy exploded. "I am sick of this coddling of Communists, this double-talk," he railed and declared his intent "to subpoena every officer in the United States, and every officer and civilian" involved in Peress's situation. Immediately following that confrontation, Adams called Stevens about how McCarthy had "upbraided" him over the letter. Stevens gave Adams permission to release his letter to the press, infuriating the senator even more.[36]

The hearing began at 10:30, with General Zwicker and his staff scheduled to follow Peress, who again invoked his constitutional rights. About 3:30 p.m., Adams witnessed McCarthy in the hallway, downing his "afternoon snort" of bourbon and thundering that there had been "some kind of Communist conspiracy" to give Peress an honorable discharge. McCarthy returned to the hearing room, now cleared of spectators and press, and began to interrogate Zwicker.[37]

Ralph Zwicker was a war hero. Senator Charles Potter, who had lost both legs in France, recalled the legend that, following D-Day, Zwicker had picked up the carbine from one of his fallen men and carried it for the next thirteen months. His awards included the Silver Star, the Legion of Merit, the Bronze Star, and the British Distinguished Service Order; his troops had contributed to the liberation of Paris and the rest of France. Potter's memory was so vivid because, at the time, he had been suffering in the bitter cold in Luxembourg and heading for France "for my meeting a few weeks later with a land mine at Colmar." After the war, Zwicker had served under Eisenhower at NATO, and, in 1953, had received his first star as brigadier general. Potter recalled that Zwicker's commanding officers had called him "exceptionally able" and "superior." In short, he was one of Ike's boys.[38]

In fact, Zwicker was not a supporter of Irving Peress. He had first identified the dentist as suspect on October 21, 1953, had repeatedly evaluated Peress negatively and had been outraged that Congress had, in effect, promoted him to the rank of major. Regardless, Zwicker had informed McCarthy privately on the morning of the eighteenth that John Adams had instructed him to refuse to talk about Peress's history on the grounds of President Truman's executive order.[39]

In testimony, McCarthy harassed the general in what John Adams called "a savage performance." Again and again, McCarthy pressed Zwicker for details of how Peress had been promoted and honorably discharged. Repeatedly, Zwicker responded that he was not at liberty to explain due to a presidential executive order. McCarthy retorted, "Well, you know that somebody has kept this man on, knowing he was a Communist, do you not?" Zwicker: "I am afraid that would come under the category of the executive order, Mr. Chairman."

McCarthy accused the general of "hemming and hawing." Zwicker responded, "I am not hawing, and I don't like to have anyone impugn my honesty, which you just did." McCarthy snidely countered, "Either your honesty or your intelligence." Then he roared, "Who ordered his discharge?" Zwicker responded, "The Department of the Army." "Who in the Department?" the senator demanded. "That I can't answer," the general responded.

McCarthy invented a rambling story about a hypothetical commander who had done what the senator alleged Zwicker had done with Peress: "Do you think, General, that anyone who is responsible for giving an honorable discharge to a man who has been named under oath as a member of the Communist conspiracy should himself be removed from the military?" Zwicker, cool under fire, responded, "He should by all means [be] kept if he were acting under competent orders to separate that man."

McCarthy moved in for the kill: "You have a rather important job. I want to know how you feel about getting rid of Communists." Zwicker shot back, "I am all for it." McCarthy took that as a refusal to answer and snarled, "Anyone with the brains of a five-year-old child can understand that question." Pressed again on McCarthy's hypothetical general, Zwicker said, "I do not think he should be removed from the military." McCarthy took the final, bizarre step: "Then, General, you should be removed from any command. Any man who has been given the honor of being promoted to general and who says, 'I will protect another general who protected Communists,' is not fit to wear that uniform, General."

When pressed again on why he had given "an honorable discharge to a man known to be a Communist," Zwicker replied, "Because I was ordered to do so." "In other words, anything that you are ordered to do, you think is proper?" "That is correct," Zwicker snapped. "Anything that I am ordered to do by higher authority, I must accept."

At that point, it was abundantly clear who McCarthy's target was. He asked Zwicker, "What is your considered opinion of this order forbidding you to assist this committee in exposing the Communist conspiracy in the Army?" Zwicker: "Sir, I cannot answer that, because it is signed by the President. The President says don't do it and therefore I don't." He added, "I won't answer that because I will not criticize my Commander in Chief."

At 5:15, McCarthy closed the session, ordering Zwicker to appear again the following Tuesday at 10:30 a.m. He also told Zwicker to "contact the proper authority who can give you permission to tell the committee the truth about the case before you appear Tuesday." Zwicker, knowing that "proper authority" implied the five-star general who was president of the United States, stated, "Sir, that is not my prerogative, either." "You're ordered to do it!" McCarthy roared. Zwicker, the loyal soldier, said again, "I am sorry, sir, I will not do that." [40]

CHAPTER 8

SAVING ROBERT STEVENS

The day after Joe McCarthy's ferocious interrogation of Zwicker, he continued to publicly chastise the army for ignoring Irving Peress's alleged communist ties. When he learned of McCarthy's statements, Zwicker told reporters that McCarthy was guilty of "twisting everything" and presenting a version of the hearing that "was absolutely not a truthful one."[1]

Although the transcript was not yet available, details of the hearing had leaked out. At 8:00 a.m. the following day, John Adams was in Secretary Stevens's office, delivering a blow-by-blow account. Suddenly, two visibly irate generals barged into the room. Matthew Ridgway, the army chief of staff, and Charles Bolte, the vice chief of staff, had seen quotes from the testimony, including McCarthy's charges that Zwicker was a "disgrace to the Army" and "not fit to wear the uniform." "This," Ridgway thundered, "is going too far!"[2]

At 9:38 a.m., the mortified Stevens called Zwicker at Camp Kilmer to give him "a vote of confidence." "I deeply resent such comments as Sen. McCarthy made to you yesterday," Stevens said. Zwicker was appalled to learn that the secretary had not yet decided if he would be required to return to testify on Tuesday. He warned Stevens that officer morale could be severely damaged if another soldier's "character is impugned as mine was yesterday"—especially if government officials "are doing nothing to refute those statements." Zwicker bitterly complained that "so-called Communists" were permitted counsel while army officers were not. When asked about his health, he growled, "I am feeling fine, and I will feel a whole lot better if I can wrap this rascal up."[3]

Troubled by that conversation, Stevens contemplated defying McCarthy. After consulting with William Rogers, Stevens and John Adams decided to visit the members of McCarthy's committee, starting with the Democrats. At 2:30 p.m., they met with Senators McClellan and Symington in McClellan's office. They agreed that Symington should write McCarthy a letter requesting that no hearing be held on Tuesday. The party then consulted the prestigious Democratic political strategist Clark Clifford, who advised that "under no circumstances should we permit a subordinate officer of the Army to take on Senator McCarthy in a sort of contest." Any confrontation, he said, "should be on the top levels." Stevens and Adams also called on Republican senators Dirksen, Mundt, and Potter. Potter promised to do his part to get the Tuesday hearing canceled. He said he could not comprehend "what it was that McCarthy had against the Army."[4]

"WE'LL FIGHT!"

At the White House on the morning of February 19, the nervous Joseph Alsop had secured a meeting with Sherman Adams for the purpose of sharing urgent information. Alsop read aloud from his notes detailing the positions and influence of communists during Ike's tenure supervising postwar Germany. Adams asked, "Why do you think I need to know this, Mr. Alsop?" The journalist said that he and his brother Stewart believed that McCarthy's next target was the president himself. They were considering publishing the information to inoculate the public against McCarthy's use of it. Before going with the story, they wanted to know if the administration truly intended to fight McCarthy. "Alsop," Adams responded, "we'll fight." "Well, that was all I came to find out, Governor," Alsop said.

"Leaving my notes with you, I have forgotten the conversation already."[5]

By February 20, the newspapers had published Stevens's February 16 letter to McCarthy refusing to turn over the records regarding the promotion and discharge of Peress. General Zwicker, not trusting army officials to protect him, released excerpts from the adjutant general's letter ordering him to proceed with Peress's discharge—an order he had had to obey. He also provided his own account of how McCarthy had charged that he was "a disgrace to the uniform."[6]

The previous evening, Roy Cohn had called John Adams to say that they now had an FBI report with "the most damning evidence" on Peress. In response, at 9:40 a.m. on the twentieth, Stevens called McCarthy, telling him about his discussions with subcommittee members. "Joe," Stevens said, "I am going to try to prevent my officers from going before your committee, until you and I have an understanding as to the kind of abuse they are going to get." McCarthy raged, "Just go ahead and try it, Robert. I am going to kick the brains out of anyone who protects Communists." If Stevens made that decision, McCarthy threatened, "I guarantee you will live to regret it."

McCarthy continued, "I don't give a goddam whether an officer is a general or what he is, when he comes before us with the ignorant, stupid insulting aspect of those who appeared, I will guarantee you that the American people will know about it." Stevens responded that he had told McCarthy's fellow subcommittee members that he "was not going to let General Zwicker appear on Tuesday." McCarthy growled, "I am all through with all this covering up of communists. I am sorry Bob Stevens is one that is doing it too. You can consider yourself subpoenaed for 10 o'clock, Tuesday morning." He slammed down the phone.[7]

After reporting to the other subcommittee members about his conversation with McCarthy, Stevens arranged with Jerry Persons to go to the White House for consultation with Sherman Adams. After returning, Stevens talked with the columnist James Reston, who had heard about McCarthy's calling Zwicker "a disgrace to the uniform." Stevens confirmed that he had decided against permitting the senator "to put General Zwicker on public display next Tuesday." Reston asked the big question: "Has the President been apprised of this?" Stevens dissembled, "Not as far as I know." He worried to Reston that the transcript of Thursday's session with Zwicker was "being rather carefully edited" by McCarthy and his staff. The headline on Reston's column the next day read, "Officers Ordered to Defy M'Carthy and Not Testify." Reston reported, "The Army was in touch not only with members of Senator McCarthy's office today but also with the White House on the run-in with McCarthy." [8]

After talking with Reston, Stevens spoke more candidly with Deputy Defense Secretary Roger Kyes about his discussion with Persons and Sherman Adams at the White House. "Everybody in authority," he said, "is fully informed." Stevens said that they had decided to "play it by ear" for the moment and he would be informed of "any decision at a high level" regarding whether he should personally testify on Tuesday. Stevens of course was referring to the president, who was still in California. The delay in making a decision was probably to allow for consultation with Eisenhower. [9]

By midday February 21, word came down to Stevens from the White House. At 6:00 p.m., the secretary of the army released a crisply worded statement, probably edited by Seaton or Hensel, that began, "I have directed Brigadier General Ralph W. Zwicker, of Camp Kilmer, NJ, not to appear before Senator McCarthy on Tuesday." Zwicker, the statement continued, had "suffered humiliating treatment only because he carried out actions which were his official duty." Stevens repeated his own willingness to appear, if requested, in the general's place. While pledging cooperation with congressional committees to rid the army of subversives, the secretary declared himself certain "that the American people do not believe in unwarranted abuse of our loyal officers any more than I do." [10]

Stevens later boasted to the journalist Arthur Hadley that he had not "asked anybody's approval or clearance" to issue the statement. That was untrue, but the secretary was ready to mount his white horse with the journalist. "It was time for me, Stevens, to make a statement; do the job myself," he told Hadley. That afternoon, Stevens called Senator Karl Mundt and invited him to ride with him to Valley Forge, Pennsylvania, the following day, where both were to receive Freedoms Foundation awards. During the trip, Mundt suggested to Stevens that they organize a luncheon meeting with McCarthy and the other Republicans on his subcommittee.[11]

AN "ALOOF" PRESIDENT?

The morning papers on Monday, February 22, reported that Stevens was headed for a "public showdown" with McCarthy, due to the mistreatment of General Zwicker. William Lawrence of *The New York Times* noted that Zwicker had been praised by General Eisenhower for his heroism in the campaign in Europe and had recommended Zwicker's division for a presidential citation.[12]

At 12:40 p.m., Senator Potter confirmed to John Adams that the Tuesday hearing had been postponed. Zwicker was taking no chances on his unpredictable superiors. In a telephone interview that evening, the general protested that he had been treated more harshly than a former communist who had testified. He emphasized that he had informed McCarthy that he was complying with a presidential directive in declining to answer questions.[13]

Amid this furor, the press noted with disdain that Eisenhower was in California, playing golf. A *New York Times* reporter in Palm Springs characterized the president as holding himself aloof from the dispute. Jim Hagerty, in California with the president, seemed to confirm that impression. When asked if the army secretary had been in contact with the president, Hagerty said he had not, although he conceded that Stevens had possibly communicated with Secretary of Defense Wilson and Sherman Adams. However, according to Hagerty, the president had not expressed his personal view regarding the dispute between the army and Senator McCarthy. Once again,

Eisenhower's penchant for camouflage contributed to the myth that he would rather play golf than pay attention to weighty matters.[14]

The February 23 papers carried the unedited text of McCarthy's interrogation of Zwicker. By all accounts, Eisenhower was privately furious over McCarthy's abuse of Zwicker. Ike, when preferring to disguise his involvement in a controversial matter, frequently employed surrogates to communicate with those on the front lines. A favorite messenger was Paul Hoffman, the Studebaker chairman and his golfing partner in Palm Springs. At 11:25 a.m. that day, Hoffman tried to call Stevens. He missed him, so he left a message commending Stevens for his courage and calling it "wonderful" that Stevens "was doing battle with McCarthy" and "doing a great job."[15]

About 2:30 p.m., Stevens received a call summoning him to what John Adams later called "a council of war" on Capitol Hill. Stevens and Adams stopped at the White House to pick up congressional aides Jerry Persons and Jack Martin. When they arrived at the Capitol, other power brokers were waiting: Richard Nixon, William Rogers, William Knowland, and Everett Dirksen. Persons, who had instigated the meeting, announced that his objective was to cancel the hearing, now rescheduled for Thursday.

Dirksen called the abuse of Zwicker "outrageous" and the Schine-Cohn affair "unpardonable." Claiming he was McCarthy's best friend in the Senate, Dirksen wanted McCarthy to do three things: end his arbitrary use of subpoenas and one-man hearings, cease his abuse of the army, and fire Roy Cohn. But John Adams later believed that Dirksen betrayed him by failing to deliver that message to McCarthy, instead promising McCarthy that he would ask the administration to fire Adams. Months later, Dirksen would repeatedly propose such a compromise scenario: fire both Adams and Cohn and end the conflict. As they prepared to leave the meeting, Nixon said, "Remember, this meeting never occurred."[16]

Later that afternoon, Senator Mundt called the Pentagon and asked Stevens's executive officer, Colonel Kenneth BeLieu, to convey the urgent message to Stevens "that tomorrow we are setting up a lunch at the Capitol for him and the Republican members of the committee—McCarthy, Dirksen, Potter, and me." Mundt added, "No one else is to know."[17]

Henry Cabot Lodge knew nothing about that planned luncheon. On February 23, he penned an "eyes only" message to Eisenhower that would be waiting on the president's desk when he returned from California the following morning. Focused on 1956, Lodge bluntly asserted that although ostensibly McCarthy's fight was with the army, it was "actually a part of an attempt to destroy you politically." He foresaw a rising tide of pressure for FBI checks of army officers and employees of other executive departments preliminary to McCarthy's taking on the White House itself.

Given that danger, he urged the president to use Stevens as his lightning rod. Stevens's job should be "to defend the Army before the public and before the Congress and do it with skill and vigor." As long as the president was in a political struggle with McCarthy, "all questions to the Army should come through Secretary Stevens"—not the president—and Stevens should avoid any appearance of denying the right of Congress to investigate the army. Lodge lamented that although Zwicker's stand "was perfectly correct," he was not a skilled debater and "it was very easy for McCarthy to make him look stupid." "Debaters should be met by debaters," he wrote. "It is not fair in war for debaters to meet Generals or in peace for Generals to meet debaters." Then with foresight, he suggested that the Peress situation "can be the occasion for bringing the entire question to a head." What they needed was "a little help from a friendly Senator, a little luck and a little skill on the part of Sec. Stevens."[18]

That "friendly senator" would be Republican Ralph Flanders of Vermont, who was then planning a public attack on McCarthy. "A little luck" might be taking shape over at CBS, where the journalist Edward R. Murrow was finalizing plans for a televised program about McCarthy. As for Stevens demonstrating "a little skill," that was more problematic. Unknown to Lodge or anyone else in the administration, Stevens had committed himself, once again, to a secret negotiation with McCarthy the following day.

"SURRENDER!"

At 7:45 a.m. on February 24, the president's plane landed at National Airport. By 8:00 a.m., Eisenhower, rested and refreshed, was at the White House, and at 8:30, he presided over a meeting with Republican legislative leaders.

At midday, Stevens was working with Struve Hensel and John Adams on his statement to use in testimony before McCarthy's subcommittee. Suddenly, about 1:00 p.m., without explanation, he rose and left the room. "Where's he gone?" asked Hensel. Adams responded, "He's going to a secret lunch on the Hill." When Stevens arrived at the Capitol, he was shocked to find a crowd of reporters clustered outside the dining room. He "opened the door and walked in alone: without a lawyer, without even an accompanying aide as a witness." Stevens had unwittingly walked into what press secretary Jim Hagerty later called "a bear trap."[19]

The senators in the group included McCarthy, Dirksen, Potter, and Mundt. The luncheon discussion, over fried chicken, went on for an estimated two hours. Stevens and McCarthy exchanged heated words about the abuse of officers and Stevens's discussions with other committee members. Eventually, group exhaustion spawned a desire for the creation of a document of understanding. Using a typewriter in the room, Karl Mundt typed up a draft, making numerous changes. It was signed by both Stevens and McCarthy and was, as Mundt recalled, "attested to by the signatures of all Senators present."[20]

The memorandum of understanding covered three main points; the first cited "complete accord" between the army and the subcommittee that communists "must be rooted out of the Armed Services"; the second documented "complete agreement" that the secretary of the army would complete the Peress case, identify the names of persons responsible, and make those persons available to the subcommittee. Finally, the next appearance of General Zwicker would be "deferred" until Senator Symington returned from Europe; if the subcommittee decided at that time to call Zwicker, Stevens pledged that he would be available.

The memorandum contained not one word about what Stevens had come into the room seeking: assurances that army officers who testified would be treated with respect, although Stevens thought he had received verbal assurances to that effect. However, the group apparently persuaded him that including such guarantees in the memorandum might cause McCarthy to renege on the agreement. When the doors opened, an estimated fifty reporters and photographers flooded into the room; plates and coffee cups were still left over from the lunch. The cameras caught McCarthy and Stevens sitting side by side on a green leather sofa, smiling and shaking hands.[21]

When asked by reporters, Stevens expressed confidence that army officers would not be abused in the future. At 4:30 p.m., back at the Pentagon, Stevens called together twenty-one of his top officers and associates and announced that he had achieved an agreement whereby they would be protected from mistreatment like that visited upon General Zwicker. Seaton listened to Stevens's account in growing discomfort. Struve Hensel handed Seaton a wire service copy of the luncheon memorandum of understanding. When the meeting broke up, Seaton joined Stevens as he walked out the door. According to William Ewald, who undoubtedly heard the story directly from Seaton, Seaton said, "Bob, you've been had."[22]

The president's first day back at the White House was a busy one. Somehow, however, Ike found a few moments to read Henry Cabot Lodge's "eyes only" memorandum warning him that McCarthy's assault on army heroes, e.g., Ralph Zwicker, was "part of an attempt to destroy you politically." Eisenhower called Lodge in New York, asking him to talk with Bob Stevens. Once again, by using an intermediary, he would maintain the fiction that he and the secretary were not in communication. However, neither he nor Lodge knew about the lunch agreement Stevens had just signed.[23]

When Lodge reached Stevens at 5:10 p.m., his initial assignment from the president was to coach the secretary on his testimony the next day. However, he was surprised when Stevens informed him, "By the way, Cabot, the hearing is off." He reported that he had gone to lunch with McCarthy and the other Republicans "at their request." Lodge listened in stunned silence as the secretary recited the three parts of the agreement he had signed. Stevens maintained that he had "fought the good fight" to ensure that military personnel were "treated decently." When Stevens declared that "the Republicans talked very frankly to Joe," Lodge skeptically asked, "They did?" Stevens replied, "Yes."

Shocked by this revelation, Lodge played his presidential card. He said that after reading his memorandum to Eisenhower on McCarthy, the president had "called me this morning . . . and asked me if I could talk to you on the phone." He told Stevens that McCarthy's investigation of the army was "preliminary to an attempt to destroy the President politically. There is no doubt about it. [McCarthy] is picking the Army because Eisenhower was in the Army."

Lodge punched holes in Stevens's hopes about the outcomes of the noon meeting. "I know these guys and I know how their minds work," he said. "The crowd that supported Senator Taft at the convention in 1952 are all now revolving around Joe. And this is basically an attempt to destroy Eisenhower." The confused secretary protested, "But it was his top legislative leaders who were talking to me." Lodge countered that those men were "inclined to appease" McCarthy.

Having punctured Stevens's balloon, Lodge focused on using the Cohn-Schine relationship against McCarthy. He had evidently seen John Adams's written report, sent to Sherman Adams on February 16. "You have that documentation there on boy S," he said, "and I think you ought to get that in shape; edit it up so it is in shape for publication." Stevens responded, "We are doing that." Only days after receiving the Adams report, the White House had apparently ordered Struve Hensel and Fred Seaton to edit and fact-check it for release to the media. Lodge believed that release of the Schine story could be "a devastating thing. And all we need to do is find a good . . . thing to get it out." That, the ambassador concluded, would be "a great public service."[24]

Stevens had now been warned he had been "had" by both Seaton and Lodge. Increasingly unnerved, he called Karl Mundt to seek a copy of the memorandum of understanding. Stevens put on a brave face with the senator. "Actually I have accomplished what we set out to do, and that was to get our fellows treated right by that committee," he asserted. Mundt's response was not encouraging: "If we can avoid stirring it up by Joe." At that, Stevens broke down. "I am going to be in the ash can," he moaned but still dared to hope that, as a result of the meeting, "we will get along a lot better." Regarding "the Schine matter," Mundt advised Stevens to "treat him like he was anybody's boy now."[25]

Stevens's panic escalated; he called his unidentified White House contact, probably Jerry Persons, repeatedly between 5:30 and 6:00 p.m. He phoned Ralph Zwicker, feebly explaining that he could not guarantee that the general would not be called to testify again; however, he was "satisfied" that the other Republicans on the subcommittee would ensure that officers received "fair and appropriate treatment." Zwicker fretted about "getting it straight on the things he called me. And I am not satisfied that that has been straightened out." Stevens promised to support whatever the general wished to do to correct the record.[26]

At 6:38 p.m., Seaton called Stevens to tell him how bad the situation was. Reporters had buttonholed Hensel and Seaton, insisting that Mundt, when asked if the treatment of officers had been discussed, had "denied it categorically." Seaton had dodged the question by saying, "I wasn't at the meeting." Stevens protested, "I certainly did tell Joe McCarthy in no uncertain terms I thought he had abused General Zwicker very badly." Seaton countered that the news wires and the major newspapers "all seemed to have a unanimity about it." Any story they would write would "not be too satisfactory." That was an understatement; the press had already adopted a powerful word to characterize what Stevens had done: "Surrender."

Stevens was now in a state of sheer panic. The longer he talked with Seaton, the closer he got to breaking down. The secretary stared into the abyss. "If it turns out I am a yellow-belly and McCarthy is a hero," he would go back to the senators, "tell them this is more than we in the Army can take" and try to get them to approve another kind of statement. Seaton tried to calm him: "I wouldn't want to say it was going to be that bad." Stevens sighed, "I think it will be bad." Seaton then urged the secretary to prepare a statement "because I don't believe you have any choice in the matter if you want to avoid that sort of public opinion." He bluntly warned Stevens, "Any corrective measures will have to be taken tomorrow."[27]

That night, Stevens frantically called Mundt to tell him he had "made a mistake" in agreeing to the memorandum and that he intended to issue a statement repudiating it. Mundt recalled attempting to dissuade Stevens, "without success." Colonel BeLieu took the distraught secretary home and called his friend the journalist Arthur Hadley to come to the Stevens residence to help with the secretary. Hadley arrived to find "a shattered Stevens" who was "drinking too much." In that condition, Stevens was juggling phone calls, including one to Jim Hagerty about 10:00 p.m. He wanted to put out his statement and resign, but Hagerty urged him to "cool off overnight." Hagerty fumed to his diary, "Someone let Stevens walk right into a bear trap, and now I'll have to work like hell to get him out of it." He knew that Eisenhower would also have to "work like hell" on it.[28]

BeLieu and Hadley finally persuaded Stevens to go to bed. "We know this is a mess," they agreed. "Stevens will probably be destroyed and McCarthy become bigger than ever. The Army is in for a long, bad time with failing morale." Then the two men did something extraordinary: they ghosted a statement for Stevens and put it out, falsely claiming that the secretary had "drafted the statement just before he went to sleep." That worked with some news outlets but not with John Finney at United Press, who, Hadley recalled, was "the type of reporter who will check inside the Pearly Gates before he decides to enter." Finney said, "Arthur, I can't take that story without talking to Stevens." After some arguing, they told him to wait, went upstairs, awakened Stevens, and coached the secretary to mouth to Finney, "John, I'm going to fight." Inebriated and half asleep, Stevens repeated on the phone: "I'm going to fight."[29]

A FALSE IMPRESSION

The morning of February 25, Eisenhower was embroiled in a fiasco that, contrary to appearances, was not of his own making. *The New York Times* ran a devastating front-page photograph of McCarthy whispering in Stevens's ear. William Lawrence concluded that Stevens had "reversed his previous stand and abandoned his defiance of the McCarthy investigating committee." Again, "surrender" was the handy one-word label for what had transpired.

More important, Lawrence reported that the army secretary's "about-face reflected a high Administration policy decision." That was obvious, he concluded. "The Administration decision to drop its public fight with Senator McCarthy because of charges he had mistreated Army officers in questioning them was taken a few hours after President Eisenhower had returned to Washington from his Palm Springs, Calif. golfing vacation." Arthur Krock, usually inclined to give Eisenhower the benefit of the doubt, declared that Stevens's capitulation to McCarthy was the result of "the high policy decision of the Administration."

That misimpression was not erased by Karl Mundt's statement to the press that President Eisenhower had known nothing about the meeting. When asked if he was aware of reports that the president had sent word that he wanted the dispute settled privately, Mundt replied, "I'm sure not."[30]

Stevens, thanks to Hadley's and BeLieu's ghosted statement, was reported the next morning to be "steaming mad" at the implication that he had surrendered to McCarthy; he was quoted as insisting that McCarthy had agreed not to abuse army officers in the future. Meanwhile, over at the Pentagon, the hungover Stevens was, as John Adams described him, "brokenhearted." He lamented that "yesterday I was a hero; today I am a dog." Officers greeted one another in the hallways, waving white handkerchiefs. McCarthy was rumored to be strutting around the Capitol, boasting of his victory; he reportedly quipped to one reporter, "Want a commission? I can get it for you!" Then McCarthy winked, grinned, and administered a small kick.[31]

According to Hagerty's diary, the allegation that the luncheon agreement was "high administration policy" linked to the president's return from California "kicked up a mess." The 8:30 a.m. staff meeting ended early so Sherman Adams, Hagerty, Persons, Jack Martin, and Gerald Morgan could meet with Nixon and Rogers about it.[32]

About the time that meeting began, Stevens called Senator Dirksen at home. The secretary was desperate. "I am going to have to do something," he said. "It may get drastic." He had been "absolutely crucified and the Services along with me." He asked Dirksen to reassemble his senators, minus McCarthy, and issue a statement to correct what had been "so misunderstood by the press." Dirksen asked whom the secretary had talked with; Stevens said he had told Nixon, Mundt, and Persons about the press depicting him as "a yellow-belly" who had "capitulated" to McCarthy. Dirksen responded, "Let me call Karl."[33]

Dirksen did not want to pass up the chance to work both sides of the street. He headed for the White House where, apparently at Eisenhower's behest, he agreed to contact his Republican colleagues to see if they could agree to issue a second statement testifying to Stevens's "integrity and ability" in dealing with the Peress issue and confirming that army officers would be treated with "proper respect." He repeated his previous pledges to work to get Cohn fired, to end one-man hearings, and to strip McCarthy of the authority to issue subpoenas without a majority vote by the subcommittee. According to Nixon, when Dirksen attempted to secure an agreement, "McCarthy proved adamant." The president then ordered Nixon to take charge of drafting a statement Stevens could issue from the White House.[34]

"VERY MAD AND GETTING FED UP"

By now the president was, in Hagerty's words, "very mad and getting fed up." That states it mildly; Eisenhower was in the midst of a full-blown presidential temper tantrum. This was, the president thundered, about "his Army" and his hatred for McCarthy's tactics.

"This guy McCarthy is going to get into trouble over this. I'm not going to take this one lying down!" He raged. "My friends tell me it won't be long in this Army stuff before McCarthy starts using my name instead of Stevens'. He's ambitious. He wants to be president. He's the last guy in the world who'll ever get there, if I have anything to say."[35]

About 9:30 a.m., Sherman Adams told Stevens to wait for a call from the White House. The frantic army secretary found the waiting unbearable; he made no fewer than ten calls to the White House. Seaton, seething about the situation, was assigned to be Stevens's handler. Stevens had once again violated the president's orders that Seaton was to be the designated liaison with McCarthy. John Adams recalled that Seaton had "growled" at him, "Don't ever let this happen again. Don't get into these things and wait until there is a mess and expect *us* to get you out." Adams speculated about who "us" was—Persons, Nixon, Sherman Adams—or "the President himself?" Adams would have had no doubt had he been at the White House. The president was in command mode. At 12:35 p.m., he met off the record with Nixon, Sherman Adams, and Persons. By 3:00 p.m., he had cleared his personal schedule to address the situation, and he ordered Stevens to come to the White House.[36]

Prior to departing, Stevens accepted a call from General Lucius Clay, an Eisenhower confidant. When Clay asked how he was, Stevens said, "I am a little sunk." "Have they let you down from up above?" Clay asked. Stevens responded, "Yes, but not the Boss." "I had everything in great shape, the flag at the mast," he claimed. But "the President wasn't in it in any way, shape or form." He blamed the president's "political advisors," who, he insisted, had "pulled the carpet completely from under me; and they dropped it right in the President's lap—right where I didn't want it."

Clay surmised, "Mainly the Senate people?" "Yes, plus Jerry." Clay commented that Persons "is always for armistice. I personally think this has hurt the party one hell of a lot." Clay declared himself ready "to come down to tell the Boss my views." Stevens responded, "Now is the time if there ever was one." Clay decided, "I am going to have a talk with him, and I just don't think this can be allowed to drop now."[37]

A few minutes later, Clay was on the phone to his old comrade in arms. Eisenhower was furious, ranting nonstop about "this fracas." "None of us knew about this meeting yesterday," he growled. "You can imagine my astonishment in reading of it this morning. Got my men in—we checked up—know that [Stevens] got agreement and assurance to say, 'Under those conditions my boys will come down & testify like anybody else.' He is now in state of shock & near hysteria. He made [an] error in agreeing too quickly." Clay agreed, "They were just too smart for him."

The president fumed that "one of the worst things" was that this "happened on [the] day I came back from Cal[ifornia]. We didn't know about the meeting, but they say I came back to tell Stevens to go." Clay confirmed that the "initial impression" was "that you instructed Stevens to settle this thing." Ike shot back, "Nothing could be further from the truth!"

Then Clay warned Eisenhower, sounding much like Lodge. McCarthy, he said, had become "too powerful—people [are] scared to do anything about him. I am willing to bet he has information on honorable discharges while you were Chief of Staff." Eisenhower denied that possibility. Clay warned the president not to underestimate the damage McCarthy's innuendos could inflict. Ike smelled presidential ambitions in McCarthy's actions. The senator, he grumbled, was "calling all Democrats traitors, knowing that will defeat us in the long run because we must have Democrats to win. Consequently, he will go around & pick up the pieces. He's crazy if he believes that."[38]

The intensity of Eisenhower's anger reverberated throughout the White House. As John Adams put it, the president's "own White House operatives and his Senate allies like Mundt, Knowland, Dirksen, even his own Vice-President—had let him down." Ike read with rising rage a column that alleged he was "now sharing command of the Army with McCarthy." His wrath rose to a new level when he called for and read the transcript of McCarthy's interrogation of General Zwicker.[39]

"100 PERCENT!"

At midafternoon on February 25, Bob Stevens left for the White House, accompanied by Fred Seaton. When they arrived, the task force was gathered in the East Wing. The group had grown to include Roger Kyes, the acting secretary of defense (Wilson was out of the city), William Rogers, Gerald Morgan, Hagerty, Persons, Sherman Adams and his assistant Bernard Shanley, and Richard Nixon. "We worked all afternoon in Person's East Wing office," Nixon recalled, "while Eisenhower, probably to relieve the tremendous anger he felt, practiced chip shots on the South Lawn."[40]

At Eisenhower's direction, Nixon supervised the drafting. Stevens later described Nixon "wadding up and hurling the various drafts until the group settled on just the right mix of forcefulness and restraint." After drafting a statement, Hagerty and Shanley argued that the president needed, in person, to "back up fully the Stevens statement." Shanley suggested that the secretary deliver his statement in the Oval Office in Eisenhower's presence—a proposal the president apparently vetoed.[41]

Finally, about 5:30, a group including Sherman Adams, Kyes, Nixon, Stevens, and Hagerty marched up to the presidential study on the second floor of the living quarters of the White House. They presented the draft document to the president. Eisenhower reviewed the statement for a full thirty minutes, providing his own edits that, Hagerty noted, "made it stronger." He decided that Stevens should deliver the statement himself from the White House. He authorized Hagerty to tell reporters, once Stevens read the statement, that he fully supported it.[42]

About 6:15, Stevens addressed the waiting reporters. Eisenhower's edits had eliminated any defensive or emotional statements and employed the crisp, quasi-military language characteristic of the Eisenhower writing style. Citing the memorandum of understanding from the February 24 luncheon, the secretary set out "to make certain things clear. I did not at that meeting and have not receded at any time from any of the principles upon which I stand." It was his duty, he said, to uphold the rights of army personnel "in circumstances where they are unable to protect those rights."

Then came the strong, unwavering statement, employing the president's emphatic "shall" (rather than "will") to voice a soldierly statement of duty: "I shall never accede to the abuse of army personnel under any circumstances, including committee hearings. I shall never accede to them being brow beaten or humiliated." Nor did the secretary intend that they be deprived of counsel, "as was the case with General Zwicker." Stevens cited "assurances" he had received from the members of the subcommittee that "they will not permit such conditions to develop in the future." Had there been no such assurances, "I would never have entered into any agreement whatsoever." If such mistreatment happened again, the secretary made his position "perfectly clear": "I shall once again take all steps at my disposal to protect the rights of individuals in this Department."

Jim Hagerty rose and announced, "On behalf of the President, he has seen the statement. He approves and endorses it 100 percent." [43]

CHAPTER 9

EISENHOWER IN COMMAND

Dwight Eisenhower had crossed a political Rubicon with his "100 percent" endorsement of Robert Stevens's statement. He now intended to maintain behind-the-scenes command of the confrontation with McCarthy until the battle was over. The morning of February 26, Jim Hagerty recorded in his diary, "Everybody jittery around here. Can't beg off when going is tough." Ann Whitman described her boss as "fretted" over four troublesome issues that day. The first two involved legislation regarding "wetbacks," the term used in the 1950s for Mexican illegal immigrant agricultural laborers, and bills in Congress to provide funding "for school buildings throughout the country."

The remaining two were both critical and time sensitive. The Bricker Amendment, an attempt to circumscribe the president's authority to make treaties and agreements abroad, authored by Republican Senator John W. Bricker (Ohio), was scheduled for climactic votes that very day in the Senate. Finally, McCarthy, the president noted in his diary, was "grabbing headlines and making people believe he is driving the Administration out of Washington."[1]

Hagerty described McCarthy's reaction to Stevens's statement as "pretty rough." The senator charged that Stevens had made a "completely false statement." He was adamant that when army officers "are not frank and truthful—whether military personnel or not—they will be examined vigorously to get the truth about Communist activities." "If it will be unpleasant to tell the truth," he growled, "I can't be responsible."

Hagerty had fully briefed reporters on the drafting of Stevens's statement. William Lawrence of *The New York Times* described the details of the White House operations, including the president spending thirty minutes personally editing the final document. His intervention, the columnist concluded, "underlined the gravity of the latest crisis" in the nation's capital. James Reston provided more detail about how, amid the furious activity in the East Wing, "the President changed out of his brown business suit, put on his golf slacks, went out to the back lawn of the White House, and practiced his pitch shots."[2]

That was an expression of the president's management style. When addressing a nasty problem, Eisenhower would issue orders. Then, knowing that no one could work effectively with him hovering over them, he would withdraw and leave his subordinates to their work, sometimes resorting to golf to alleviate his own tensions. Nevertheless, however much he appeared to delegate, he would have the final word. As a result, Stevens's statement was crisp, blunt, and unapologetic. The president had validated John Adams's observation that Eisenhower "could be in control while appearing to loaf."[3]

STATUS OF THE SCHINE REPORT

The club in the presidential closet—the detailed account of the privileges sought for G. David Schine by Roy Cohn and Joe McCarthy—commanded more of the president's attention in the following days. Professor Fred I. Greenstein of Princeton University wrote that Lodge, Brownell, and Sherman Adams had all confirmed to him that Eisenhower "was well aware of the Cohn-Schine abuses and was countenancing the strategy of using them as the vehicle for attacking McCarthy." Henry Cabot Lodge's conversation with Stevens on February 24 revealed that only days after receiving it, Eisenhower had apparently ordered his man in the Pentagon, Fred

Seaton, to edit John Adams's cumbersome forty-one-page report into a form appropriate for publication. On February 26, Richard Nixon confirmed to the columnist Arthur Krock—off the record—that Eisenhower had approved using a report "two inches thick" to get Roy Cohn fired.[4]

That day, General Lucius Clay revealed that he too knew about the Schine report, probably from conversation with Eisenhower. In a phone call, he urged Stevens to "let that Adams story leak out." Stevens repeated what he had told Lodge: "That is being, you might say, staffed carefully with that thought in mind." Clay urged that the report be released "in the next couple of days" because "right now is the psychological moment to do it; and if it is not done now, it will be too late." Stevens responded that any decision on releasing the report would be made at "a higher echelon" but promised to pass on the suggestion.[5]

As well as he knew Eisenhower, Clay did not fully appreciate his genius for timing critical operations. In fact, February 26 was not the right "psychological moment" to release the Schine report. The political storm surrounding the White House's rescue of Stevens would have buried the story. Besides, Adams's crude compilation was, in the judgment of Seaton and Hensel, not ready for the media. The original version contained too many land mines that McCarthy could exploit.

Eisenhower intended that the release of the Schine report wait until it was in pristine form, for the moment that Lodge called "good"—the tipping point when public and congressional opinion would be primed to take a fresh look at the Wisconsin senator. Ike once explained to his brother Milton in another context, "I have believed it wise, if not almost necessary, to retain as long as possible a position of flexibility—that is, to wait until the last possible moment before announcing any positive decision."[6]

However, Eisenhower had decided who would be his lightning rods for this operation. John Adams learned from Struve Hensel that his role in the preparing the Schine report would be only supportive. "I knew then that the decision had been made," Adams concluded.

"The Army was going to counterattack against McCarthy, and my diary was the ammunition, and Stevens and I were obviously going to lead the charge."

To play his sacrificial role, Adams had to be squeaky clean. He recalled that Seaton had the FBI investigate "if there were any skeletons in my closet they might have missed on earlier security checks." They found none, but the inquiry made him nervous. When Seaton informed him that "the FBI hadn't found any dirt on me," Adams asked to see the report. Seaton responded, "Oh no. It's confidential." Adams glumly concluded that "it was all arranged." Years later, the army counsel was still bitter that he "was not included in any of the conferences at which my fate was decided."[7]

The right moment for release of the Schine report hinged in part on other matters, above all the outcome of the debate over the Bricker Amendment to the Constitution in the Senate. The amendment had been introduced in 1951. The best-known version declared that no treaty could be implemented by the government unless Congress passed enabling legislation; it also placed limits on executive agreements. Truman had adamantly opposed this infringement on the president's authority to conduct foreign policy, and Eisenhower, the most international of modern presidents, opposed it as well. Eisenhower had accused Bricker of being "almost psychopathic on the subject."[8]

On February 25, the day of Eisenhower's rescue of Robert Stevens, the vote was 50 to 42 on Senator Bricker's version, well short of the two-thirds required for a constitutional amendment. However, back in January, Democratic senator Walter F. George of Georgia had introduced an amendment that, although more moderate, would still limit the president's authority to make executive agreements. Eisenhower noted in his diary on February 26 that George's amended version appeared to have the necessary two-thirds vote for passage.[9]

However, it failed, thanks in part to Senator Ralph Flanders of Vermont, Sherman Adams's good friend; their close relationship had developed when they were neighboring governors in New Hampshire and Vermont. Flanders, who was secretly planning a public attack on McCarthy, had been on record supporting a modified amendment similar to that proposed by Senator George. Surprisingly, he reversed himself and voted against the amendment on the final ballot. That reflected Flanders' growing alliance with the White House.

However, even with Flanders's opposition, the vote tally moved toward a successful two-thirds outcome. Suddenly, just as the roll call neared its completion, Harley Kilgore, a West Virginia Democrat who was apparently inebriated, staggered into the chamber and cast his vote against the George amendment. That made the final vote 60 to 31 in favor (senators present and voting); the proposed constitutional amendment had failed.[10]

With a Bricker-type amendment off the congressional agenda for the remainder of the year, the Eisenhower forces could turn their attention more fully to McCarthy. In Ralph Flanders, they had found the "friendly senator" that Lodge had told Eisenhower would be essential to setting the stage for a counterattack.[11]

Those clandestine plans were not visible to the press, which assumed that rhetorical denunciation of McCarthy—something Eisenhower would never do—was imperative. Robert Stevens, a *Washington Post* editorial concluded, was not at fault in the situation. "The real and inescapable issue is McCarthyism and the Administration's relation to it." Eisenhower, though "personally repulsed by the gangrenous infection," had been counseled "that he must not tangle frontally with McCarthy unless he is sure he can win." The editorial called on the president to "disavow, in the most unequivocal terms, McCarthyism and everything it stands for." The editorial quoted a Balkan proverb: "You are permitted in a time of great danger to walk with the Devil until you have crossed the bridge." It concluded that if Eisenhower chose to "walk with the Devil"— meaning McCarthy—"he will walk alone."[12]

A SMILING, DANGEROUS PRESIDENT

On February 27, when reporters asked McCarthy about his reaction to the president's support of Stevens, he denied that there were any great differences between himself and the White House. "Eisenhower said he was against browbeating witnesses—I am too," he asserted. Nevertheless, he called off a one-man hearing he had scheduled for the next day in New York.[13]

In fact, Eisenhower was covertly urging Senate leaders in both parties to curb McCarthy's ability to conduct one-man hearings. The proposal was that the three other Republican senators on the McCarthy subcommittee "be on hand whenever the Wisconsin senator presides at a hearing." *The New York Times* reported that, "according to reliable information," the Senate leadership had launched the effort "partly because of the intervention of President Eisenhower." Granting that he had seen some such reports, McCarthy said, "I doubt whether the President intends to prevent me from digging into Communists. I don't think he wants to curb my powers."[14]

Eisenhower tried to prepare his troops for the coming confrontation. Nixon recalled the president telling staff at lunch that his boxing instructor at West Point "used to hit him clear across the ring." Unless he "got up smiling every time, the boxing instructor would turn his back and walk out of the room." Some of his people, the president believed, "were actually afraid of McCarthy." Ike "wanted to see smiling faces around him." That fit William Ewald's apt description years later of Eisenhower's method of dealing with adversaries: "Don't see, don't feel, don't admit, and don't answer; just ignore your attacker and keep smiling."[15]

Eisenhower delivered a comparable pep talk to Republican congressional leaders the morning of Monday, March 1. He deplored their tendency to be "grim and downhearted" regarding what had happened with Stevens, the army, and McCarthy. He urged them, "Let's go out and grin at the world. It's about time we developed a sense of humor."

Eisenhower told the leaders that he anticipated numerous questions about Stevens and McCarthy at his Wednesday news conference. He "would not challenge the right of Congress to investigate" but "we can't defeat Communism by destroying the things in which we believe"—a statement he would frequently repeat in the days ahead. He reviewed the details of Stevens's involvement in the luncheon meeting "under a vow of secrecy," emphasizing that Stevens "did not even tell me about it." At the luncheon, Ike said, Stevens had agreed to a memorandum "that was terrible in its effect."[16]

For all the president's cheerleading, Nixon remembered that "by this time, Eisenhower's reaction to the whole incident had become very emotional." The vice president thought that Ike had been embarrassed by Stevens's blunder and the resulting news stories and "was offended by McCarthy's tactics, techniques, and personality." Nixon was worried; he believed that the statement the president planned to make at his news conference "would cause Eisenhower and the party more trouble than he or his White House staff and liberal friends who were urging it could imagine."[17]

To some extent, all this was a smoke screen to obscure what was going on behind the scenes. The previous afternoon, February 28, Eisenhower had met alone with Stevens at the White House; after the recent fiasco, the secretary was being kept on a short leash. Stevens had finally learned his lesson; he would no longer attempt to negotiate unilaterally with Joe McCarthy. For that meeting, the president's appointment schedule bore a prefix rarely used in listing an off-the-record meeting—"strictly."[18]

On Monday morning, Stevens followed up on his discussion with Eisenhower, discussing at length with Struve Hensel the John Adams "diary" and documents detailing the privileges sought for David Schine. Hensel had concluded that "it wouldn't be the sensible thing to release the information" yet because the current version contained irrelevant details and some of it "was a little bit dated." However, he worried that "the story would leak out" and was "apprehensive to the point that I am not sure we can sit on it." Adams, he said, had given out "a lot of copies" and "every day he thinks of a new one who has seen it." They still needed documentation and to get "all of the facts." The men agreed that it was time to consult the commander of the operation. "Let me grab hold of Seaton and see what his view is," Hensel concluded. Stevens concurred: "I thought maybe you and Fred would have an idea."[19]

TERROR AT THE CAPITOL

That same day, the newspapers reported that the night before, Irving Peress's home had been stoned by hoodlums. Peress angrily blamed "the terrorism that stems from McCarthyism." He charged that "fascist hoodlums threw rocks through our windows, narrowly missing our children and endangering their lives." Peress observed that the attackers had acted "in the true tradition of the Storm Troopers of Hitler."[20]

Peress was not the only one under siege. On Sunday morning, Roy Cohn, sitting with his father in New York, read a column in *The New York Times* by Arthur Krock, whom Cohn characterized as a "White House confidant." Krock wrote that the Eisenhower administration was pressing the Republican members of the McCarthy subcommittee to join with the Democrats and fire Cohn. The Eisenhower forces, he asserted, blamed Cohn for the assault on the army because of his relationship with David Schine. Most important, Krock, channeling his off-the-record conversation with Richard Nixon, mentioned "a record of Cohn's interventions with the Army with respect to [David] Schine that will become public." Cohn recalled Stuart Symington's one-word warning: "Crossfire."[21]

Then, in the afternoon of Monday, March 1, terror struck in the spectators' gallery of the House of Representatives. Four Puerto Ricans—three men and a woman—listened to the debate; then, suddenly, at 2:32 p.m., they brandished guns and opened fire. Bullets riddled the table of the House majority leader and the chairs around it. Five congressmen—Alvin Bentley of Michigan, Ben Jensen of Iowa, Clifford Davis of Tennessee, George Hyde Fallon of Maryland, and Kenneth Roberts of Alabama—were wounded, Bentley most critically. Capitol police quickly subdued three of the shooters, and the fourth was apprehended at a nearby bus station. "Those people just shoot wildly, just shoot into a crowd," the president mused to Speaker Sam Rayburn. "Probably blindly insane." Ike did not mention that, the previous November, the Secret Service had uncovered a plot by Puerto Rican extremists to harm him and Ambassador Henry Cabot Lodge.[22]

Nothing upsets the Washington news cycle quite as precipitously as unexpected violence. The attack in the House momentarily pushed the Army-McCarthy contest aside. Anne O'Hare McCormick of *The New York Times* reflected that Americans were accustomed to hearing about acts of terror abroad. "But," she continued, "when it breaks out in the ordinarily sedate Congress of the United States, the almost unguarded citadel of government by law, Americans are stunned and incredulous. It is as if the solid ground opened and for a shocked instant we caught a whiff of the bitter political passions boiling up in other sections of the world."[23]

The columnist Walter Lippmann, in words appropriate today, noted how impossible it was "to provide perfect protection against a terrorist . . . who is willing to die in the attempt." He could not resist tying the episode to the demagoguery of McCarthy, who "has never as yet caught an important spy, in fact any spy." The reason, Lippmann argued, was that "McCarthy does not know, or is pretending not to know, that spies do not have red bulbs attached to their foreheads which light up and blink so that nobody shall miss seeing them." The "important spies," he concluded, "are people who are not easily suspected, who wear highly protective camouflage, and are not easily detected."[24]

The news from the House of Representatives overshadowed other stories that would have normally commanded more attention. For example, March 1 was also the date the United States tested a deliverable hydrogen bomb on Bikini Atoll in the Marshall Islands in the Pacific. The predicted yield was five megatons, but the operation, dubbed "Bravo" spun out of control, yielding three times that amount. More than two hundred persons lived in an area affected by radiation, and a Japanese fishing boat was snowed with radioactive ash.[25]

The administration also announced that Scott McLeod, the State Department security officer and reputed McCarthy admirer, had been stripped of his authority over personnel. The press viewed the move as a slap at McCarthy. McCarthy rose to the bait, telling the press that he had drafted a letter to Secretary Dulles asking why the action had been taken.

An easy-to-miss paragraph was tacked onto the end of the McLeod report in *The New York Times*. It began, "Senator Fred Seaton of Nebraska, now Assistant Secretary of Defense, spent an hour in consultation at the White House." Reportedly, Seaton had played a prominent role in producing "the Presidential statement backing Mr. Stevens in his stand that he would not accede to any abuse of Army witnesses." The Washington media had begun to figure out that Seaton was Eisenhower's field general in the contest with McCarthy.[26]

A CRITICAL DAY: MARCH 2, 1954

Despite the terrorist attack in Congress, March 2 was a day of feverish strategizing in the White House against McCarthy. Robert Kieve noted in his diary that the issue "took up most of the discussion in this morning's staff meeting," focused on the president's news conference scheduled for the following day. Sherman Adams informed the staff that the president had "very definite ideas" about how to approach the Army-McCarthy conflict and "no one on the staff is likely to influence the P[resident]'s thinking on this issue very much, nor the expressing of that thinking in tomorrow's press conference."

Ike made certain that his key advisers knew what was going on. National Security Advisor Robert Cutler reflected that, while he had been meeting that morning with the president, Eisenhower had radiated a "great inner calm that makes the rest of us feel like babbling children." To Cutler, Ike had called the McCarthy-Stevens flap "a newspaper issue" that "would be quickly replaced by some other matter." Eisenhower knew what most of the staff did not: that over at the Pentagon, Seaton and Hensel were laboring on the Cohn-Schine document that would soon become that "other matter."[27]

Eisenhower actively stage-managed the buildup toward action against McCarthy. At 10:00 a.m., he met with RNC chairman

Leonard Hall. Afterward, Hall met with reporters in the White House. He repeated Ike's concern that the Stevens-McCarthy issue was diverting attention from the president's legislative program. Hall, who had previously called McCarthy an "asset" to the party, now asserted that he could not endorse Senator McCarthy's abuse of generals who were "fighting communism just as conscientiously as he is."[28]

In the late morning, Eisenhower sat down with Henry Cabot Lodge for an off-the-record discussion, followed immediately by one with Robert Stevens. Lodge's handwritten notes reflect the issues he discussed with the president. Hall should be replaced, he wrote, because the RNC chair's performance often left the president "just putting out fires." Eisenhower, he continued, had men making "strategic decisions for which they are not fitted by experience." "The Pres[ident] must be [a] political leader," he scribbled, but he needed help. Lodge concluded that "nothing will be solved" by putting a strong political advisor under Sherman Adams. During his two months in the White House, Lodge, an experienced political operator, had felt he "was not used & in fact excluded." He concluded his notes with a pithy cooking metaphor: "Politics is not the frosting on the cake; it is the egg in the cake."[29]

Meanwhile, Eisenhower pursued legal issues relevant to his campaign against McCarthy. He called William Rogers about the president's authority "to protect people against McCarthy," especially personnel lower on the chain of command. "Suppose I made up my mind that McCarthy is abusing someone in a Dep[artmen]t," he asked, "what is constitutional for me to do in this regard?" Rogers promised to deliver a memorandum by 9:30 the following morning and actually delivered two by nightfall. The first delineated the powers of the president to withhold information from congressional committees. The second memorandum traced the precedents for such actions back to George Washington.[30]

Finally, that same day, Lodge's "good" thing that might set the stage for releasing the Schine report surfaced. Edward R. Murrow informed his *See It Now* staff that a program on McCarthy would be aired on March 9. He ended his March 2 broadcast by deploring the country's "retreat into unreasoning fear" and pledging to "deal with one aspect of that fear next week." By March 2, and probably before, the White House knew that Murrow was planning a television broadside about McCarthy.[31]

"THE YELLOW SON OF A BITCH"

At precisely 10:30 a.m. on March 3, a solemn Dwight Eisenhower stepped to the podium in the ornate Victorian-era Indian Treaty Room of the old State Department Building. James Reston described the president as "ruddy, wearing a new light gray spring suit, a white shirt and a red-and-blue foulard tie"; he was attired in patriotic colors for nonmilitary battle. More than two hundred reporters were present.[32]

The twenty-first-century reader will be surprised at the brevity of Eisenhower's opening comment about the shootings in the House of Representatives. He noted the visit of the governor of Puerto Rico the previous day and expressed his regrets "at the tragic events on Capitol Hill 2 days ago." That was all. Perhaps his calm demeanor was rooted in the fact that the perpetrators had been quickly apprehended. In any event, on this day in 1954, he had other priorities relating to the Army-McCarthy conflict.

The president launched into a lengthy statement—without using the senator's name—about the Peress case, his "complete and full expression on one incident of recent weeks." The army, he said, had "made serious errors in handling the Peress case," but new procedures would prevent the repetition of such problems. He denied that he or the White House had encouraged Stevens to surrender: "Neither in this case, nor in any other, has any person in the executive branch been authorized to suggest that any subordinate, for any reason whatsoever, violate his convictions or principles or submit to any kind of personal humiliation when testifying before congressional committees or elsewhere."

He then made three "observations." The first was a pledge that his administration would be "unceasingly vigilant" about "subversive penetration." The second was aimed directly at McCarthy, asserting that "we are defeating ourselves" by combating communism with "methods that do not conform to the American sense of justice and fair play." The third stated simply that "the conscience of America," mediated through the Congress, would determine if "we are exercising proper vigilance without being unfair."

Eisenhower then turned to the abuse of army witnesses—again without mentioning McCarthy. He commented that, in his "many years in the Army," he "never saw any member of the Congress guilty of disrespect toward the public servants who were appearing before him." He asserted "that our military services and their leaders have always been completely loyal and dedicated public servants, singularly free of suspicion of disloyalty." He soberly added that "in this tribute to the services, I mean to include General Zwicker, who was decorated for gallantry in the field."

The president stated that he expected government employees, civilian or military, "to respond cheerfully and completely to the requests of the Congress and its several committees," but the Congress bore the responsibility "to see to it that its procedures are proper and fair." Finally, he cited problems confronting the nation "of vital importance" that were "both foreign and domestic in character." He deplored any diversion from "these grave problems," including subversion, "through disregard of the standards of fair play recognized by the American people."

"And that," President Eisenhower stated with an air of finality, "is my last word on any subject even closely related to that particular matter." The president's wishes could not have been plainer; he would not answer any questions about Zwicker, Stevens, or McCarthy.[33]

That was a tough prescription for journalists who had entered the room anticipating a sensational presidential denunciation of Senator McCarthy. A *Chicago Tribune* correspondent, Willard Edwards, told William Ewald that Joseph Alsop had leaned over to whisper, "Why, the yellow son of a bitch!" Reporters like Alsop, hungering for an anti-McCarthy tirade, missed the subtlety of what they had just heard.[34]

"A WITLESS MAN IN A POSITION OF POWER"

McCarthy did not. He fired off an angry, insulting response: "If a stupid, arrogant or witless man in a position of power appears before our committee and is found aiding the Communist party, he will be exposed." He took his sarcasm to a new level: "The fact that he might be a general places him in no special class as far as I am concerned. Apparently the President and I agree on the necessity of getting rid of Communists. We apparently disagree only on how we should handle those who protect Communists." McCarthy was taunting not just General Zwicker but the general in the White House.[35]

The Washington press corps was severely critical of the president's news conference statement. James Reston opined that Ike had "turned the other cheek today" and McCarthy had "struck him about as hard as the position of the President will allow." Advance hints from the White House that the president was prepared "to put things straight" had turned out to be false; once again, Eisenhower had been "the genial conciliator." Nor was it a surprise that McCarthy had "not only defied the President but patronized him."[36]

The Washington Post's editorial writer echoed the "other cheek" theme with the caveat that "Senator McCarthy's arrogance may yet save President Eisenhower from the worst consequences of his own timidity." Eisenhower had delivered a "condemnation of sin," but McCarthy, instead of endorsing the president's "weaseling" principles, was "forcing on the President the fight he has so far declined to accept."[37]

The most devastating response to the president's statement was Herblock's cartoon in *The Washington Post* depicting a ferocious, grinning McCarthy with a bloody meat cleaver in his hand, confronting a downhearted Eisenhower, who, pulling a white feather from his scabbard, warned McCarthy, "Have a care, sir."[38]

However, McCarthy's statement showed he had understood Ike's hidden message. Eisenhower had gambled that blending a specific attack on McCarthy's methods with a refusal to give the senator the attention he craved would push him over the edge of civility. The tactic had worked. In response to the president's statement, McCarthy displayed a stunning lack of respect for General Zwicker, for the popular general in the White House, and for the presidency itself.

One newspaper got the impact of Eisenhower's strategy partly right. *The Washington Star* reported that McCarthy had given the impression that "General Eisenhower may be a nice fellow but probably is not too bright." The conclusion: "It is doubtful that a more arrogant and insulting statement has ever been made by any Senator concerning a President of his own party." [39]

The following morning, Jim Hagerty noted that the president was "upset at [the] press reaction" and that the stories in *The Washington Post* and *The New York Times* had "really hit below the belt." Hagerty had released a film to radio, television, and movie newsreels. "Hell," he groused to his diary, "with slanted reporters, we'll go directly to the people." [40]

Herbert Brownell understood Eisenhower's strategy; they had obviously discussed it previously. The day following the president's news conference, the attorney general sat down with reporters for an off-the-record discussion. John Crider, a *Wall Street Journal* correspondent, wrote Sherman Adams that his liberal colleagues had endeavored to "pin Herb down that Ike was wishy-washy in his statement of principles in the tussle with McCarthy." Brownell had steadfastly maintained that it was "too early to tell how effective the President's statement was."

Crider also reported that a colleague in charge of a national lecture agency had informed him recently that he "was amazed at the change of public sentiment" toward McCarthy. A year earlier, lecturers around the country had found it "unsafe to suggest there was anything wrong with the man." Now audiences were asking "What are we going to do about this fellow McCarthy?" If that report was accurate, he opined, it might "confirm the correctness of Ike's handling of the situation. . . . For him to have lowered himself to Joe's level might have endangered his own position." The tipping point had arrived. [41]

TOWARD A POLITICAL D-DAY

Eisenhower understood that he was in the early stages of all-out war. At a specially called cabinet meeting, he cautioned cabinet members to avoid blunders in the tense days ahead. They were instructed to take care not to retain subordinates who could be subject to attack but to handle their cases with "fairness, justice, and decency." Having done so, every cabinet member was then obligated to protect subordinates from abuse and threats. In short, department heads were to clean house, be fair, protect their subordinates, and not buckle to pressure from "*any* source"—implying McCarthy. Eisenhower, echoing Lodge's counsel, also instructed the cabinet members not to make political speeches, implying the need to avoid any mention of McCarthy. Instead, they should focus addresses and articles on "the positive aspects of the broad Administration program for creating a better, more prosperous and stronger United States." He emphasized that he had done precisely that with his own statement on McCarthy and Stevens.[42]

On March 6, Lodge, back in New York, sat down to write a final "eyes only" report to the president, based on his notes from their discussion on March 2 and summarizing his "two months tour of duty as your adviser at the White House." "Dear General," he began. "The plain fact is that there is a gap in your organization because there is no one whose primary responsibility is political strategy for you." Though Eisenhower, as president, might sometimes decide to disregard political strategy, he "should always know what it is."

Lodge, in effect, restated a decades-old management truism, "What is everybody's responsibility is nobody's." "You have delegated political strategy to everyone in general and no one in particular," he wrote. As a result, "ideas about political strategy are put to one side and are often not even discussed." He warned that "an opponent such as Senator McCarthy will out-think this kind of system every time. It is a system which is continually running around putting out fires after they have started."

He drove the point home: if political strategy was "nobody's business" in the White House, "that means that you must do it yourself." Though Ike had rescued Stevens, he "should not have to pick up the pieces." The fight," Lodge concluded, "should have been McCarthy versus Stevens, not McCarthy versus Eisenhower. The fact that it is McCarthy versus Eisenhower is a major victory for McCarthy." He expressed a grudging admiration for McCarthy, who "had his television script, press statement and everything ready to get an equal play with you on your statement." Eisenhower, he concluded, urgently needed a single individual assigned to be the political strategist; that person "should think about nothing else."[43]

In his present circumstances, Eisenhower had already accepted Lodge's premise that "you must do it yourself." Actually, in Fred Seaton, Eisenhower had identified a man who might eventually fill the bill—a public relations expert with senatorial experience who was committed to protecting the president. However, at that moment, Seaton was on a presidential mission that even Lodge did not fully comprehend, plotting an attack on McCarthy's vulnerable flank, manned by Roy Cohn.

"HALF MCCARTHY AND HALF EISENHOWER"

On the day Lodge made his final report to the president, Eisenhower's former and subsequent electoral opponent, Adlai Stevenson, made a play for the headlines. Stevenson understood that it was in his political interests to continue to tie Eisenhower to McCarthy. Stevenson was scheduled as the featured speaker at a $100-a-plate Democratic dinner in Miami, Florida. The night prior, he hinted to reporters that it was time Democrats charged the president with "full responsibility" for the actions of all Republicans, including Joe McCarthy.[44]

At the dinner, Stevenson was at his eloquent best. "We are witnessing the bitter harvest of slander, defamation, and disunion planted in the soil of our democracy," he said. He called it "wicked" and "subversive"—a carefully chosen word—"for public officials to try deliberately to replace reason with passion; to substitute hatred for honest difference; to fulfill campaign promises by practicing deception; and to hide discord among Republicans by sowing the dragon's teeth of dissension among Americans." Stevenson excoriated McCarthy's impugning of "the loyalty and patriotism" of Democrats with his incantation of "twenty years of treason," delivered "under the auspices of the Republican National Committee." "Extremism produces extremism," he declared, "Lies beget lies."

Stevenson proclaimed that "those who live by the sword of slander also may perish by it, for now it is also being used against distinguished Republicans." The governor reeled off a stunning list of respected Americans hounded by McCarthy and his cronies, climaxing with "the President himself patronized." Stevenson called McCarthyism "a malign and fatal totalitarianism" that was sweeping the country "because a group of political plungers has persuaded the President that McCarthyism is the best Republican formula for political success."

Stevenson echoed Lincoln's "house divided" speech with a phrase that would dominate the next day's headlines: "A political party divided against itself, half McCarthy and half Eisenhower, cannot produce national unity—cannot govern with confidence and purpose." [45]

Back in Washington that night at the White House correspondents' dinner, the "jittery" Robert Stevens sat with Jim Hagerty. Hagerty was keeping an eye on the secretary, who, he had noted in his diary, was "developing [a] persecution complex—highly irrational—beginning to talk himself into [a] position where he actually thinks he is [a] big hero." That night, he found Stevens "very unstable and excited," loudly proclaiming he was "all alone in this fight." Hagerty thought to himself, "Someone better ride herd on him but good." [46]

At another table, the president engaged in relaxed conversation with Robert Donovan of the *New York Herald Tribune* and Admiral Lewis Strauss, the chairman of the Atomic Energy Commission. Eisenhower was visibly pleased when Irving Berlin sang a new song, "Gee, I Wish I Was Back in the Army." Reportedly, the line in the song that most amused Ike was "There's always someone high up where you can pass the buck."[47]

In fact, Eisenhower had just passed the buck down the chain of command to Strauss. Just prior to the program's beginning, the AEC chair suggested, to Donovan's surprise, that the journalist introduce Secretary Stevens to the crowd. Donovan looked over at Eisenhower, who had apparently planted the suggestion. "Well, I'll tell you what," Ike said with a grin. "If you do, I'll be first on my feet applauding." So Donovan asked Stevens to take a bow, and Eisenhower, *The New York Times* reported, "quickly joined in clapping vigorously."[48]

Dwight Eisenhower had just sent another signal to Joe McCarthy.

CHAPTER 10

A POLITICAL D-DAY

The morning of March 7, 1954, a New York Times headline declared, "Stevenson Says President Yields to 'M'Carthyism.'" The status of the increasingly tense relationship between the president and the junior senator from Wisconsin remained a subject of intense speculation. Arthur Krock described the GOP as desperate to avert "an all-out conflict" between Eisenhower and McCarthy, fearing its impact on the fall elections. Eisenhower's public support for abused officers such as Ralph Zwicker could only mean that, unless accorded adequate respect, he would order "such officials to decline thereafter to appear before McCarthy." Krock, who knew Eisenhower better than most other journalists, recognized that, in a showdown, "McCarthy may be the one to retreat."[1]

James Reston, however, concluded that Eisenhower was "playing a waiting game," gambling "that the American people will get bored with the Wisconsin Senator or that he will discredit himself or come to an abrupt political end." McCarthy, Reston wrote, "has already won a considerable victory" and "tilted successfully with the President himself." He was wrong; the president was not waiting, except for the right moment—only days away—to spring his planned assault on McCarthy.[2]

That Sunday, Edward R. Murrow and the *See It Now* team

reviewed a near-final edit of the program on McCarthy, scheduled for March 9. Fred Friendly, then a news producer at CBS, asked the assembled staff, "Is there anyone in this room who, in their past, has done anything that could be used to hurt Ed?" Murrow worried that he might not attract a substantial audience; CBS, though permitting the broadcast, was unwilling to finance its advertising. "I want to advertise it in *The New York Times*, make sure people look at it," Murrow fretted. He eventually persuaded British media baron Sidney Bernstein and Friendly, Murrow's boss, to finance the advertising out of their own pockets. Murrow expected no support from the Eisenhower administration. He characterized Eisenhower's statement at his March 3 news conference as "watered-down sweet reason." He was cynical: "The White House is not going to do, and not doing to say, one goddamned thing." [3]

RESPONDING TO STEVENSON

Joe McCarthy announced that he would demand equal radio and television time to respond to Adlai Stevenson's March 6 address. Eisenhower was not about to let that happen. At 8:15 a.m. on March 8, the impatient Eisenhower met with Republican legislative leaders and launched a discussion of who should respond to Stevenson's Saturday-night speech. Ike started with one premise: McCarthy was not an option. He looked directly at Richard Nixon and said, "I am going to make a suggestion, even though he is present, that I think we probably ought to use Dick more than we have been." Nixon could "take positions which are more political than it would be expected that I take. The difficulty with the McCarthy problem is that anybody who takes it on runs the risk of being called a pink. Dick has experience in the communist field, and therefore he would not be subject to criticism." [4]

Sometime that morning, Eisenhower pulled the reluctant Nixon, along with Hagerty, into his private office and coached the vice president on his speaking assignment. Nixon, he said, should not attack Stevenson or McCarthy directly. The president wanted the address billed "not as rebuttal" but a talk on "Republican leader-ship." Nixon was hesitant, but Eisenhower would not take no for an answer. Later, when the president heard that Nixon had expressed concerns, he phoned him. The address, he told Nixon, should not be "answering anybody—our own publicity shouldn't mention Stevenson & McCarthy." Nixon should be "positive," pushing program, not personalities. Nixon, he said, should feel free to come to him "for help if necessary."[5]

Hagerty recorded in his diary that, following the legislative meeting that morning, the president "called the Republican leaders into his office and laid down the law." "Let's stop this nonsense," he said, "and get down to getting [our] program passed." Hagerty described the president as "dead set [on] stopping McCarthy." He intended to push GOP chairman Leonard Hall to request equal time from NBC and CBS to answer Stevenson, but "with party spokesmen," not McCarthy. Eisenhower characterized McCarthy as a "pimple on [the] path of progress." Hagerty was pleased; "Ike really made up his mind to fight Joe from now on in."[6]

Eisenhower called Hall and pressed him to contact the networks immediately in order to preempt McCarthy. If the networks were reluctant, Hall was to notify the president so Eisenhower could per-sonally "get in touch with [William] Paley and [David] Sarnoff," his friends running CBS and NBC, respectively. "Get busy right away," Eisenhower ordered. "This is a good job for you." By 3:00 p.m., Hall was back in the Oval Office, reporting that he had secured radio and television time for the Republican response to Stevenson.

That afternoon, Hagerty and Bernard Shanley talked with the president as he changed clothes, preparing to practice golf shots on the White House lawn. They agreed that the next day, Hagerty should "leak" the evolving story of their action against McCarthy, underscoring the president's press conference statement, the deci-sion to strip Scott McLeod of authority over State Department per-sonnel, and Hall's achievement in denying McCarthy the chance to respond to Stevenson for the Republican Party. "Tomorrow"—March 9—would be a providential day to send the message that

Eisenhower, in Hagerty's words that morning, had "made up his mind" to go after Joe McCarthy.[7]

The administration was prepared to announce another action designed to get under McCarthy's skin. In 1953, when he had raised a fuss about allegedly procommunist books in overseas libraries, McCarthy had offered to provide copies of his own books. On March 8, Theodore Streibert, the USIA director, sent the senator a letter stating that, following "a careful review of your books," the agency had found that "they are not well adapted to the special purposes served by our overseas libraries." Hagerty would save the public announcement for a moment when he thought it would do the most damage to McCarthy.[8]

Eisenhower managed to squeeze time into this hectic day to respond to Henry Cabot Lodge's March 6 report, urging him to appoint a full-time political strategist to the White House staff. "You can get no argument from me when you advance this contention," he wrote. The merits of Lodge's argument that, without such a person, "you must do it yourself" had been obvious that very day. Eisenhower lamented that the administration had "so much to be bragging about" and regretted "that we allow situations to arise where we have to go around wearing sack cloth and ashes."[9]

About 6:00 p.m. the evening of March 8, Robert Stevens answered a call from Senator Stuart Symington. Symington, not one to mince words, stated, "I would like to see the report on Schine sometime, if the Army is willing to release it." Stevens replied, "Stuart, I doubt very much that they are." His use of "they" underlined the fact that he was not in charge of the project. He told Symington said that the report was not quite "pulled together." Symington growled, "I understand it has been pulled together, and I don't want to see it pulled apart before we get a chance to look at it. Naturally, it is of great interest to us." Again Stevens hedged, saying "I doubt very much whether it would be available, Stuart." When he continued to respond ambiguously to the senator's entreaties, Symington asked whether he needed to go to "a higher authority?" Stevens danced around that possibility, stating that the report was "a hell of a lot of stuff." Finally Symington gave up for the moment and asked that his request be kept "private between you and me."[10]

Symington was not wrong about the status of the project. By the time he called Stevens, the thirty-four-page, carefully edited report was virtually complete. His call was most likely the result of a purposeful leak designed to create the appearance that senators—not the army or, more important, the White House—were forcing release of the report.

Symington was not the only senator who had been primed to seek a copy of the Schine document. That same evening, Defense Secretary Wilson, apparently at the instigation of Fred Seaton, phoned Senator Charles Potter, telling him about the Schine report and that the Democrats were demanding copies; he urged Potter to make his own formal request. In response to Wilson, Potter wrote him that night, seeking "all the facts" regarding attempts to gain "preferential treatment for Private Schine." Showing how closely the White House was monitoring the operation, Sherman Adams informed Jim Hagerty about Potter's request. "That ought to kick up [a] fuss," Hagerty surmised, "and start [the] ball rolling to get rid of Roy Cohn." John Adams sarcastically recalled how "miraculously" Potter's letter had appeared on the desk of the secretary of defense. "This was," Adams concluded, "a phony exercise."[11]

"A FRIENDLY SENATOR"

On March 9, the newspapers reported that the Republican National Committee had "sidetracked Senator Joseph R. McCarthy and assigned Vice President Richard M. Nixon to deliver the Administration's reply" to Adlai Stevenson's charge that the party was "half McCarthy and half Eisenhower." Nixon would make his response at 10:30 p.m. on March 13. *New York Times* correspondent William Lawrence, apparently briefed by Hagerty, reported that Nixon's assignment had been orchestrated by Eisenhower. McCarthy was undaunted; he threatened to take legal action to force the radio and television networks to grant him time to respond to Stevenson. "Mr. Nixon," he stated, "is speaking for the party. I am speaking for myself." [12]

In Palm Springs the week of February 17, Ike had played golf as the guest of Paul Helms, a California baking-industry executive. In a March 9 letter to Helms, Eisenhower wrestled one last time with the efficacy of his strategy for confronting Joe McCarthy. He had returned to Washington from California "to find a plateful of problems and headaches." McCarthy, he said, could make "a few extraordinary and outlandish charges in the papers, and the whole United States abandons all consideration of the many grave problems it faces in order to speculate on whether McCarthy has it within his power to destroy our system of government."

To Helms, Eisenhower recalled his commitment, throughout his professional life, "to avoid public mention of any name *unless it can be done with favorable intent and connotation*; reserve all criticism for the private conference, speak only good in public." "This," he stated—as if arguing with himself—"is not namby-pamby" but "sheer common sense." Ike protested—again, almost to himself—that he had not acquiesced in or approved of McCarthy's methods. "I despise them," he wrote. "Nevertheless, I am quite sure that the people who want me to stand up and publicly label McCarthy with derogatory titles are the most mistaken people that are dealing with this whole problem." [13]

Eisenhower had chosen another, clandestine path. Events were already in motion; and there was no going back. Senator Ralph Flanders, the Republican from Vermont, had lunched at the White House the previous week with his old friend and former gubernatorial colleague Sherman Adams. They had surely discussed Flanders's plan to deliver the most important address of his senatorial career. Adams had either recruited Flanders on behalf of the president—a likely scenario—or, at minimum, had strongly encouraged him. [14]

The afternoon of March 9, Flanders rose on the Senate floor and announced his intention to offer some "advice to the junior senator from Wisconsin." He asked a loaded question about Joe McCarthy: "To what party does he belong? Is he a hidden satellite of the Democratic Party, to which he is furnishing so much material for quiet mirth?" Flanders answering his own question, intoned, "One must conclude that his is a one-man party, and that its name is 'McCarthyism.'"

Flanders likened McCarthy to an overly zealous housecleaner, frenetically cleaning out the grimy corners of the house of government bequeathed to his party by the Democrats. "Is the necessary housecleaning the great task before the United States," he asked, "or do we face far more dangerous problems, from the serious consideration of which we are being diverted by the dust and racket?"

Flanders catalogued the march of communism in the world—in Korea, Indochina, Europe, Latin America, and "other trouble spots in Asia and in Africa." "In truth," he observed, "the world seems to be mobilizing for the great battle of Armageddon." In that apocalyptic struggle, "what is the part played by the junior senator from Wisconsin?" His words dripped with sarcasm: "He dons his war paint. He goes into his war dance. He emits his war whoops. He goes forth to battle and proudly returns with the scalp of a pink Army dentist."[15]

It was a short speech, designed for ready reference for reporters and others, including Eisenhower, to whom Flanders had sent advance copies. Most important, the speech had been delivered by a Republican senator—the very people Eisenhower had insisted all along must ultimately deal with McCarthy—with ridicule perfectly designed to provoke an imprudent reaction from McCarthy. When Hagerty heard that McCarthy, who had returned that day from his speaking tour, had responded to Flanders with sarcasm, he noted in his diary, "Joe getting reckless."[16]

Having read the speech in advance, Eisenhower wrote Flanders, "I was very much interested in reading the comments you made in the Senate today. I think America needs to hear from more Republican voices like yours." Flanders told reporters that he had that night received "a letter of praise from President Eisenhower." He insisted that his campaign against McCarthy would "not split the party"; it was "something like either concealing a cancer or operating on it. I am operating on it." Indeed he was, with the enthusiastic endorsement of the president of the United States.[17]

"WE WILL NOT WALK IN FEAR"

Another advance copy of the Flanders speech had been delivered to Edward R. Murrow. As the journalist put the final touches on his *See It Now* script, he inserted the "war paint" segment of Flanders's remarks. At 10:30 p.m. Eastern Time on March 9, Murrow looked into the camera and began, "Good evening. . . . Because a report on Senator McCarthy is by definition controversial, we want to say exactly what we mean to say, and I request your permission to read from the script whatever remarks Murrow and Friendly may make." He then offered McCarthy the option of making a response in a subsequent broadcast.

The show was a montage of video footage as Murrow painted a portrait of an unrepentant demagogue. "Our working thesis tonight is this question," he stated. "If this fight against Communism is made a fight between America's two great political parties, the American people know that one of these parties will be destroyed, and the Republic cannot endure very long as a one-party system."

In measured phrases and images, Murrow, explored the senator's operations "as a one-man committee" who had "demoralized the present State Department" and leveled charges of conspiracy against the army. He noted in particular McCarthy's allegation that General Ralph Zwicker was unfit to serve and his humiliation of the secretary of the army at the February 24 luncheon. Murrow granted that congressional committees had legitimate investigative roles, but, he noted, "the line between investigating and persecuting is a very fine one and the junior Senator from Wisconsin has stepped over it repeatedly."

A half hour later, Murrow closed with devastating eloquence. "We must not confuse dissent with disloyalty," he said, reading directly from his script. "We must remember always that accusation is not proof and that conviction depends upon evidence and due process of law." In a few words, he plumbed the depths of the paranoid psychology on which McCarthyism thrived: "We will not walk in fear, one of another. We will not be driven by fear into an age of unreason, if we dig deep in our history and our doctrine, and remember that we are not descended from fearful men—not from men who feared to write, to speak, to associate and to defend causes that were, for the moment, unpopular." Murrow concluded, "This is no time for men who oppose Senator McCarthy's methods to keep silent." Though the United States was committed to defending freedom around the globe, "we cannot defend freedom abroad by deserting it at home." [18]

It is dangerous to assume that, because things happen at the same time, one is the cause of the other. However, the circumstantial evidence for the White House's exploitation of the two events on March 9—the Flanders speech and the Murrow broadcast—is compelling. The army, with Seaton in charge, clearly delayed distribution of the Schine report until after Flanders and Murrow had delivered their attacks. As A. M. Sperber, Murrow's biographer, put it, "The convergence of events March 9 was near-uncanny." [19]

Edward R. Murrow would not have colluded with a White House he held in some disdain. However, the plan for the broadcast was no secret. The Eisenhower people—Jim Hagerty in particular—considered CBS CEO William Paley and President Frank Stanton "good friends." Now, with the Flanders speech and Murrow's program grabbing headlines, the Eisenhower forces had met the requirements for action that Henry Cabot Lodge had considered essential: "a little help from a friendly senator" and a "good" thing—Murrow's powerful broadcast—to trigger release of the Schine report. [20]

A CRITICAL NEWS CONFERENCE

The morning of March 10, the White House staff focused on the president's news conference at 10:30 a.m., especially his response to the Stevenson speech. The staff advised the president to characterize Stevenson's charge that the party was "half Eisenhower and half McCarthy" as "nonsense"—counsel Ike readily embraced.[21]

At the news conference, UPI's Merriman Smith asked if the president saw "a need for any additional Republican reply on a nationwide basis to Adlai Stevenson other than Vice President Nixon's speech on Saturday?" Eisenhower responded, "Well, I don't sense any particular need myself" and expressed his admiration for the vice president. ABC's Martin Agronsky asked about the report "that you personally chose the Vice President to respond to Mr. Stevenson, and communicated your wishes to Mr. Hall; is that correct?" Eisenhower suddenly developed a faulty memory. He vaguely recalled a meeting, "and I don't remember that I was one the one who suggested it . . . but I certainly concurred heartily." Then came the predictable question about Stevenson's charge that the Republican Party was "half Eisenhower and half McCarthy." Ike was ready: "I say nonsense." He did not elaborate.

Roscoe Drummond asked about the Flanders speech and "whether you find yourself in substantial sympathy with it, or what your reaction is to it if that is not correct?" There was no foggy response this time; Eisenhower spoke resolutely, asserting that "the Republican Party is now the party of responsibility." He stated that Flanders had been justified in noting "the danger of us engaging in internecine warfare." Flanders, he continued, "is doing a service when he calls the great danger to that kind of thing that is happening." The president commended Flanders for "calling attention to grave error in splitting apart when you are in positions of responsibility and going in three or four different directions at once is just serious, that's all."

Anthony Leviero of *The New York Times* jumped up to ask, "Mr. President, I wonder if you would put that much on the record, the answer to that question." Eisenhower smiled, mentioned the news conference transcript, and muttered that Jim Hagerty could "see how any errors of grammar, of which I was guilty, when I stated it." Following laughter, he conceded, "You can put it in."[22]

"USE MY INFLUENCE ON MR. H"

Following the news conference, Eisenhower discussed the anti-McCarthy operation under way at the Pentagon with his advisers. He believed the moment had arrived to act. The president, Hagerty noted, was "in [a] fighting mood" and "has had it as far as Joe is concerned."

Eisenhower told Hagerty, "You can use my influence on Mr. H to get him to release it." "It" clearly was the Schine report and "Mr. H" undoubtedly referred to Struve Hensel. That was a direct presidential order. Ike did not mention Seaton, who surely already knew Ike was ready to launch the attack. Later that day, Hensel called Stevens regarding the "narrative," confirming that they "were under pressure to get it out." The report would be ready "shortly before noon," and he strongly urged Stevens to review it. When Stevens asked about the sources of the pressure, Hensel, probably fulfilling an unwritten commitment to provide the president with deniability, spoke not of the White House but mentioned requests from Democratic senators Richard Russell of Georgia and Republican senator Charles Potter of Michigan. Hensel and Seaton "had spent yesterday with Rogers and Brownell of Justice, and time with the Secretary [Wilson] last night." At 11:00 a.m., Seaton called Stevens, pressing upon him the urgency of looking at the report because "we are getting great pressure from the hill."[23]

Charles Wilson was apparently spooked by what Seaton and Hensel shared with him the evening of March 9. The next morning, knowing that the release of the Schine report was imminent, he called McCarthy and invited him to lunch at the Pentagon. They talked for two hours and met with the press afterward. Aside from agreeing that they had "no arguments" regarding the handling of communists drafted into the armed forces, Wilson was unusually quiet. McCarthy did most of the talking, praising Wilson as a man "who has been combating Communists longer than I have." Wilson commented that "he had not come to Washington to engage in quarrels with anyone."[24]

Roy Cohn later recalled McCarthy's account of the luncheon with Wilson. McCarthy "had barely pulled his chair up to the table" when Wilson informed him that a "shocking" and "thoroughly documented" report had been compiled about the "favored treatment" Cohn had sought for Schine. Wilson had told McCarthy that "he would be powerless to keep it from getting out unless I [Cohn] resigned at once." When Cohn asked McCarthy how he had responded, McCarthy boasted, "What do you think I told him? I told him to go to hell."[25]

Eisenhower was furious about Wilson's unauthorized luncheon with McCarthy. In Jim Hagerty's words, that luncheon hurled "a monkey wrench" into the president's "carefully prepared plans." When he informed the president, Ike leaned back in his chair and let loose with a number of "goddams." Then he said to Hagerty, "You know, Jim, I believe Cabot Lodge is dead right when he says we need acute politicians in those positions. They are the only ones who know enough to stay out of traps—the only ones who can play the same kind of game as those guys on the Hill." Hagerty described Eisenhower as "greatly disturbed"; the president called him several times to find out what had been said at the news conference. He fumed to Hagerty, "If they are cooking up another statement, then, by God someone is going to hear from me—but good."

Hagerty called Seaton to ask, "What's going on over there?" Seaton shot back, "Listen, if you think you have troubles, come over to the Pentagon." Hagerty commiserated, concluding afterward that Seaton was "doing [a] good job." But when Ike read reports of Wilson and McCarthy's postluncheon news conference, he relaxed. "Just a lot of words," he said. "No use to have that luncheon at all."[26]

According to Cohn, he and McCarthy ran into Stuart Symington in the corridor of the Senate Office Building that afternoon. Symington told them he had just received a "strictly confidential" copy of the report detailing "improper activities" on behalf of Schine. Cohn recalled that as Symington "turned to walk away he whispered for my ear his reminder, last made two months before: 'Crossfire!'"[27]

That evening Eisenhower attended a stag dinner at the Sulgrave Club for Senators Knowland and Homer Ferguson of Michigan. Ike was grinning when he shook Vice President Nixon's hand and said, "I hope you are taking plenty of vitamins for that speech you are going to make Saturday night." The president was not smiling when he talked with a group that included Senators Dirksen and McCarthy. Nixon noted "considerably more coolness in [Ike's] attitude toward McCarthy than he previously had evidenced at social functions."[28]

On March 10 another shot was fired in the escalating barrage of anti-McCarthy salvos emanating from 1600 Pennsylvania Avenue. The National Guard announced that Roy Cohn, a guardsman for seven years, had been ordered to report to Camp Kilmer, New Jersey, for training from June 12 to 25. Ironically, Cohn would undergo his training under the command of General Ralph Zwicker.[29]

"IT'S A PIP"

On March 11, the morning newspapers reported on the president's press conference, highlighting his endorsement of Senator Flanders's speech and his characterization of Stevenson's "half McCarthy" allegation as "nonsense." A companion story, somewhat bizarre, also hit the news. On Wednesday, McCarthy and Flanders had reportedly encountered each other in the Capitol basement. McCarthy had given Flanders a "hug"—perhaps an overstatement describing the senator's habit of throwing his arm around the shoulders of colleagues. Flanders had tried to be cordial, saying "Hello, Joe, I'm glad to see you." McCarthy had allegedly said, "Ralph, I looked up your record. You voted less for the Republican than any man in the Senate." Flanders invited McCarthy to "get the figures ready and put them in the record." McCarthy had his facts wrong; *The New York Times* reported that, in the past year, Flanders had supported his party more consistently than had McCarthy. In a final, surreal twist, when Flanders arrived at his seat on the Senate floor McCarthy approached him and "put his arms around him from the rear, pretending to choke him." Then he patted Flanders on the shoulder and walked away.[30]

Over at the Pentagon, there was controlled panic. John Adams called Stevens at 9:40 a.m. to tell him that Senator Potter was, at that moment, reporting to Seaton and Hensel about a meeting that the Republicans, including Knowland and Bricker, had held "with Joe in secret last night." Potter had taken his copy of the Schine report to the meeting. According to Adams, the senators had "laid it on pretty violently" with McCarthy, recommending he fire a staff member (presumably Cohn) and pressuring McCarthy "to get off the Army's neck." Neither Stevens nor Adams knew the precise plans or when the report would be released; they were not in the inner circle with Seaton and Hensel. Adams said, "I have a personal feeling that it [the Schine report] will never see the light of day."[31]

That meeting with Republican senators had gotten Joe McCarthy's attention. About 1:30 p.m., he called Seaton. Instead of yielding to the pressure to fire Cohn, McCarthy had decided to launch a counterattack. Reflecting on his luncheon with Secretary Wilson, he argued that Wilson "should get [the] full story" by hearing McCarthy's perspective: "I called you to get all of the story." Seaton smoothly replied, "You have no argument with me on this." He added, "The Secretary had nothing to do about putting out [the] report."

McCarthy's objective was to delay delivery of the report and persuade Seaton to include his response. "You are public relations advisor on this. Make it appear they want to get both sides." He said he had "stuff available" that Seaton could "incorporate" into the report, including memoranda and "written notations on any dealings with the Army." Seaton shrewdly placed responsibility for releasing the report beyond the Pentagon, saying that the army "has been bombarded on all sides from Senators and Congressmen." McCarthy roared back that the "Army should not make [a] report without checking with me." He offered to make his information "available by tonight or tomorrow morning."

That conversation reinforced what Seaton had already decided:

it was imperative to get the report out that day, March 11, as planned. McCarthy knew too much and might manage to mitigate its impact. Seaton, the smooth operator, knew just what to say; he told the senator he would "personally guarantee" that McCarthy's request to include additional material would be passed on to his superiors and that such information would be available "for inclusion by tomorrow." But he knew that tomorrow would be too late.[32]

Copies of the thirty-four-page Schine chronology were scheduled for delivery just after working hours. After McCarthy hung up, Seaton met with Stevens, undoubtedly to report on the conversation with McCarthy. Following that meeting, Stevens gave the army press aide, Colonel Lloyd Lehrbas, a heads-up that "this whole business is going to break." He had learned from Seaton "that they will probably be sent up there around 5:00 to all the senators that have asked for a copy of this report" and to the press shortly thereafter. "Therefore," he surmised, "it will probably all break in the morning papers." The report would be "finally released by Seaton, who is really carrying the ball on it now."[33]

At 4:10 p.m., Stevens phoned Seaton to ask if the report was ready, and Seaton said it was. However, Seaton reported that McCarthy had "sent me a message . . . a document that he thought I would be extremely interested in." He had also received word that McCarthy, then on the Senate floor for the vote on a bill on Alaskan and Hawaiian statehood, "was trying to reach me." Stevens confirmed that the target time was 5:00 p.m. "Or a little before," Seaton said. "If there is any hold on it, I had better get in touch with you." He asked, "You will be here until 5:00?" Stevens responded, "Yes."[34]

The activity in Seaton's and Hensel's offices accelerated in an effort to get the report out before McCarthy could act. At 4:35 p.m., Seaton called Stevens to tell him that he had informed McCarthy that the report "would be delivered to the Hill this afternoon" in response to "long-standing requests" from other senators.[35]

At 4:56 p.m., Stevens called Hensel to verify that he understood the procedure for release of the report. "I have instructed our people not to give out any copies of this thing," he said. Hensel asked if, "copies are going to the senators?" Stevens responded, "Yes." Hensel asked, "But you gave nothing to the press?" Stevens replied affirmatively, showing he understood that "the motivating force must come from the Senate" in order to maintain the appearance that "we are not handing this stuff out to pick a battle with McCarthy." The report would be released in its entirety to the press when the senators, ready with copies and primed, demanded it. Stevens asked Hensel, "Will you be talking with Fred [Seaton] again?" Hensel responded, "He is going to duck out, and he thought you were." That, too, was part of the plan. When calls began to flood into the Pentagon from the McCarthy camp and the news media, the operation's commanders planned to be unavailable.[36]

Over in the White House, Jim Hagerty knew, as did his boss, that the "Army report on Schine-Cohn-McCarthy [is] going up on [the] Hill today." He had read it with a public relations expert's eye. "It's a pip," he confided to his diary; "shows constant pressure by Cohn to get Schine soft Army job, with Joe in and out of threats." He believed that the report "should bust things wide open." No one was closer to the president on the McCarthy operation, with the exception of Seaton. If Hagerty had seen the final version, so had Ike.[37]

As Fred I. Greenstein accurately stated a generation ago in *The Hidden-Hand Presidency,* the Schine chronology was released by the army, "ostensibly on its own but actually at White House instigation." However, Eisenhower, even in his memoirs, never acknowledged his role. Instead, he wrote that "the Army"—not the White House—had "moved over to the attack." Regarding the Schine report, he wrote, "The Army put it to use." He did not mention Fred Seaton, who had been operating under his orders.[38]

Seaton retained the schedule for delivery in his "Eyes Only" file, gathered at Eisenhower's direction. Copies were to be distributed between 5:20 and 5:40 p.m. on March 11 to two chairmen of House committees and eleven senators, including McCarthy. Six senators who were not on McCarthy's committee and one additional House chairman would receive copies in the morning. William F. Knowland, the Republican majority leader, would not get his copy until the next day at 11:00 a.m. The White House did not intend to permit the unpredictable Knowland, so frequently a McCarthy supporter, to see the report before it got to the press.[39]

That night, Eisenhower hosted a stag dinner including some of his best friends, prestigious business executives, his brother Milton, Sherman Adams, and Fred Seaton. Perhaps the commander in chief's invitation on that special night constituted a modicum of recognition for Seaton's clandestine service that day.[40]

PART 3

1954: VINDICATION

CHAPTER 11

"A WAR OF MANEUVER"

The morning of March 12, Jim Hagerty warned the White House staff; if asked, they were to state that "they didn't know anything about [the] Army report on Schine-Cohn-McCarthy." He cheerfully noted in his diary that the document was getting "big play in papers" and the headlines were "taking play away from Mc-Carthy."[1]

"Big play" was an understatement. The papers published the entire text of the thirty-four-page document, rigorously edited and fact-checked by Seaton and Hensel: the July 1953 effort to secure a commission to assign Schine to duty in New York; McCarthy's subsequent attack on the army regarding alleged subversives at Fort Monmouth; the constant, abusive phone calls and ugly encounters with Roy Cohn; the pressure for special passes whenever Schine was assigned weekend or night duty; and Cohn's threats, using "vituperative language," to "wreck the army" and get Secretary Robert Stevens and John Adams fired. The report ended with the February 16 phone call requesting that General Ralph Zwicker be made available for testimony two days later.[2]

That day, the man at the center of the storm, Private G. David Schine, was at Camp Gordon in Georgia, enduring what the newspapers called "a rugged soldier's training." He was "sleeping in an undisclosed spot in Georgia's piney woods" about twelve miles from the camp.[3]

AN ANGRY MAJORITY LEADER

The president was pulled out of his cabinet meeting at 10:10 a.m. to take an angry phone call from William Knowland. The Senate majority leader had seen the papers and was furious that he and other Republican leaders had not received a copy of the Schine report. Eisenhower pleaded ignorance; the report had been issued, he claimed, because members of the McCarthy committee had demanded it. "Someone just said there is a report about a man named Cohn," he said. "I don't know a damned thing about it." Eisenhower sounded clueless. "There has been a blunder and I am sorry," he said. Defense Secretary Charles Wilson was out of town, but Eisenhower said he would ask Deputy Secretary Roger Kyes to call the majority leader.

The president, besides feigning his own ignorance, purposely avoided mentioning the men who were truly knowledgeable: Seaton, Hensel, and Stevens. Kyes, who had recently announced his intention to resign, could plead a lack of knowledge, but his assignment was to pour oil on troubled waters, a task he performed with consummate skill. "I am very disturbed to know that someone in our outfit did a flap on you," he told Knowland. "I am just as shocked as you." He added, "I personally don't know about this Schine document. I have not read its contents." Kyes claimed not to know "who specifically handled it" and pledged that "someone will be in trouble." He promised to let the senator know when the report would be delivered. In fact, it was scheduled for delivery within the hour, as planned.[4]

Hagerty's diary leaves little doubt that Eisenhower himself had decided to delay delivery to Knowland. Ike was not upset with anyone in the Pentagon for what he had labeled a "blunder" when talking to Knowland. In fact, he sounded downright pleased. "You know, Jim, I suppose if those leaders had seen the report, it would have never gotten out in the papers," he said. "They always want to play everything the hard way—compromise, compromise—nuts!"[5]

MCCARTHY FIGHTS BACK

About noon that day, Stevens called Hensel to take the temperature of the operation. McCarthy had scheduled a news conference for 1:00 p.m. at the Pentagon, he said, "so the blast will be coming over at lunch." It was a "blast," all right; McCarthy was ready to fight. He christened the army report "blackmail" and declared that he did not intend to fire Roy Cohn. Cohn sat "pale-faced" beside McCarthy and labeled the charges in the report "untrue." "No improper influence," he said, "was ever exerted by me or by anybody else to my knowledge on the Army in behalf of Mr. Schine." Cohn denied that he had ever threatened "to wreck the Army, Stevens or any other such thing."[6]

Then McCarthy distributed documents he claimed would "throw a different light on the whole episode." Overnight, his staff had produced eleven memoranda that mixed occasional fact with outright fabrication. Years later, *Chicago Tribune* reporter Willard Edwards, a McCarthy staff intimate at the time, told William Ewald he had witnessed a half-dozen of McCarthy's secretaries typing furiously through the night to reconstruct events and backdate memoranda.[7]

According to McCarthy biographer Thomas Reeves, the McCarthy memoranda portrayed Robert Stevens and John Adams as "the foulest of villains," truly guilty of "blackmail." In a memorandum dated December 9, subcommittee director Frank Carr had complained to McCarthy, "I am getting fed up with the way the Army is trying to use Schine as a hostage to pressure us to stop our hearings on the Army." The press highlighted an unsigned memorandum alleging that Stevens and Adams, in return for McCarthy's ending his investigation of the army, had offered to provide "dirt" on communists in the navy and air force—a claim the army fiercely denied. A Roy Cohn memorandum, also dated December 9, alleged that Adams had followed through on that alleged bargain by providing information on "a large number of homosexuals" at an air force base.[8]

However, the McCarthy forces remained on the defensive. Bipartisanship bloomed among the senators on McCarthy's subcommittee, supporting the contrived scenario that senators had demanded the army's report. Senator John McClellan, on behalf of the Democratic members, confirmed that the army had released the thirty-four-page document "pursuant to the request made more than a month ago." He and Republican senator Charles Potter both called for "an immediate executive session of the subcommittee." Potter charged that the report carried "shocking charges" and, if it was accurate, "Mr. Cohn should be removed immediately."[9]

McCarthy's staff scrambled to get on top of the story. On March 12 the senator composed a telegram to Stevens denying he had ever urged the army to give Schine a special commission or special treatment. To Stevens's amusement, McCarthy's secretary had lost that document. In great embarrassment, she called Stevens to seek a copy. The next day Stevens and Hensel agreed to send one, keep the original, and write an answer, which was composed after they met with Seaton over lunch.[10]

McCarthy's telegram was reported in the Sunday papers. The senator claimed he had "an unbreakable rule" that neither he nor anyone on his staff would attempt "to interfere with or influence the Army in its assignments." No one on his staff, he stated, had "any authority to request any consideration for Mr. Schine other than what other draftees get." In his response, Stevens effectively accused McCarthy of lying: "Am astounded [at] your wire of March twelve suggesting that you never urged the army to confer on David Schine a direct commission or to treat him specially after his induction as a private." He reinforced the manufactured stimulus for releasing the Schine report: "You also know that you never made any claim to me that you or anyone else was being blackmailed" until the report had been issued "in reply to requests by members of the Senate."[11]

A CONFIDENT COMMANDER

Shortly after lunch on March 12, Eisenhower escaped the political ruckus for the peaceful environment of Camp David. At such moments, he preferred to keep controversy at a distance, leaving his subordinates to tiptoe across the hot political coals. He was confident that his operation against McCarthy was proceeding, in Jim Hagerty's terms, according to "carefully prepared plans." He wrote William Robinson, an executive of the *New York Herald Tribune*, how pleased he was that editorial writers had begun to understand that the president "cannot be one of the parties in a gutter brawl." Ike embraced the big picture. "There is a certain reactionary fringe of the Republican Party," he said, "that hates and despises everything for which I stand or is advanced by this Administration." He pondered that the Republican Party might have to face "the complete loss of the fringe of Old Guarders," except for procedural matters. However, he concluded, "I, for one, have always thought that we cannot afford to appear to be in the same camp with them." [12]

IKE DEPLOYS THE VICE PRESIDENT

Flanders's and Murrow's assaults on McCarthy had been delivered on March 9, the Schine report released on March 11. An every-other-day drumbeat of anti-McCarthy publicity would continue on Saturday night, the thirteenth, with Richard Nixon's televised address. Ostensibly, Nixon was responding to Adlai Stevenson's March 6 address charging that his party was "half Eisenhower and half McCarthy."

On Friday, Nixon, seeking seclusion to prepare his speech, checked into a hotel room and left word that he should be interrupted "only in case of an emergency." Nevertheless, his work was disrupted twice. The first time was by a call from William Knowland, still irate over the distribution of the Schine report. Nixon had just started back to work when the White House called. Eisenhower wanted him to come to the Oval Office to discuss his speech. Feeling frustrated, Nixon did as requested. When he arrived, Ike lectured him to make the case that Republicans had "a progressive, dynamic program which benefited all the people." He urged the vice president to cite the fact that the president "had commanded 5 million troops in Europe." Eisenhower culminated his speech-making micromanagement by advising the vice president to "work a smile or two into the program." [13]

Ike got what he wanted. Nixon delivered a soaring hymn of praise for Dwight Eisenhower. He asserted that the president "is not only the unquestioned leader of the Republican Party but he has the confidence and support of the great majority of Americans, Republicans and Democrats alike." However, the country was being distracted from the president's program by men who, "by reckless talk and questionable method, made themselves the issue instead of the cause they believe in so deeply." Excepting a mild allusion at the outset, Nixon did not mention the name of Senator Joseph McCarthy.

The name the vice president invoked repeatedly was Eisenhower's. Ike was, he said, "not only an American leader; he is a world leader." He talked about having watched the president make "great decisions during the past year" and proclaimed, "I have never seen him mean, I have never seen him rash, I have never seen him impulsive. I have never seen him panicked. And I have never seen him make a decision which was motivated by political purposes." Ike's only concern, he maintained, was "what is good for America." Nixon crowned his rhetorical homage with "I think we are lucky to have this man as President of the United States." [14]

Meanwhile, McCarthy defended himself against a rising torrent of criticism. In a Saturday-night speech in Wisconsin, he warned he would "get rough" with his adversaries: "I don't care how high or low those who scream at what we are doing." James Reston concluded that "Senator McCarthy is getting careless"; instead of asking people about communists, "he is asking them whether they think he tells the truth. That is a reckless question." William Lawrence found McCarthy on the defensive in response to "a series of crushing defeats within his own Permanent Subcommittee on Investigations," engineered by a White House pushing for the dismissal of Roy Cohn. The *New York Times* editors concluded that "as the week ended, it could be said that the legend of Senator McCarthy's invincibility has been punctured." They invoked a military metaphor befitting the five-star general in the White House: "This has been a war of maneuver rather than of desperate assault, but the outcome begins to appear. We are coming in out of the wilderness." [15]

That Sunday, Roy Cohn appeared on *Meet the Press* and lied shamelessly. He insisted that he "did not ask for preferential treatment for Dave Schine at any time." Schine, he said, had a legitimate need to "devote himself to completing this committee work in which he was involved." The army had "reneged" on the agreement to permit that service. Cohn asserted, "At no time did I or anybody else on the committee ever suggest that he should be relieved from KP or any other unpleasant duty that any draftee had to go through."[16]

AGITATION FOR HEARINGS

By March 15, the *New York Times* reporters had figured out that "the key men in the Army's fight with Senator Joe McCarthy" were John Adams, Fred Seaton, and Struve Hensel; Seaton was "calling the signals," and Hensel "is planning strategy for the expected hearings on Capitol Hill." Adams, identified as potentially "the key witness" in any hearings, was a busy man that day. On orders from Seaton and Hensel, he was plowing through McCarthy's eleven memoranda line by line, refuting their assertions in detailed memoranda to Hensel.[17]

Meanwhile, Hensel and Seaton kept Stevens on a short leash. In a phone call, Hensel warned him to "say nothing to the press." Hensel had just received "two hundred–odd pages of undigested testimony" about Schine's and Cohn's behavior at Fort Dix—especially Cohn's persistent pressure for weekend passes and exemptions from KP duty for Schine. "It is a bad story," he told Stevens. "It is the story of demoralization of at least one company by these two brash kids." Hensel urged Stevens, before speaking to the press about the Fort Dix report, to "check this with Fred Seaton."[18]

William Ewald provided a vivid description of the situation in mid–March 1954: "So there at the moment the Great Debate rested: The Army's meticulously expurgated list of facts, in chronological order; the eleven McCarthy memos—self-serving, crudely written, questionably dated rejoinders; Stevens' innocuous, wordy, always amiable, frequently irrelevant recollections; Adams' fact-engaged, detailed retorts, descending at times into niggling quibbles over who paid the bills and why a single private should do Sunday KP. The controversy often turned on the Army's undocumented word against McCarthy's purportedly contemporaneous written evidence."[19]

Amid growing agitation to hold hearings, the question became whether the Senate Armed Services Committee would stage them—a solution preferred by the administration—or whether McCarthy's own subcommittee would do it. However, Republican Leverett Saltonstall of Massachusetts, the Armed Services chairman, was up for reelection and wanted nothing to do with the controversy. The members of the subcommittee's parent committee, Government Operations, had no stomach for the fight. Eisenhower's decision to keep William Knowland out of the loop proved costly. Hensel told Stevens that "the present disposition of the Majority Leader in the Senate seems to be to start in this committee—the McCarthy one."[20]

A DECISION ON HEARINGS

On March 16, the stage was set for a stormy, three-hour meeting of McCarthy's subcommittee. McCarthy stated his willingness to step down as chairman and testify under oath but was adamant that he be granted the right to cross-examine other witnesses—an issue that would remain unresolved for the moment. He got his way on most matters. The seven-member subcommittee would be reorganized as a "special committee" to conduct the investigation. McCarthy would step down from the chair in favor of Karl Mundt, the man whom cynical reporters had labeled "the Tortured Mushroom" or "The Leaning Tower of Putty." All other subcommittee matters would be set aside while the hearings were held. Roy Cohn was not formally suspended, but the group agreed that new counsel should be secured for the hearings. The *New York Times* editors asserted that this plan was "a little like saying that Mr. McCarthy has now graciously agreed to investigate himself."[21]

The issue, much debated, was whether the hearings would be closed to the public. McClellan and Symington insisted on open hearings. Dirksen was reluctant, arguing that the inquiry could have only two outcomes—the termination of Roy Cohn or John Adams or both—and open hearings were not essential. But Charles Potter joined with McClellan, justifying public hearings on the grounds that "somebody has committed perjury and I don't know who." Ironically, the formal motion for public hearings was offered by McCarthy.[22]

Almost immediately, the decision to hold public hearings dictated that the sessions would be televised. Minority Leader Lyndon Johnson had instructed McClellan, the subcommittee's senior Democrat, to insist on televised hearings, no matter what else they conceded. Subsequently, Hagerty would confide to his diary, "Ike wants hearings open and televised."[23]

The next morning, the newspapers reported the decisions made by the McCarthy subcommittee, especially to televise the hearings. The spotlight was shared by Jim Hagerty's planted story that the USIA had rejected McCarthy's books on communism as "not suitable reading" to include in the holdings of overseas libraries. Once again, the Eisenhower operation got under the senator's skin. "If I was really interested in getting these books into the libraries," McCarthy grumbled to the press, "I presume I could accomplish that by joining the Communist Party."[24]

Hagerty's operation continued to roll out negative McCarthy-related stories. The New York City selective service director revealed that Roy Cohn had been deferred from military service twice, in 1945 and 1946, and had avoided induction until the government ended the draft in 1947. Two days before the draft was resumed on June 24, 1948, Cohn had enlisted in the National Guard, which made him no longer subject to the draft.[25]

At his March 17 news conference, Eisenhower was questioned about whether he believed McCarthy's charge that "your Secretary of the Army made threats against the Senate committee and offered to turn in the Navy and the Air Force if he could get a favor from the committee." He responded with military crispness, "Now, when you ask me whether I believe Secretary Stevens, of course I do. If I didn't believe him, if I didn't have faith and confidence in him, he wouldn't be where he is; I believe in him."

When asked if the controversy was damaging the morale of army officers, Ike drew on his own experience to assert that army leaders, when unjustly accused, experience "a mixture of anger, resentment, and rather a great deal of sadness." He delivered a subtle dig at McCarthy: "They are not articulate; they are not around making speeches in commercial clubs or all that sort of thing." But such officers "are people to whom I think we owe a lot." He called for distinguishing between "anyone we think may have made a mistake and may have made a blunder, and these great armed services."

Near the end of the news conference, Eisenhower was asked if he thought a time would ever come "in which events do not require us to ask a question about unwise investigators?" Responding to laughter, he countered that he had told an "associate" (probably Hagerty) that morning, "You know, if one name comes up I am going to ask permission whether we couldn't have one press conference without this particular subject coming up." That line generated more laughs. Ike had still managed to avoid mentioning the name of Joe McCarthy.[26]

A STORY "HALF-TOLD"

John Adams and Joe Alsop had agreed in February that the report Adams had shared about David Schine was off the record. However, Alsop titled his March 15 column "McCarthy-Cohn-Schine Tale Was Half-Told." He reported that Cohn's "disgusting obscenities" had been deleted, as had intimations as to the nature of the McCarthy-Cohn-Schine relationship. Struve Hensel told Stevens that Robert F. Kennedy, the counsel for the Democrats and brother of Senator John F. Kennedy, had tried to pump him about what had been "half-told." "Either Joe's memory is awful damn good," Hensel muttered, "or Joe has a copy—no matter what John Adams says."[27]

Adams himself no longer had a copy of his original documents. He recalled how, right after the release of the Schine report, "Fred

Seaton appeared in my office and demanded that all the copies of my diary of the Schine pressure be handed over to him on the spot." Adams had called Sherman Adams twice, trying to get his original documents back, but the chief of staff had put him off, saying they were deposited "in a good safe place."[28]

Seaton was now on the Washington hot seat; key people knew that he had been the field general in the distribution of the Schine report. After reading Alsop's "half-told" column, Senator Syming-ton called Seaton to seek the real "dirt." Symington had heard that Seaton had "heavily censored" the report, and he demanded "the uncensored version." Seaton smoothly sidestepped the question, as-serting that he had not censored the report since "in fact there ac-tually was not a report. There was a collection of memoranda and papers—some totally unrelated to the subject." However, he con-fessed, "there was some unpleasant language taken out."

Symington was not persuaded by Seaton's verbal footwork, so Seaton resorted to the strategy he had employed with McCarthy on March 11, promising to relay the senator's request higher up the chain of command. "As far as I am concerned," he said, "anything the com-mittee asks for that is within my power to get, the committee gets." That "within my power" phrase provided the shrewd newspaperman with an escape hatch. Symington persisted, "I would like to get it all."

Symington gave up. "Telling you how to act on the Hill is like trying to tell a Grandmother how to suck eggs," he said to Seaton. "If they ask you something and you don't know the answer, tell them you don't know but will be glad to get it." Symington noted that newspaper editorials thus far indicated that the public response to the Army's revelations "might not be bad for you."[29]

Seaton handled the press with comparable skill. A few days later, the *New York Times'* "Random Notes" reported that "the White House is not complaining" about the release of the Schine report. "Just to keep the record straight," the article continued, "the White House neither approved publication of the report nor knew any-thing about it." The *Times* noted that when the army had submitted the report to the Defense Department, it had "left the decision to

Fred A. Seaton, Assistant Secretary of Defense. Mr. Seaton took the decision on his own, without checking at the Executive Mansion, and he has not heard from anybody there about it yet." That, of course, was pure fiction, probably propagated by Seaton himself. Notably missing in this account was any mention of Defense Secretary Charles Wilson. By denying that he had checked at "the Executive Mansion," Seaton had avoided mentioning the president's name. The newspaper did not ask the obvious question: "Who granted Fred Seaton that authority?" [30]

"SIT IN JUDGMENT ON HIS OWN CASE"

The morning of March 20, C. D. Jackson was "hot and bothered about McCarthy" and the plan for the senator to be "both investigator and investigated" in the upcoming hearings. Jackson persuaded National Security Advisor Robert Cutler to join him in accosting the president about the issue. In their presence, Eisenhower called Karl Mundt and asked him how long he expected the hearings to last. Mundt, in what would prove to be a remarkable miscalculation, responded that, once they secured staff, "less than a week."

Ike, labeling the question "confidential," wondered aloud about the propriety of having someone on the hearings committee "involved as deeply as the Senator?" McCarthy had insisted on remaining a member, but Mundt promised that the army could interrogate him. Eisenhower cautioned him that he, Dirksen, and Potter "must not let anything be put over on them." Mundt thought the Democrats would help to keep the process honest by insisting on televised hearings. Ike's final caution: "Push; & remember there's honor & decency at stake right now." [31]

Following his phone call to Mundt, Eisenhower agreed with Jackson and Cutler to send a follow-up letter to him. Jackson composed a draft and showed it to Herbert Brownell, who "gloomed" on the idea, but Fred Seaton was "all for it." Meanwhile, Ike had second thoughts; he had allowed agitated aides to push him into violating his principles for handling McCarthy.

Dwight D. Eisenhower, campaigning in Milwaukee, Wisconsin, on October 3, 1952, tried unsuccessfully to avoid shaking hands with Senator Joseph McCarthy. *Dwight D. Eisenhower Presidential Library*

Vice President Richard Nixon advised Eisenhower about McCarthy and Washington politics. *Dwight D. Eisenhower Presidential Library*

Eisenhower consults with Secretary of State John Foster Dulles (left) and Charles "Chip" Bohlen, Eisenhower's choice as ambassador to the Soviet Union, whose nomination McCarthy opposed. *Dwight D. Eisenhower Presidential Library*

McCarthy consults with his chief counsel, Roy Cohn, who pushed McCarthy to investigate the US Army. *Getty Images*

G. David Schine was a consultant to McCarthy's investigations subcommittee before being drafted into the army. The privileges McCarthy and Cohn sought for him precipitated the Army-McCarthy hearings. *Karl E. Mundt Foundation*

Eisenhower with
Army Secretary
Robert Stevens.
*Dwight D. Eisenhower
Presidential Library*

John G. Adams, army
counsel, compiled a
key report detailing
McCarthy and Cohn's
efforts to obtain
special privileges for
Private Schine. *US
Army, courtesy Harry S.
Truman Library*

Eisenhower with Press Secretary James Hagerty, a confidant on handling McCarthy. *Dwight D. Eisenhower Presidential Library*

Assistant Secretary of Defense Fred Seaton oversaw Eisenhower's covert campaign against McCarthy. *Dwight D. Eisenhower Presidential Library*

H. Struve Hensel, Pentagon general counsel, collaborated closely with Seaton in the campaign against McCarthy. *Seeley G. Mudd Library, Princeton University, and the US Navy*

Henry Cabot Lodge, Jr., ambassador to the United Nations, was a confidential adviser to Eisenhower regarding McCarthy and other political matters. *United States Senate Historical Office*

Senator Karl E. Mundt (R–South Dakota), chaired the Army-McCarthy hearings. *Karl E. Mundt Foundation*

On February 18, 1954, Senator McCarthy charged that World War II hero General Ralph W. Zwicker was "not fit" to wear the uniform of the US Army.
The National Archives

"Have A Care, Sir"

HERBLOCK
©1954 THE WASHINGTON POST CO.

This Herblock cartoon, dated March 4, 1954, portrayed McCarthy as ruthless and Eisenhower as too cautious, which is how many in the media regarded the two men.
Herb Block Foundation

Senator Everett Dirksen (R–Illinois) tried repeatedly to make a deal that would end the Army-McCarthy hearings. *The Dirksen Congressional Center*

Edward R. Murrow attacked McCarthy on his *See It Now* television program on March 9, 1954, not long before the Army-McCarthy hearings began. *Tufts University*

Senator Ralph Flanders (R–Vermont) criticized McCarthy on the floor of the US Senate and eventually introduced a censure resolution. *United States Senate Historical Office*

Joseph Welch, the Boston lawyer who represented the army during the Army–McCarthy hearings, charged that Senator McCarthy had "no sense of decency." *Karl E. Mundt Foundation*

The televised Army–McCarthy hearings gripped the nation's attention from April 22 to June 17, 1954. *Karl E. Mundt Foundation*

When Jackson showed the president his draft, he was shocked to discover his boss "had pretty well made up his mind not to send it and got very angry when I told him that this time he was morally involved." Eisenhower had outsourced the matter, calling William Knowland "to ask what progress [is] being made in [the] McCarthy matter." Knowland informed the president that he had urged Mundt and Potter that "McCarthy not be allowed to vote or question in the Army-McCarthy inquiry." The majority leader said he would issue a statement saying that "Senator McCarthy should voluntarily withdraw" from such a role and keep the hearings "completely impartial." Ike responded, "Everybody in the United States will approve what you said." He called Jackson to inform him that Knowland would make "an appropriate statement on this subject." Jackson grumbled to his diary that only Symington had spoken out, endorsed by Knowland, "and later the Pres. will do a me-too. Not pretty." [32]

Nevertheless, Eisenhower would do it his way. His hand was evident in GOP chairman Leonard Hall's statement that Senator McCarthy "should not participate in the hearings." "The Senator," Hall stated, "should step down and should not examine witnesses." It was rumored, according to William Lawrence, "that President Eisenhower was ready at his news conference tomorrow morning, to put new momentum behind the drive to divorce the Wisconsin Senator from any active role in investigating himself or his counsel, Roy M. Cohn." Jim Hagerty encouraged reporters to ask the president about the issue at his press conference. However, that morning a *New York Times* editorial conceded that McCarthy would probably win his demand for the right of cross-examination. In that event, there would be "no doubt that he is still master of the McCarthy subcommittee that is investigating McCarthy." [33]

The morning of the news conference—March 24—Hagerty had "a bitter argument" with Jerry Persons over whether the president should take a stand on McCarthy's presence on the subcommittee and his right to cross-examine witnesses. Persons called that a "matter for the Senate" and urged that the president not "get into it." Persons was so angry that he refused to attend the staff meeting.

An argument ensued, even without Persons present; C. D. Jackson called that discussion "bitter."

In that quarrel, Hagerty muted his comments because, he noted in his diary, "I knew how [the] Pres[ident] felt." He, Cutler, and congressional liaison Gerald Morgan went into the Oval Office to brief the president. Eisenhower, the press secretary recalled, "stopped them dead in [their] tracks," saying "Look, I know exactly what I am going to say. I'm going to say he can't sit as a judge and that the leadership can[not] duck that responsibility." Ike articulated the resolve that had governed his actions since January: "I've made up my mind you can't do business with Joe and to hell with any attempt to compromise." Afterward, C. D. Jackson called his "let the dust settle" colleagues "criminally negligent." "There is a killer abroad in the streets," he confided to his diary, "and they say to the President, 'This is an unpleasant passing political incident.'"

Eisenhower was not about to indulge in Jackson's kind of hyperbole. However, as he and Hagerty walked to the press conference that morning, the president laughed and said to his press secretary, "The two Jerrys"—meaning Persons and Morgan—"didn't look very happy this morning." When Hagerty hesitated to comment, Eisenhower stated, "I know, Jim. Listen, I'm not going to compromise my ideals and personal beliefs for a few stinking votes. To hell with it." Hagerty responded, "Mr. Pres[ident], I'm proud of you."[34]

At the press conference, Merriman Smith, probably prompted by Hagerty, asked about the president's "feelings" regarding McCarthy's participation in the hearings and the senator's insistence "on the right of cross-examination in an investigation of the dispute between his committee and the Army." Eisenhower, denying he was talking about "a particular situation," crisply delivered his prepared statement: "I am perfectly ready to put myself on record flatly, as I have before, that in America, if a man is a party to a dispute, directly or indirectly, he does not sit in judgment on his own case, and I don't believe that any leadership can escape responsibility for carrying on that tradition and that practice." Everyone in the room knew who "he" was.[35]

Eisenhower's growing self-assurance aside, there were dangers in the course he had chosen. Swede Hazlett, Ike's boyhood friend, fretted in a letter that, although Ike made "light" of the Wisconsin senator, "your most dangerous foe is our demagogic friend (or should I have omitted the 'r'?)." "I have no doubt," he continued, "that, when it suits his purposes, he will attack you directly. He'll paint you redder than red (I understand he is stocking ammo from that Russian 'good-will era' when you were in Berlin)." [36]

Such warnings had become commonplace. About a week later, Ike's brother Milton reported on a dinner conversation with Symington. The senator claimed that he had seen "documents which he says would prove that McCarthy in good time will directly attack you. First, he will go after CIA and try to discredit the two Dulles brothers. Then he will go after many who served under you in the German occupation task." The senator had concluded, "There is bad stuff in the [McCarthy] files on both." Eisenhower was suspicious of Symington's motives. He scribbled a note stating that Symington's message constituted "an artificial buildup to urge me to act in a personal way." That was something the president did not intend to do. He was committed to battle and was not about to second-guess his course of action. [37]

ANOTHER "CHICKEN LUNCH"?

In such a situation, rumors abound. On March 25, Jim Hagerty was "boiling mad." *The Washington Post* reported that the army had waived requirements and promoted David Schine to investigator's school at Camp Gordon. Hagerty called Fred Seaton, who labeled the story, if true, "deliberate sabotage, and if I can find out the Pentagon source of [that] story, he won't be with us any longer." Later, Seaton called back to tell the press secretary that the army was "flatly denying" the story. Hagerty was appreciative, noting in his diary, "Good job by Fred—lot of guts."

Hagerty did not know that, at lunch that day, his own intestinal fortitude would be tested. He had been invited to dine at the office of J. Mark Trice, the secretary of the Senate, along with Jerry Persons, Gerald Morgan, and Jack Martin, the key White House conservatives in the McCarthy confrontation. When Hagerty walked in, he was shocked to see senators Joe McCarthy, Karl Mundt, Herman Welker, Iowa's Bourke Hickenlooper, Nevada's George Malone, and several other Republican lawmakers. Later, William Knowland dropped by to shake hands. Like Robert Stevens on February 24, Hagerty had walked into a trap.[38]

The gathering was purely social for a while. Hagerty was relieved when McCarthy, Mundt, and Malone departed. However, Welker and Hickenlooper then proposed that "both Cohn and Adams resign and [the] case be dropped." That was the compromise Everett Dirksen had repeatedly advocated. Hagerty listened quietly, as did his White House colleagues, understanding that it was a last-ditch effort to derail the planned hearings. He departed without comment.

The press secretary, who undoubtedly consulted with Eisenhower, then called in Persons and Morgan and told them he was going to put out the word that there had been no White House approval of that luncheon. He called it "a put up job and don't know whether our boys are in on it." The next day, William Lawrence, fully briefed by Hagerty, reported that the rumor of a "settlement by resignations" had been denied by "the highest Administration officials." He had acquired names and details "according to a reliable source [of] who was present at the luncheon." The luncheon effort and Karl Mundt's public insistence that McCarthy was not a "principal disputant" in the controversy reinforced the Wisconsin senator's pet assertion: "This isn't my case—it is a case involving my chief counsel and the Army legal counsel." The New York Times reported that, according to "a high Administration source"—undoubtedly Hagerty—"no such deal is cooking."[39]

Roscoe Drummond's column on March 26 addressed what he called "a new mess" in Washington. "What do you think of the manner in which the Republican Party is conducting itself in Washington today?" he asked. "Sen. Joseph R. McCarthy continues to spread the impression that the Eisenhower administration is either deliberately or stupidly 'coddling Communists.'" He predicted that "unless this spectacle comes to an end soon, the Republicans will lose one or both houses of Congress in November." In 1952, the Republicans had pledged to clean up the "mess in Washington" left by the Democrats; now there was another "mess in Washington" presenting "Republican government as quarrelsome, unproductive and legislatively nearly impotent."

Eisenhower read that column and passed it on to Hagerty, calling it "a remarkable piece" that "ought to be read by every Republican. Why not get [Leonard] Hall to reproduce & send out wholesale?" Later that day, the RNC chairman stated that, in regard to the 1954 election, "McCarthy has done more harm than good." He granted that McCarthy's "Senate effectiveness has diminished in the past few weeks."[40]

WHO ENLISTED TOM DEWEY?

Meanwhile, Karl Mundt's search for counsel for the hearings had bogged down. Mundt asked three high-ranking government officials for assistance: Chief Justice Earl Warren, Attorney General Herbert Brownell, and J. Edgar Hoover, none of whom thought it proper to help him find an attorney for the subcommittee. William J. Jameson, the president of the American Bar Association, declined to take the job after consulting with his sixteen-member board. Consequently, as the month ended, Mundt was forced to postpone the commencement of hearings.[41]

The press covered Mundt's stalled search for counsel but paid little attention to the question of an attorney for the army. John Adams could not serve because he would be a witness. Neither could Hensel, given his deep involvement in the preparation of the Schine report. Furthermore, McCarthy claimed he had information regarding Hensel's alleged profiteering during World War II. Though Hensel had cleared himself with the attorney general, it was obvious that the Pentagon needed to go outside its ranks to find a tough attorney to cope with McCarthy, Cohn, and the subcommittee's legal team.[42]

Secretly, Governor Thomas E. Dewey of New York had been enlisted to assist the US Army in its search for counsel. Who authorized Dewey to recruit an attorney for the army? The most likely candidates were Dewey's former associates John Foster Dulles and Attorney General Brownell. However, on the evening of March 31, Dewey had called Dulles and revealed that he had already been recruited. The next day, Dulles told Brownell that Dewey had been coy, saying only that "he had to find trial counsel for this McCarthy business." Brownell said he had told the governor "he was crazy to do it" and speculated incorrectly that Hensel had possibly enlisted him. But Fred Seaton knew Dewey well.[43]

There is only one credible answer as to who chose or, at minimum, approved Dewey: Dwight D. Eisenhower. Dewey was unlikely to have involved himself in the search for army counsel without a green light—or, more likely, a personal request—from the president. There is no record that Eisenhower questioned Dewey's involvement because he must have sanctioned it. Typically, he transmitted such requests, especially if politically explosive, through a trusted friend or a credible subordinate, most likely, in this case, Fred Seaton.

Therefore, while Senator Mundt's subcommittee was still floundering in its search for counsel, the army was not. Over in the Pentagon, Robert Stevens knew the choice was imminent. Near the end of the month, he asked Seaton, "How are you coming on a lawyer?" Seaton responded, "Ours? There's no need to worry." About that time, Seaton informed Hensel, "I've been talking with Tom Dewey. He recommends a lawyer in Boston named Welch. Do you know him?" Hensel said he did and declared, "He'd be a natural. I should have thought of it myself."[44]

Late in the day on March 31, Stevens tried to call Seaton, who was unavailable; he was at National Airport, picking up a visitor. The visitor was a Boston attorney named Joseph Nye Welch.

CHAPTER 12

COUNTDOWN

On April 1, the US government reached an agreement with Joseph Welch to represent the army. Welch was sixty-three, a highly successful trial lawyer and partner at the Hale and Dorr firm in Boston. He was over six feet tall and meticulous about his dress; he wore bow ties and three-piece suits and projected a folksy, eccentric persona. An Iowan by birth, he had attended Grinnell College and earned a law degree at Harvard. He was known for his wit, jocular personality, and deceptive brilliance. He had, Roy Cohn observed, "an unerring instinct for the jugular." [1]

In Ewald's account of Welch's recruitment, one day in late March, a phone rang in Welch's office. Bruce Bromley, a friend and former judge on the New York State Court of Appeals, was on the line. Bromley had called about "an extremely sensitive subject." Welch was requested to go to New York City to a room in a club, where a certain gentleman would be waiting. When Welch walked in, he was greeted by the governor of New York, Thomas E. Dewey. [2]

Years later, Herbert Brownell confirmed that Governor Dewey had played a "decisive part in the selection. . . . As far as I know, the decision to select counsel for the Army was in the hands of Sherman Adams at the White House." Brownell knew that anything of consequence that Sherman Adams did, he executed on behalf of

Eisenhower. A handwritten note in large letters in the Adams Papers at Dartmouth College reinforces the evidence: "Fred Seaton—Joe Welch—Dewey recommended. He came down—talked with Wilson." The problem, the chief of staff noted, "was to get Wilson to agree." At the bottom of the page, Adams wrote, as if in relief, "Finally."[3]

Once Wilson signed off, Stevens, Seaton, and Hensel could orchestrate Wilson's announcement of the appointment. It is unlikely that Welch met with the president. He would soon spend extended time with the president's key field commanders in the struggle with McCarthy: Seaton, Hensel, and Hagerty.

ORGANIZING THE TEAM

Early the afternoon of Thursday, April 1, Seaton, Hensel, Stevens, and Welch were all in Seaton's office. The group decided that a meeting with Welch's entire team was essential prior to issuing an announcement. The next morning, Fred Fisher, a young attorney in Welch's office, read a memorandum from his boss. He and a colleague, James St. Clair, were directed to fly to Washington, DC, immediately and bring luggage for a week to ten days. They were further instructed, "Flower in buttonhole, Pentagon, River entrance, Room 3E, Mr. Fred Seaton." Fisher was given a direct phone number to call to contact Governor Dewey in event of any difficulty. At National Airport in Washington, a Seaton aide met the attorneys and ushered them into a waiting limousine. They were hustled through "the maze of the Pentagon" and into a room where Welch awaited them. Welch then explained that they had been summoned to Washington "in the greatest secrecy" because the Pentagon wanted to announce Welch's appointment the next afternoon.[4]

The Friday-morning papers revealed that another Boston attorney, Samuel P. Sears, had been engaged as counsel for the hearings subcommittee. According to *The New York Times*, his nomination "precipitated a storm on Capitol Hill." Sears, it turned out, was a fervent McCarthy advocate who had applied for the job in violation of subcommittee rules and had lied about making public statements supporting the senator. On April 5, the subcommittee officially terminated the relationship with Sears. Because of the furor over the Sears appointment, the announcement of Welch's selection avoided intense scrutiny.[5]

About 6:00 p.m. that day, following the news conference announcing Welch's appointment, the attorneys left with Seaton and Hensel for the Carlton Hotel, where they all relaxed in a cocktail lounge. When the Pentagon officials left for a few moments, Welch looked his colleagues in the eye and said, "Boys, we're in the kind of lawsuit that is different from anything you've known." He warned that "even the lawyers will be on trial. If there is anything in any of your lives that might be embarrassing for you, it better come out now—even tax returns." St. Clair knew of nothing, but Fisher revealed that he had been a member of the National Lawyers Guild at Harvard and had joined an affiliated group after graduation. The guild had been accused of communist ties, and Fisher had resigned in 1950.

Welch pondered that. "This is serious, Fred, it can be very serious. I don't think you can stay after this." When Seaton and Hensel returned to the table, Welch informed them, and almost immediately Seaton and Hensel left to make phone calls. Later, the group repaired to a hotel room and over drinks discussed the problem. Fisher recalled that Seaton and Hensel "were very much on edge."

Fisher's membership in the Guild almost certainly would come out at the hearings. They considered a strategy whereby if McCarthy attacked Fisher, "Joe Welch would become very outraged and turn the attack against the Senator." However, the consensus emerged that it was too dangerous to take the chance; Fisher would have to return to Boston. St. Clair also asked to be removed from the case, but Seaton and Hensel were "adamant" that Welch and St. Clair should not withdraw. They decided to consult with Jim Hagerty and accept whatever decision he made. Seaton tracked down Hagerty, asking him to meet them at Hensel's home in Georgetown.

When the group arrived, Hagerty was waiting for them. Following intense deliberation, he promised the attorneys that if McCarthy abused them, they "could count on a friend in the White House—his boss, the President." The upshot was that Fisher would return to Boston but Welch and St. Clair would remain on the case. Welch told Fisher that he was "the luckiest of the three" because Welch and St. Clair could not know what awaited them in the hearings. Welch, although he had agreed to take the case pro bono, foresaw a big payoff for his law firm. "What a case!" he said. "A million dollars couldn't buy all the publicity." [6]

IKE'S ANTIFEAR CRUSADE

The New York Times of Sunday, April 4, reflected the president's evident command of the situation that had put McCarthy's fortunes at "a cross-roads." Unlike previously, "the real strength" of the anti-McCarthy forces, the editors said, "is that they are anchored in the White House." The Schine report had been released on March 11, "evidently with the President's knowledge." The Republican National Committee, "with the President's approval," had chosen Richard Nixon over McCarthy to respond to Adlai Stevenson's March 6 speech. Sources close to the president had indicated—in language virtually lifted from Jim Hagerty's diary—that Eisenhower was "fed up" with McCarthy.

That McCarthy's fortunes were in decline was undeniable. In a January 1954 Gallup Poll, the senator's favorable-to-unfavorable ratio had been 50 to 29 percent. By March 15, three days after the release of the Schine report, it was down to 46 to 36 percent. The poll published on April 4 reported, for the first time, more negative than positive respondents to McCarthy: 48 percent negative to 36 percent positive, with 16 percent undecided. A small news story that weekend symbolized the deteriorating McCarthy-Cohn fortunes; down in Georgia, Private G. David Schine had been rejected for training as a military police criminal investigator. [7]

Once Welch was hired and the announcement was imminent, Eisenhower could escape from the prehearing clamor in Washington. About noon on April 2, he and Mrs. Eisenhower departed for

Camp David, where Ike intended to spend the weekend in preparation for a Monday-evening speech. The address would be his "fear
speech," designed to drain energy from the McCarthy movement
by reassuring the American people. That was a great mission of the
Eisenhower presidency in 1954: to lower the level of fear at home
and abroad, thereby protecting American democracy from extremism and avoiding another, more cataclysmic world war.

A week earlier, Hagerty and Eisenhower had discussed the speech
"at length" and the president's plan for "a package deal," with Herbert Brownell reporting later on what the administration was doing
to combat communism. Ike planned to "speak only from notes and
nothing else—15 minutes." The address, he said, "should take [the]
Red play away from McCarthy and put it back on [a] decent level." [8]

The president's Camp David notes were a rich litany of the
sources of fear among the American people, including "the inten-
tions of the Men in the Kremlin," weapons of mass destruction, the
"possibility of depression," and the threat of communist subversion
at home and abroad. Ike made specific notes about how he would
handle McCarthy's contribution to a climate of fear without using
the senator's name. [9]

That Monday morning, Eisenhower fretted his way through a
legislative leadership meeting. "I am speaking off-the-cuff tonight,"
he told Republican congressional leaders. "I'll probably faint from
stage fright." Brownell's address on Friday would "lay out [the]
whole Red set up," emphasizing the FBI, which enjoyed great prestige with the American people. Ike could not resist a dig at McCarthy. He had learned from Brownell's script that "there were about
6/10,000ths of 1% of subversives in the Armed Services." That, the
president concluded, showed "what a silly business this screaming of
the Armed Forces being full of Communists was." [10]

That night, Eisenhower delivered his "fear" address in a new
format; he sat on the edge of his desk, arms folded, smiling, with a
flag to his right, and spoke from notes, not a script, without a teleprompter. One reviewer commented that, in contrast to the president's past efforts, "the improvement was great indeed." The format

"enabled General Eisenhower to achieve relaxation" and "television's most desired quality—naturalness."[11]

What Ike called "off-the-cuff" remarks were, in fact, thoroughly rehearsed and, given their fidelity to his Camp David notes, memorized. For a president not renowned for his speaking skills, the talk was a tour de force. Among other subjects, he discussed the fear "of Communist infiltration into our own country, into our Government, into our schools, into our unions, into any of our facilities, any of our industries, wherever they may be, and where those Communists could damage us."

Then he addressed McCarthy's methods and "the fear that we will use intemperate investigative methods, particularly through congressional committees, to combat communistic penetration." He observed "that there can be very grave offenses committed against an innocent individual, if he is accused, possibly, by someone having the immunity of congressional membership. He can lose his job. He can have scars that will be lasting. But in the long run," Eisenhower assured his listeners, "you may be certain of this: America believes in, and practices, fair play, and decency and justice." No reasonably informed citizen could doubt that he was talking about McCarthy.[12]

THE GENERAL'S "FRIEND"

At 8:15 on Tuesday morning, Ike was so pleased with how his television address had gone that he summoned Jim Hagerty to alter his original plan to cancel Wednesday's news conference. He wanted to hear all the newspaper reports. "That's what I've been telling you boys for a long time," he lectured his press secretary. "Just let me get up and talk to the people. I can get through to them that way. I don't feel I do when I have to read a speech or use that damn teleprompter." Ike called Herb Brownell, cautioning him to avoid any "political overtones" in his Friday address. He should make it "a factual presentation" focused on "bragging on [the] FBI and his subordinates."[13]

April 6 was the evening of Joe McCarthy's response to Edward

R. Murrow's March 9 *See It Now* telecast. McCarthy reiterated his standard anticommunist rhetoric, talked about the "Major Peress scandal," and alleged that Murrow "as far back as twenty years ago was engaged in propaganda for Communist causes." The line from McCarthy's broadcast that concerned the White House was his charge that there had been an "eighteen-month deliberate delay" in the US development of the hydrogen bomb; McCarthy demanded to know if the delay had been perpetrated by "loyal Americans or traitors."[14]

At his news conference the next day, Eisenhower went directly to questions. The inevitable McCarthy question was asked: "A certain senator" had charged that "there had been a delay of 18 months in the production of the hydrogen bomb" and that it was "due to subversion in the Government." Ike brushed off the question, saying "No, I know nothing about it. I never heard of any delay on my part, never heard of it." When pressed again on McCarthy's charge, he insisted, "I don't know of any speech; I get from here the first knowledge that there was a speech." That was another dig at McCarthy, conveying to the senator that the president deemed his address unimportant.

In reference to McCarthy's *See It Now* broadcast, Eisenhower was asked, "Mr. President, would you care to say anything to us about the loyalty and patriotism of Edward R. Murrow?" By reflex, Eisenhower sought to avoid saying anything about McCarthy and Murrow's broadcast: "I am going to say nothing at all about that. First of all, I don't comment about people, I don't comment about things of which I know nothing."

Then Ike realized what he had done: if he left it there, the headlines the next day would say he had doubts about Murrow's loyalty. He owed too much to the journalist for his eloquent denunciation of McCarthy on March 9. "I will say this," he amended. "I have known this man for many years; he has been one of the men I consider my friend among your profession." The president's refuge when in a tight spot was often to invoke World War II. He recalled that when Murrow had been reporting on the war from London, "I always thought of him as a friend." It was an extraordinary moment for Eisenhower to call any journalist "my friend." [15]

Once Samuel Sears resigned, the hearing subcommittee moved quickly to replace him. On April 7, Ray H. Jenkins of Knoxville, Tennessee, was announced as the subcommittee's unanimous choice. Everett Dirksen called him "the best trial lawyer in East Tennessee." Subcommittee members were relieved to find no record of public statements by Jenkins about McCarthy. "We asked," Dirksen said, "in effect, whether he had ever stolen a horse or burned down a barn" or done anything else "that might rise later to haunt this committee," but "we were satisfied there was not." The committee set a target date of April 21 to begin hearings. [16]

Meanwhile, Herbert Brownell was busy preparing his remarks designed to follow up on the president's televised address. His task was to report on what the administration was actually doing to combat communism. The president micromanaged the drafting of Brownell's speech, much as he had Nixon's March 13 address. After reviewing a draft, he called Hagerty into his office. Perhaps recalling the mistake he and Brownell had made with the Harry Dexter White speech in November, Eisenhower emphasized, "Tell Herb that he must remain above partisanship. He has a good speech. He'd spoil it if the people listening think it is political." [17]

Brownell did his duty. Focusing on the threat of "Communist infiltration here at home," he extolled the FBI's "quiet, painstaking work" in penetrating communist groups. As a result, "36 active Communist leaders have been convicted and sentenced to jail for conspiring to advocate the overthrow of our Government by force and violence." He warned that communists could exploit people outside the party, and "for that reason, we have adopted the Employee Security Program and under it have removed hundreds of such employees who were security risks."

As Ike wished, Brownell's presentation was rigorously factual, almost to the point of tedium. Once again, the Eisenhower team had stolen the spotlight from McCarthy without mentioning his name, while invoking the glamor of the FBI. The president's editing had toned down what Hagerty called a "deliberate crack at McCarthy" to a patriotic commitment to be "basically fair in accordance with the traditional American concepts of due process of law" and "a careful regard for individual dignity and freedom and the preservation of personal liberty." The next day, the *New York Times* editors praised the attorney general's speech and were impressed that the FBI had so effectively infiltrated subversive organizations that "the Communist Party in this country doesn't know which of its Communist members to trust." [18]

THE OPPENHEIMER LAND MINE

Another threat to Eisenhower's anti-McCarthy operation had surfaced on April 8, the day prior to Brownell's broadcast: the Atomic Energy Commission had stripped J. Robert Oppenheimer, frequently called "the father of the atom bomb," of his security clearance. Oppenheimer had headed the Manhattan Project, developing the first nuclear device; following the war, he had become an adviser to the AEC.

The action against Oppenheimer had not yet been announced. Jim Hagerty and Robert Cutler discussed their fear that McCarthy "would be able to make a lot of hay on it." Hagerty fretted, "It's just a question of time before someone cracks it wide open and everything hits the fan." Oppenheimer had a huge reputation in the scientific world; suspension of his security clearance would touch off a "chain reaction" at a moment when, Hagerty believed, McCarthy had his "back to [the] wall" and "could easily get out from under by splashing this one." [19]

How to get out ahead of McCarthy on the Oppenheimer issue? In near desperation, Hagerty enlisted AEC chairman Lewis Strauss to persuade *The New York Times* to delay announcing Oppenheimer's suspension in return for detailed information that would assist the paper in writing an in-depth story. On April 10, Hagerty noted that the "Oppenheimer business" was "all the work" that got done that day. He and Sherman Adams briefed the president, who "listened gravely," then asked if "the record will be spelled out?" The staff worked furiously on a draft of an AEC statement, which they presented to Eisenhower at 11:30 a.m. "He looked serious," Hagerty noted, removed his glasses, "and chewed them" while reading. Hagerty also showed Eisenhower an Associated Press story about McCarthy saying he would "soon" discuss "publicly" the causes of the eighteen-month delay in the development of the hydrogen bomb. Eisenhower instructed the staff to "stick carefully to the facts" and follow "orderly procedure." He was concerned that they "handle this so that all our scientists are not made out to be Reds. That god-damn McCarthy is just likely to try such a thing."[20]

The Oppenheimer case preoccupied the president's team throughout the weekend. After Brownell and Hagerty debriefed Strauss on the reasons for the AEC's action, Brownell expressed skepticism, saying that he "would have to see the President on this one." He thought that the only possible criminal action against Oppenheimer would be for perjury. "No one has proved any espionage," he said, "just bad associations." That conclusion haunted the White House; "guilt by association" was a staple of McCarthyism. Eisenhower had lectured the public on television about the destructiveness of fear. Now people in his administration had turned the fear of communist subversion into an action damaging the reputation of a man who had served his country with distinction.[21]

The sleep-deprived Hagerty characterized April 13 as "a rough day." The word on Oppenheimer had gone out on the wire services the previous night, and Hagerty's phone had rung constantly from 10:30 p.m. until 6:30 a.m. Hagerty called Strauss, and they agreed to hold any formal AEC statement until later in the day. The news about Oppenheimer's suspension was already in *The New York Times*, making use of the details generated by Hagerty's efforts. The article chronicled Oppenheimer's questionable associations, his hiring of alleged communists or former communists, his contradictory testimony to the FBI about attending communist meetings, his failure to report in timely fashion on an attempt by the Soviet Union to secure scientific information from him, and his opposition to the development of the hydrogen bomb. Oppenheimer, who had had not denied his communist associations in the 1930s and '40s, provided a forty-three-page response to the allegations.[22]

The press would soon be clamoring for a statement from the White House. At 9:00 a.m., Strauss, Brownell, Assistant Press Secretary Murray Snyder, Hagerty, and Persons met with Sherman Adams to argue about its content. Strauss and Hagerty warned that any delay in revealing the steps taken resulting in suspension "would start us off on the wrong foot and we would have to admit it later anyway." Hagerty informed the president that the AEC statement was ready for release, and Eisenhower said, "Get it out as soon as possible." By 12:30, Strauss had cleared the release with his other commission members, and it was released at 1:30 p.m.[23]

It was Oppenheimer's opposition to the H-bomb that the White House feared McCarthy would exploit. Later that day in Arizona, McCarthy called the Oppenheimer suspension "long overdue" and commended Strauss and the AEC for their action. The senator stated that the previous spring, he had conducted his own investigation about the delay in developing the H-bomb. He claimed that two White House aides had convinced him that "it would not be wise to hold public hearings at that time because of the security measures involved."[24]

Traveling in the West, McCarthy continued to command headlines; reporters pressed the senator about whether he was trying to capture control of the Republican Party and run for president. The senator's answer to both questions was "No." When asked if he was "deliberately provoking a fight with the President," he denied it. "I may say the President has never indicated to me that he was unhappy about digging Communists out."[25]

Meanwhile, McCarthy won a twenty-four-hour delay in starting the hearings so he could deliver a speech in Houston on Texas Independence Day. That moved the hearings to April 22. Karl Mundt announced procedures that would "limit the range of the investigation," a proposal to which Senator John McClellan had agreed.

Mundt confidently predicted that "the public hearings probably would run about ten days."[26]

THE INDICTMENT OF MCCARTHY

April 13 was also the day the papers reported that Senator Karl Mundt had requested both sides to file in writing "the precise charges and the proof they intend to offer through documents and witnesses." Mundt observed that the enterprise had increasingly assumed the character of a trial, not just a congressional hearing. The two brilliant trial lawyers, Jenkins and Welch, would feel right at home in such proceedings.[27]

On April 13, the Eisenhowers left for Augusta, Georgia. Ike intended to go where reporters would be less able to ask him questions about the Army-McCarthy hearings or the Oppenheimer case. When Congress was in session, he normally scheduled a weekly news conference, but there would be none this week.

On April 14, in response to Karl Mundt's requirement, the army released twenty-nine formal charges against Joseph McCarthy and Roy Cohn. Joe Welch understood the importance of beating the McCarthy forces to the punch with the accusations; it also took attention away from the Oppenheimer story. His well-written document went well beyond the comparatively antiseptic, chronological report issued on March 11, portraying McCarthy as the principal protagonist in the dispute. He had designed the document to repudiate McCarthy's protestation that the dispute was a conflict between only Roy Cohn and John Adams. Based on this new document, the editors at *The New York Times* confirmed that what "everybody knows to be the fact, is that Mr. McCarthy is up to his neck in this battle." Now, with this bill of particulars, there was no longer much doubt about the army's—and indirectly Eisenhower's—intent: to place the junior senator from Wisconsin on trial for his political life.

The army's indictment was devastating; repeatedly, it hung the scandal of the Cohn-Schine relationship around Joe McCarthy's neck. "The Department of the Army," it read, "alleges that Senator

Joseph R. McCarthy as Chairman of the Permanent Subcommittee on Investigations," along with his chief counsel, Roy Cohn, had "sought by improper means to obtain preferential treatment for one Pvt. G. David Schine, United States Army, formerly chief consultant of this subcommittee." McCarthy's name was invoked again in item one, which said that "on or about July 8, 1953 Senator McCarthy sought to obtain a direct commission in the United States Army for Mr. Schine." In the remaining twenty-eight charges, the dates and specifics tumbled, one after the other, in a chillingly precise recitation of the repetitive wielding of improper influence. McCarthy's name was cited more than a dozen times, the indictment contending that Cohn had, at all times, been acting under the senator's authority. No allegation was more damaging than number 24, stating that Cohn, "upon learning that Private Schine might be assigned to overseas duty, threatened to get the Secretary of the Army fired and cause the subcommittee to 'wreck the Army.'"[28]

The army's "bill of particulars" was supposed to be withheld from the press until McCarthy and his associates released their own, but it quickly leaked; the entire text appeared in the papers on Friday, April 16. McCarthy refused to file his countercharges until the subcommittee took action on the "news leak." It turned out that Democratic Senator Symington was the source, and McCarthy accused Symington of violating a Senate rule.

At the Pentagon, Joe Welch and his team could take satisfaction in their work to that point. They had put McCarthy and Cohn on the defensive. It was no accident that the leaked information had gone to Jim Hagerty's favorite White House reporters. Nor had Symington's action in releasing the document been thoughtless. With McCarthy in the eye of the storm, Welch chose that moment to quietly release the news that Frederick G. Fisher, Jr., of his law firm had been withdrawn from the case due to his previous membership in the National Lawyers Guild. That news was buried, almost unnoticed, at the end of *The New York Times* story about the army's new document.[29]

While McCarthy railed against Symington's disclosure, he was out of state, unavailable to Roy Cohn. Therefore, Cohn leaked his own telegram to Senator Mundt, complaining that the army's twenty-nine allegations "contain many false, misleading and distorted statements, as well as the outright omission of highly relevant events." He blamed the accusations on the army's "long-standing attempt to stop our investigation of instances of Communist infiltration in the Army." [30]

Karl Mundt knew he had the proverbial tiger by the tail. Understanding that his friend and political ally Joe McCarthy was facing a trial of dimensions he had not anticipated, he called a news conference and suggested that the senator "remove himself entirely from the investigation." Mundt suggested that McCarthy "submit in writing any questions he might have for witnesses." [31]

MCCARTHY GETS HIS WAY

Mundt was down to the wire in defining McCarthy's role in the hearings. McCarthy had returned from Texas, and, on Sunday, April 18, Mundt announced that subcommittee investigators would meet with the Wisconsin senator on Monday to set "ground rules." McCarthy was still adamant about his right to cross-examine witnesses; he threatened to appeal on the Senate floor if the subcommittee asked him to withdraw as a member.

As usual, he got his way; agreement was finally achieved in a three-hour closed-door session. McCarthy accepted some limits on his questioning rights, provided they were "equal to those accorded the other side." He also promised to file a detailed response to the army's twenty-nine-point set of charges. Mundt still hoped to complete the hearings in ten days to two weeks. [32]

G. David Schine showed up that day on Capitol Hill, fresh from Georgia, looking "trim and tan"; he spent some hours in the offices of the McCarthy subcommittee, presumably being questioned by Ray Jenkins, the subcommittee counsel. When pursued by reporters afterward, he bounded up a Senate Office Building stairway three steps at a time, literally running to jump into a waiting limousine with his father, J. Myer Schine.

McCarthy, scrambling to regain his footing, played the Struve Hensel card. The senator apparently believed that Hensel, more than anyone else, had been responsible for issuing the March 11 report on privileges sought for Private Schine. He told reporters that Hensel would be a principal target of his questioning. On Tuesday, April 20, he issued a set of forty-six charges; one highlight was the allegation that John Adams had impeded the investigations into communists in the army, acting "with the influence and guidance of H. Struve Hensel." While masterminding the preparation of the March 11 report, Hensel "was himself under investigation by the subcommittee for misconduct and possible law violation" when he had held "a top procurement post" in the navy, illegally profiting to the tune of $56,526.34. Therefore, Hensel's effort to block investigation of those charges was the real reason behind the army's attacks on McCarthy and Cohn.[33]

McCarthy had finally attacked someone who would not be intimidated. A few minutes after he aired those charges, Hensel responded with headline-grabbing rhetoric, calling the allegations "barefaced lies." He threatened McCarthy with a lawsuit "if the Senator makes those charges without the protection of senatorial immunity." He charged that McCarthy had "reached a high mark of scandalous malice and the low mark of cowardly irresponsibility." Hensel immediately asked the Pentagon's security officer to request J. Edgar Hoover and the FBI to review all of his records and background. That day, Gould called the District of Columbia police, asking them to "pay close attention to Mr. Hensel's house at night." At the bottom of the memorandum recording Gould's call was a single handwritten word: "McCarthy."[34]

Wednesday, the day before the hearings were to begin, was a tense day at the White House. Bernard Shanley tried to see Sherman Adams at 8:00 a.m., but, he recorded, Adams "wouldn't open his mouth." Shanley already knew the chief of staff was on edge because "he had been a little rough with me the day before." Key personnel were just as jittery at the Pentagon, where Hensel was consulting with Joe Welch, undoubtedly regarding McCarthy's allegations. One good sign for the Eisenhower forces: the Gallup Poll reported that 46 percent of the respondents tended to agree with Robert Stevens on the charges, 23 percent with McCarthy.[35]

The first hearing session was scheduled to begin at 10:30 a.m. on Thursday, April 22. On Wednesday, *The New York Times* had published the procedural rules. Though he would not vote or otherwise deliberate with the subcommittee, McCarthy and his counsel "shall have the same right to cross-examine as the members of the subcommittee." The army's case was scheduled to go first, including a statement by Secretary Stevens. The hearings were to be televised in full on three networks plus highlights on radio and local television.[36]

On April 22, at dawn, television technicians invaded the ornate marble-walled, high-ceilinged Senate Caucus Room on the third floor of the Senate Office Building. They lugged in equipment, set up scaffolds to hold bulky television cameras, and tested floodlights. Shortly before 10:00, the large oak doors were flung open and politicians, lawyers, photographers, reporters, and staff people flooded in. Built to handle an audience of three hundred, the room soon held a crowd estimated at five hundred to eight hundred.

As the moments ticked away toward beginning, John Adams, whose professional life had careened wildly for months toward that moment, recalled the scene: "Around a coffin-shaped table sat the principals, the subcommittee, various lawyers and counsel Jenkins. At the end of the table were McCarthy, Cohn, and subcommittee director Carr, protected by two plainclothesmen. Immediately next to the McCarthy group sat the Army group, Stevens, myself, and Special Counsel Welch. A phalanx of generals sat behind Stevens. Struve Hensel, still one of the accused, sat next to us, with his lawyer." After so many weeks, Karl Mundt was finally ready. When the red lights on the television cameras told him that America was watching, the senator, Adams recalled, "picked up a glass ashtray and rapped for order." The time was 10:35 a.m.[37]

About noon that day, the president and Mrs. Eisenhower boarded their plane back to Washington, DC. The general was ready to return to the front to oversee Operation McCarthy.

CHAPTER 13

THE EISENHOWER-MCCARTHY HEARINGS

A single word characterizes each of the key actors in the hearings drama that unfolded on April 22. "Shocked" was the word for Joe Welch, who, according to Thomas Reeves, "took one look through the doorway and recoiled in horror" at the "utter confusion" in the hearing room; it teemed with hundreds of spectators, photographers jumping "up and down to get pictures," and television cameras following every move.[1]

"Ambushed" aptly describes Karl Mundt's feelings that day. The South Dakota senator had been drafted by the subcommittee to preside over the circus because, he believed, "behind the scenes, secret meetings at the White House and Capitol Hill were held." He later reflected that "the Big Name actors onstage were marionettes pulled by unseen, and often unidentifiable, forces on the dark side of the curtain."[2]

"Cynical" was an appropriate word for Roy Cohn. His relationship with David Schine was being dragged through the mud. The inquiry, he wrote not long before his death, "had nothing to do with what it said it was doing." The hearings, he believed, were not about him and Schine or his threats to "wreck" the army. "The real purpose, of the whole shebang," he lamented, "was to wipe out McCarthy. Joe knew, I knew that."[3]

"Angry" described Struve Hensel, who had accused McCarthy of "barefaced lies" when the senator charged that Hensel had masterminded the Schine report as a means of covering up his own corruption. John Adams, sitting near Hensel, was "bitter"; the army counsel believed that he and Stevens had been set up to be sacrificial lambs. "If the fall guy role for me was hard, it was even more difficult for Secretary Stevens," he recalled. "Jittery" was the word Jim Hagerty frequently applied to Robert Stevens, an apt description for the secretary's emotional, often impulsive response to stressful situations.[4]

After calling the session to order, Mundt presented the mission of the hearings: to determine whether McCarthy and his aides had "sought by improper means to obtain preferential treatment for one Private G. David Schine" and whether the US Army had held Schine "hostage" to force McCarthy's subcommittee to end its investigation of communist infiltration in the army.[5]

To characterize McCarthy's approach to the hearings as "aggressive" would be an understatement. Mundt instructed subcommittee counsel Ray Jenkins to call his first witness; at that moment—seventeen minutes into the hearing—McCarthy's nasal baritone broke the spell: "A point of order, Mr. Chairman. May I raise a point of order?" Robert Stevens and John Adams, he said, could not speak for the army because they were "Pentagon politicians." He called it "a disgrace" and an insult to "the millions of outstanding young men in the Army" to permit those men, "who are trying to hold up an investigation of Communists, label themselves as the Department of the Army." He got no ruling from the chair at that moment. James Reston opined the next day that McCarthy "could not help it. When the red lights on those TV cameras go on, the Senator automatically produces sound."[6]

Stevens was scheduled to testify after lunch. He stood proudly in front a phalanx of uniformed, decorated army generals, clearly visible to the television audience. A sympathetic journalist described the scene: "For just a moment, the little man with the glasses and the burlap-colored hair was bigger than anybody in the whole crowded room." "First," Stevens began, "it is my responsibility to speak for the

Army. The Army is about a million and half men and women, in posts across this country and around the world." "That was when," the reporter wrote, "you could shut your eyes and almost hear the bugles."

McCarthy erupted, "Mr. Chairman, a point of order. Mr. Stevens is not speaking for the Army." The magic moment was gone; Stevens "fell back into his niche as a displaced gentleman, stoutly backing his Army but somewhat embarrassed by the whole thing." As usual, McCarthy got his way. The chair ruled that "for the purpose of this inquiry, he [Stevens] speaks for himself, for Mr. Adams and for Mr. Hensel." That sickened John Adams. "McCarthy is in charge," he thought to himself. "He may be sitting here along with the others being investigated, but really he's in charge." [7]

Stevens plowed ahead, labeling as "absolutely false" McCarthy's charge that the army had sought to "blackmail" the subcommittee into ending its investigation. He obediently repeated Fred Seaton's formula for shifting responsibility—that the Schine report had been issued in response to senatorial requests. He called McCarthy's "tireless effort to obtain special consideration and privileges" for Schine a "perversion of power." Ending his statement, Stevens declared, "I am proud to have had this chance to speak for the Army today. This Army is of transcendent importance to this nation and the friends of freedom and justice and peace around the world." [8]

A PURPOSELY BUSY PRESIDENT

"Busy"—purposely busy—was the word for Dwight Eisenhower on April 22. Though he was not in the hearing room, the columnists Joseph and Stewart Alsop called the president "the seventh principal," in addition to McCarthy, Stevens, Cohn, John Adams, Carr, and Hensel. However, Ike had arranged a hectic travel schedule that would make it difficult for anyone to ask him about the hearings. When his plane landed at National Airport, the president immediately motored to Constitution Hall to greet the annual convention of the Daughters of the American Revolution. Afterward, he spent less than ten minutes at the White House before flying to New York to address the annual dinner of the American Newspaper Publishers Association.[9]

On that first night of the hearings, Eisenhower chose to deliver a sharply worded sermon to the publishers on the evils of sensationalism in the press. Ostensibly, the speech was not about McCarthy—but, of course, it was. Ike had often complained that the press had a guilty conscience about McCarthy. Having built him up, the media wanted the president to destroy a monster of their own making. His address was chock full of references to "the facts," employing the term a dozen times. He accused the papers of placing "a premium upon clichés and slogans. We incline to persuade with an attractive label; or to damn with a contemptuous tag. But catchwords are not information. And, most certainly, sound popular judgments cannot be based upon them. . . . Freedom of expression is not merely a right," the president concluded, "its constructive use is a stern duty. Have we, have you as publishers, the courage fully to exercise the right and perform the duty? Along with patriotism—understanding, comprehension, determination are the qualities we now need. Without them, we cannot win. With them, we cannot fail."[10]

Ike later complained to Swede Hazlett that he had received "a number of criticisms" from publishers in attendance that night, protesting "Why should he attempt to tell us about our business?" He wished he could respond, "When have you hesitated to tell me how to run my business?" Ike argued that "any hurt feelings must be because someone felt the shoe fit—but uncomfortably."[11]

That shoe pinched Walter Lippmann's journalistic foot. Lippmann wrote a disdainful column, referring repeatedly to Eisenhower as "the general"—never as "the president." "The general" believed that newspapers "have made McCarthy powerful by giving too much space and too many headlines to him." The prestigious pundit argued; "General Eisenhower is quite mistaken. . . . McCarthy's charges of treason, subversion, espionage, corruption, perversion are news which cannot be suppressed or ignored." He concluded, "General Eisenhower himself has a heavy responsibility for the things he complains about."[12]

Nevertheless, Eisenhower did not intend to remain in Washington and field questions about the hearings. He arrived back at the White House at 11:30 p.m. and departed the next morning for Kentucky to visit Abraham Lincoln's birthplace en route to Augusta, Georgia. The president spoke movingly there of Lincoln's "forbearance in the extreme—patience," paying indirect homage to his own approach to Joe McCarthy.[13]

That exit allowed Ike and Hagerty to avoid questions on the big news the second day of hearings, when Stevens revealed that he possessed the transcript of a phone call from McCarthy seeking privileges for David Schine; indeed, the army had fifty to a hundred such transcripts. The room shook with laughter when Stevens recalled McCarthy's wisecrack that Roy Cohn "thinks that Dave ought to be a general and operate from a penthouse on the Waldorf-Astoria." The news of the phone transcripts set off hours of wrangling that resulted in the passage of a motion to subpoena the documents in question.[14]

INDOCHINA IN CRISIS

The crisis in Indochina, where the French were on the verge of defeat, was an unwanted passenger on the president's plane. John Foster Dulles informed Eisenhower that the French foreign minister, Georges Bidault, was "a man close to the breaking point." Bidault believed that the only alternatives were using B-29s to bomb the Viet Minh rebels at Dien Ben Phu or give up and negotiate an armistice. Eisenhower was forced to truncate his trip and return to Washington on April 25 to address what Jim Hagerty called a "situation getting very grave." Arriving back in Washington at 9:15 p.m., the president read updated reports on Indochina deep into the night. Hagerty noted pessimistically that the French expected Dien Bien Phu to fall within a week.[15]

On Monday morning, April 26, Eisenhower plunged into meetings, with Indochina—not the Army-McCarthy hearings—the main item on the agenda. The president confirmed that the French forces at Dien Bien Phu "could not hold out for more than a week and would fall possibly sooner." No mention was made of an unspoken issue: if Eisenhower could be blamed for losing Indochina to the communists, McCarthy could exploit that issue, just as he had charged General George C. Marshall with the loss of China.

In spite of his preoccupation with the crisis in Indochina, the hearings were on the president's mind. He complained to congressional leaders that he feared that the American people would conclude that Congress is focused on "nothing but McCarthy." "The worst thing about this McCarthy business," he said, "is that the newspapers are all saying that the leadership in the Republican Party has switched to McCarthy and we are all dancing to his tune." [16]

"Worried" was the word for Fred Seaton, the president's man in the Pentagon, in the wake of the subpoena for the Pentagon's monitored telephone transcripts. Seaton fretted on his personal notepad about whether the subpoena was aimed at "*ALL* monitored conversations." He was relieved when Attorney General Brownell advised Sherman Adams that the transcripts should be limited to the principals in the hearings and, in particular, urged that the administration deny any demand for "telephone conversations with the White House or the Department of Justice." Limiting the transcripts to the "principals" in the investigation—McCarthy, Stevens, Cohn, John Adams, Carr, and Hensel—conveniently left out Fred Seaton. [17]

DOCTORED EVIDENCE

On April 27, at McCarthy's urging, Ray Jenkins asked Stevens if he had asked Private Schine to pose for a picture with him. Stevens could not recall. Jenkins produced a 14-by-20-inch photo showing the two beside Stevens's plane in Fort Dix, New Jersey; the secretary appeared to be smiling at the private. The next day, only seconds after the session began, Joseph Welch signaled Chairman Mundt. "Mr. Welch, a point of order?" Mundt asked. Welch responded, "I don't know what it is but it's a point of something." Granted permission, he continued, "My point of order is that Mr. Jenkins yesterday was imposed upon and so was the Secretary of the Army by having a doctored or altered photograph produced in this court-room as if it were honest."[18]

The public relations officer at McGuire Air Force Base had found the original photograph, which included a third person, Colonel Jack Bradley. The picture showed Stevens smiling at Bradley, not Schine. Welch's instinct for the jugular was fully on display: "I charge that what was offered in evidence yesterday was an altered, shamefully cut-down picture so that somebody could say to Stevens, 'Were you not photographed alone with David Schine?'" The Democrats demanded "the facts," and Jenkins, embarrassed, dismissed Stevens and called to the stand the man who had given him the doctored photograph—Roy Cohn—who claimed not to have known about the alteration.[19]

Finally, on April 30, the seventh day of the hearings, James Juli-ana, a McCarthy aide, took responsibility for the photo but insisted he had not been ordered to cut out Bradley. Welch prodded Juliana about the origins of the photograph. "Did you think it came from a pixie?" he asked, slyly alluding to the fact that the photo had been prepared on Roy Cohn's orders. McCarthy saw a chance to disrupt the questioning and asked, "Will the counsel for my benefit de-fine—I think he may be an expert on that—what is a pixie?" Welch responded, "Yes, I should say, Mr. Senator, that a pixie is a close rel-ative of a fairy. Shall I proceed, sir? Have I enlightened you?" As the room erupted in laughter, McCarthy shot back, "As I said, I think you may be an authority on what a pixie is."[20]

That laughter reflected the fact that the hearings were already steeped in innuendo. In the 1950s, "fairy" was a common pejora-tive term for "homosexual." Welch had subtly reminded the crowd of the whispered story behind the privileges sought for Schine. McCarthy's snide rejoinder suggested, "You must be one too."

Regardless of the facts about the Cohn-Schine relationship, numerous participants in the Army-McCarthy drama believed the men were lovers. Fred Seaton retained, in his "Eyes Only" docu-ment collection, a handwritten note on his official notepaper, bear-ing the name, address, and phone number of a former chauffeur of Schine. The man had apparently volunteered, if needed, to testify about driving Cohn and Schine on trips between Fort Dix and New York and claimed that there had been "sex acts in the back of the car." Though the chauffeur never testified, Seaton's retention of the document reflects how far the Eisenhower forces contemplated going to defeat Joe McCarthy.[21]

Then a second piece of doctored evidence surfaced. The afternoon of May 4, with Stevens testifying, McCarthy reached into his briefcase and produced a document dated January 26, 1951, apparently dictated by FBI Director J. Edgar Hoover. The senator alleged that the letter disclosed possible espionage at Fort Monmouth, New Jersey, but the army had paid no attention to the warning. Welch stated that "the mere fact that we have an impressive-looking purported copy of such a letter does not impress an old-time lawyer." He shrewdly added, "I would like to have Mr. J. Edgar Hoover say that he wrote the letter and mailed it."[22]

The next morning, McCarthy's attempt to align himself with the popular FBI director exploded in his face. Robert A. Collier, a ten-year FBI veteran, testified that Hoover had flatly denied that the letter was authentic. The paragraphs in the McCarthy letter were apparently drawn from a longer memorandum Hoover had dictated on the date in question. Collier reluctantly agreed with Welch that the document was "a carbon copy of precisely nothing" and "a perfect phony."[23]

The Eisenhower forces piled more humiliation on the senator. When Chairman Mundt asked the attorney general whether the entire Hoover memorandum could be released, Brownell ruled against it and, in effect, charged McCarthy with "unauthorized use" of confidential FBI reports. Welch grilled McCarthy about how he had secured the "phony" letter, expressing "an absorbing curiosity to know how in the dickens you got hold of it." When McCarthy refused to answer, Welch reminded the senator that he had sworn "to tell the truth, the whole truth and nothing but the truth." McCarthy would admit only that it had come from a confidential informant. In effect, he invoked his own version of the constitutional amendment he loved to vilify: the Fifth.[24]

THE SPECTER OF PERJURY

Then Robert Stevens got blindsided. On May 4, Arthur Krock, in *The New York Times*, questioned the accuracy of Stevens's testimony. The army secretary had testified that following his lunch agreement with the Republican senators on February 24, "I went back to the office and then I went home. And I don't think I saw anybody, except some of my own staff that afternoon." Krock resurrected a February 26 James Reston column that detailed how, in fact, Stevens had met with a group that included "Acting Secretary of Defense Kyes, Gen. Matthew B. Ridgway, Assistant Secretary of Defense Seaton, H. Struve Hensel" and other army officers.[25]

Armed with that revelation, Karl Mundt called the subcommittee into executive session on May 6 to question Fred Seaton. Given Seaton's relationship with the White House, that was a moment of peril for the administration. At 10:10 a.m. in room 248 of the Senate Office Building, Ike's henchman in the Pentagon was sworn to tell "the truth, the whole truth, and nothing but the truth."

Those who worked closely with Seaton knew better than to underestimate him. On that occasion, he exhibited a highly selective memory. His answers were punctuated with phrases such as "not so far as I remember" or "no, not to the best of my memory." He provided the information in the narrowest possible framework, without elaboration.

Roy Cohn seized the chance to find out how the administration had arranged to disclose its knowledge of his activities on behalf of Private Schine. "Were you present at any such discussion, at any time when there was any mention of that made?" Cohn asked. Seaton: "No, I certainly don't recall it, Roy." Asked when he had first learned about the Adams report, Seaton was vague: "Well, I can't exactly pinpoint it." "Whose idea was it to keep this report?" Cohn inquired. Seaton said that "to the best of my knowledge, it was Mr. [John] Adams." Cohn pressed the central question: "Whose idea was it to issue the report?" Again, Seaton—the man who, on March 11, had actually engineered its release—just could not recall. He remembered that "Senator Potter subsequently wrote a letter to the secretary, the contents of which I don't remember at the moment, but it had to do with that general subject, and a report was then sent to Senator Potter."

Cohn pressed Seaton about McCarthy's phone call the day the Schine report was released. To whom had Seaton transmitted the senator's request to include his documents? Seaton stonewalled: "Well, I don't remember specifically." Cohn tried again to pin Seaton down. "Did you ever hear any discussion in the Defense Department or particularly with Mr. Stevens or Mr. Adams, or Mr. Hensel, or any of them, concerning the fact that the issuance of this report would result in discrediting Senator McCarthy?" Seaton disingenuously responded, "No, I can't say that I did, Roy."

Thoroughly frustrated, Cohn snapped, "Why were they getting out this report, Fred?" "My understanding," Seaton coolly responded, "is that [it] was gotten out in order to satisfy the request from members of Congress who had demanded the report." When Cohn asked how many senatorial requests they had received, Seaton stated, "Well, to the best of my memory, it was someplace between fifteen and ten." Cohn pushed harder: "How many of those requests had been made on the solicitation of Mr. Stevens, Mr. Adams or anyone from the Army?" Seaton quietly responded, "I wouldn't know any that were, but I know nothing about that, Roy." Fortunately, Cohn's question had left Seaton himself out of the equation.

Seaton's testimony confirmed that a meeting had taken place on February 24 in Secretary Stevens's office. However, he made it sound so inconsequential that it was not worth remembering. He recalled only "a very short discussion"—"five minutes"—among Stevens, Kyes, Hensel, and himself about the memorandum of understanding Stevens had signed at his luncheon. "There was no material discussion" about the negative press reports, and "no decision was reached, or anything else." Seaton smoothly polished off his antiseptic account of that tumultuous day in the Pentagon: "The three of us walked down the hall, Kyes went into his office, Hensel into his, and I went into mine." [26]

Cohn had not outmanuevered Eisenhower's field commander in

the Pentagon's anti-McCarthy operation. The next day, when Stevens was forced to recant his previous testimony, McCarthy accused him of perjury, but no one so accused Fred Seaton.[27]

AN ANGRY PRESIDENT

Eisenhower and Hagerty knew that failure to hold a news conference when the president was in town would generate speculation about Indochina and the Army-McCarthy hearings. So they scheduled a session for 9:00 a.m. on April 29. After making noncommittal responses to questions about Indochina, the president showed irritation at two McCarthy-related questions. He "wore a look of incredulity" when informed that a congressman had quoted RNC chairman Leonard Hall to the effect that he had scheduled Senator McCarthy for three solid months of campaigning for Republican candidates. "Leonard Hall?" Ike snapped. The reporter responded, "Yes, sir." Eisenhower retorted, "Leonard Hall hasn't said that to me." The room rocked with laughter.[28]

Another question hit even closer to the president's anti-McCarthy nerve. Arthur Sylvester of the *Newark News* noted Stevens's testimony about the "pressure by Mr. McCarthy in behalf of Private Schine" and asked if Secretary Wilson had ever taken the matter up with the president. That question reaped the five-star general's scorn: "You mean talking about this private?" Sylvester responded, "Yes, and pressure being put on him." At that, Eisenhower spat out, "I never heard of him. I never heard of him." A *New York Times* reporter wrote that the president "appeared indignant and angry and his audience broke into laughter." But, the journalist added, "The President did not join in the merriment." No wonder the reporters laughed. It was unbelievable, a week into the Army-McCarthy hearings, to suggest that the president of the United States had not heard of G. David Schine.

Finally, another correspondent asked, "Mr. President, as a former commanding general of the United States Army, what do you think of all the excitement at the Capitol over the privileges granted this private?" The president was described as "flushed and glaring," and "his jaw was set." Following a silence, a reporter wrote, "The President drew up his shoulders and clenched his hands together, and when he answered, it was in a deeply husky voice": "I trust that you ladies and gentlemen will excuse me for declining to talk at all about something that—the whole business—that I don't think is something to talk about very much. I just hope it is all concluded very quickly. That's all." With that, Eisenhower strode rapidly out of the room. Merriman Smith barely had time to voice his usual benediction: "Thank you, Mr. President."[29]

The president's comment that he hoped the hearings would be "concluded very quickly" inevitably generated rumors. The next day, when asked if anyone at the White House had tried to call a halt to the Army-McCarthy hearings, Hagerty told reporters, "There is nothing to it."[30]

A DEAL TO END THE HEARINGS?

Republican senators on the McCarthy subcommittee made numerous attempts to shut down the Army-McCarthy hearings. Eisenhower's concluding comment at his April 29 news conference appeared to support the conclusion that the president wanted them terminated. If key participants wanted them ended, why did they continue?

In fact, every time Eisenhower had an opportunity to exercise his influence to truncate the hearings, he refused. Television was not kind to McCarthy. As John Adams recalled, McCarthy "looked grotesque close-up, his face covered with cream-colored pancake makeup to disguise his heavy beard for the television cameras. Though he was fleshy with whiskey weight, and his shirt would be soaked through by noon, his sharp nose made him look like a hawk as he descended on Stevens. His voice was usually a tight whine, and he occasionally emitted a strange, high giggle." Stevens, on the other hand, Adams noted, was "freshly shaven; his gray hair was neatly combed," and his gray double-breasted suit "was beautifully cut and neatly pressed." He looked, Adams suggested, "like the men who pass the collection plates in at prosperous Presbyterian churches, which he did when he was home in Plainfield, New Jersey."[31]

Eisenhower had made a cold-blooded decision: the hearings were proving so destructive to McCarthy's reputation that he wanted them to continue until, politically, the senator was ground into dust— even if it damaged the Republican Party in an election year. Herbert Brownell, who knew Ike's mind on the issue, wrote that, when Republican leaders sought to end the televised hearings, "we in the administration recognized the damage that live coverage of the hearings was causing McCarthy and recommended their continuation."[32]

That intent remained covert. Ike postured otherwise with people who did not know his secret plan. Charles Potter claimed that when he visited the White House, the president had asked, "When is it going to end, Charlie?" On May 6, Ike wrote Harry Bullis, a General Mills executive, that he hoped the hearings would be "brought speedily and effectively to an end."[33]

Everett Dirksen spearheaded the effort to end the hearings. His formula for making peace focused on firing both Roy Cohn and John Adams, as he had proposed all along. That would reinforce McCarthy's contention that the fundamental conflict was Adams-Cohn, not Army-McCarthy. Dirksen made his first big effort the night of Monday, May 3: he sought to limit testimony primarily to Stevens and McCarthy and take the remaining sessions behind closed doors. He presented his scheme to the other three Republican senators on the subcommittee and all agreed, including McCarthy.[34]

Welch initially agreed to discuss the proposal. However, the next day, after consulting with Jenkins, he concluded, "We were unable to invent a magic formula for shortening the hearings" and declared, "We must plough the long furrow." Welch repeated more than once, "I want all the facts developed." Dirksen called Welch's clarification "a change of heart," and McCarthy smartly asserted that the attorney had "welched." On May 5, Welch repeated that he "would not be satisfied with a formula whereby Senator McCarthy would follow Mr. Stevens and be subjected to an examination and cross-examination and that the hearing would then be ended."[35]

That Eisenhower had vetoed an early end to the hearings became apparent in his May 5 news conference, after Stevens's and Welch's rejection of the Dirksen proposal. His first question that day addressed the issue: "Mr. President, last week you expressed the hope that there would be an early end to the Army-McCarthy hearings. Yesterday the Army counsel objected to a Republican proposal to cut them short. . . . Do you still favor a quick end to those hearings?"

Eisenhower joked about his stormy exit from the April 29 news conference, noting "that my appearance upon answering seemed to be more important than what I had to say, so I will try to be very careful." Once the laughter subsided, he resumed his carefully rehearsed statement: "I did say that I hoped that these hearings would be quickly concluded; but by the word 'concluded,' I meant, of course, with effective answers to whatever were considered by the committee to be the main issues involved, and from the principals concerned." That comment sounded remarkably like Welch's statement that he wanted "all the facts developed." The president closed the discussion: "I am going to say just one more thing about it, and then I wouldn't be surprised that I would bar questions of this nature"—pausing for more laughter—"for a few weeks at least."

Suddenly, Edward J. Milne of the *Providence Journal* leaped to his feet and, mimicking McCarthy, shouted, "Mr. President, point of order!" That "one more thing" was a question Jim Hagerty had undoubtedly planted. When the laughter waned, Milne asked "whether or not Secretary Stevens, who is now in his tenth day on the stand, has your full backing in his course of conduct?" All in the room knew that Stevens's "course of conduct" the previous day had been to reject Dirksen's plan to curtail the hearings. Eisenhower delivered a crisp, unequivocal response: "Secretary Stevens was selected for his present job with great care, upon the recommendation of people that have known him for a long time. His record was carefully examined. I know of nothing that would cause me to lose confidence in Secretary Stevens' administration of the Army, and on that basis I'd back him up to the limit."[36]

But the movement to end the hearings was still active. Ike sought a contingency plan in case that happened. The moment he emerged from the May 5 news conference, he phoned Herbert Brownell to ask his "shot-gun opinion": if the hearings produced nothing "that disciplines this man [McCarthy] or limits his power in any way"—to Ike, the reason for the hearings—"could the President get away with ordering *no* member of [the] Executive Branch to go before [the] Committee?" In other words, what would his options be if the McCarthy forces succeeded in ending the hearings and the senator returned to his investigations? Brownell apparently affirmed the president's authority to invoke executive privilege.[37]

The news on May 7 transformed the international and political landscape. On that day, Eisenhower learned that Dien Bien Phu had fallen; the French had suffered a humiliating defeat. Though he had not yet decided against military intervention, Eisenhower had "grave doubts" about the efficacy of air strikes and the introduction of additional ground troops. Above all, he did not intend to violate the American "tradition of anticolonialism" by supporting France's efforts to maintain portions of its empire. Years later, writing his memoirs, Eisenhower was still irritated that, on the day of the fall of Dien Bien Phu, the lead story in a major newspaper had focused on "Senator McCarthy's demand for a test of the Executive's right to bar secret data to congressional investigators."[38]

MORE VETOES

Roy Cohn recalled that Dirksen made a second effort the following week—around May 8—to close down the hearings "at once." Any additional witnesses would testify behind closed doors, and all testimony would be released to the public. Cohn narrated an elaborate anecdote "with mystery-story overtones, involving a young man in a hotel room"—Cohn—"awaiting a telephone call" informing him that the hearings were history. Cohn had agreed to a plan whereby he and John Adams would resign simultaneously and announce that they were "taking the step at a personal sacrifice" to "save the taxpayers' money and serve the nation." Cohn got the approval of

McCarthy who allegedly said, "Besides, nobody is going to win this thing." Cohn endured "a lonely, day-long wait" at the Mayflower Hotel. Then, about dark, the phone rang and Cohn was informed that the army had rejected the proposal.

According to Cohn, Dirksen was furious. The senator had rushed to the White House and demanded that "the Administration insist on the Army's agreeing to the plan," but the White House "refused to bring any pressure on the military. If that was how the Army wanted it, Dirksen was told, that's the way it had to be." Dwight Eisenhower had exercised his second pocket veto.[39]

Dirksen would make one final, dramatic attempt. Jim Hagerty knew something was afoot on May 10, when Walter Winchell took him to lunch "as an emissary of [the] McCarthy group." Winchell wanted Hagerty to lobby the president, calling it "a good idea to call off [the] Army-McCarthy hearings and to recommend that they be taken off television." Knowing what Ike wanted, Hagerty told Winchell he "could not give such a word" and used the excuse that "we would not interfere with Senate proceedings."[40]

Everett Dirksen presented his new plan the morning of Tuesday, May 11. The plan had four components: (1) that Stevens conclude his testimony and McCarthy then testify, with public hearings recessed upon the conclusion of his testimony; (2) that other witnesses be examined only in executive session, with the testimony released immediately to the public; (3) that Ray Jenkins interview prospective witnesses and report on whether anyone else should testify in public sessions; and finally that (4) Senator McCarthy—in Roy Cohn's words—"at the conclusion of his testimony, be authorized to resume the regular hearings on matters not related to the present controversy."[41]

On the morning of May 11, Jim Hagerty noted that the White House was under "great pressure to try to take hearings into executive session after McCarthy's testimony." The congressional aides in the White House believed "it would be a good idea." Hagerty thought "it would be terrible," and the president "agrees with me." Eisenhower had called Charles Wilson, he noted, "and told him not to put any pressure at all on Stevens along these lines but to tell Stevens to 'do what you think is right.'" By that point, Wilson and Stevens knew what that instruction from the White House boss really meant.[42]

McCarthy announced his acceptance of the plan, and the hearing was plunged into debate over the proposal. Stevens initially stated that "at the present time we do not subscribe to the idea of putting witnesses into executive session." Close to noon, Mundt made a passionate plea to the principals to "search their souls and consciences" during the noon hour. He boxed himself in by stating to "all parties" that he would, in the name of equity, vote "no" if any one of those directly involved, including the army, objected.[43]

Strangely, after lunch, Joe Welch returned without Robert Stevens. The secretary, supposedly suffering from a virus infection, had gone home. However genuine his illness, his absence was convenient, protecting him from another stressful encounter and freeing him to consult the Pentagon and the White House. When pressed about whether Stevens was still opposed to the Dirksen resolution, Welch stalled, saying he would try to reach the secretary by phone. Mundt offered Welch the use of a private phone, but Welch preferred a pay phone, probably to avoid anyone listening in on the conversation and provide an opportunity to consult others besides Stevens.

When Welch returned, he stated, "Mr. Chairman, due to the wonderful invention of television, the Secretary was able to follow what had happened." Stevens was therefore "ready to talk." "Wonderful!" exclaimed Mundt. "And what was Mr. Stevens ready to say?" Welch said, in effect, that Stevens had said "No." When the perplexed Mundt sought clarification, Welch declined to answer for Stevens, so he left to make another pay phone call.

When Welch returned, he quoted Stevens: "I continue in my view that the proposed resolution would not result in fairness." The vote was three nos by the Democrats, three yeses by the Republicans except for Mundt, who kept his commitment: "The chair votes no. The motion fails." Hagerty noted later in the day that the army's negative response "came [as] a great surprise to everyone on the Hill and at the White House—not to Sherman Adams and myself." That meant it was no shock to the president.[44]

Roy Cohn believed that the administration had lost, in Dirksen, "a valuable ally in the hearings." He later recalled seeing the senator running his fingers through his hair in obvious distress. "Roy," he said, "I've just about had it with those people. I'm fed up with them. I offered them a chance to get off the hook and they were stupid enough not to take it."[45]

The next day, Hagerty recorded that Ike was "getting pretty sick and tired of McCarthy." When Jerry Persons argued that Stevens had "made a mistake" in not ending the hearings, the president "disagreed violently." He gave Stevens credit for standing firm. "I think Stevens did exactly right," he said. "Here he had been on the stand for thirteen days and if [this] plan [had] been successful the other witnesses, except McCarthy, would have been testifying behind closed doors. McCarthy would then be at liberty to come out of the hearings and tell reporters anything he wanted even though they had [a] transcript. He would have [a] forum while [the] Army would not. Anyway, I'm glad the Army is fighting him right down the line." That candid rhetoric reflected presidential veto number three.[46]

There may have been a fourth. On November 10, 1979, a young attorney, Ann M. Lousin, was seated next to Robert Stevens at a dinner to organize the Chicago chapter of the Supreme Court Historical Society. Lousin, a graduate of Welch's alma mater, Grinnell College in Iowa, engaged Stevens in animated conversation over drinks and dinner. Stevens told Lousin that late in the Army-McCarthy hearings, McCarthy had personally contacted him and asked for a meeting. He had asked Stevens to consider announcing that "for the security of the country, we are ending the televised hearings." Stevens had taken the proposition to Eisenhower, who had listened. Then Ike had slapped the desk and shouted, "No! Now we have the bastard right where we want him!"[47]

CHAPTER 14

PROTECTING THE PRESIDENT

The morning of Wednesday, May 12, Joseph and Stewart Alsop's column identified "two great dangers" confronting the Eisenhower administration: "the grim crisis in Indochina" and "the domestic political crisis that is currently spilling over in the McCarthy-Army hearings." Though Indochina dominated the opening questions at the president's news conference that morning, the reporters quickly turned to Joe McCarthy.[1]

One journalist asked about the attorney general's ruling that Senator McCarthy had released classified FBI information "without authorization." Eisenhower responded, "Well, the question is of two parts. One involved the Senator"—as close as Ike ever came to using McCarthy's name—but he declined to comment "on that particular incident." Otherwise, he called any release of classified information "reprehensible," especially "involving the security of our country." Robert Spivack asked if the president thought that members of "this McCarthy spy network" should "be regarded as security risks?" Ike snapped, "That is a question I don't believe I will answer."[2]

JANUARY 21 RISES AGAIN

Henry Cabot Lodge was worried. On May 7, he wrote an "eyes only" letter to the president. Joe Welch had informed him that he might be called to testify "concerning a meeting which I attended in January in Herbert Brownell's office." He believed that such testimony "would be utterly destructive of the integrity of the presidential office" and a violation of "the spirit of the Constitution" to require testimony from a presidential adviser. Lodge intended "to decline to give testimony in that capacity." Eisenhower assured Lodge that his position was "exactly correct" and he was certain that Herbert Brownell "would agree with this view."[3]

Discussion of the January 21 meeting was something the White House wanted to avoid at all costs. It had included close advisers to the president: Brownell, Rogers, Sherman Adams, Lodge, and Gerald Morgan. That gathering had, in effect, launched the secret campaign against McCarthy, commencing the compilation of the privileges sought for G. David Schine and leading to the publicized report that had spawned the Army-McCarthy hearings. It had been, in Lodge's words, Eisenhower's "first move" against McCarthy. McCarthy knew about that meeting, and it was only a matter of time until he exploited it. The drama now would revolve around the effort to avoid revealing the contents of that meeting and any implication of the president's involvement.[4]

John Adams had also been present at that meeting. As he prepared to testify, he was described by one reporter as "a man who does not get enough sleep." Adams was a bundle of nerves. He had been convinced he was being followed and had begun switching cabs and walking through alleys. "Everyone thought their home phones were being tapped," he recalled. Adams once accosted a man who was rummaging through his desk. He received anonymous, threatening phone calls, including a bomb threat.[5]

On May 12, Adams opened Pandora's box, implicating the president and his adviser. Before testifying, he counseled with Struve Hensel. "I'm worried about it," he told Hensel. "I don't see any way

I can keep the White House out of it if they ask the right questions." Hensel, who had accused McCarthy of "barefaced lies," roared, "Pull 'em all in! Why should you be stuck out there all by yourself? Hell, pull 'em all in!" That is precisely what Adams did.[6]

Adams began his testimony in the firm belief that "the Republican majority was more interested in saving McCarthy than in establishing the truth." Worried that he could be charged with perjury, Adams planned to "recount, day by day, the abuse heaped on me by Cohn." He detailed Cohn's constant agitation about Fort Monmouth and his unrelenting pressure to grant David Schine long weekends off at Fort Dix. What had generated headlines, he later recalled, "was not Cohn's abuse or McCarthy's silence. It was my revelation, at the end of the day, that the White House played a role in the fight against McCarthy." Adams described "a sudden stir in the committee room" when, referring to the January 21 meeting, he revealed the names of the people in attendance. The newspapers highlighted Adams's testimony that "Governor Adams asked me if I had a written record of all of the incidents with reference to Private Schine." When Adams said he had none, the president's chief of staff "thought I should prepare one." John Adams also testified that, afterward, participants in the meeting had visited Dirksen, Potter, and Mundt. That revelation upset the Democrats on the subcommittee. A demand to subpoena the January 21 participants was now inevitable.[7]

"DON'T TALK ANYMORE ABOUT THAT MEETING"

On May 13, Jim Hagerty noted in his diary that Eisenhower "feels very strongly" on the issue of subpoenas for subordinates and had declared, "This is one we will fight out right up and down the line." Ike had ruminated whether to send Sherman Adams before the subcommittee "to give his name, his title and then refuse to answer all questions under Presidential order" or dispatch Herbert Brownell with the same message. For Eisenhower, that was the political equivalent of a prisoner of war providing name, rank, and serial number.

"McCarthy," Hagerty noted, "may be bluffing but if [an] attempt is made to subpoena White House personnel, we will fight it."[8]

The president took two actions on May 13 in preparation for the looming showdown. First, he wrote Secretary of Defense Wilson, ordering him to instruct all employees who testified before the Government Operations Subcommittee "not to testify to any conversations or communications, or produce any documents" involving "official transactions between an employee of the Department of Defense and any person either within that Department or any other part of the Executive Branch of the Government." Wilson was traveling in the Far East, but that letter would empower Acting Secretary Robert B. Anderson to silence John Adams about the details of the January 21 meeting.[9]

The president's other action—a secret one—was also channeled through Anderson, who wrote Army Secretary Robert Stevens:

> At the instruction of The Honorable Sherman Adams, the Department of the Army is to deliver at once to the Honorable Fred A. Seaton, Assistant Secretary of Defense, for his prompt transmittal to the White House each and all stenographic notes, transcriptions, or other records or memoranda concerning conversations and communications between any of the principals of the Army-McCarthy hearings, employed within this Department or within the Executive Branch of the Government, regarding any matters which are involved in the subject of inquiry before the Subcommittee of the Senate Committee on Government Operations.

Thus began the impoundment of documents that Fred Seaton would thereafter retain.[10]

The issue of the January 21 meeting haunted Eisenhower's cabinet meeting on the morning of Friday, May 14. Ike said he was "quite clear in his own mind" that testimony should not be allowed regarding "security information or other basic national interests" and—the linchpin—"personal advice exchanged between superior and subordinate in the Executive Branch." Such advice was "a privileged matter," and cabinet members should cite his orders against testifying "about advice offered in a personal relationship." Referring to the January 21 meeting, he said that a subpoena might be issued for the president's staff. Though Ike wanted "to avoid a major fight between the Executive and the Legislative" based on "the captious challenge of one Senator," he drew a constitutional line: the president would protect "the privacy of personal advice."[11]

That morning, as John Adams prepared to depart the Pentagon for Capitol Hill, Fred Seaton called. "Don't talk anymore about that meeting. These are orders. Written instructions will follow." Adams's anxiety escalated; while he was testifying on May 13, his car, parked in front of his apartment building, had been stolen. Now, on May 14, he was being ordered to go back to the hearing and refuse to talk.[12]

At the hearings, the senators—especially the Democrats, angry that the Republican senators had known about the January 21 meeting and they had not—were ready to pounce. One reporter called the scene at the May 14 hearing "the strangest since the hearings began." Another concluded that the administration's instruction to John Adams not to talk about the meeting "appeared likely to unite the committee Republicans and Democrats in a challenge to the Executive Branch."[13]

Stuart Symington opened that confrontation. "Why was Ambassador Lodge at the meeting on January 21?" he asked. Adams responded, "I don't know, sir. I did not arrange for his presence." At that moment, Joe Welch objected, stating Anderson's order: "This was a high-level discussion of the executive department and this witness has been instructed not to testify as to the interchange of views on people at that high level at that meeting."[14]

Symington asked where Adams had gotten his instructions to refuse to talk. Adams said he had received them from Acting Secretary of Defense Robert B. Anderson; he did not mention Fred Seaton. "Clearly the finger was beginning to point at the White House," Adams recalled. "A constitutional confrontation loomed." Adams himself had no doubt about the real origins of the order: "I had been gagged, of course, because the White House wanted to stay out of this unseemly brawl."[15]

Senator McClellan demanded that the witnesses at the January 21 meeting "be subpoenaed and brought here to tell what they know about it." He wondered if there had been "someone higher" than John Adams or Robert Stevens "directing their actions" and whether McCarthy and his aides had been "smeared." Symington agreed that the January 21 meeting had been "perhaps the most important conference of all because it is where much, if not most of all this business started."[16]

Suddenly, Everett Dirksen announced that he wanted to testify about the visit John Adams and Gerald Morgan had made to his office on January 21. Adams endured "a moment of terror." Dirksen, to Adams's surprise, had kind words for both Morgan and him, but McCarthy smelled blood. He asked Dirksen if that had been "the moment of blackmail," when Adams had threatened to release the Schine report unless the committee quashed the subpoenas for loyalty board members. Adams, "paralyzed with fright," thought he "was going to have a heart attack." He saw himself being "indicted for perjury . . . Dirksen had only to say yes to McCarthy, and I could go to jail."

Dirksen, Adams recounted, "went right up to the edge—and pulled back." He found his memory "slightly vague" and was not sure he had learned "that a report was going to be circulated." Adams had been saved by a single word: "report"; at that point, there had, strictly speaking, been no report, only a verbal account. Mundt and Potter testified similarly. All three Republican senators declined to validate McCarthy's claim that Adams's sharing the allegations about Schine constituted "blackmail."[17]

"I'LL FIGHT THEM TOOTH AND NAIL"

When gearing up for a major action, Ike often resorted to golf. At midafternoon on Friday, May 14, he and Jim Hagerty headed for Burning Tree Country Club. There they discussed the status of his legislative program, the situation in Indochina, and the Army-McCarthy hearings—especially Senator McClellan's "threat to subpoena White House staff members and bring them before the Committee." The president, Hagerty recalled, "would not stand for this one minute." Those were his "confidential advisors," and "Congress had absolutely no right to ask them to testify in any way, shape or form about the advice they were giving to him at any time on any subject." Ike thundered, "If they want to make a test of this principle, I'll fight them tooth and nail up and down the country. It is a matter of principle with me and I will never permit it." He said he would again "tell all members of the staff to keep out of this controversy, to have nothing to say on it." The president decreed that that Hagerty would be "the spokesman on all questions dealing with McCarthy." [18]

The next day, the newspapers highlighted the "gag order" the White House had imposed on John Adams. William Lawrence noted that "efforts to find out whether President Eisenhower himself gave the orders for Mr. Adams not to testify were unavailing." Jim Hagerty had responded "No comment" to that "and all other questions dealing with the McCarthy-Army controversy."

Meanwhile, Eisenhower made a decision; the executive privilege order Herbert Brownell and William Rogers had been refining since late 1953 would be issued on Monday morning, May 17. He and Mrs. Eisenhower departed for Camp David on Saturday morning, leaving the team—Sherman Adams, Brownell, Assistant Attorney General Lee Rankin, and other White Houses advisers—to put finishing touches on the order. Sherman Adams scheduled breakfast with the president and the team for 7:15 a.m. Monday morning to review the document. [19]

That weekend, Walter Lippmann called McCarthy's threat to subpoena White House advisers another episode in "one of the great constitutional crises of our history" involving "flagrant and systematic trespass upon the constitutional prerogatives of the President, and it goes on and on because he does not defend his rights." Arthur Krock wrote that "the issue has been brought close to the President's person by the revelation that John G. Adams is under high Executive instruction to withhold certain facts that the entire subcommittee considers to be relevant." However, the columnist concluded, "As yet the President is aloof." [20]

Behind the scenes, Eisenhower was anything but aloof. An unnamed Republican Senate leader stated that he expected President Eisenhower to prevent his advisors from testifying; then "the fat will be in the fire." The May 16 *New York Times* quoted Karl Mundt to the effect that the Eisenhower administration "might be on sound ground" in refusing to give details about the January 21 meeting. McCarthy blustered, insisting that it was "urgent" for the subcommittee to "get a complete story about the Justice Department's part" in the January 21 meeting; he supported McClellan's demand that the participants be subpoenaed. Mundt again demonstrated his feeble grasp of the situation, predicting that the hearings could now "move a lot more rapidly" and end "in the next ten days or less." [21]

On Monday morning, the president met with his advisers over breakfast to review the written order. Ike read the letter, approved it, and said he would sign it at 8:30 and send it immediately to Robert Anderson, the acting secretary of defense, authorizing Hagerty to release it to the press at 9:00 a.m. The attorney general's ten-page memorandum, designed to accompany the letter, traced the precedents for executive privilege from George Washington through Harry Truman. The Republican congressional leaders were scheduled to meet right after Eisenhower signed the letter. The president said he would present the letter to them as an "accomplished fact" so they could not oppose it or insist on changes.

At that meeting, Eisenhower grumbled that he had attempted to stay out of the "damn business on the Hill"; however, it was "the threatened subpoena of his confidential advisors that made it necessary for him to act." He explained his action, which was not open for discussion: "I have issued instructions to the Secretary of Defense which order him to keep confidential any advisory discussions in the administrative side of this government." The president was blunt: "Any man who testifies as to the advice he gave me won't be working for me that night." [22]

EXECUTIVE PRIVILEGE

The same morning, John Adams prepared to step into an army car outside the Pentagon to transport him to the hearings. He was handed an envelope with two documents in it: the president's letter and the attorney general's memorandum, with instructions to read the letter at the hearings. Adams resentfully concluded that the president "was invoking Executive Privilege to shut me up." To be precise, it was to shut him up about the January 21 meeting. Eisenhower had not mentioned that meeting to the congressional leaders. That was because—something the president was loath to admit—it had been his meeting, although he had not been present. However much the White House sought to deny it, that meeting had generated the decision to develop the Cohn-Schine report that had eventually led to the Army-McCarthy hearings. Now the president and the attorney general had skillfully buried that fact in constitutional principle.[23]

However, when Adams took the stand to testify, the hearing was already in turmoil. That was because Eisenhower and Brownell had hatched a one-two punch designed to throw McCarthy off balance. That morning, Brownell had stated that criminal prosecution might be instituted against those involved in the "preparation and dissemination" of the fraudulent letter from J. Edgar Hoover. That was a shot across McCarthy's bow, designed to intimidate him just before Adams presented the president's executive privilege letter.[24]

When the smoke cleared, Adams read the one-page letter aloud. Eisenhower bowed to congressional prerogatives whereby, if requested, departments or agencies must furnish relevant information to committees. The letter presented an elegant separation-of-powers argument: that "the persons entrusted with power in any one of the three great branches of Government shall not encroach upon the authority confident to the others. The ultimate responsibility for the conduct of the Executive Branch rests with the President."

"Throughout our history," the letter continued, "the President has withheld information whenever he found that what was sought was confidential or its disclosure would be incompatible with the public interest or jeopardize the safety of the Nation." Eisenhower stressed the necessity for executive-branch personnel "to be completely candid in advising with each other on official matters" and said it was improper "that any of their conversations or communications, or any documents or reproductions, concerning such advice be disclosed." Therefore, the secretary of defense was ordered, regarding the issues now before the subcommittee, to instruct those employees that "they are not to testify to any such conversations or communications or to produce any such documents or reproductions. This principle must be maintained regardless of who would be benefited by such disclosures."

The president concluded with a carefully parsed paragraph that exempted from his order communications directly *between* "any of the principals"—McCarthy, Cohn, Stevens, Adams, Hensel, and Carr—in the Army-McCarthy hearings. It clearly left out the participants in the January 21 meeting, including John Adams, who, on that particular date, had been acting in an advisory capacity. When he finished reading, Adams looked up and stated, "The letter is signed by Dwight D. Eisenhower." A terrible silence ensued. The president's bombshell had completely disrupted the hearings. The presidential hand was no longer "hidden." [25]

Karl Mundt was upset. Later, in his unpublished manuscript, the South Dakota senator complained that, as result of the president's letter, "the lid was put on." John Adams, he wrote, had been put "under wraps and the wheels of the investigation ground to a slow halt." He recalled that he had "had a feeling we were shadow boxing, that the witnesses who should be testifying were not there, that the Secretary of the Army, Mr. Stevens, and John Adams were mere puppets and somewhere in the dim misty background were the real actors pulling the strings and whispering the cues." [26]

Years later, Roy Cohn, near death, contended that Eisenhower's action had proved that the army had not acted independently: "The White House was quarterbacking this game to get Joe and had been all along." He asserted, "Under the guise of protecting the separation of powers . . . President Eisenhower made the Mafia rule of *omerta*"—the gangster's "code of silence"—into "a constitutional principle." Eisenhower had decreed that "nobody in the executive branch was permitted to testify to Congress about anything he or she discussed within the executive branch." Cohn's verdict: "Nothing close to this had ever been done before by a President of the United States." The president who had declared, "I won't get into the gutter with that guy," had "gutted the Constitution."[27]

In the face of the president's action, both the Democrats and Republicans on the hearing committee floundered. Senator McClellan suggested that, as a result, "these hearings are terminated." Dirksen could not see how the committee could reach a conclusion "with the proof incomplete." McCarthy felt blindsided: "I must admit that I am somewhat at a loss to know what to do." He railed against this "Iron Curtain." "Who," he demanded, "who is responsible for the issuance of the smear that has held this committee up for weeks and weeks and weeks and has allowed Communists to continue . . . with a razor poised over the jugular vein of the nation?" Then he stalked out of the hearing room.[28]

When McCarthy returned, he demanded a week's recess to figure out how to respond to this new development. A contentious subcommittee executive session lasted from 1:30 p.m. to 3:00, with Dirksen finally moving to recess the hearings until the following Monday, May 24, in the hope that the president's order could be clarified or changed. Potter seconded, insisting that the vote did not mean "this would end the hearing." The motion passed 4 to 3 on a party-line vote.[29]

When Cohn later asked McCarthy why he thought Eisenhower would go so far, the senator replied, "Too much was coming out and he had to stop the show." According to Cohn (and confirmed by Sherman Adams), Everett Dirksen had gone to the White House "to try to convince the President to change his mind." Eisenhower, Cohn wrote, "refused to allow us to establish for the record the full truth about that fateful January 21 meeting when plans were drawn to destroy Joe McCarthy." For all his biases, his analysis was largely accurate.[30]

Also—no small matter to Dwight Eisenhower—May 17, 1954, was the day that the Supreme Court, in *Brown v. Board of Education*, ruled that racial segregation in schools was unconstitutional.

SENDING THE SECRETARY INTO BATTLE

There was no great outcry by the public or Congress against Eisenhower's order. It had thrown the McCarthy forces into such disarray that they desperately needed the recess to regroup. Senator Symington called the postponement a "transparent device" to conclude the inquiry, but Chairman Mundt denied that the recess "even remotely implies a discontinuation of the hearings." McCarthy complained, "We can't possibly resume the hearings unless we are allowed to get all the facts." On May 18, Jim Hagerty, when asked if the president might modify his order, replied tersely that "the President issued his letter yesterday—period." Asked if the president's letter had been intended to terminate the hearings, he snapped, "I can think of nothing that would be a more silly question." [31]

Senator McClellan denied that any failure to modify the president's order would mean the hearings would be "terminated." "My position is the same as always," he stated. "The hearings should not end until all the principals have been heard." A primary "principal," Joe McCarthy, had not yet testified. McCarthy continued to maintain, "I think the President will rescind the order," a prospect *The Washington Post* called "unlikely." [32]

Once again, Eisenhower did not intend to stay in town to answer questions. By midday on May 18, he was airborne for Charlotte, North Carolina, to participate in the ceremonies celebrating the 189th anniversary of the signing of the Mecklenburg Declaration of Independence—an oft-disputed precursor of the 1776 declaration—and to celebrate Armed Forces Week. On the way to the airport, he ordered Hagerty to manage the fallout from his order so it would appear constitutional, giving no hint of the real significance of the meeting in Brownell's office. He "did not intend to modify in the slightest degree his order to the Defense Department" but wanted the January 21 meeting framed as strictly limited to discussion of subpoenas for loyalty board members, "not to take over from Stevens the conduct of the investigation." Any implication that his order was intended to close down the hearings was "just stupid and silly," but he would be firm that "confidential advice" from his advisers would not be provided to Congress.

Eisenhower took a guest with him on the presidential plane that day: Robert Stevens. The president did not intend to give the unpredictable army secretary a chance to stay in Washington and talk to reporters. When it was announced that Stevens would accompany the president, Hagerty observed that the reporters "did not believe this was the only reason—and they were right." Hagerty provided the press with a cosmetic reason for the secretary's presence: that the president wanted to give "public support to him by having him as [a] guest on [the] plane and appearing with him on [the] platform." However, Ike had a confidential plan that he, Hagerty, and Stevens would hammer out in the privacy of the presidential aircraft.

Eisenhower deemed it politically imperative to distance himself from the January 21 meeting. He delegated Hagerty to negotiate with Stevens about "his willingness to issue a statement on his own behalf." Eisenhower sealed the deal in person. "The President and I," Hagerty chronicled, "talked to Stevens alone on the plane and outlined this plan and procedure." Like the dispassionate commander in World War II who had sent men into battle to die, Eisenhower chose to deploy a bureaucratic foot soldier to take enemy fire.[33]

Once in Charlotte, in return for that commitment, President Eisenhower gave Stevens the admiring public attention he craved. The secretary, Hagerty noted, got "a big hand" when the president introduced him. Ike "supported him to the hilt with photographs eating together" and by shaking hands with him at both the Charlotte and Washington airports. Upon Ike's return to the White House, Sherman Adams and Hagerty met with Eisenhower to discuss whether to hold a press conference on May 19. They decided to go ahead; otherwise, in Hagerty's words, it "would look as if the President were trying to run away from the situation."[34]

At 10:30 a.m. on May 19, Eisenhower strode purposefully into the news conference and went quickly to questions. Regarding the *Brown v. Board of Education* decision, the president said, "The Supreme Court has spoken and I am sworn to uphold the constitutional processes in this country; and I will obey." He intended that as a soldierly statement of duty, without elaboration. Eisenhower was not about to climb out on another major constitutional limb only forty-eight hours after invoking executive privilege in the Army-McCarthy hearings.

Eisenhower was asked if his letter invoking executive privilege would make it "impossible to get at the whole truth in the controversy" and, if so, whether he would "rescind or at least relax that order." He was prepared: "First I have no intention whatsoever of relaxing or rescinding the order, because it is a very moderate and proper statement of the division of powers between the Executive and the Legislative." He was "astonished" that anyone would suggest that the order "be used as a reason or excuse for calling off hearings." It was, in effect, Eisenhower's fifth veto of any attempt to end the hearings.

Therefore, as he had planned, Eisenhower resolutely asserted that the imminent subpoenas for loyalty board members were "the purpose of the January 21 meeting," camouflaging his personal involvement. "They," he began, distancing himself from the issue, "asked an advisor or two of mine to be there." He noted that the meeting had been in the attorney general's office, not the White House. Ike contended that his May 17 order had avoided sidetracking that meeting into "a relationship between the President and his advisors that had no possible connection with this investigation." He asserted that he had simply been trying to keep the investigation "on the rails."

The president repeated the word he had carefully parsed at his May 5 news conference, hoping the investigation would be "concluded" soon but "conclusively so that the principals tell their stories openly and fully." He declined to specify which "principals" he was citing—again avoiding McCarthy's name—but noted that only "some of them have been questioned."

Then the president revealed the bargain he had negotiated on the plane to North Carolina: Secretary Robert Stevens would issue a statement "about the disassociation between his administration of the Army and this meeting of last January 21st." When asked whether the authority for the army's response to the investigation had "passed from Stevens to a higher level at the January 21st meeting," Eisenhower stated that "at that meeting there was no attempt made, there was nothing brought up that could intimate such a thing." For a reporter listening closely, that comment revealed that the president knew precisely what had transpired in the attorney general's office on January 21.

Gould Lincoln of *The Washington Star* asked the big question: "Mr. President, would it be correct to say that the White House OK'd the preparation and submission of the Army report on Senator McCarthy and Mr. Cohn?" Eisenhower's blunt response: "It would not." Since the "preparation and submission" of that report had taken place in the Pentagon, the president's statement, however misleading, sounded superficially credible.

After discussion of the Supreme Court decision in *Brown*, David Sentner of Hearst Newspapers peeled one last layer off the January 21 question: "Mr. President, did you say whether you were aware in advance of the calling of the so-called conference on January 21st?" Eisenhower stalled: "The what?" Sentner repeated the question. Suddenly Ike's memory failed him—although Herbert Brownell revealed in his memoirs that he had discussed the January 21 meeting with the president both in advance and afterward. "Well," said the president evasively, "I wouldn't answer it in any event because, after all, we do come to a place here where you can't go into detail; but my memory wouldn't serve me anyway. I couldn't remember such a thing." Whatever his flaws, Eisenhower did not have a bad memory.

Asked for his judgment of the impact if the hearings were called off at this time, Ike reinforced veto number five: "Well, I don't think the facts have been brought out." He repeated his earlier statement, word for word, that he still wanted to hear "all of the principals

telling their story." Though he wanted "to see this thing settled conclusively," it needed to be done in a manner "so that we do know
the facts" and "let the chips fall where they may." [35]

ORCHESTRATING A COVER-UP

Jim Hagerty called this press conference "one of the best" the
president had held, "forceful and to the point." He called Herbert
Brownell immediately to report on what their boss had said. "That
makes my job a lot easier," the attorney general responded. Brownell
was expecting Senator Mundt and Ray Jenkins shortly for lunch, a
meeting undoubtedly arranged as part of the Eisenhower strategy.
Hagerty's diary reveals that he had already phoned a recording of
the president's remarks to Fred Seaton "so he could get up Stevens'
statement saying [the] Army had sole responsibility." [36]

The operation was typical of General Ike—carefully timed, with
near-military precision. A half hour after the president's press conference had begun, Stevens had been scheduled to deliver his statement. Mundt and Jenkins would lunch with the attorney general
soon thereafter, allowing sufficient time for them to hear about the
president's and the secretary's statements.

At 11:30, Robert Stevens released his carefully composed statement, drafted by Fred Seaton and designed to get his commander
in chief off the hook. The secretary began, "I wish to make it perfectly plain that the decision and the acts on the part of the Army
concerning the controversy presently being heard by the Senate
Subcommittee were the decisions and acts of the Department of the
Army alone. At no time did the Army or I as its Secretary receive
any orders from anyone in respect to the preparation or presentation of the Army's case. Specifically, the conference of January 21
was only for the purpose of obtaining an interpretation of existing
directives." [37]

Later, Brownell called Hagerty to report that Mundt and Jenkins "had dropped their request for modification of [the] Executive Order" upon hearing of the president's remarks and Stevens'

statement that "the Army had sole responsibility" and that no "higher ups" had been in charge. The two men had left "in good spirits," and, Brownell informed Hagerty, "they were in favor of the Administration, at least when they walked out of my door." [38]

Did the president lie to the press on May 19, 1954? Yes, he did. The best that can be said is that it was a strategic deceit. He was determined not to give McCarthy grounds for making the president, not himself, the issue. Otherwise, the resulting scandal could have threatened Eisenhower's presidency and provoked a constitutional crisis. Any attempt by a president to destroy the prestige of a prominent US senator risked violation of the separation of powers—the very constitutional doctrine Eisenhower had invoked in his May 17 executive order. The newspapers the next day quoted Eisenhower's saying "Let the chips fall where they may." Clearly, he did not want them falling anywhere near the Oval Office.

Stevens's statement defused the efforts to pin responsibility for the Schine report on the White House or prematurely end the hearings. Karl Mundt's public response was that the hearings "will resume Monday—period." He appeared to accept the premise that the army alone had been responsible for the charges made against McCarthy and his aides. [39]

JOE MCCARTHY IN TROUBLE

That McCarthy was in trouble was undeniable; he had been tumbling toward political purgatory since March 11, when the Schine report had been released. By May 24, his "unfavorable" rating in the Gallup Poll had risen to 49 percent, with 35 percent favorable. At that point, his narrow path to redemption rested on his own testimony. During the one-week recess, McCarthy searched almost desperately for an issue that would have traction. He claimed that he had attempted to see the president on his issues with the army between January 22 and February 24; Jim Hagerty checked and told reporters, "I know of no request by the Senator at that time for an appointment with the President." When the senator criticized the administration's foreign policy in a speech, Eisenhower ranted angrily about Republican senators who lacked "the guts to defend the Administration—Boy! We really need a few good hatchet men on our side up there!"[40]

The afternoon of May 20, *New York Times* reporter William Lawrence dropped in on Hagerty to inform him, off the record, that McCarthy had charged that, by refusing to allow confidential advisers to testify, the administration was "resorting to the Fifth Amendment." Hagerty hoped that the news would make Ike so mad that the president would let him "burn McCarthy's ears off." However, Hagerty's temper cooled, and at the next morning's staff meeting, he reported the president's decision "not to answer McCarthy's Fifth Amendment charges." Ike he said, "did not want to have daily arguments with McCarthy from the White House." Hagerty echoed the president's persistent argument: "That would just build him up and would be what he would want."[41]

In the Sunday, May 23, *New York Times*, Lawrence, perhaps influenced by Hagerty, emphasized that McCarthy's potential criminal problems arising from his use of the fraudulent letter from J. Edgar Hoover. McCarthy's "Fifth Amendment" charge got little traction; neither did his innuendo that the administration "must have something to hide." Back in Wisconsin, he warned the president in a speech that continued hearings would result in the "suicide" of the Republican Party. McCarthy got laughs when he characterized the president as "an honest man" who "has millions of things to do, and should not be tied up in the question of who shined Schine's shoes."[42]

PERJURY?

The consensus quickly emerged that Eisenhower was constitutionally within his rights to invoke executive privilege. Arthur Krock declared the action "so clearly within his constitutional province" that the subcommittee members had "quickly left the Senator from Wisconsin alone" in his demand for subpoenas for White House advisers. "The Secretary's assertion of full responsibility," he wrote, "both before and after the high Executive conference [on January 21], and the President's certification of this statement, got the subcommittee's inquiry back on the track." Krock knew better than to accept Stevens's statement literally; back on February 26, Richard Nixon had told Krock—off the record—about a report "two inches thick" that Eisenhower had approved using to get Roy Cohn fired. Perhaps Krock, like other journalists at the time, believed that the political demise of a demagogue like McCarthy justified casting a blind eye toward Eisenhower's deception.[43]

The resumption of the hearings on May 24 was uncomfortable for Robert Stevens. The public statement the secretary had issued on May 19 was one thing; testifying similarly under oath was another. Prior to the recess, he had flatly testified, "I don't know who decided to prepare [the Schine report]." When McCarthy had asked if the secretary had ordered the Schine report allegations distributed to Congress and the public, Stevens had stated, "No, sir; I did not order them put out."

But, John Adams recalled, Stevens "had to eat his words." Stevens stated, "The responsibility for these charges being put out is mine, completely." Thus he fulfilled his secret agreement with Eisenhower. McCarthy hounded Stevens, declaring that the secretary either had a "bad memory" or was guilty of "perjury." When Stevens suggested that some of John Adams's activities related to the Schine case constituted independent actions, McCarthy pounced: "Do you expect anyone with an ounce of brains to believe that?"[44]

Walter Lippmann's column the following week stripped the artifice off the administration's charade. Secretary Stevens, he opined, had to have been acting "under the authority of Secretary Wilson and the President." "What then," he asked, "was the point of allowing McCarthy to muddle up the hearings and call Stevens a liar with all the hullabaloo about whether Stevens had or had not had orders from higher up?" The columnist found it incredible that Stevens had been "treated as if perhaps he were somebody else's Secretary of the Army."[45]

John Adams, although uneasy, did his part that Monday afternoon. When the senators asked whether Sherman Adams had ordered him to prepare the chronology, Adams called it a "suggestion" rather than an "order." That day, following the hearing, he went to Stevens's office to discuss his frustrations, but the secretary gave him "a drill sergeant's dressing down" for complaining about his lot. Adams left the meeting feeling depressed. "I was alone now," he wrote in his memoirs. "Seaton avoided me" and was always "busy."

John Adams believed that Karl Mundt, his fellow South Dakotan, wanted to charge him with perjury. When he completed his testimony on May 24, Mundt recalled "a practice the chair had followed back in 1948." That was when Mundt had asked Alger Hiss, later imprisoned for perjury, a question he then repeated to Adams: "I would like to ask you before you are dismissed and unsworn whether you feel that you have now had a complete and full and fair opportunity to testify before this Committee?"[46]

CHAPTER 15

"NO SENSE OF DECENCY?"

At the end of the day on May 24, the Army–McCarthy hearings finally returned to the subject that had launched the inquiry in the first place: the privileges sought for Private G. David Schine. Major General Cornelius Ryan, the commanding general at Fort Dix, testified that Schine had been treated as "a man apart" from other draftees. The private had been granted sixteen weekend passes for alleged "committee business," compared to the average of three or four for other draftees.

DROPPING CHARGES

Then, unexpectedly, over the objections of Joe Welch and the Democrats, the Republicans voted to dismiss the charges against subcommittee director Frank Carr and Struve Hensel due to insufficient evidence. Hensel had been included based on McCarthy's allegations that the Pentagon counsel had profited illegally while serving as a procurement office with the navy. The army had included Carr in the hope that he might be more forthcoming in testimony than McCarthy. The decision to drop the charges was another transparent attempt to truncate the hearings before McCarthy testified.

Jim Hagerty believed the Republicans had "just cut their throats" by that action, and Eisenhower agreed. "If they were going to drop the charges on Hensel and Carr," the president fumed, "they should have made McCarthy publicly admit then and there that he was withdrawing his charges. . . . Anything less is just stupid and cowardly." Hagerty believed the Republicans had taken the action to get McCarthy "off the spot" because Carr might "break down" and "spill a lot of beans." Ike was disgusted. "I hope you tell all our people at the White House," he said, "that it's about time they stopped trying to have me work with guys like Mundt and the rest. They're not for us, they never were, and never will be." [1]

The next morning, Hagerty learned that Everett Dirksen, who had made so many attempts to shorten the hearings, was the architect of the decision to drop the charges. According to Charles Potter, Dirksen, who had met with the president the previous Friday, had told his colleagues they should dismiss the charges because "that was the way the President wanted it." Furious, Eisenhower denied the story and dispatched congressional aide Jack Martin to demand that Dirksen retract his statement. Ike had stated at his news conference that the hearings should end "only after all the principals had an opportunity to tell their story openly and fully." For the president, those "principals" included Carr and Hensel, both of whom the army's attorneys were anxious to have testify. [2]

Hagerty called what Dirksen had done a "squeeze play," and the president agreed. To the press, Dirksen denied that dismissal of the charges by the Republicans was a "whitewash." *The Washington Post* concluded that dropping the charges proved that the subcommittee, "despite Mr. Mundt's temporary elevation to the chairmanship, remains under the influence of Senator McCarthy." [3]

JOE MCCARTHY AND ADOLF HITLER

On May 4, McCarthy had produced without authorization a letter allegedly written by J. Edgar Hoover, placing the senator in jeopardy of possible criminal charges. When Senator McClellan suggested that both McCarthy and his informant "might be guilty of a crime,"

McCarthy blustered, "If anyone wants to indict me, they can go right ahead." Then the senator took a momentous step; he challenged government employees to disobey their superiors and report directly to him—a clear shot at the president's May 17 executive order. He asserted that the oath government employees took "to protect and defend this country against all enemies, foreign and domestic" was a commitment that "towers far above any Presidential secrecy directive." The 2 million federal employees, he declared, should deem it "their duty to give us any information which they have about graft, corruption, communism, treason" and disregard any "loyalty to a superior officer."[4]

Eisenhower was outraged when he heard about McCarthy's challenge to federal workers. However, his initial response the morning of May 28 was coldly methodical. He drafted a statement that was issued in the name of Attorney General Brownell. The statement, released at the White House at 11:00 a.m., declared, without mentioning the senator's name, "The executive branch has sole and fundamental responsibility to enforce laws and presidential orders. . . . That responsibility cannot be usurped by any individual who may seek to set himself above the laws of our land, or override orders of the President of the United States to federal employees of the executive branch of government."[5]

Afterward, Eisenhower called Hagerty into the Oval Office and vented his rage at "the complete arrogance of McCarthy." Pacing behind his desk, he spoke in "rapid fire order." McCarthy's challenge to federal employees to disobey their superiors, he thundered, "amounts to nothing but a wholesale subversion of public service." Eisenhower delivered what was, for him, the ultimate condemnation. "McCarthy," he said, "is making exactly the same plea of loyalty to him that Hitler made to the German people. Both tried to set up personal loyalty within the Government while both were using the pretense of fighting Communism. McCarthy is trying deliberately to subvert the people we have in Government, people who are sworn to obey the law, the Constitution and their superior officers. I think this is the most disloyal act we have ever had by anyone in the Government of the United States."

Following that angry outburst, Eisenhower cooled off, sat down at his desk, and speculated as to whether the question might come up at his next news conference; Hagerty thought it would. The rage resurfaced: "Make sure it does because I'll tell you now what I'm going to say. I am going to tell the newsmen that in my opinion this is the most arrogant invitation to subversion and disloyalty that I have ever heard of. I am going to also say that if such an invitation is accepted by any employee of the Government and we find out who that employee is, he will be fired on the spot if a civilian and court martialed on the spot if a military man."

Ike and Hagerty decided that the press secretary should enlist his allies in radio, television, and the newspapers to educate the public on the issue. Late in the afternoon, Hagerty found Eisenhower chipping golf shots on the back lawn and urged him to listen to Edward R. Murrow's radio program that night. Hagerty noted with satisfaction that Murrow and other commentators had accepted the Eisenhower-Brownell statement, treating it "quite properly as a fundamental Constitutional fight between the Administration and McCarthy."[6]

BEGINNING OF THE END

Finally, on May 27, Roy Cohn began his testimony. On the stand, he once again described David Schine as a "hostage" to attempts to end the investigations. He cited a threat by John Adams to have Private Schine sent overseas if the investigation of the army was not terminated. Cohn repeated his charge that the Cohn-Schine report constituted blackmail. He also reinforced the allegation that Stevens and John Adams had offered to provide information on communists in the air force and navy if McCarthy would drop his investigation of the army.[7]

There was a big stir when word of the Eisenhower-Brownell statement was communicated to the hearing on the morning of the twenty-eighth. McCarthy, in response, dug the hole deeper, restating his invitation to federal employees to share information. "I have stated and I will continue to state," he declared, "that my Democrat

colleagues will not get the names of the loyal Government em-
ploye[e]s who give us the evidence of threats that has been growing
over the last twenty or twenty-one years." At last, McCarthy had
extended his "twenty years of treason" mantra to twenty-one years
to include the Eisenhower administration. Hagerty declared in his
diary that the "fight is now joined." As he put it, "Has a United
States Senator, or anyone, a right to publicly urge the formation of a
personal Gestapo within the Administrative Branch of the Government, including the military?"[8]

That Saturday morning, Robert Stevens met secretly with the
president. Stevens, the good soldier, was still the anxious, jittery man
who so frequently needed reassurance. He wanted to know what
Eisenhower would think if J. Edgar Hoover testified about the "pur-
loined" letter McCarthy had produced on May 4. Ike muttered that
he was trying to keep the hearings "poison out of his system" and
instructed Stevens to contact Herbert Brownell or William Rogers.
He already knew that Brownell would probably not allow Hoover
to testify.

Eisenhower looked at the nervous, exhausted man in front of
him. Stevens, almost heroically, had done what the president had
asked, at the risk of his reputation and a charge of perjury, by taking
sole credit for the Schine report. Perhaps the general recalled talking
with soldiers fresh from battle; he suggested that Stevens and his
family "go away for a vacation after this thing is over."[9]

The columnist Roscoe Drummond believed the last days of the
Eisenhower-McCarthy confrontation had arrived. In his May 31
column, he wrote, "The most significant political fact in Washington today is that President Eisenhower and Senator McCarthy have
reached an open breach." He argued that no other interpretation
was credible in the face of "the cold, blunt, explicit reply of the
White House" to the senator's call for employees to feed him information, regardless of presidential orders.[10]

That evening Eisenhower was scheduled to deliver a speech at
the Columbia University bicentennial celebration dinner in New
York City. He was still seething about McCarthy. While preparing

his remarks, the president told Hagerty that he intended to make it "a finished fight with McCarthy" over the senator's call for federal employees to provide him with information. He "believed the question was a fundamental Constitutional one and [he] was going to the people with it." [11]

Eisenhower's speech that night was chock full of barbs at McCarthy but, as usual, couched in principle, without mentioning the senator's name. The president warned against confusing "honest dissent with disloyal subversion" and issued a clarion call to "drive from the temple of freedom all who seek to establish over us thought control—whether they be agents of a foreign state or demagogues thirsty for personal power and public notice." He concluded that whenever citizens come to "view every neighbor as a possible enemy . . . a free society is in danger." [12]

When Hagerty released the president's speech, the wire services pressed him as to whether Eisenhower had been talking about McCarthy; Hagerty declined to comment. He noted in his diary that the speech had gotten a "wonderful reception" at the dinner, interrupted twenty-five times by applause. The president had sat at the same table with William Paley, the president of CBS, who pledged he would give orders to all his newscasters on radio and television to plug the speech. [13]

FLANDERS STRIKES AGAIN

On May 28, in the midst of the president's rage over McCarthy's challenge to federal workers to betray their superiors, Eisenhower had asked Hagerty if they could "feed a speech to Senator Potter to be delivered on the floor of the Senate on this subject?" Instead, the White House repeated the successful pattern of the second week in March, when Senator Ralph Flanders and Edward R. Murrow had set the stage for the issuance of the Schine report by the army.

At Hagerty's instigation, Murrow used his May 28 radio program to defend the president's response to McCarthy's challenge to government employees to violate the orders of their superiors.

The White House apparently decided that Senator Flanders, Sherman Adams's good friend, was the better choice for the speech Ike wanted. Flanders needed no encouragement; he was eager to go after McCarthy once again.[14]

On June 1, Flanders rose in the Senate and denounced McCarthy as a "menace." In language that echoed Eisenhower's private rant to Jim Hagerty, he accused McCarthy of acting like Hitler. Flanders's attack made some listeners wince, particularly when the senator addressed the subject most Washington pundits and politicians had avoided. "The real heart of this mystery," he stated, "concerns the personal relationships" between Roy Cohn and David Schine. He noted that Cohn seemed to have a "passionate anxiety" to keep Schine as a staff person. "Why?" Flanders asked provocatively. "Does the Assistant [Cohn] have some hold on the Senator?"[15]

Cohn was deeply offended by the speech. He was convinced that Flanders had used the word "passionate"—along with the Vermont senator's questioning what "hold" Cohn had on McCarthy—to suggest homosexual relationships. "McCarthy was aware of the homosexual stories [about himself]," Cohn wrote, "and he laughed them off." Cohn connected Flanders's innuendos to Joe Welch's use of "fairy" in his exchange with McCarthy on April 30 over the cropped photograph of Schine and Stevens.[16]

At his news conference on June 2, Eisenhower implemented a milder anti-McCarthy strategy than he had threatened in his Oval Office rant. He reminded reporters that "a few days ago," the attorney general, "at my direction, prepared a statement with respect to Executive responsibility in maintaining the proper and constitutional division between the authority and responsibilities of the Executive and the Legislature. At my direction, Mr. Hagerty published that. Now, that constitutes the last word I have got to say on this subject, unless something happens that makes me think I have to say something more." One reporter ignored the president's prohibition; twenty minutes into the session, he asked whether the president thought McCarthy was hurting his program. Eisenhower swallowed, glared at the journalist, and called for the next question.[17]

MCCARTHY CHALLENGES SEATON

That day at the Army-McCarthy hearing, McCarthy made another attempt to rescue his deteriorating prestige. First, he claimed he possessed the names of 133 communists who had infiltrated the nation's hydrogen bomb defense plants; the allegation resembled his charges about the State Department in West Virginia in 1950 that had first brought him national exposure. The next day, he alleged that the Defense Department was uninterested in his information on spies in defense plants; he had directed his secretary to call Assistant Secretary of Defense Fred Seaton to request a meeting during the noon recess, but, he claimed, he had heard nothing from Seaton.

That was a setup, perhaps aimed at smoking out Seaton on his role in producing the report that had launched the hearings. Seaton had been out of his office when McCarthy's secretary had phoned. When he had returned the call, McCarthy had not been available, nor had McCarthy returned Seaton's call the next morning. Responding to McCarthy's claim that the Pentagon was not interested, Seaton did something unusual for him; he went public, writing the senator a letter detailing his repeated efforts to contact him, indicating his willingness to meet, and emphasizing that he would "be pleased to receive the names of those communists working in defense facilities." Seaton's letter, published in its entirety in *The New York Times*, effectively defused the situation. His quick action rescued the White House from adding him to the list of advisers to the president protected by the president's May 17 executive order. In his May 6 testimony, he had disguised his role in developing the Schine report, but, given Robert Stevens's recent testimony, a subpoena to Seaton at this time might have opened a floodgate of perjury charges.[18]

Behind the scenes, the role of the man Ike called his "reserve division" continued to grow. On May 13, Seaton, on White House orders, had begun collecting documents on the Army-McCarthy controversy. On Friday, June 4, Sherman Adams formalized that arrangement, and transmitted the president's order that "Assistant

Secretary of Defense, Fred Seaton, is hereby designated as the President's representative for custody of documents impounded under the President's letter to the Secretary of Defense, dated May 17, 1954." That letter had formally implemented the president's executive privilege order.[19]

The order formalized Seaton's collection of the Pentagon's phone call transcripts related to McCarthy, published verbatim in the Sunday papers on June 6. They included the call to Robert Stevens on February 20, when McCarthy had threatened, "I am going to kick the brains out of anyone who protects Communists."[20]

WELCH VS. MCCARTHY

McCarthy had managed to drag out the proceedings so that, by the end of the first week in June, almost two months after the hearings began, he had not yet formally testified. His favorite delaying tactic was to pick a fight with a witness or another senator. On June 7, McCarthy and Stuart Symington got into a row, based on a transcript of Symington's call to Stevens; McCarthy accused the Missouri senator of hatching "a plot" to destroy President Eisenhower and the Republican Party. Symington heatedly responded that he had acted as an "American," not as a "Democrat," in advising Stevens. McCarthy scoffed at Symington, calling him "Sanctimonious Stu" and implying that he was building his case to run for president in 1956.[21]

On June 8, the Republicans made a final attempt to close down the hearings. The plan was to call no witnesses after Joe McCarthy—who had not yet testified—a plan senators claimed had been approved by both the army and McCarthy. This time, Eisenhower would exercise no veto; the hearings had already done McCarthy sufficient damage.

With the end in sight, Joseph Welch, the courtly gentleman with the instinct for the jugular, was circling his prey, preparing to inflict some final wounds. He baited McCarthy, saying that he was "appalled" by his tactics. The senator, he said, had a "genius for creating confusion, throwing in new issues, making new accusations, and creating turmoil in the hearts and minds of the country that I find troublesome. And because of your genius, sir, we keep on, just keep on, as I view it, creating these confusions. Maybe I am over impressed by them. But I don't think they do the country any good." McCarthy's shrewd rejoinder was that he was confident that Welch meant he had "a genius for bringing out facts that may disturb the people."[22]

At the hearing that began on June 9, Roy Cohn was still on the stand. Welch sarcastically explored the "committee work" that Cohn and David Schine had allegedly performed on weekends while Schine was at Fort Dix and "the minimal work product that came out of it all." McCarthy watched his counsel squirm under Welch's implications about the intimacy of that relationship. Welch taunted Cohn as to whether he would "hurry" to act "before sundown" if he discovered a communist somewhere.

McCarthy came to his counsel's rescue. The senator's ponderous nasal voice interrupted Welch, and Chairman Mundt asked, "Have you a point of order?" McCarthy responded, "Not exactly, Mr. Chairman, but in view of Mr. Welch's request that the information be given once we know of anyone who might be performing any work for the Communist Party, I think we should tell him that he has in his law firm a young man named Fisher . . . who has been for a number of years a member of an organization which was named, oh years and years ago, as the legal bulwark of the Communist party."

Welch had expected an attack on Fred Fisher because of his past association with the National Lawyers Guild. But, as Fisher later recalled, they had settled on a strategy whereby if McCarthy attacked Fisher, "Joe Welch would become very outraged and turn the attack against the Senator." However, the situation had become complicated; two days prior, Roy Cohn had struck a deal with Welch, to which McCarthy had agreed, that if the senator did not mention Fisher, Welch would not discuss Cohn's lack of military service. Now, to Cohn's distress, McCarthy had violated that agreement. Both Welch and McCarthy were armed and ready for a showdown.[23]

John Adams recalled that "a hush fell over the room" when Mc-Carthy hurled the Fisher accusation. McCarthy rumbled, "I have hesitated to bring this up, but I have been rather bored with your phony requests to Mr. Cohn here that he personally get every Communist out of government before sundown. Therefore, we will give you the information about the young man in your own organization."

Welch sat with his head in his hands, staring at the table; then he addressed Mundt: "Mr. Chairman, under these circumstances, I must have something approaching a personal privilege." Mundt replied, "You may have it, sir. It will not be taken out of your time." McCarthy was pacing about, ordering aides to retrieve the file on Fisher. Three times Welch tried to get his attention, to which McCarthy finally snapped, "I can listen with one ear." Welch countered, "I want you to listen with both." He began, "Until this moment, Senator—" only to be interrupted again by McCarthy barking orders to aides. Welch had carefully scripted his response, so he began a second time, using precisely the same words.

"Until this moment, Senator, I think I never really gauged your cruelty or your recklessness. Fred Fisher is a young man who went to the Harvard Law School and came into my firm and is starting what looks to be a brilliant career with us." He noted that he had learned from Fisher about his membership in the National Lawyers Guild and decided to withdraw him from the team. "Little did I dream," he continued, "you would be so reckless and cruel as to do an injury to that lad. . . . I fear he shall always bear a scar needlessly inflicted by you. If it were in my power to forgive you for your reckless cruelty I would do so. I like to think that I am a gentle man, but your forgiveness will have to come from someone other than me."

McCarthy appeared to be reading a newspaper. When Welch ended his statement, McCarthy resumed his attack on Fisher. After some back-and-forth in front of the very uncomfortable Roy Cohn, McCarthy started to speak again and Welch interrupted in a commanding voice, "Let us not assassinate this lad further, Senator. You have done enough. Have you no sense of decency, sir, at long last? Have you left no sense of decency?"

McCarthy persisted in bemoaning Fisher's subversive associations, but Welch knew when to quit. He said, "Mr. McCarthy"—no respectful "Senator" this time—"I will not discuss this with you further. . . . I will not ask Mr. Cohn any more questions. You, Mr. Chairman, may, if you will call the next witness." The attorney had perfectly timed his tirade to set the stage, after six long weeks of hearings, to fully discredit the senator from Wisconsin.[24]

The audience applauded at length. Welch walked out of the hearing room, followed by a herd of reporters. McCarthy was left in the room, looking forlorn, as if he needed someone to talk to. He looked at some of his aides, threw up his hands, and asked, "What did I do?" In the hallway, Welch told reporters, "I am close to tears." McCarthy, he said, had tried to "crucify" Fisher because he had made "one mistake." "I don't see how in the name of God you can fight anybody like that," he lamented. "I never saw such cruelty . . . such arrogance." McCarthy retorted to reporters, "Too many people can dish it out but can't take it." But the news media had chosen their champion; *The New York Times* ran a picture of the soulful, tearful Joe Welch, holding a handkerchief to his face.[25]

Later, according to John Adams, after the crowd had dispersed, Welch asked a fellow attorney in an unemotional voice, "Well, how did it go?" Adams believed that Welch had set a trap for McCarthy. Despite his earlier agreement with Cohn, Welch's taunting of Cohn to name and clean out communists "by sundown" had been designed to get under McCarthy's skin. Adams recalled that Winston Churchill, when asked how he spent his spare time, responded, "I rehearse my extemporaneous speeches." Adams concluded, "So, I think, did Joe Welch."[26]

McCarthy then began his testimony, repeating his charges of communist influence in the army and how he had been "blackmailed" to end his investigation. Meanwhile, on Ike's orders, Jim Hagerty had secured a half hour of time on the evening of June 10 for a presidential speech before the National Citizens for Eisenhower Congressional Committee chairs. Eisenhower and Hagerty scheduled the president's news conference for that day, one day after

Welch's triumphant confrontation with McCarthy. The president was ready for the hearings to end; they had done the damage he wanted. It was time to move on with a news conference focused on foreign affairs and a speech highlighting the president's legislative program. At the news conference, Eisenhower was pressed by reporters about whether he would endorse all Republican candidates, implying McCarthy's allies, who were up for election in the fall. The president vaguely discussed the need to elect people who would assist in meeting governing responsibilities. "But I imagine that you could probably pull out of the hat some specific question that could be most embarrassing; I hope you won't do that." That remark was greeted with laughter.[27]

The president's speech that night was televised. His only reference to McCarthy-type subjects involved his legislative proposals to enhance internal security and his commitment to "plug loopholes through which spies and saboteurs can now slip." That oblique reference to McCarthy's crusade underscored that his speech—in the midst of McCarthy's testimony—was simply Ike's latest effort to steal the spotlight from McCarthy.[28]

RALPH FLANDERS INVADES A HEARING

Ralph Flanders was frustrated; the senator complained that his speeches against McCarthy were garnering only marginal attention in the press. On June 11, the aggressive seventy-three-year-old Vermont senator hijacked what remained of McCarthy's dignity.

As Ray Jenkins, the subcommittee's hearings counsel, was questioning McCarthy, Flanders burst into the hearing room. Without permission from Chairman Mundt, he strolled over to McCarthy and—in full view of the television cameras—handed the senator a letter. Mundt later called the action "without precedent in the history of the Senate." "This is to inform you," Flanders said to McCarthy, "that I plan to make another speech concerning your activities in the Senate this afternoon . . . I would be glad to have you present." The letter informed McCarthy that Flanders would introduce Resolution No. 261 on the floor of the Senate that day, charging McCarthy with "unbecoming conduct" and demanding his removal from his committee chairmanships.[29]

As the hubbub subsided, Senator Mundt called out, "The committee will be in order." McCarthy responded, "Will the Chair ask Mr. Flanders to remain?" When Mundt complied, McCarthy continued, "Mr. Flanders"—not the respectful "Senator"—"you have just handed me a letter and I read it." He sneered, "Number 1, I will be unable to be present because I will be testifying. Number 2, I don't have enough interest in any Flanders' speech to listen to it. Number 3, Senator, may I have your attention? Number 3, you have gone on the Senate floor and have indicated you have information of value to this committee. You suggested the committee is not getting at the heart of this matter." He called Flanders's June 1 address on the Senate floor "an extremely scurrilous speech." When Flanders attempted to leave the room, McCarthy roared, "Let me finish, Mr. Flanders. At that time you did not have the courtesy that you have today of letting me know that you are speaking. I think, Senator, if you have any information of value to this committee, what you should do is what my Republican colleagues have done, what I am doing now—take the oath, raise your right hand, let us cross-examine you."

Mundt finally recovered and asked Flanders to "retire to the rear of the room," where other spectators were sitting. "I am sorry," Mundt said. "We can't permit this kind of feuding to go on here." Flanders shot back, "I retire under compulsion." McCarthy countered that he had "no feud with Mr. Flanders" and suggested that the senator's attack "was not the result of viciousness, but perhaps senility." He later told reporters, "I think they should get a man with a net and take him to a good quiet place."[30]

On Sunday, Flanders appeared on NBC's *Meet the Press*, charging that McCarthy was "fighting communism with fascism," close to Eisenhower's comparison of McCarthy to Hitler. Flanders said he would give McCarthy three and a half weeks to respond to his charges, but with Senate adjournment scheduled for July 31, that would leave very little time. Flanders faced an uphill fight. Senator

Knowland, the Republican majority leader, had already labeled the Flanders resolution a "mistake" and declared it "not justified." Knowland argued that dealing with his motion might derail the passage of President Eisenhower's legislative program. When he heard about Knowland's opposition, Eisenhower grumbled to Herbert Brownell, "Knowland is the biggest disappointment I have found since I have been in politics."[31]

Flanders's motion to deprive McCarthy of his committee chairmanships was a first step toward censure. Did the White House put Flanders up to the maneuver? It is likely; the similarities between the president's and the senator's rhetoric were striking. The timing and style of the senator's actions were intriguingly reminiscent of his speech on March 9.

On June 15, *The Washington Post* published a small story headed "Flanders' Home Given Police Guard."[32]

ENDING THE WAR

Compared to the drama of the confrontation with Welch and the Flanders intrusion, the final days of the Army-McCarthy hearings were anticlimactic. On the fifteenth, Roy Cohn concluded his testimony with an emotional statement calling Joe McCarthy "a great American." "I have never known a man who has less unkindness, less lack of charity, in his heart and soul," he declared. On June 16, Welch and McCarthy had their bitterest exchange since the confrontation on June 9. Welch rebuked McCarthy for trying to act as both judge and witness in alleging that the army's charges were false and dishonest. McCarthy called the charges against his staff "completely unfounded. . . . They are guilty of only one crime—namely, that they fight communism." When he accused Welch of failing to understand that threat, Welch's voice rose: "I work at an address (the Pentagon) where there are men without limbs, who lost them fighting communism." "Don't tell me," he declared, "that the United States Army doesn't fight Communists. You do not have a monopoly, sir, in that field."[33]

The biggest news at the hearing the final day—June 17—was Senator Charles Potter's call for perjury investigations. Potter was convinced that the testimony had been "saturated with statements which were not truthful and which might constitute perjury in a legal sense." He even suggested that "there may have been subornation of perjury," an accusation that did not exempt the White House.

Senator Karl Mundt gaveled the final hearing to closure at 6:32 p.m. The hearings had lasted 36 days, had been televised for 187 hours, and had generated 7,424 pages of transcripts. Ironically, it was also the day that the army ordered Private G. David Schine to report to Fort Myer, Virginia, to receive his formal orders before returning to Camp Gordon, Georgia. In spite of all their efforts to be together—so pivotal to the origins of the Army-McCarthy hearings—Roy Cohn and David Schine would continue to be separated.[34]

BENEDICTIONS

John Adams sat in his office alone, watching the television screen and fretting about Senator Potter's call for the investigation of perjury. "My door was closed; my phone almost never rang; I had little to do; I just sat there . . . contemplating my own bleak future." Robert Stevens, he wrote, "had been giving me the silent treatment for weeks." Joseph Welch, he believed, "wasn't really representing me." Adams took only limited satisfaction from Welch's success in humiliating McCarthy "since I was going down the drain too."[35]

Robert Stevens, who had sacrificed himself for the president, was more upbeat. "The integrity of the Army was at stake," he told reporters. "I don't feel like it's at stake any longer." He confirmed that he had no plans to resign and would serve as long as the president and Secretary Wilson believed he could be of service "to them and to the country."[36]

As the hearings ground to a halt, the columnist Roscoe Drummond asserted, "Everybody is being hurt" by the hearings, and "nobody is being really helped. The outcome can hardly fail to be inconclusive. The country is being hurt; the government is being hurt; America's reputation around the world is being undermined; the precision fabric of a decent society is being rent." Nevertheless, he recognized the damage to McCarthy. "Few correspondents who have followed these hearings believe that he will ever recover the political influence and the power to intimidate he has exercised so long." He noted that "all the public opinion polls show Mr. McCarthy's political influence declining and the public's political distrust increasing." Drummond hinted at the truth behind the headlines: "These hearings show Mr. Eisenhower that the President must fearlessly protect the executive branch of the government from congressional usurpation." [37]

Ike believed that he had done precisely that. As he reportedly told Stevens when McCarthy made a last desperate attempt to truncate the hearings, "We've got the bastard exactly where we want him." Joseph and Stewart Alsop understood that truth, despite the wide acceptance of the mantra that "nobody won." On the Sunday after the hearings ended, the Alsops wrote, "There is to be no more appeasing of McCarthy. On the contrary, McCarthy is to be recognized for what he is—the President's most dangerous enemy—and treated accordingly." [38]

Eisenhower had reached that conclusion months earlier; implementing it had been more complex than either the journalists or White House staff had understood. The general in the Oval Office, the veteran of so many battles, had decided that what was required was a disciplined, deceptive campaign, agile enough to respond to new circumstances and carried out by loyal foot soldiers such as Sherman Adams, Henry Cabot Lodge, Herbert Brownell, Fred Seaton, and eventually, in their own ways, Robert Stevens and John Adams. It required, in the prescient term Fred I. Greenstein coined a generation ago, a "hidden hand." [39]

Eisenhower's news conference on June 16 lasted only twenty minutes; reporters asked no questions about McCarthy, the hearings, or the Flanders resolution. The most insistent queries were aimed at whether the president intended to run again in 1956. Ike, with a grin, called that a question that "has never yet been discussed in the White House since I have been there." Ray Scherer of NBC quoted Sherman Adams, who had said that, besides losing Congress in November, there were "two other contingencies under which you might not offer yourself for re-election, but he didn't name them." "A funny thing," Ike responded, Adams had told him that morning he probably would get a question about "two secret contingencies that I haven't told you about, and someday I am going to tell you." "So," Ike concluded to laughter, "I am just as ignorant as you are."[40]

On the way back from the news conference, Eisenhower expressed his "amazement" to Jim Hagerty that the reporters had respected his edict two weeks earlier that he was not going to talk about McCarthy. That the reporters were more interested in Eisenhower's future political plans than McCarthy's spoke volumes about the impact of the hearings.[41]

On June 19, *The New York Times* carried the tiniest of news stories, a few short lines buried on page seven. The previous day, Joe Welch and James St. Clair had "visited President Eisenhower at the White House." Welch had gone to the White House "at the invitation of James C. Hagerty, White House Press Secretary, who has known Mr. Welch for several years." That was a cover story, as Hagerty had apparently met Welch for the first time on April 2. Hagerty confided to his diary that he "got them in to see the president." Welch told Eisenhower that "if the hearings had accomplished nothing else," they had kept McCarthy "in front of the television sets" so the public could "see how disgracefully he acted." Eisenhower agreed.[42]

The rationale for Welch's visit to the White House was more Eisenhowerian subterfuge. Under the guise of visiting Hagerty, Ike and the attorney could talk candidly about Joe McCarthy. And Eisenhower could perpetuate the fiction that someone other than the president of the United States had "killed" Joe McCarthy.

EPILOGUE

On June 11, 1954, Vermont senator Ralph Flanders had disrupted the Army-McCarthy hearings, announcing his intent to try to strip Joseph McCarthy of his committee chairmanships. When that effort failed to get traction, Flanders introduced a censure resolution, making three charges: that McCarthy had abused the Gillette-Hennings subcommittee of the Rules Committee that had investigated McCarthy's charges against public officials (including George C. Marshall) in 1951 and 1952; that he had sent Roy Cohn and David Schine on a European trip that had embarrassed the nation and the Senate; and that he had abused witnesses, such as General Ralph Zwicker. Cohn realized that he was on a political sinking ship, and on July 20, he resigned. McCarthy called Cohn's resignation a victory for the communists and their sympathizers. On August 2, the Senate voted 75 to 23 to form a six-member select committee to investigate the charges against McCarthy.[1]

The six members of the new committee were selected by Majority Leader William Knowland and Minority Leader Lyndon B. Johnson. The Democrats included Edwin C. Johnson of Colorado, John Stennis of Mississippi, and Samuel J. Ervin, Jr., of North Carolina. Knowland selected Frank Carlson of Kansas, Francis Case of South Dakota, and Arthur Watkins of Utah, whom Knowland appointed as chairman. When Knowland informed Watkins, the senator departed the majority leader's office "committed to an ordeal." The new committee announced that it would add to Flanders's charges McCarthy's misuse of the J. Edgar Hoover letter, his invitation to government employees to provide him with classified information, and his abuse of fellow senators in the course of his investigations.[2]

IN PRAISE OF MARSHALL

Two days after the Senate approved the select committee, Eisenhower belatedly attempted to remedy the egregious mistake he had made during his 1952 campaign, when he had failed to stand up for George C. Marshall. McCarthy was still persecuting Marshall. The senator had entered a letter into the Congressional Record from Harry Woodring, secretary of war under Franklin Roosevelt, asserting that General Marshall "would sell out his grandmother for personal advantage."

At the president's August 4 news conference, Edward T. Folliard of *The Washington Post* quoted the Woodring letter and asked, "Mr. President, what do you think of that appraisal of General Marshall?" George Marshall, Eisenhower replied, "has typified all that we look for in what we call an American patriot." Marshall had been a soldier who said, in effect, "I am here to serve and not to satisfy personal ambition." Eisenhower extolled Marshall's "brilliant record, always serving to the best of his ability." He deplored the Woodring letter, asserting that it was "a sorry reward" to suggest that Marshall "is not a loyal, fine American, and that he served only in order to advance his own personal ambitions. I can't imagine anyone that I have known in my career of whom this is less so than it is in his case."

As usual, Ike delivered his statement without mentioning McCarthy by name. Perhaps he wanted to encourage the new select committee investigating McCarthy's conduct to remember the senator's slurs against Marshall. However, he kept the censure process at arm's length, treating the deliberations as "a matter of the Senate."[3]

THE COMMITTEE PROCESS

The select committee held nine public hearings between August 31 and September 13; television coverage and still photos were prohibited. On September 27, it released a sixty-eight-page report unanimously recommending censure. Once the report was released, the Senate agreed to adjourn and take up its recommendations after the congressional elections. Reflecting on his experience chairing the committee, Arthur Watkins wrote, "I have never suffered such intense and continuing distress."[4]

On November 2, 1954, the Democrats won both houses of Congress by narrow margins. Vice President Nixon suggested that the administration's conflicts with Senator McCarthy had cost the support of "pro-McCarthyites" in three Midwestern states: Illinois, Michigan, and Wisconsin. McCarthy ascribed the Republican defeat to public resentment "against the jungle war which powerful elements of this Administration waged against those of us who were trying to expose and dig out Communists." In a postelection Gallup Poll the public rejected, 49 to 24 percent, the proposition that the Watkins committee had treated the senator unfairly.[5]

On November 9, McCarthy released the text of a speech asserting that the communist party had made "a committee of the Senate its unwitting hand-maiden." "I shall demonstrate," he declared, "that the Watkins Committee has done the work of the Communist Party" and used "Communist methods" to manufacture "a plausible rationalization for advising the Senate to accede to the clamor for my scalp."[6]

On November 10, the day debate began on the select committee's report, McCarthy inserted the "hand-maiden" speech into the Senate record. That day, he repeatedly disrupted the debate, raising unanswerable questions and reading from the Senate's record and newspaper clippings. The debate became so acrimonious that McCarthy's colleagues warned him that his harsh attacks on the integrity of the select committee might add charges to the censure resolution. Outside Senate sessions, McCarthy got under Watkins's skin by repeatedly calling the chairman "a coward."[7]

The next day, hundreds of McCarthy supporters besieged Capitol Hill, carrying small American flags and wearing badges declaring "I like McCarthy." They visited their senators and packed the galleries. Senator Leverett Saltonstall of Massachusetts told reporters that sixty people had called on him, bearing the signatures of four thousand McCarthy supporters.[8]

On November 17, McCarthy entered Bethesda Naval Hospital to be treated for traumatic bursitis in an elbow. Supporters visited him, pleading for him to do something magnanimous that might extract him from the situation. At one point Everett Dirksen thought he had persuaded his colleague to sign an apology, but McCarthy finally responded, "No, I don't crawl. I learned to fight in an alley."[9]

But by November 29, McCarthy was ready to end the fight he knew he was losing. Expressing regret for "discourteous and offensive words," he said he was prepared "for whatever action the Senate may take on this resolution of censure." However, he continued, "my efforts to expose Communist infiltration in Government will continue regardless of the outcome of the censure vote." McCarthy asked for "unanimous consent" that the debate be terminated at 3 p.m. on December 1, followed by a vote. The Senate accepted McCarthy's proposal, although the final vote spilled over another day.[10]

On December 1, huge bundles of petitions opposing McCarthy's censure were delivered to the Capitol; armed guards stood over them with pistols drawn while samples were delivered to Vice President Nixon, the Senate's presiding officer. That day, McCarthy's Senate allies made three attempts to modify the charges against him. Dirksen offered a substitute resolution stating that there was no legal foundation for censure, but it was defeated 66 to 21. Mundt proposed language that "deplored and disapproved" what McCarthy had said about other senators but would not censure him; that motion lost 74 to 15. Senator Styles Bridges proposed a resolution that would have exonerated McCarthy completely, but his motion lost 68 to 20.[11]

The draft censure resolution had become increasingly cosmetic. The counts against McCarthy had been reduced to three: his refusal to cooperate with the Gillette-Hennings committee investigating his charges against public officials, his "contemptuous" treatment of its members, and his "reprehensible" conduct toward Brigadier General Ralph Zwicker. Gone was any mention of the privileges sought for Private G. David Schine, the issue that had spawned the Army-McCarthy hearings. At 6:44 p.m., a preliminary vote on the first two counts passed 67 to 20. The vote on the count condemning abuse of General Zwicker was deferred until the next day.[12]

That night, in a television interview, McCarthy declared, "I don't think the American people are at all fooled. They know I am being censured because I dared to do the dishonorable thing of exposing Communists in Government." Asserting that censure "won't stop us," he announced he planned to resume hearings the following week.[13]

The big news on December 1 was Republican majority leader William Knowland's announcement that he intended to vote against McCarthy's censure. Knowland argued that censure might inhibit the investigative powers of the Senate. Jim Hagerty recalled that at that news, Eisenhower "literally hit the roof." The president stormed, "What's the guy trying to do? Here he personally picked the Committee to draw up the censure charges, he vouched for their honor and integrity and then he turns around and votes against them, using this phony reason of investigative curtailment."[14]

THE DAY OF RECKONING

Eisenhower normally conducted news conferences on Wednesday mornings. However, he scheduled one for Thursday, December 2, at 2:30 p.m., smack in the middle of the Senate's final debate on McCarthy's censure. He had decided, once again, to steal the spotlight from McCarthy.[15]

Inevitably, a reporter asked about the censure debate. "I have no comment on that," the president said. "This is a matter of the Senate, as I understand it, determining what is required in the preservation of the dignity of the Senate." Another journalist inquired whether the president perceived a growing split between fervently anticommunist Republican conservatives and the administration. Ike insisted that he saw "no connection between trying to be tough on communism and still being progressive."[16]

With only three counts left in the draft resolution, the focus in the Senate turned to McCarthy's abuse of General Zwicker. That charge was dropped after Lyndon Johnson informed Arthur Watkins that a number of southern senators opposed it. Instead, the Senate substituted McCarthy's rhetorical abuses of the select committee, condemning him for calling it a "lynch party" practicing "deliberate deception" and "fraud" and calling the chairman "a coward." The resolution had been reduced to a narrow recital of McCarthy's transgressions against the dignity of the US Senate.

Even the term "censure" did not survive the final debate. In the phrase concluding each section, McCarthy "is hereby censured" had been replaced by "is hereby condemned." Vice President Nixon, with the approval of the body, changed the title of the resolution to conform with the use of "condemned" in the body of the resolution.

The final vote came at 5:03 p.m.; it was 67 in favor, 22 opposed. All 22 "no" votes were Republican, half of the 44 Republican senators voting. Joe McCarthy voted "present."[17]

POSTSCRIPT

On Friday evening, December 3, about 6:00 pm., Eisenhower called Jim Hagerty to say, "Senator Watkins got quite a kicking around on the Hill from McCarthy and his side." The president wanted Watkins to know that "I am for him one hundred percent" and invited the senator to the White House for a personal visit. They met the next morning for about forty minutes. Watkins told Ike he would regret "to his dying day that they could not go through with censure on the Zwicker business." The president commented that there were "a lot of misguided people in this world" and that McCarthy was only "a champion of McCarthy."

After Watkins left, Eisenhower and Hagerty agreed to issue a statement saying that the president had congratulated him on a "very splendid job." Ike later told Hagerty that the news stories "were just exactly what I wanted to see in the paper, and I don't particularly care what the Old Guard thinks about it." [18]

For McCarthy, Eisenhower's public praise for Watkins was the last straw. On December 7 at 11:40 a.m., he walked into the first hearing of his subcommittee in months and delivered a statement. "The President of the United States," he said, "has taken it upon himself to congratulate Senators Flanders and Watkins who have been instrumental in holding up our work." The president had praised "those who hold up the exposure of communists in one breath and in the next breath urges patience, tolerance and niceties to those who are torturing American uniformed men." McCarthy apologized to the American people for supporting Eisenhower for president. He recalled that he had assured voters that if they elected the general, "they could be assured of a vigorous, forceful fight against Communists in Government. Unfortunately in this, I was mistaken." [19]

McCarthy had now broken openly with Eisenhower. Once again, faithful to his unwavering policy, Eisenhower did not respond. Rhetorically, he had ignored McCarthy for two years; that had always been his way of saying to the senator, "You don't really matter." Now, outflanked by the White House and humiliated by his senatorial colleagues, that tactical message had become unassailable fact. Joe McCarthy did not matter anymore.

AFTER CENSURE

Following condemnation by his colleagues, McCarthy remained in the Senate, but his influence was a shadow of what it had been. Due to the Democratic victory in November 1954, he no longer chaired a committee. "Now," John Adams recalled, "when McCarthy stood up to speak on the Senate floor, the chamber would empty." When he sat down with other senators in the Senate Dining Room, "his colleagues would make lame excuses and leave." The bands of reporters who had once hung on his every word were gone. [20]

In a June 1955 legislative leaders' meeting, Eisenhower discussed McCarthy's ongoing efforts to regain his status. McCarthy had criticized the president for agreeing to talk with Soviet leaders at a Big Four (United States, USSR, United Kingdom, France) meeting in San Francisco. He had introduced a resolution calling for the United States to negotiate solely "about the liberation of the countries [in Eastern Europe] now held captive by the Communists—and nothing else." Neither Ike nor his congressional leaders took the senator's resolution seriously. Ike boasted that he "could know more about Europe in five minutes than McCarthy could in fifteen years." Then he repeated the truism making the rounds in Washington. "It's no longer McCarthyism," he said. "It's McCarthywasm." [21]

In late 1955, McCarthy called and asked John Adams to come to his home. As they sat down, Joe poured six ounces of gin. "He looked awful." Adams recalled. "He had lost about forty pounds, and his hands shook. He was having trouble drinking, and gin trickled from the corners of his mouth when he took a sip." It was a strange, superficially friendly visit, "as if the Army-McCarthy hearings had never happened." When McCarthy walked Adams to the door, John said, "So long, Joe." He described the man he left at the door as "the cadaverous visage of McCarthyism, standing silently in the shadows, slowly dying." [22]

On May 2, 1957, Senator Joseph R. McCarthy died—the victim, according to his death certificate, of "hepatitis, acute, cause unknown." He was forty-eight years of age. [23]

IN IKE'S OWN WORDS

On November 23, 1968, Eisenhower edited an article he had drafted for publication in *Reader's Digest*. The essay elaborated on an enduring theme in the Eisenhower White House, decrying "extremism" and exalting "moderation" and "the middle way" as the "common sense" way to get things done.

On that day, four months before his death, Eisenhower reviewed the words he had previously written; that earlier draft included harsh language about McCarthy that, as president, he had adamantly refused to use in public. Discussing "extremists," he had written, "The worst of these during my administration was Senator Joseph McCarthy." Though some extremists were "sincere men" and "honest in their convictions," he concluded, "Joe McCarthy was not. He was a vicious demagogue, who in his thirst for personal publicity wrecked the lives and careers of many decent people." Now Eisenhower thought better of that statement and scribbled a note to his editor, asking that it be eliminated.

Eisenhower still wrestled with how candid to be about McCarthy's extremism. "Actually," he wrote, "I yearned in every fiber of my being to do precisely what my critics were urging—to issue a ringing denunciation of the senator and all his evil works." Ike, the cautious editor, crossed out "evil." He explained that he had decided that a rhetorical attack would only make McCarthy "a hero and a martyr." "I continued to refuse to get down in the gutter," Eisenhower wrote, "with one of the worst extremists of this century." He crossed out the latter phrase, instead stating that he had refused to fight McCarthy on the senator's "own terms."

Eisenhower did not reveal any details about the deceptive operation he had employed to destroy the Wisconsin senator. Still, he could not resist a hint: "What a lot of people even today don't know is that behind the scenes I was doing all I could to assist those who were wrongly accused, and in many cases my efforts were effective. Also, although I did not mention McCarthy's name publicly, I spoke out time after time against the despicable kind of tactics he was using."

Ike recalled that once the struggle with McCarthy was over, a former aide and critic of his approach to McCarthy confessed to the president: "By gosh, Mr. President, you *were* right about McCarthy." Smiling, Eisenhower responded, "Sometimes I am." [24]

Dwight D. Eisenhower died on March 28, 1969; his article "We *Must* Avoid the Perils of Extremism" was published the following month. For all his editing, Dwight Eisenhower had finally—publicly—denounced Joe McCarthy.

ACKNOWLEDGMENTS

A generation ago, the two men to whom this book is dedicated—William Bragg Ewald Jr. and Fred I. Greenstein—blazed the trail on Dwight Eisenhower's role in the Joseph McCarthy saga. Their insights were largely ignored by historians thereafter, although Greenstein's iconic "hidden hand" characterization of Eisenhower's leadership outlived its original context. Both men personally urged me to proceed with this project.

Ewald had first access to the documents Fred A. Seaton, assistant secretary of defense during the Army-McCarthy hearings, collected on Eisenhower's orders. I am indebted to the Seaton family who, upon Fred Seaton's death, donated his "eyes only" file to the Eisenhower Presidential Library in Abilene, Kansas. I am grateful to the Eisenhower Library staff and archivists for editing and organizing those documents for effective research. The living members of the Seaton family made contributions to my research. Fred Seaton's son Don and his nephews Ed and David provided context from their personal experiences, supplementing Gladys Seaton's oral history.

Former Eisenhower aides provided important perspectives. I am indebted to Bill Ewald's son William Ewald III for facilitating conversations with his father. Douglas Price, a campaign aide in 1952, sent me documents relating to Eisenhower's controversial appearance in Milwaukee, Wisconsin. Robert Kieve, a White House speechwriter, provided a copy of his personal diary. White House assistant Stephen Benedict provided insight into the personal lives of those serving in the Eisenhower White House.

Some treasured colleagues have supported and improved my work. Irwin F. Gellman made constructive suggestions, counseled me through difficult moments, and assisted with insight on Richard Nixon's role. My colleagues at the annual Eisenhower Academy in Gettysburg, Pennsylvania—Daun van Ee, Michael Birkner, Keith Olson, and George Colburn—have provided ongoing insights and advice. Van Ee reviewed the manuscript and facilitated access to the Eisenhower published papers he had edited. Carol Hegeman, the director of the Eisenhower Academy for the National Park Service, first invited me to participate in the Academy and connected me with these scholars.

I am particularly indebted to Duane Krohnke, a retired Minneapolis attorney and authority on Joseph Welch, his fellow alumnus at Grinnell College in Iowa. Duane provided me with documents unavailable elsewhere, especially Fred Fisher's account of the hiring of Welch as Army counsel for the Army-McCarthy hearings. Duane also connected me with Ann M. Lousin, a Chicago attorney, and Nancy Welch, Welch's granddaughter, both of whom provided important information about Welch and McCarthy.

Ambassador Avis Bohlen, Ambassador Charles Bohlen's daughter, provided important information on the Bohlen family and early access to her introduction to her uncle Charles Thayer's memoir. Arthur Hadley, a *Newsweek* journalist in the 1950s, provided perspectives on McCarthy and Army secretary Robert Stevens. John P. Burke at the University of Vermont, provided an interview Fred Greenstein had conducted with Herbert Brownell Jr., Eisenhower's attorney general. Brownell's daughter Ann Brownell Sloane has both encouraged my work and provided insights into her father's role. The Eisenhower family has been consistently supportive of my work on the Eisenhower legacy. Thomas C. Reeves and Richard M. Fried, McCarthy biographers, have advised me. Michael S. Mayer's

2009 book of profiles on key figures in the Eisenhower administration has been an indispensable resource.

Colleagues nearby provided vital assistance. Dalene McDonald, the director of Southwestern College's Deets Library, arranged for my access to the files of *The Washington Post*, and her staff facilitated dozens of interlibrary loan requests. Nan Myers at Wichita State University's Ablah Library facilitated extended access to the transcripts of the Army-McCarthy hearings. James A. Shepherd, the former provost at Southwestern College and now president of Thomas University in Georgia, educated me about the traditions of military deception that Eisenhower applied to his conflict with McCarthy.

No serious scholar of the Eisenhower presidency can function without the assistance of the wonderful staff at the Dwight D. Eisenhower Presidential Library in Abilene, Kansas. Karl Weissenbach, the former director, and his successor, Tim Rives, have supported my research and promoted my Eisenhower books. Archivist Christopher Abraham was helpful in the early stages of my research. Retired long-time archivists David Haight and Jim Leyerzapf advised me. The research-friendly condition of the Eisenhower archives can be attributed, in no small part, to their decades of dedicated labor.

Other document collections were critical. The Massachusetts Historical Society in Boston facilitated my research in the Henry Cabot Lodge Papers. The Seeley-Mudd Library at Princeton University provided documents online. The Dartmouth College Library facilitated my research in the Sherman Adams papers. The Karl E. Mundt Archives at Dakota State College in South Dakota made the senator's unpublished memoir available. The University of Rochester in New York and Syracuse University libraries facilitated my research in the Thomas E. Dewey and Ralph E. Flanders papers.

Prologue, a publication of the National Archives, gave my scholarship on Eisenhower and McCarthy exposure in the October 2015 issue. *Prologue* published photographs that are now included in this book. Other sources of photographs include the document sites above, the Senate Historical Office and the Herbert Block

Foundation. The assistance of Kathy Struss at the Eisenhower Library in identifying photographs has been exceptional.

I save some special credits for last. I never would have published with Simon & Schuster without the advocacy of my agent, Will Lippincott. My editor, Bob Bender, counseled me through the process of completing the manuscript, and skillfully edited it. His assistant, Johanna Li, has provided superb technical assistance.

Then there is my wife, Grace. She has edited every word, provided wise feedback, and supported me personally in ways that cannot be adequately shared here. In fairness, her name should be on the book.

NOTES

ABBREVIATIONS

ACW: Ann C. Whitman

AEC: AtomicEnergy Commission

AWD: Allen W. Dulles

BSP: Bernard Shanley Papers, Dwight D. Eisenhower Presidential Library

CDJP: C. D. Jackson Papers, Dwight D. Eisenhower Presidential Library

CF/OF: Central Files/Official File, Dwight D. Eisenhower Presidential Library

DDE: Dwight D. Eisenhower

DDEP: *The Papers of Dwight David Eisenhower*, ed. Louis Galambos and Daun van Ee, Johns Hopkins University Press, 1970–2003

DDEPL: Dwight D. Eisenhower Presidential Library

FASP: Fred A. Seaton Papers, Dwight D. Eisenhower Presidential Library

FRUS: *Foreign Relations of the United States*

HCLP: Henry Cabot Lodge, Jr., Papers, Massachusetts Historical Society

HEW: Department of Health, Education, and Welfare

IIA: International Information Administration

JEH: J. Edgar Hoover

JFD: John Foster Dulles

JFDP: John Foster Dulles Papers, Dwight D. Eisenhower Presidential Library

JHP: James Hagerty Papers, Dwight D. Eisenhower Presidential Library

LC: Library of Congress

MHS: Massachusetts Historical Society

NSC: National Security Council

OH: Oral history

OSANSA: Office of Special Assistant for National Security Affairs

PC: Press conference

PPP: *Public Papers of the Presidents,* American Presidency Project, University of California, Santa Barbara, online

RG: Record Group

RNC: Republican National Committee

SGMML: Seeley G. Mudd Manuscript Library, Princeton University

UN: United Nations

USIA: United States Information Agency

VOA: Voice of America

WH: White House

WHOSS: White House, Office of the Staff Secretary, Dwight D. Eisenhower Presidential Library

PREFACE

1. I am indebted to Michael J. Birkner, "Eisenhower and the Red Menace," *Prologue*, Fall 2001, for clarifying the distinction between 1953 and 1954.

2. In Fred Greenstein's iconic phrase, Ike employed a "hidden hand" to destroy Joe McCarthy; see Fred I. Greenstein, *The Hidden-Hand Presidency: Eisenhower as Leader* (Baltimore: Johns Hopkins University Press, 1982).

3. Two authors who made a particular effort to rehabilitate McCarthy's reputation are M. Stanton Evans, *Blacklisted by History* (New York: Three Rivers Press, 2007), and Arthur Herman, *Joseph McCarthy: Reexamining the Life and Legacy of America's Most Hated Senator* (New York: Free Press, 2000).

4. William Bragg Ewald, Jr., *Who Killed Joe McCarthy?* (New York: Simon & Schuster, 1984); FASP, Eyes Only.

5. Alexis Coe ran into the same denial of access to McCarthy correspondence and related the experience in a column, "Senator, Let Us Read Your Letters," *The New York Times*, Oct. 27, 2015; I was denied access in October 2013.

6. I am indebted to my Southwestern College colleague Provost James A. Sheppard for educating me about military deception of the type in which Eisenhower was thoroughly schooled.

7. Ewald, *Who Killed Joe McCarthy?*, 242.

8. For a thorough discussion of this issue, see George C. Edwards III, *The Strategic President: Persuasion and Opportunity in Presidential Leadership* (Princeton: Princeton University Press, 2009).

9. W. H. Lawrence, "New Role for M'Carthy," *The New York Times*, Jan. 10, 1954; Lawrence, "Senate Enmeshed," *The New York Times*, Jan. 7, 1954.

10. Eisenhower, remarks at the National Defense Executive Reserve Conference, Nov. 14, 1957, *PPP.*

PROLOGUE

1. Douglas R. Price, e-mail to author, Sept. 4, 2011; Price, a personal aide to General Eisenhower in the campaign and later serving with the Republican National Committee, provided supporting documents for his account of the motorcade's organization.

2. Milton Eisenhower, interview with Herbert Parmet, June 19, 1969, DDEPL, OH-531, 26.

3. William Bragg Ewald, Jr., *Who Killed Joe McCarthy?* (New York: Simon & Schuster, 1984), 23.

4. McCarthy's June 14, 1951, speech is excerpted at length online in J. Bradford Delong, "A Historical Remembrance: George C. Marshall," 2008; Thomas C. Reeves, *The Life and Times of Joe McCarthy* (New York: Stein & Day, 1982), 372–75; David M. Oshinsky, *A Conspiracy So Immense: The World of Joe McCarthy* (New York: Oxford University Press, 2005), 197–200; Ewald, *Who Killed Joe McCarthy?*, 25; Arthur Herman, *Joseph McCarthy: Reexamining the Life and Legacy of America's Most Hated Senator* (New York: Free Press, 2000), 189–90; Harold B. Hinton, "Marshall U.S. Foe, M'Carthy Charges," *The New York Times*, June 15, 1951.

5. W. H. Lawrence, "Eisenhower to Back M'Carthy If Named, but Assails Tactics," *The New York Times*, Aug. 23, 1952; Reeves, *The Life and Times of Joe McCarthy*, 436–37.

6. Ewald, *Who Killed Joe McCarthy?*, 32–34; Robert Cutler, *No Time for Rest* (New York, Little, Brown, 1966), 288; W. H. Lawrence, "Eisenhower Wants Koreans to Bear Brunt of Fighting," *The New York Times*, Oct. 3, 1952; Thomas C. Reeves, in *Distinguished Service: The Life of Wisconsin Governor Walter J. Kohler, Jr.* (Milwaukee: Marquette University Press, 2006), 282–83, accepts that Eisenhower and McCarthy had a stern conversation. According to Reeves, McCarthy told Kohler that Eisenhower did not bring up the paragraph of praise for Marshall he had planned for the speech.

7. Ewald, *Who Killed Joe McCarthy?*, 46; Sherman Adams, *First-Hand Report: The Inside Story of the Eisenhower Administration* (London: Hutchinson, 1961), 40–41.

8. Ewald, *Who Killed Joe McCarthy?*, 47.

9. The words of praise deleted from the speech and a transcript of the speech are in the speech-writing assistant Stephen G. Benedict Papers, B4 (1), DDEPL; Jeffrey Frank, *Ike and Dick: Portrait of a Strange Political Marriage* (New York: Simon & Schuster, 2013), 74–75.

10. W. H. Lawrence, "Eisenhower Scores President on Reds," *The New York Times*, Oct. 4, 1952; Bill Lawrence, *Six Presidents, Too Many Wars* (New York: Saturday Review Press, 1972), 194–97; Ewald, *Who Killed Joe McCarthy?*, 47.

CHAPTER 1: THE FIRST CONFRONTATION

1. Fred I. Greenstein, interview with Sherman Adams, cited in Michael J. Birkner, "Eisenhower and the Red Menace," *Prologue*, Fall 2001, 202.

2. DDE to G. Hauge, 09-15-53, *DDEP*, no. 417; DDE to Brownell, July 2, 1953, *DDEP*, no. 294; Eisenhower described his Soviet relationships after the war in *Crusade in Europe* (New York: Doubleday, 1949), 438, 460–67.

3. DDE diary, April 1, 1953, *DDEP*, no. 118; Dwight D. Eisenhower, *The White House Years: Mandate for Change* (Garden City, NY: Doubleday, 1963), 268.

4. Shanley diary, approx. March 20, 1953, BSP, B1, IV (3), 743; Eisenhower always refused to discuss running for a second term, but even following a massive heart attack and surgery in 1955–56, he did so. Insofar as possible, he wanted his presidential ambitions cloaked in a call to duty.

5. "Enter the 83rd," *The New York Times*, Jan. 4, 1953.

6. "Cohn, Veteran Investigator at 25," *The New York Times*, Jan. 3, 1953; for more information on Cohn, see William Bragg Ewald, Jr., *Who Killed Joe McCarthy?* (New York: Simon & Schuster, 1984), 49–51; Sidney Lion, *The Autobiography of Roy Cohn* (Secaucus, NJ: Lyle Stuart Inc., 1988), 113; Thomas C. Reeves, *The Life and Times of Joe McCarthy* (New York: Stein & Day, 1982), 463–66; David M. Oshinsky, *A Conspiracy So Immense: The World of Joe McCarthy* (New York: Oxford University Press, 2005), 253–56; Herbert Brownell, Jr., *Advising Ike: The Memoirs of Attorney General Herbert Brownell* (Lawrence: University Press of Kansas, 1993), 257.

7. C. P. Trussell, "Party Margin Slim," *The New York Times*, Jan. 4, 1953.

8. John D. Morris, "Senate Votes Fund to Start Inquiries," *The New York Times*, Jan. 31, 1953; "McCarthy to Double Investigating Staff," *The Washington Post*, Jan. 15, 1953; "The M'Carthy Inquiry," *The New York Times*, Feb. 1, 1953.

9. DDE, Inaugural Address notes, Feb. 27, 1953, WHOSS, Minnich Series, B1, Misc.; DDE diary, Jan. 16, 1953, *DDEP*, no. 1057. A man of action, Eisenhower was also an excellent wordsmith and often his own best editor.

10. DDE, Inaugural Address, Jan. 20, 1953, *PPP*; W. H. Lawrence, "President's Plan," and James Reston, "Inaugural Is Held to Extend U.S. Commitments to World," *The New York Times*, Jan. 21, 1953.

11. Throughout this book, the author often refers to the president's schedules and appointments, most of which are not explicitly cited; see the Dwight D. Eisenhower Daily Appointment Schedule, available at DDEPL, also available online from the Miller Center of Public Affairs, University of Virginia, website.

12. Clayton Knowles, "G. O. P. Seeks Brownell Plan for Solving Snag on Wilson," *The New York Times*, Jan. 19, 1953; Justin Hyde, "GM's 'Engine Charlie' Wilson Learned to Live with a Misquote," *Detroit Free Press*, Sept. 14, 2008.

13. DDE, Transition Journal, Jan. 20, 1953, HCLP II, Carton 6, off-site (23), SH14, VE9; DDE diary, Jan. 20, 1953, HCLP, Lodge-Eisenhower Correspondence, Reel 28; Harold B. Hinton, "Wilson Severs Ties to General Motors," *The New York Times*, Jan. 16, 1953.

14. Harold B. Hinton, "Approval Is Likely," *The New York Times*, Jan. 23, 1953; John D. Morris, "Senate Approval of 2 Wilson Aides Remains in Doubt," *The New York Times*, Jan. 25, 1953; Clayton Knowles, "Eisenhower Likely to Hold Up 2 Wilson Aides," *The New York Times*, Jan. 26, 1953; Arthur Krock, "Wilson Case Bad Start for New Administration," *The New York Times*, Jan. 25, 1953.

15. Emmet John Hughes diary, July 16, 1953, SGMML.

16. JFD to Brownell, Jan. 28, 1953, JFDP, Tel. Call Series, B1 (4); Cabinet Meeting, Jan. 30, 1954, Cabinet Series, B1, DDEPL; WHOSS, Cabinet Series, Minnich Series, B1, Misc.-C (1), DDEPL; Ewald, *Who Killed Joe McCarthy?*, 48.

17. "Bedell Smith: A Good Choice," *The New York Times*, Jan. 12, 1953; Jeff Broadwater, *Eisenhower and the Anti-Communist Crusade* (Chapel Hill: University of North Carolina Press, 1992), 55.

18. "A Splendid Appointment," *The New York Times*, Jan. 13, 1954; Bernard Shanley diary, BSP, B1, IV (1), 599; William S. White, "Conant Replies to His Critic," *The New York Times*, Feb. 4, 1953; McCarthy to DDE, Feb. 3, 1953, DDEPL, Name Series, B22, McCarthy; Persons to Stephens, Feb. 4, 1953, DDEPL, Name Series, B22, McCarthy; Ewald, *Who Killed Joe McCarthy?*, 53, 56–57; White, "Committee Backs Conant and Smith," *The New York Times*, Feb. 5, 1953; "Senate Confirms Smith and Conant," *The New York Times*, Feb. 7, 1953; Brownell, *Advising Ike*, 253–55; Irwin F. Gellman, *The President and the Apprentice: Eisenhower and Nixon, 1952–1961* (New Haven: Yale University Press, 2015), 102.

19. Charles E. Bohlen, *Witness to History, 1929–1969* (New York: Norton, 1973), 312; Charles Bohlen interview, Dec. 17, 1970, Columbia University Oral History Project, OH-136, DDEPL; "Bohlen May Get Red Post," *The New York Times*, Feb. 1, 1953; James Reston, "6 Career Officers Picked," *The New York Times*, Feb. 6, 1953; Eisenhower, *Mandate for Change*, 212; Reeves, *The Life and Times of Joe McCarthy*, 468.

20. Eisenhower, *Mandate for Change*, 212–13; DDE to Taft, March 18, 1953, *DDEP*, no. 92.

21. William S. White, "Bohlen Defends Yalta Pact," *The New York Times*, March 3, 1953; Ewald, *Who Killed Joe McCarthy?*, 57–58.

22. Robert Cutler, *No Time for Rest* (New York: Little, Brown, 1966), 320–21; Hughes diary, March 4, 1953 SGMML. Ann Whitman, Eisenhower's secretary, was supposedly Cutler's source for Ike's choice of colors on a hard day.

23. DDE, President's Statement to Soviet People, March 4, 1953, *PPP*.

24. "Message Conveying Condolences on Death of Stalin," March 5, 1953, PPP; "Smith and Bohlen Sat Up with Soviet 'Sick Friend,'" *The New York Times*, March 6, 1953.

25. *Mandate for Change*, 267; White, "Move to Denounce Soviet Is Shelved," *The New York Times*, March. 11, 1953.

26. Drew Pearson, *Drew Pearson Diaries, 1949–1959*, ed. Tyler Abell (New York: Holt, Rinehart, 1974), March 5, 1953, 254; Oshinsky, *A Conspiracy So Immense*, 288.

27. JFD to S. Adams, March 13, 1953, JFDP, White House Memoranda Series, B8, Security Matters, McLeod, Bohlen (4); "McCarthy Joins Fight," *The New York Times*, March 14, 1953; William S. White, "Senate G. O. P. Is Split," *The New York Times*, March 14, 1953; "Bohlen Foes Push Fight," *The New York Times*, March 15, 1953; Clayton Knowles, "M'Carran Opposes Bohlen," *The New York Times*, March 16, 1953.

28. JFD to Lourie, JFD to Wiley, March 16, 1953, Taft and JFD, March 16, 1953, JFDP, Tel. Call Series, B1 (2); JFD to S. Adams, March 16, 1953; JFD conversation with President, March 16, 1953; DDE and JFD, March 16, 1953, all three in JFDP, Tel. Call Series, B10 (White House).

29. JFD to Bohlen, March 16, 1953, JFDP to Wiley and Taft, March 17, 1953, both in JFDP, Tel. Call Series, B1 (2).

30. Dulles to DDE, March 17, 1953, JFDP, Tel. Call Series, B10 (White House); Bohlen, *Witness to History*, 323; introduction by Avis Bohlen to 2nd edition of Charles Thayer, *Bears in the Caviar* (Montpelier, VT: Russian Life Books, 2015), 16. The account is based on Thayer's diary, Charles W. Thayer Collection, Harry S. Truman

Library, Independence, MO. For a detailed account of the origins of the perception that the State Department was a nest of striped-pants homosexuals, see Robert D. Dean, *Imperial Brotherhood: Gender and the Making of Cold War Foreign Policy* (Amherst: University of Massachusetts Press, 2001), 97–145; highlights from the FBI report on Bohlen are recounted on 123–24, 134–35.

31. McCarthy, speech, approx. March 17, 1953, JFDP, White House Memoranda Series, B8, Security Matters, McLeod, Bohlen (4); William S. White, "Dulles to Evaluate F.B.I. Bohlen Study," *The New York Times*, March 17, 1953; James Reston, "Dulles Facing Test Today," *The New York Times*, March 18, 1953; Ewald, *Who Killed Joe McCarthy?*, 58.

32. JFD to Stephens and S. Adams, March 18, 1953, JFDP, Tel. Call Series, B10 (White House); Ewald, *Who Killed Joe McCarthy?*, 57; Oshinsky, *A Conspiracy So Immense*, 287; Bohlen, *Witness to History*, 322.

33. Jay Walz, "Dulles Says Clearing Bohlen Was Job for Him," *The New York Times*, March 23, 1953; Arthur Krock, "Another Proof That McCarthy Isn't the Boss," *The New York Times*, March 19, 1953; Ewald, *Who Killed Joe McCarthy?*, 57–58; Bohlen, *Witness to History*, 324.

34. William S. White, "Senate Unit Backs Bohlen," *The New York Times*, March 19, 1953; Ewald, *Who Killed Joe McCarthy?*, 57–58; Reeves, *The Life and Times of Joe McCarthy*, 470; Oshinsky, *A Conspiracy So Immense*, 289; DDE, News Conference, March 19, 1953, *PPP*.

35. JFD to AWD, March 21, 1953, JFDP, Tel. Call Series, B1 (2); Bohlen, *Witness to History*, 323; Dean, *Imperial Brotherhood*, 134–35.

36. "Ex–F.B.I. Man Picked for Security Chief," *The New York Times*, Feb. 26, 1953; Oshinsky, *A Conspiracy So Immense*, 262–64.

37. S. Adams to JFD, March 19, 1953, two calls, JFDP, Tel. Call Series, B10 (White House).

38. JFD to McLeod, S. Adams, Hagerty, Brownell, DDE, March 20, 1953, JFDP, White House Memoranda Series, B8, Security Matters, McLeod, Bohlen (4).

39. Dulles to Hagerty, Lourie, and S. Adams, March 20, 1953, JFDP, Tel. Call Series, B10 (White House).

40. JFD to McLeod, March 20 and 21, 1953, Brownell, March 20, 1953, JFDP, White House Memoranda Series, B8, Security Matters,

McLeod, Bohlen (4); Oshinsky, *A Conspiracy So Immense*, 290; Ewald, *Who Killed Joe McCarthy?*, 58.

41. William S. White, "Dulles Holds Firm," *The New York Times*, March 21, 1953; Murray Marder, "Secretary Is Accused of Security Over-riding," *The Washington Post*, March 21, 1953; John D. Morris, "M'Carthy Balked in Bohlen Fight," *The New York Times*, March 23, 1953.

42. JFD and Brownell, March 21, 1953, JFDP, Tel. Call Series, B1 (2); JFD Memorandum for Phleger, March 23, 1953, JFDP, White House Memoranda Series, B8, Security Matters (3); Conversations—DDE, JFD, Brownell, March 22, JFDP, Tel. Call Series, B8, Security Matters, McLeod, Bohlen (3); Brownell to DDE, March 23, 1953, DDE diary, B4, Phone Calls (2), DDEPL; JFD and Taft, March 23, 1953, JFDP, Tel. Call Series, B1 (2).

43. William S. White, "G. O. P. Chiefs Join to Score M'Carthy," and James Reston, "Main Issue in Bohlen Case," *The New York Times*, March 24, 1953; Reeves, *The Life and Times of Joe McCarthy*, 472; Oshinsky, *A Conspiracy So Immense*, 290.

44. JFD, phone conversations with Taft, Brownell, and Wiley, March 24, 1953, JFDP, Tel. Call Series, B1 (2), and White House Memoranda Series, B8, Security Matters (3); Brownell, *Advising Ike*, 255.

45. JFD, Taft to JEH, Brownell, March 24, 1953, JFDP, Tel. Call Series, B1 (2).

46. Notes by Reap and McCardle, March 24, 1953, JFDP, White House Memoranda Series, B8, Security Matters (3); William S. White, "2 Senators Study F. B. I. Bohlen Data," *The New York Times*, March 25, 1953; Reeves, *The Life and Times of Joe McCarthy*, 472; Oshinsky, *A Conspiracy So Immense*, 291; Brownell, *Advising Ike*, 255.

47. McCarthy, speech, March 25, 1953, JFDP, White House Memoranda Series, B8, Security Matters, McLeod, Bohlen (2); Gellman, *The President and the Apprentice*, 93–94.

48. William S. White, "Bitterness Marks Debate on Bohlen," *The New York Times*, March 26, 1953, Bohlen, *Witness to History*, 330; Reeves, *The Life and Times of Joe McCarthy*, 474; Oshinsky, *A Conspiracy So Immense*, 291–92.

49. DDE, News Conference, March 26, 1953, *PPP*; William S. White,

"President Terms Bohlen Best Man," *The New York Times*, March 26, 1953; Reeves, *The Life and Times of Joe McCarthy*, 473.

50. "M'Carthy Insists Bohlen Is Unfit," *The New York Times*, March 29, 1953; Robert Albright, "Vote Termed Personal Victory for President," *The Washington Post*, March 28, 1953; the "no more Bohlens" quote is cited in Reeves, *The Life and Times of Joe McCarthy*, 475, taken from William S. White, *The Taft Story* (New York: Harper, 1954), 239; Ewald, *Who Killed Joe McCarthy?*, 58–59.

51. "Bohlen Sworn In," *The New York Times*, March 30, 1953; Shanley diary, approx. March 20, 1953, BSP, B1, IV (3), 743.

CHAPTER 2: "DON'T JOIN THE BOOK BURNERS!"

1. "Greek Shipowners to Stop Red Trade," *The New York Times*, March 29, 1953; Edward Ryan, "Greek Owners of 242 Ships Bar Red Trade," *The Washington Post*, March 29, 1953; Thomas C. Reeves, *The Life and Times of Joe McCarthy* (New York: Stein & Day, 1982), 486.

2. "Two Secretaries of State," *The Washington Post*, March 31, 1953; William S. White, "M'Carthy Loses a Battle," *The New York Times*, March 29, 1953; Joseph Alsop, "Matter of Fact," *The Washington Post*, April 1, 1953; David M. Oshinsky, *A Conspiracy So Immense: The World of Joe McCarthy* (New York: Oxford University Press, 2005), 292–95.

3. Stassen to JFD, March 30, 1953, JFDP, Tel. Call Series, B1 (1); C. P. Trussell, "Stassen Charges M'Carthy Impedes Red Cargo Curbs," *The New York Times*, March 31, 1953; Murray Marder, "Stassen Says McCarthy Harmed U.S.," *The Washington Post*, March 31, 1953; Oshinsky, *A Conspiracy So Immense*, 295–96; William Bragg Ewald, Jr., *Who Killed Joe McCarthy?* (New York: Simon & Schuster, 1984), 161; Michael Birkner, "Eisenhower and the Red Menace," *Prologue*, 33, no. 3 (Fall 2001), 202.

4. McCarthy to DDE, March 31, 1953, Name Series, B22, McCarthy, DDEPL; DDE to McCarthy, April 1, 1953, *DDEP*, no. 112; Irwin F. Gellman, *The President and the Apprentice: Eisenhower and Nixon, 1952–1961* (New Haven: Yale University Press, 2015), 94–95; Reeves, *The Life and Times of Joe McCarthy*, 486–87.

5. State Department Press Release, Apr. 1, 1953, JFDP, Gen. Corres. & Memo. Series, B3 (Me). Dulles assigned an aide to record verbatim what the senator said to reporters; notes on McCarthy & press, Apr. 1, 1953, JFDP, Gen. Corres. & Memo. Series, B3 (M3); State Department Press Release, Apr. 1, 1953, JFDP, Gen. Corres. & Memo. Series, B3 (Me); Arthur Krock, "In the Nation: Just a Little Careless," *The New York Times*, Apr. 3, 1953; Joseph and Stewart Alsop, "Matter of Fact," *The Washington Post*, Apr. 15, 1953; Murray Marder, "Thanks Him for Data on Aid to Reds," *The Washington Post*, Apr. 2, 1953; Reeves, *The Life and Times of Joe McCarthy*, 487; Oshinsky, *A Conspiracy So Immense*, 296–97.

6. DDE, News Conference, April 2, 1953, *PPP*; Murray Marder, "Ike Is Calm," *The Washington Post*, Apr. 3, 1953; Reeves, *The Life and Times of Joe McCarthy*, 487; Oshinsky, *A Conspiracy So Immense*, 297; Ewald, *Who Killed Joe McCarthy?*, 70.

7. Bullis to DDE, CF/OF, B317, 99–R, Joe McCarthy, DDEPL; DDE to Bullis, May 18, 1953, *DDEP*, no. 193; DDE to Phillips, June 5, 1953, *DDEP*, no. 229.

8. Ewald, *Who Killed Joe McCarthy?*, 147–48; William Bragg Ewald, Jr., *McCarthyism and Consensus: The Credibility of Institutions, Policies and Leadership*, vol. 13 (New York: University Press of America, 1986), 15; Milton S. Eisenhower, *The President Is Calling* (Garden City, NY: Doubleday, 1974), 317, and in an Columbia University Oral History Series interview, OH-292, DDEPL; Birkner, "Eisenhower and the Red Menace," 201.

9. DDE to Edgar Eisenhower, April 3, 1953, DDE diary, B3 (3), DDEPL.

10. Reeves, *The Life and Times of Joe McCarthy*, 477–78.

11. Sokolsky to JFD, Feb. 12, 1953, JFDP, Tel. Call Series, B1 (4); Edward Ranzal, "M'Carthy Sifting Voice of America," *The New York Times*, Feb. 13, 1953; Edward Ranzal, "McCarthy Lays 'Sabotaging' of Foreign Policy to 'Voice,'" *The New York Times*, Feb. 14, 1953; Reeves, *The Life and Times of Joe McCarthy*, 478–79; Oshinsky, *A Conspiracy So Immense*, 266–78.

12. JFD to Adams, Feb. 16, 1953, and JFD to DDE, Feb. 19, 1953, JFDP, Tel. Call Series, B10 (White House); Shanley diary, Feb. 18, 1953, BSP, B1, IV (1), 644, 648–50; Hughes diary, Feb. 24, 1953, SGMML.

13. Martin Merson, *The Private Diary of a Public Servant* (New York: Macmillan, 1955), 1–2, 6; Hagerty, press release, Feb. 24, 1953, CF/OF B131, 8-D-2, Voice of America, DDEPL; C. P. Trussell, "Educator Is Asked to Head the 'Voice,'" *The New York Times*, Feb. 24, 1953; JFD to DDE, Feb. 24, 1953, JFDP, Tel. Call Series, B10 (White House); DDE to Johnson, Feb. 24, 1953, *DDEP*, no. 55.

14. "The Nation," *The New York Times*, Feb. 22, 1953; Report on Overseas Libraries, "Books by Avowed Communists," n.d., 1953, CF/OF, B130, 8-D, International Information Administration (4), DDEPL; Oshinsky, *A Conspiracy So Immense*, 277–78.

15. "'Voice' Aide Ruled Suicide," *The New York Times*, March 6, 1953; Wayne Phillips, "Harassing Feared by 'Voice' Suicide," *The New York Times*, March 7, 1953; "Text of Letter Left by 'Voice' Suicide," *The New York Times*, March 7, 1953; "Suicide Cleared by McCarthy," *The Washington Post*, March 8, 1953; Oshinsky, *A Conspiracy So Immense*, 271.

16. Walter Waggoner, "New Ruling Permits 'Voice' to Use Communist Writings," *The New York Times*, March 19, 1953.

17. C. P. Trussell, "New 'Voice' Likely to Replace Agency," *The New York Times*, March 21, 1953.

18. JFD to Diplomatic & Consular Offices, April 2–3, 1953, Congressional Security Investigations, *FRUS*, vol. I, 1437–39; JFD to Lourie, April 3, 1953, JFDP, Tel. Call Series, B1 (1); Reeves, *The Life and Times of Joe McCarthy*, 488–90; Oshinsky, *A Conspiracy So Immense*, 279. Nicholas von Hoffman, *Citizen Cohn: The Life and Times of Roy Cohn* (New York: Bantam Books, 1992), 187–90, discusses evidence pro and con as to whether Cohn and Schine were lovers.

19. In later years Roy Cohn was widely assumed to be "gay"—a term rarely used in the 1950s—and he died of AIDS in 1986; Schine, on the other hand, married a former Miss Universe in 1957 and fathered six children. In that era, prominent gay men often married, raised families, and maintained lifelong secrecy about their orientation, whether gay or bisexual. At minimum, Roy Cohn was infatuated; nothing else adequately explains the obsessive behavior toward David Schine that would eventually threaten his legal and political ambitions; for more on Cohn, see Sidney Lion, *The Autobiography of Roy Cohn* (Secaucus, NJ: Lyle Stuart, 1988).

20. Dillon to Smith, Apr. 7, 1953, Congressional Security Investigations, *FRUS*, vol. I, 1441–42; German Press and Radio Comments on Cohn and Schine, Apr. 22, 1953, *FRUS*, vol. I, 1455; "Aides of M'Carthy Open Bonn Inquiry," *The New York Times*, Apr. 7, 1953; Murray Marder, "M'Carthy's 'Junketeering Gumshoes' Flayed," *The Washington Post*, Apr. 30, 1953; "Investigators in Vienna," *The New York Times*, Apr. 11, 1953; a slightly different account of the hotel incident is reported in Drew Pearson, "McCarthy's Men Get Attention," *The Washington Post*, Apr. 22, 1953.

21. "Gold Dust Twins," *The Washington Post*, Apr. 21, 1953.

22. John B. Oakes, "Inquiry into McCarthy's Status," *The New York Times*, Apr. 12, 1953.

23. JFD to Hughes and Jackson, March 13, 1953, JFDP, Tel. Call Series, B10 (White House); Robert S. Kieve diary, March 18 and Apr. 15, 1953; Kieve, a White House speech writer assisting Emmet Hughes, shared his personal diary with the author.

24. Hughes diary, Apr. 10–15, 1953, SGMML; Kieve diary, March 18, 1953, details the arduous process of writing Eisenhower's speeches.

25. Robert Cutler, *No Time for Rest* (New York: Little, Brown, 1966), 322; Hughes diary, Apr. 16, 1953, SGMML.

26. DDE, "The Chance for Peace," speech to the American Society of Newspaper Editors, Apr. 16, 1953, *PPP*.

27. Cutler, *No Time for Rest*, 322; "Eisenhower Suffers Mild Food Poisoning," *The New York Times*, Apr. 17, 1953; Report on speech, June 4, 1953, WHOSS, Minnich Series, B1, Misc.-F; Anne O'Hare McCormick, "Abroad," *The New York Times*, Apr. 18, 1953; "Leaders of 2 Parties on 'Hill' Praise Talk," *The Washington Post*, Apr. 17, 1953; "World Leaders Praise Speech by Eisenhower," *The Washington Post*, Apr. 18, 1953.

28. Yugoslavia Embassy to State Department, Apr. 17, 1953, *FRUS*, vol. I, 1446; "McCarthy Aides Visit London," *The New York Times*, Apr. 21, 1953; Drew Pearson, "McCarthy's Men Get Attention," *The Washington Post*, Apr. 22, 1953; "Cohn and Schine Return," *The New York Times*, Apr. 22, 1953; "Trailed, Cohn Charges," *The New York Times*, May 4, 1953; "Trailing of Cohn Denied," *The New York Times*, May 5, 1953.

29. For details on the Soviet spying operation during the Cold War, see John Earl Haynes, Harvey Klehr, and Alexander Vassiliev, *Spies: The Rise and Fall of the KGB in America* (New Haven: Yale University Press, 2009).

30. Legislative Leaders, Jan. 26, 1953, Legislative Series, DDEPL; DDE, State of the Union Address, Feb. 2, 1953, *PPP*; Birkner, "Eisenhower and the Red Menace," 200.

31. For a detailed examination of the security program, see Herbert Brownell, Jr., *Advising Ike: The Memoirs of Attorney General Herbert Brownell* (Lawrence: University Press of Kansas, 1993), 230–51; Walter Lippmann, "Today and Tomorrow," *The Washington Post*, Feb. 5, 1953; Birkner, "Eisenhower and the Red Menace," 199.

32. Brownell, *Advising Ike*, 247–48; for the plight of homosexuals during the period, see David K. Johnson, *The Lavender Scare* (Chicago: University of Chicago Press, 2004), and Robert D. Dean, *Imperial Brotherhood: Gender and the Making of Cold War Foreign Policy* (Amherst: University of Massachusetts Press, 2001); Birkner, "Eisenhower and the Red Menace," 199.

33. Legislative Leaders, Apr. 27, 1953, DDE diary, B4, Staff Notes, DDEPL; Press Release, Executive Order 10450, Morgan Files, B7, Security Program (3) DDEPL; "Text of Executive Order," *The New York Times*, Apr. 28, 1953; Murray Marder, "New Federal Security Plans Stiffens Tests," *The Washington Post*, Apr. 28, 1953; Birkner, "Eisenhower and the Red Menace," 199.

34. DDE diary, May 1, 1953, *DDEP*, no. 168.

35. "Taft Reported in Fair Condition," *The New York Times*, May 22, 1953; DDE to Taft, May 21, 1953, *DDEP*, no. 202.

36. DDE diary, May 14 and June 1, 1953, *DDEP*, nos. 188, 222; Gellman, *The President and the Apprentice*, 93.

37. Cabinet Meeting, June 5, 1953, WHOSS, B1, C-5 (1); Joseph and Stewart Alsop, "Matter of Fact," *The Washington Post*, June 14, 1953.

38. Shanley diary, Nov. 19, 1953, B2, VI (2), 1280, BSP.

39. Remarks at Dartmouth College Commencement, June 14, 1953, *PPP*; Edward Folliard, "Must Know Communism to Whip It," *The Washington Post*, June 15, 1953. In addition to the anti-McCarthy quote, an account of Eisenhower's interaction with two other

degree honorees on June 14 is found in Anthony Leviero, "Eisenhower Backed on Book Ban Talk," *The New York Times*, June 17, 1953; Gellman, *The President and the Apprentice*, 97, quotes Richard Nixon, following the Dartmouth speech, pushing McCarthy to wind up his IIA investigation: "You should not be known as a one-shot senator."

40. DDE, News Conference, June 17, 1953, *PPP*; Anthony Leviero, "Eisenhower Backs Ban on Some Books," *The New York Times*, June 18, 1953; Chalmers Roberts, "Ike Explains Statement," *The Washington Post*, June 18, 1953.

41. Joseph and Stewart Alsop, "Matter of Fact," *The Washington Post*, July 1, 1953; Eisenhower said those very words at a cabinet meeting on June 26, 1953; WHOSS, Cabinet, B1, C5 (3); Cabinet Series, B2; Shanley diary, BSP, IV (5), 969.

42. Shanley diary, n.d., BSP, B1, IV (1), 625–625e.

43. Notes on Cabinet meeting, Feb. 12, 1953, recorded Feb. 19, WHOSS, Minnich Series, B1, Misc.-R; the process reviewing the case is discussed in Brownell, *Advising Ike*, 244–45.

44. DDE, Statement by the President, Feb. 11, 1953, *PPP*; Birkner, "Eisenhower and the Red Menace," 201.

45. Shanley diary, June 15, 1953, BSP, B2, IV (5), 939-a.

46. DDE to John Eisenhower, June 16, 1953, *DDEP*, no. 246; AWD to JFD, June 17, 1953, JFDP, Tel. Call Series, B1 (1).

47. Cabinet Meeting, June 19, 1953, WHOSS, Minnich Series, B1, C-5 (2), and June 20, 1953, B1, Misc.-H.

48. JFD to Brownell, June 19, 1953, JFDP, Tel. Call Series, B1 (1).

49. "Six Justices Agree," *The New York Times*, June 20, 1953; Shanley diary, June 19, 1953, BSP, B2, IV (5), 950a–51.

50. DDE, Statement by the President, June 19, 1953, *PPP.*

51. William Conklin, "Pair Quiet to End," *The New York Times*, June 20, 1953; the controversy over whether the executions were justified has continued down to the present, represented by recent books including Ronald Radosh and Joyce Milton, *The Rosenberg File*, 2nd ed. (New Haven: Yale University Press, 1997); Walter Schneir and Miriam Schneir, *Final Verdict: What Really Happened in the Rosenberg Case* (Brooklyn: Melville House, 2010); and Sam Roberts, *The*

Brother: The Untold Story of the Rosenberg Case (New York: Simon & Schuster, 2014).

CHAPTER 3: "YOU'RE IN THE ARMY NOW!"

1. Cabinet Meeting, June 26, 1953, WHOSS, B1, C5 (3), and Cabinet Series, B2, DDEPL; Shanley diary, BSP, B2, IV (5), 969, DDEPL; "You're in the Army Now" came out in 1917 (when Eisenhower was in the infantry), music by Isham Jones, lyrics by Tell Taylor and Ole Olsen. The music appeared in several movies and cartoons about the US Army, including one of the same name in 1941.

2. John G. Adams, *Without Precedent: The Story of the Death of McCarthyism* (New York: Norton, 1983), 67–68; Peter Kihss, "Witness, on Einstein Advice, Refuses to Say He Was Red," *The New York Times*, Dec. 17, 1953; "Einstein Criticized," *The New York Times*, June 14, 1953.

3. "New Hearings Set on 'Red' Book Issue," *The New York Times*, June 24, 1953; "M'Carthy Calls 23 for Book Inquiry," *The New York Times*, June 28, 1953; "Eisenhower Attacked," *The New York Times*, June 24, 1953.

4. DDE to Downs, June 24, 1953, *DDEP*, no. 47; "Confusion on 'Book Burning' Grows," *The New York Times*, June 28, 1953; Emmet John Hughes, *The Ordeal of Power: A Political Memoir of the Eisenhower Years* (New York: Atheneum, 1963), 94; Gladwin Hill, "Eisenhower Assails 'Zealots,'" *The New York Times*, June 27, 1953.

5. Cabinet Meeting, June 26, 1953, WHOSS, Cabinet, B1, C5 (3); Cabinet Series, DDEPL, B2; Shanley diary, BSP, IV (5), 969, DDEPL.

6. DDE, News Conference, July 1, 1953, *PPP*; "Ike Questions Need of Purging Mystery Books," *The Washington Post*, July 2, 1953; C. P. Trussell, "Eisenhower Hints a New Book Order," *The New York Times*, July 2, 1953.

7. DDE to Brownell, July 2, 1953, *DDEP*, no. 294; DDE to Sulzberger, Oct. 5, 1953, *DDEP*, no. 452.

8. "Veteran Red Hunter Joins M'Carthy Unit," *The New York Times*, June 19, 1953; C. P. Trussell, "3 on McCarthy Panel Assail Aide for 'Shocking' Attack on Clergy," *The New York Times*, July 3, 1953; Trussell, "Republican Senator Attacks McCarthy's Aide," *The New York Times*, July 4, 1953; "M'Carthy Aide Scores Clergy," *The Washington*

Post, July 2, 1953; Murray Marder, "McCarthy Committee Splits over Article," *The Washington Post*, July 3, 1953; "Church Groups Hit Red Clergy Charge," *The New York Times*, July 5, 1953; "Clerics Vehement on 'M'Carthyism,'" *The New York Times*, July 6, 1953.

9. C. P. Trussell, "McCarthy Balks Colleagues, Refuses to Oust Matthews," and "Senators Predict Matthews Ouster," *The New York Times*, July 8–9, 1953; Murray Marder, "Matthews' Dismissal Blocked by McCarthy," *The Washington Post*, July 8, 1953.

10. Hughes diary, July 8–9, 1953, SGMML; Shanley diary, July 9, 1953, BSP, B2, V (1), 1014–15; "Texts of Documents in Matthews Case," *The New York Times*, July 10, 1953; Sherman Adams to JFD, July 9, 1953, JFDP, Tel. Call Series, B10, White House, (3).

11. DDE, President's Message to NCCJ leaders, July 9, 1953, *PPP*; Edward Folliard, "Charge Held in Contempt," *The Washington Post*, July 10, 1953.

12. Shanley diary, July 9, 1953, BSP, B2, V (1), 1015; Hughes diary, July 7–8, 1953, SGMML; William Bragg Ewald, Jr., *Who Killed Joe McCarthy?* (New York: Simon & Schuster, 1984), 72; Irwin F. Gellman, *The President and the Apprentice: Eisenhower and Nixon, 1952–1961* (New Haven: Yale University Press, 2015), 97–98.

13. "Overreach," *The Washington Post*, July 11, 1953; C. P. Trussell, "Eisenhower Scores Attack on Clergy," *The New York Times*, July 10, 1953; "The President Strikes Back," *The New York Times*, July 11, 1953.

14. Shanley diary, July 9, 1953, BSP, B2, V (1), 1015; Hughes diary, July 15, 1953, SGMML; Ewald, *Who Killed Joe McCarthy?*, 72.

15. DDE to Nixon, July 10, 1953, *DDEP*, no. 310.

16. Shanley diary, July 10, 1953, BSP, B2, V (1), 1020–23; Cabinet Meeting, July 10, 1953, WHOSS, Minnich Series, B1, Misc.-H.

17. July 10, 1953, WHOSS, Minnich Series, B1, Misc.-McCarthy; Shanley diary, July 10, 1953, BSP, B2, V (1), 1023; "M'Carthy at White House," *The New York Times*, July 11, 1953.

18. "Democrats Quit M'Carthy's Group," *The New York Times*, July 11, 1953; Murray Marder, "Democrats off M'Carthy Committee," *The Washington Post*, July 11, 1953; C. P. Trussell, "Bolters Spur McCarthy Plea," *The New York Times*, July 17, 1953; Murray Marder, "Democrats Reject Bid," *The Washington Post*, July 17, 1953; "M'Carthy

Scored by G. O. P. Member," *The New York Times*, July 21, 1953; Murray Marder, "2d Staff Aide of McCarthy Under Attack," *The Washington Post*, July 14, 1953; William S. White, "M'Carthy in the Middle," and Arthur Krock, "President Gets Tough and Finds It Pays Off," *The New York Times*, July 12, 1953.

19. DDE to Hazlett, July 21, 1953, *DDEP*, no. 332.

20. DDE, News Conference, July 22, 1953, *PPP*; "President's Progress Report," *The New York Times*, July 23, 1953.

21. Johnson to DDE, July 3, 1953, CF/OF, B130, 8-D, IIA (2); Murray Marder, "Johnson Quits as U.S. News Chief," *The Washington Post*, July 7, 1953; Walter H. Waggoner, "The State Department Sings a Variation on an Old Theme," *The New York Times*, July 9, 1953; Statement by Robert Johnson, July 9, 1953, CF/OF, B130, 8-D, IIA (2); "Some Banned Books Are Restored," *The New York Times*, July 8, 1953; McCarthy to Johnson, July 9, 1953, CF/OF, B130, 8-D, IIA (3); "New Book Order M'Carthy Target," *The New York Times*, July 10, 1953.

22. On June 1, 1953, Eisenhower sent the Congress Reorganization Plan No. 8, "relating to the establishment of the United States Information Agency," http://uscode.house.gov; the history of the USIA is detailed in Nicholas J. Cull, *The Cold War and the United States Information Agency: American Propaganda and Public Diplomacy, 1945– 1989* (Cambridge, UK: Cambridge University Press, 2008), see p. 91 for Eisenhower's submission of the legislation; McCardle-Jackson phone conversation, July 18, 1953, JFDP, Tel. Call Series, B1, July–Oct. 1953 (5); DDE to Conant, July 20, 1953, CF/OF, B130, 8-D, IIA (4; DDE, Statement by the President, July 30, 1953, *PPP*; Anthony Leviero, "Streibert Named Information Chief," *The New York Times*, July 31, 1953.

23. DDE, Address to American People, July 26, 1953, *PPP*.

24. "M'Carthy Planning Shift in Inquiries," *The New York Times*, July 26, 1953; William S. White, "Position of M'Carthy in Politics Is Shifting," *The New York Times*, July 26, 1953.

25. "U.S. Continues Aid," *The New York Times*, Aug. 2, 1953; "M'Carthy Critical on Aid," *The New York Times*, Aug. 3, 1953; C. P. Trussell, "M'Carthy Attacks Allen Dulles Aide," *The New York Times*, Aug. 5, 1953; Trussell, "M'Carthy Hunting Print Shop Leaks," *The New York*

Times, Aug. 12, 1953; Trussell, "Printer Is Quoted on Access," *The New York Times*, Aug. 13, 1953; Luther Huston, "U. S. Printing Aide Silent at Inquiry," *The New York Times*, Aug. 19, 1953; Huston, "Rothschild Linked to Seizing of Code," *The New York Times*, Aug. 21, 1953; "Hearings Start on Coast," *The New York Times*, Aug. 22, 1953.

26. NSC, 153rd Meeting, July 9, 1953, *FRUS*, 1952–54, vol. I, 1953.

27. Wilcox interview, 1973, Columbia Oral History Project, quoted in *FRUS*, 1952–54, vol. I, 1467.

28. DDE to Lodge, July 9, 1953, *DDEP*, no. 309.

29. Reber to Welch, Apr. 9 and 20, 1954, FASP, Eyes Only, B5, G. David Schine case (3); J. Adams to S. Adams, Feb. 16, 1954, FASP, Eyes Only, B4, Chronology of Efforts on Behalf of Schine.

30. Stevens to Hull, March 15, 1954; Hull to Stevens, March 16, 1954, reconstruction of events for the Army-McCarthy hearings, FASP, Eyes Only, B5, G. David Schine case (1); Struve Hensel, report to Secretary Stevens after conversation with Smith, March 15, 1954, FASP, Eyes Only, B9, Telephone Notes, Secretary of the Army (19); Hensel memorandum, March 30, 1954, FASP, Eyes Only, B5, G. David Schine case (3); Fred I. Greenstein, interview with Sherman Adams, cited in Michael J. Birkner, "Eisenhower and the Red Menace," Prologue, Fall 2001, 202. James Lemuel Holloway, Jr., a four-star admiral, served as superintendent of the US Naval Academy from 1947 to 1950 and as chief of naval personnel from 1953 to 1957.

31. Author interview with Don Seaton, Nov. 14, 2012; Gladys Seaton interview, Oct. 17, 1974, OH-390, DDEPL; Shanley diary, BSP, B2, V (2), 1102; President's Appt. Schedule, July 13 and 27, 1953, Miller Center online.

32. Ewald, *Who Killed Joe McCarthy?*, 47, 229; Gladys Seaton interview, Oct. 17, 1974, OH-390, DDEPL.

33. Cabinet Meeting Minutes, July 31, 1953, Cabinet Series, B2, DDEPL; DDE, Statement by the President, July 31, 1953, *PPP*; Robert Albright, "Knowland Is Elected Senate Leader," *The Washington Post*, Aug. 5, 1953.

34. "The Nation," *The New York Times*, Aug. 30, 1953; DDE to Sidney Richardson, Aug. 8, 1953, *DDEP*, no. 379.

35. W. H. Lawrence, "U. S. Lacks Evidence Soviet Can Deliver a

Hydrogen Bomb," *The New York Times*, Aug. 21, 1953. There are numerous books on the Iranian coup, which remains highly controversial. For a firsthand account by a CIA agent, see Kermit Roosevelt, *Counter Coup: The Struggle for Control of Iran* (New York: McGraw-Hill, 1979).

36. Shanley diary, Aug. 24, 1953, BSP, B2, V (3), 1167, DDEPL.

37. Kieve diary, Aug. 17, 1953. According to Irwin F. Gellman, Richard Nixon's March 1976 unpublished memoirs at the Nixon Library in Yorba Linda, CA, describe cabinet meetings where Wilson sat next to Eisenhower and smoked; Sherman Adams, interviewed by Michael Birkner, OH-539, DDEPL; Adams's interview with Herbert Parmet confirms Eisenhower's attitude, resulting in Adams limiting Wilson's access "because Eisenhower didn't want to see him," OH-523, DDEPL.

38. DDE to Wilson, Aug. 24, 1953, *DDEP*, no. 394.

39. "U. S. Policy Aide Named," *The New York Times*, Sept. 2, 1953; "Seaton to Do His 'Best,'" *The New York Times*, Sept. 4, 1953; Anthony Leviero, "Eisenhower Sets Up Unit to Implement Security Strategy," *The New York Times*, Sept. 4, 1953.

40. "Legion Is Warned on Defense Lags," *The New York Times*, Aug. 29, 1953.

41. Hearing, Aug. 31, 1953, Executive Sessions of the Senate Permanent Subcommittee on Investigations of the Committee on Government Operations, 83rd Congress, vol. 2, US Senate website.

42. Peter Kihss, "M'Carthy Accuses 2 Army Employees," *The New York Times*, Sept. 1, 1953.

43. Peter Kihss, "M'Carthy 'Orders' Army Bare Files," *The New York Times*, Sept. 2, 1953; "Orders Still in Effect," *The New York Times*, Sept. 3, 1953; Kihss, "Army Won't Give Data to M'Carthy," *The New York Times*, Sept. 4, 1953; "First Army Denies Data to McCarthy, *The Washington Post*, Sept. 4, 1953; Ewald, *Who Killed Joe McCarthy?*, 73–74.

CHAPTER 4: THE SECRETARY AND THE SENATOR

1. Lodge to the President, Feb. 23, 1954, HCLP, Lodge-Eisenhower Correspondence, 1950–55, Reel 28, MHS; Lodge, phone call to Stevens, Feb. 24, 1954, FASP, Eyes Only, B4, Lucas (2), DDEPL.

2. Emmet John Hughes diary, July 16, 1953, SGMML; Eisenhower comment, recorded in Shanley diary, approx. March 20, 1953, BSP, B1, IV (3), 743.

3. Michael J. Birkner, "Eisenhower and the Red Menace," *Prologue*, Fall 2001, 202; William Bragg Ewald, Jr., *Who Killed Joe McCarthy?* (New York: Simon & Schuster, 1984), 3; John Adams maintains that in mid-August—more likely the first week in September—Secretary of the Army Robert Stevens, on vacation at his ranch in Montana, had heard that McCarthy was concerned about subversion at Fort Monmouth and rushed to the nearest telegraph office and wired McCarthy, John G. Adams, *Without Precedent: The Story of the Death of McCarthyism* (New York: Norton, 1983), 46–47.

4. "Stevens Ready to Aid M'Carthy," *The New York Times*, Sept. 8, 1953; "Stevens to Consult McCarthy," *The Washington Post*, Sept. 8, 1953.

5. Brownell interview with Ed Edwin, OH-157, no. 3, DDEPL.

6. Telephone Notes, Sept. 8, 1953, FASP, Eyes Only, B8, Secretary of the Army (9); Ewald, *Who Killed Joe McCarthy?*, 80; Trussel, "Stevens Will Review McCarthy's Demand," *The New York Times*, Sept. 9, 1953.

7. Rogers to Stevens, Sept. 9, 1953, FASP, Eyes Only, B4, Lucas (1); Ewald, *Who Killed Joe McCarthy?*, 80–81.

8. Hensel to Stevens, Sept. 10, 1953, FASP, Eyes Only, B5, Pike; B8, Telephone Notes, DDEPL; Seaton notes in Sherman Adams Papers, B10, McCarthy Hearings Memoranda, Dartmouth College.

9. C. P. Trussell, "M'Carthy Attacks Army's Document," *The New York Times*, Sept. 10, 1953; "Sees Pattern Repeated," *The New York Times*, Sept. 12, 1953; Ewald, *Who Killed Joe McCarthy?*, 82.

10. C. P. Trussell, "McCarthy Broke Security," *The New York Times*, Sept. 12, 1953; Stevens to Ridgway, Sept. 12, 1953, FASP, Eyes Only, B8, Telephone notes, Secretary of Army (9); Ewald, *Who Killed Joe McCarthy?*, 82.

11. Telephone Notes, Sept. 8, 1953, FASP, Eyes Only, B8, Secretary of the Army (9); C. P. Trussell, "Stevens Will Review McCarthy's Demand," *The New York Times*, Sept. 9, 1953; Grutzner, "Army Drops Clerk," *The New York Times*, Sept. 17, 1953; Ewald, *Who Killed Joe McCarthy?*, 74, 80.

12. Bishop, Memorandum for the Record, Sept. 14, 1953, FASP, Eyes Only, B6, Memos to McCarthy Subcommittee Investigation.

13. Telephone Notes, Secretary of the Army, Sept. 17, 1953, FASP, Eyes Only, B8 (10); Ewald, *Who Killed Joe McCarthy?*, 85.

14. "Seaton Sworn In," *The New York Times*, Sept. 16, 1953; Gladys Seaton interview, Oct. 17, 1974, OH-390, DDEPL; Ewald, *Who Killed Joe McCarthy?*, 82–83, 230; Adams, *Without Precedent*, 59.

15. Adams, *Without Precedent*, 50. On September 18, Secretary Stevens phoned John Adams and formally asked him to serve as the army's counsel. A businessman with his law degree from the University of South Dakota, Adams had come to Washington as a clerk for the Senate Committee on Armed Services. In 1949, he had joined the Department of Defense as assistant general counsel to H. Struve Hensel. He would begin his new position on Monday, September 28; Michael S. Mayer, *Presidential Profiles: The Eisenhower Years* (Facts on File, 2010), 4.

16. Stevens to Seaton, Sept. 17, 1953, FASP, Eyes Only, B4, Lucas (1); Ewald, *Who Killed Joe McCarthy?*, 83–85.

17. "Eisenhower Back at Capital," *The New York Times*, Sept. 20, 1953.

18. Telephone Notes, Secretary of the Army, Sept. 21, 1953, FASP, Eyes Only, B8 (10); "M'Carthy Charges Reds Duped Army," *The New York Times*, Sept. 22, 1953.

19. DDE, Address, "Forward to '54" dinner, Sept. 21, 1953, *PPP*.

20. "M'Carthy Marries Former Staff Aide," *The New York Times*, Sept. 30, 1953; John Adams incorrectly notes the wedding as taking place on August 30, Adams, *Without Precedent*, 47; Ewald, *Who Killed Joe McCarthy?*, 89; DDE, News Conference, Sept. 30, 1953, *PPP*.

21. Cabinet, Oct. 2, 1953, WHO-OSS Minnich, B1, Misc.—H, EL.

22. Roosevelt to Milton Eisenhower, n.d. (Oct. 1953), DDE to Milton, Oct. 9, 1953, Name Series, B12, Milton Eisenhower, 1952–53 (2–3), DDEPL, and *DDEP*, no. 460.

23. Harlow to DDE, Oct. 26, 1953, Name Series, B12, Milton Eisenhower, 1952–53 (2), DDEPL.

24. Stevens to Lawton, Oct. 2, 1953, FASP, Eyes Only, B4, Lucas (1); Ewald, *Who Killed Joe McCarthy?*, 90–91.

25. "Signal Corps Aides Relieved by Army," *The New York Times*, Oct.

7, 1953; "Senate Unit Queries Ft. Monmouth Aides," *The New York Times*, Oct. 9, 1953; Ewald, *Who Killed Joe McCarthy?*, 91–92.

26. "Spying Is Charged at Fort Monmouth," *The New York Times*, Oct. 13, 1953; Adams, *Without Precedent*, 53.

27. Ranzal, "Army Radar Data Reported Missing," *The New York Times*, Oct. 14, 1953; Ewald, *Who Killed Joe McCarthy?*, 92, 98–99; Adams, *Without Precedent*, 64–66; "Radar Spy Data Awaited," *The New York Times*, Oct. 22, 1953; Stetson, "M'Carthy Charges Soviets Got Secrets," *The New York Times*, Oct. 23, 1953; "Red Scientists Got Secrets," *The Washington Post*, Oct. 23, 1953; McCarthy told the press that the alleged scientist who provided the tape recording was actually thirty years of age, not nineteen.

28. Shanley diary, Oct. 13, 1953, BSP, B2, VI (1), 1196; Press release, Executive Order 10491, signed Oct. 13, released Oct. 14, 1953, Gerald D. Morgan Files, B7, Security Program (2).

29. Ranzal, "Five More Army Radar Aides Suspended," *The New York Times*, Oct. 15, 1953; "Rosenberg Called Radar Spy Leader," *The New York Times*, Oct. 16, 1953.

30. "Army Denies Tampering," *The New York Times*, Oct. 17, 1953; Johnson to Stevens, Oct. 16, 1953, FASP, Eyes Only, B4, Lucas (1).

31. Ranzal, "Radar Witness Breaks Down," *The New York Times*, Oct. 17, 1953; Adams, *Without Precedent*, 53–56; Ewald, *Who Killed Joe McCarthy?*, 94.

32. Stevens to Hoover, Oct. 19, 1953, FASP, Eyes Only, B4, Lucas; Ewald, *Who Killed Joe McCarthy?*, 95; Conklin, "Espionage in Signal Corps for 10 Years Is Charged," *The New York Times*, Oct. 18, 1953.

33. Adams to Hensel, March 24, 1954, FASP, Eyes Only, B5, G. David Schine Case (3); this memorandum of the October 20 trip to Monmouth was written by Adams in preparation for the 1954 Army McCarthy hearings; Adams, *Without Precedent*, 74–76; Ewald, *Who Killed Joe McCarthy?*, 97.

34. Conklin, "More than 12 Out in Radar Spy Case," *The New York Times*, Oct. 21, 1953.

35. Stevens to Schine, Oct. 21, 1953, FASP, Eyes Only, B4, Stevens' Calls; Ewald, *Who Killed Joe McCarthy?*, 97–98; Adams, *Without Precedent*, 58–59.

36. Cohn to Stevens, Oct. 27, 1953, FASP, Eyes Only, B4, Stevens' calls; Ewald, *Who Killed Joe McCarthy?*, 99–100.

37. Stevens to Cohn, Oct. 28, 1953, FASP, Eyes Only, B9, Tel. Notes, Secretary of Army (11).

38. Seaton to Stevens, Oct. 28, 1953, FASP, Eyes Only, B4, Lucas (2); Ewald, *Who Killed Joe McCarthy?*, 100–2.

39. Adams to Stevens, Oct. 30, 1953, FASP, Eyes Only, B5, Justice Department Position on Loyalty Boards before Congressional Committees; Ewald, *Who Killed Joe McCarthy?*, 102.

40. Cabinet Meeting, Oct. 30, 1953, Cabinet Series, B2, DDEPL; WHOSS, B1, C-8 (2); Shanley diary, BSP, B2, VI (2), 1251.

41. Adams to Stevens, Oct. 30, 1953, FAS Eyes Only, B4, Lucas, EL.

42. William Conklin, "Monmouth Figure Linked to Hiss Ring," *The New York Times*, Oct. 27, 1953; Adams, *Without Precedent*, 71–74.

43. M'Carthy Asks Unity," *The New York Times*, Oct. 22, 1953; "M'Carthy Attacks 'Bleeding Hearts,'" *The New York Times*, Oct. 29, 1953.

CHAPTER 5: THE TURNING POINT

1. The "New Look" was formalized in National Security Council document 162/2, which Eisenhower approved on October 30, 1953; for a succinct summary of the policy, see the Miller Center, University of Virginia, website.

2. Herbert Brownell, Jr., *Advising Ike: The Memoirs of Attorney General Herbert Brownell* (Lawrence: University Press of Kansas, 1993), 236–37; William Bragg Ewald, Jr., *Who Killed Joe McCarthy?* (New York: Simon & Schuster, 1984), 116–17.

3. Interview with Herbert Brownell, Jr., by Fred I. Greenstein, November 18, 1981, courtesy of John P. Burke, University of Vermont.

4. Lodge to DDE, March 6, 1954, HCLP, Lodge-Eisenhower Correspondence, 1950–55, Reel 28, MHS.

5. DDE to Brownell, Nov. 4, 1953, *DDEP*, no. 516. Daun van Ee summarizes the background of Eisenhower's past war actions toward the Soviet Union, stating the general "had endorsed Soviet-American friendship societies during the war and had halted his troops at the Elbe in order to permit the USSR to occupy Berlin. He had

traveled to Moscow in August 1945 for friendly meetings with Stalin and had given Marshal Georgy Zhukov almost every war reparation he had sought. In 1946, as Army Chief of Staff, Eisenhower had worked to cooperate with the Russians in trying to establish a combined United Nations force to police the world." Confirmed via e-mail, March 31, 2015.

6. Executive Order 10501, Nov. 5, 1953, *PPP*; Anthony Leviero, "Eisenhower Issues New Security Code," *The New York Times*, Nov. 7, 1953.

7. "Text of Brownell's Remarks," *The New York Times*, Nov. 7, 1953, and *The Washington Post*, Nov. 10, 1953; Ewald, *Who Killed Joe McCarthy?*, 118–19; Kent, "Ex-President Accused of Promoting Red 'Spy,'" *The Washington Post*, Nov. 7, 1953.

8. "Campaign on 'Red Infiltration' Issue," *The New York Times*, Nov. 7, 1953; Paul Kennedy, "Brownell Charges on White," *The New York Times*, Nov. 8, 1953; "Truman Bars 'Further Comment,'" *The New York Times*, Nov. 9, 1953; W. H. Lawrence, "Byrnes Says Truman Read Report," and "Texts of Statements by Byrnes and Brownell," *The New York Times*, Nov. 10, 1953. Byrnes, the renegade Democrat who had broken with his party to support Eisenhower in 1952, had been Truman's secretary of state when Harry Dexter White was in office. Byrnes described a meeting with Truman about the FBI report on White and said that the president had concluded that he could not withhold the commission for the position at the International Monetary Fund once a Senate committee had approved it. Brownell followed up on Byrnes's account with an additional statement justifying his speech because "I believe that the American people are entitled to know these facts."

9. Brownell, *Advising Ike*, 239; ACW diary, approx. Nov. 7, 1953, B1 (3), DDEPL; Childs, "Revival of White Case," *The Washington Post*, Nov. 11, 1953; Arthur Krock, "In the Nation," *The New York Times*, Nov. 12, 1953; author interview with Ann Brownell Sloane, March 20, 2014.

10. "The Case of H. D. White," *The New York Times*, Nov. 10, 1953.

11. W. H. Lawrence, "Truman, Byrnes Subpoenaed," *The New York Times*, Nov. 11, 1953; "A Smiling Truman Accepts Subpoena," *The*

New York Times, Nov. 11, 1953; "Text of Truman Talk," *The New York Times*, Nov. 11, 1953; Ewald, *Who Killed Joe McCarthy?*, 120–21.

12. W. H. Lawrence, "G. O. P. Chiefs Criticize Velde," and "Text of Brownell Statement," *The New York Times*, Nov. 12, 1953.

13. Herbert Brownell, Jr., interview with Fred I. Greenstein, Nov. 18, 1981, courtesy of John P. Burke, University of Vermont.

14. DDE, News Conference, Nov. 11, 1953, *PPP*; Robert Albright, "Ike Frowns on Subpoena for Truman," *The Washington Post*, Nov. 12, 1953; Irwin F. Gellman, *The President and the Apprentice: Eisenhower and Nixon, 1952–1961* (New Haven: Yale University Press, 2015), 100.

15. Reston, "Patriotism Backed," *The New York Times*, Nov. 12, 1953; Brownell, *Advising Ike*, 241, 301; Ewald, *Who Killed Joe McCarthy?*, 121–22.

16. Cabinet Meeting, Nov. 12, 1953, WHOSS, Cabinet Series; Ewald, *Who Killed Joe McCarthy?*, 122.

17. James Reston, "All Lose in White Case," *The New York Times*, Nov. 13, 1953; Reston, "Mr. Brownell Shifts the Indictment," *The New York Times*, Nov. 15, 1953.

18. Dwight D. Eisenhower, *The White House Years: Mandate for Change* (Garden City, NY: Doubleday, 1963), 315.

19. Milton Bracker, "Truman Rejects Subpoena," *The New York Times*, Nov. 13, 1953; W. H. Lawrence, "Senators to Hear Brownell Tuesday," *The New York Times*, Nov. 14, 1953; Bracker, "Truman Will Give White Case 'Facts,'" *The New York Times*, Nov. 15, 1953; Lawrence, "Truman Expected to Assert Tonight He Set Trap," *The New York Times*, Nov. 16, 1953; "Campaign on 'Red Infiltration' Issue," *The New York Times*, Nov. 7, 1953; "McCarthy Criticizes Truman," *The New York Times*, Nov. 15, 1953; Dwight D. Eisenhower, *Crusade in Europe* (New York: Doubleday, 1949), 287.

20. "Text of Address by Truman" and W. H. Lawrence, "Address to Nation," *The New York Times*, Nov. 17, 1953; Ewald, *Who Killed Joe McCarthy?*, 123–24.

21. James Reston, "Hoover Star in Hearing," *The New York Times*, Nov. 18, 1953.

22. Clayton Knowles, "Hall Asserts G. O. P. Views Communism as Big

1954 Issue," *The New York Times*, Nov. 16, 1953; Lodge to DDE, Nov. 16, 1953, HCLP, Lodge-Eisenhower Correspondence, 1950–55, Reel 28.

23. DDE, News Conference, Nov. 18, 1953, *PPP*; Ewald, *Who Killed Joe McCarthy?*, 126–27.

24. "Army Refuses Comment," *The New York Times*, Nov. 2, 1953; J. Adams to S. Adams, Feb. 16, 1954, FASP, Eyes Only, B4, Efforts on Behalf of Schine; John G. Adams, *Without Precedent: The Story of the Death of McCarthyism* (New York: Norton, 1983), 76–77; Ewald, *Who Killed Joe McCarthy?*, 119.

25. McCarthy to Stevens, Nov. 7, 1953, FASP, Eyes Only, B6, "Worknotes & Memos" (2); Ewald, *Who Killed Joe McCarthy?*, 119–20; This is William Ewald's version of this conversation, although the typed transcript at DDEPL leaves out the Waldorf reference; Ewald probably found the full quote in the difficult-to-read handwritten transcript. In his report to Sherman Adams on Feb. 16, 1954, John Adams reported other times that McCarthy privately expressed irritation about Schine but asked Adams not to tell Cohn, FASP, Eyes Only, B4, Chronology of Efforts for Schine.

26. J. Adams to S. Adams, Feb. 16, 1954, FASP, Eyes Only, B4, Efforts on Behalf of Schine; these documents include a detailed breakdown of the passes granted to Schine between Nov. 10, 1953, and Jan. 16, 1954; "Army Drafts Schine, *The Washington Post*, Nov. 5, 1953; Ewald, *Who Killed Joe McCarthy?*, 115; J. Adams, *Without Precedent*, 83.

27. "No Spies Found at Monmouth," *The New York Times*, Nov. 14, 1954; "M'Carthy to Press Monmouth Inquiry," *The New York Times*, Nov. 15, 1953; J. Adams, *Without Precedent*, 78.

28. J. Adams, *Without Precedent*, 78–80; Conklin, "Stevens, M'Carthy Trade Spy Views," *The New York Times*, Nov. 18, 1953; Ewald, *Who Killed Joe McCarthy?*, 125.

29. President's Remarks, B'nai B'rith Dinner, Nov. 23, 1953, *PPP*; Ewald, *Who Killed Joe McCarthy?*, 132–33.

30. "Text of McCarthy's Speech," "M'Carthy Accuses Truman in Reply," and "McCarthy Strikes Back at Truman," *The Washington Post*, Nov. 25, 1953; Ewald, *Who Killed Joe McCarthy?*, 133–34.

31. "Eisenhower and Truman Miss Broadcast" and Article I—No Title, *The New York Times*, Nov. 25, 1953; CD Jackson to Adams, Nov. 25, 1953, CDJP, B28, Governor Adams (2); Jackson Log, Nov. 27, 1953, CDJP, B68 (5); James Reston, "Eisenhower Staff Interprets McCarthy Speech," *The New York Times*, Nov. 26, 1953; Brownell, interview with Ed Edwin, no. 3, OH-157, DDEPL; Joseph Alsop, "Matter of Fact," and Roscoe Drummond, "The McCarthy Speech," *The Washington Post*, Nov. 27, 1953.

32. Jackson Log, Nov. 27, 1953, CDJP, B68 (5); Morris, "Eisenhowers Plan a Quiet Holiday," *The New York Times*, Nov. 26, 1953; DDE to JFD, Nov. 27, 1953, JFDP, Tel. Call Series, B10 (1); also in DDE diary, Nov. 27, 1953, Phone Calls, B5 (1), DDEPL.

33. Jackson log, Nov. 28–29, 1953, CDJP, B68 (5).

34. Jackson log, Nov. 30, 1954, CDJP, B68 (5); Shanley diary, Nov. 30, 1953, BSP, B2 VI (2), 1310–15; Robert Kieve diary, Nov. 30, 1953, provided to the author by Kieve; Ewald, *Who Killed Joe McCarthy?*, pp. 140–46, provides detail and biographical information on the participants.

35. Jackson to JFD, Dec. 1, 1953, JFDP, Tel. Call Series, B10, White House (1); James Reston, "Dulles Proclaims M'Carthy Is Wrong," *The New York Times*, Dec. 1, 1953.

36. Reston, "Dulles Proclaims M'Carthy Is Wrong"; Chalmers Roberts, "U.S. Policy Declared Jeopardized," *The Washington Post*, Dec. 2, 1963; Ewald, *Who Killed Joe McCarthy?*, 148.

37. Jackson to JFD, Dec. 1, 1953, JFDP, Tel. Call Series, B10, White House (1).

38. Kieve diary, Dec. 1, 1953, provided to the author; Jackson log, Dec. 1, 1953, CDJP, B68 (5).

39. CDJ to JFD, Dec. 2, 1953, JFDP, Tel. Call, B10, White House (1); Ewald, *Who Killed Joe McCarthy?*, 148–49.

40. Jackson log, Dec. 2, 1953, CDJP, B68 (5); Kieve diary, Dec. 2, 1953.

41. DDE, News Conference, Dec. 2, 1953, *PPP*; Ewald, *Who Killed Joe McCarthy?*, 150–51.

42. James Reston, "Eisenhower Takes Issue with M'Carthy on Policy," and W. H. Lawrence, "President Crosses a Rubicon," *The New York Times*, Dec. 3, 1953.

43. "Text of McCarthy Statement" and William S. White, "M'Carthy Insists on Red Trade Bar," *The New York Times*, Dec. 3 (listed incorrectly as Dec. 1 on Proquest), 1953; "McCarthy Denies He Intends to Seek Presidency," *The Washington Post*, Dec. 3, 1953; "An Honorable Man," *The Washington Post*, Dec. 4, 1953; "M'Carthy Fires Back at Ike and Dulles," *The Washington Post*, Dec. 4, 1953.

44. Numerous documents on the Bermuda conference are accessible in *FRUS*, vol. V, part 2, and at the State Department website; DDE, Address before U.N. General Assembly, Dec. 8, 1953, *PPP*; Kathleen Teltsch, "Eisenhower Gets Warm U.N. Reception," and A. M. Rosenthal, "Eisenhower Tries New Atomic Tack," *The New York Times*, Dec. 9, 1953; Eisenhower entitled the second volume of his memoirs *Waging Peace*.

45. William S. White, "President's Talk Weakens Critics," *The New York Times*, Dec. 10, 1953; DDE, News Conference, Dec. 16, 1953, *PPP*; Anthony Leviero, "Details Guarded on Security Risks," *The New York Times*, Dec. 17, 1953; "Ike's Speech Praised Generally on 'Hill,'" *The Washington Post*, Dec. 9, 1953.

46. J. Adams, *Without Precedent*, 83.

47. J. Adams to Stevens, Dec. 9, 1953, FASP, Eyes Only, B4, Lucas (2); Hensel to Potter, Report on Privileges Sought for G. David Schine, March 10, 1954, FASP, Eyes Only, B4, McCarthy (5); Ewald, *Who Killed Joe McCarthy?*, 155–57; J. Adams, *Without Precedent*, 82–84.

48. J. Adams to Stevens, Dec. 10, 1953, Vituperations by Cohn, FASP, Eyes Only, B4, Concurrent Memoranda, DDEPL; Ewald, *Who Killed Joe McCarthy?*, 157–58; J. Adams, *Without Precedent*, 85–86.

49. DDE to Hazlett, Dec. 24, 1953, Name Series, B18, Hazlett 1953 (1), DDEPL; *DDEP*, no. 640.

50. James Reston, "Time-Out in the Political Souffle," *The New York Times*, Dec. 13, 1953.

51. DDE, Statements by the President, Dec. 17–19, 1953, *PPP*; William S. White, "President Accents High Policy Issues," *The New York Times*, Dec. 19, 1953.

52. William S. White, "President Pledges Tougher Red Drive," *The New York Times*, Dec. 20, 1953; Gallup, "Public Votes Eisenhower as 'Man-of-Year,'" *The New York Times*, Dec. 27, 1953.

53. Roy Cohn, *McCarthy* (New York: New American Library, 1968), 111–113; Sidney Zion, *The Autobiography of Roy Cohn* (Secaucus, NJ: Lyle Stuart, 1988), 112–13.

54. "Nixon's Asia Tour," *The New York Times*, Dec. 20, 1953.

55. "To Sift Tax Cases," *The New York Times*, Dec. 31, 1953; the Proquest version of this news story erroneously shows the report date as December 20, but its content suggests that McCarthy made the comments after, not before, seeing Nixon and Rogers; Gellman, *The President and the Apprentice*, 101; Michael J. Birkner, "Eisenhower and the Red Menace," *Prologue*, Fall 2001, 201–2; Ewald, *Who Killed Joe McCarthy?*, 161; Thomas C. Reeves, *The Life and Times of Joe McCarthy* (New York: Stein & Day, 1982), 532–33; David M. Oshinsky, *A Conspiracy So Immense: The World of Joe McCarthy* (New York: Oxford University Press, 2005), 360–61.

CHAPTER 6: "EISENHOWER'S FIRST MOVE"

1. W. H. Lawrence, "M'Carthy's Focus Reported Shifted," *The New York Times*, Jan. 5, 1954; "Stories Laid to Nixon Talk," *The New York Times*, Jan. 7, 1954.

2. W. H. Lawrence, "New M'Carthy Curb Urged," *The New York Times*, Jan. 6, 1954; Irwin F. Gellman, *The President and the Apprentice: Eisenhower and Nixon, 1952–1961* (New Haven: Yale University Press, 2015), 104.

3. John G. Adams, *Without Precedent: The Story of the Death of McCarthyism* (New York: Norton, 1983), 116–17; William Bragg Ewald, Jr., *Who Killed Joe McCarthy?* (New York: Simon & Schuster, 1984), 188–89.

4. CD Jackson to S. Adams, Nov. 25, 1953, CDJP, B28, Governor Adams (2).

5. Eisenhower summarized the status of his plan, long in effect, in a conversation with Congresswoman Francis P. Bolton (R–Ohio) on June 15, 1954, ACW diary, B2 (2), DDEPL; Dwight D. Eisenhower, *The White House Years: Mandate for Change* (Garden City, NY: Doubleday, 1963), 277; Poll on McCarthy, Jan. 15, 1954, Dr. George H. Gallup, *The Gallup Poll: Public Opinion 1935–1971*, 2 vols. (New York: Random House, 1972), online.

6. Henry Cabot Lodge, Jr., *As It Was* (New York: Norton, 1976), 133; DDE, President's News Conference, Jan. 13, 1954, *PPP.*

7. DDE President's Radio and TV Address, Jan. 4, 1954, *PPP.*

8. Hagerty diary, Jan. 7, 1954, JHP, B1 (1); William S. White, "Congress Reaction Points to Red Issue in Elections," *The New York Times*, Jan. 7, 1954.

9. DDE, State of the Union Message, Jan. 7, 1954, *PPP*; W. H. Lawrence, "'Akin to Treason,'" *The New York Times*, Jan. 8, 1954.

10. W. H. Lawrence, "Senate Enmeshed in M'Carthy Curbs," *The New York Times*, Jan. 7, 1954.

11. "Permanent System Sought," *The New York Times*, Jan. 19, 1954.

12. "The Nation," *The New York Times*, Jan. 10, 1954.

13. W. H. Lawrence, "New Role for M'Carthy," *The New York Times*, Jan. 10, 1954; Lawrence, "Senate Enmeshed," *The New York Times*, Jan. 7, 1954.

14. "McCarthy Curb Doubted," *The New York Times*, Jan. 11, 1954.

15. Smith to Stevens, Jan. 12, 1954, FASP, Eyes Only, B4, Stevens' Calls; Peter Kihss, "Monmouth Expert Barred in Key Job," *The New York Times*, Jan. 12, 1954; "Monmouth Security Woes Antedate McCarthy Visits," *The New York Times*, Jan. 11, 1954; "Fort Monmouth Case," *The New York Times*, Jan. 14, 1954; "Taylor Predicts Ruin of M'Carthy," *The New York Times*, Jan. 20, 1954; Ewald, *Who Killed Joe McCarthy?*, 165.

16. William P. Rogers to Philip Young, Jan. 12, 1954, William Rogers Papers, B16 (Daily correspondence, Jan. 1954–Apr. 1954), DDEPL; Herbert Brownell, Jr., *Advising Ike: The Memoirs of Attorney General Herbert Brownell* (Lawrence: University Press of Kansas, 1993), 258; J. Adams to Rogers, Jan. 7, 1954, FASP, Eyes Only, B4; Ewald, *Who Killed Joe McCarthy?*, 166–67.

17. J. Adams, *Without Precedent*, 203–4.

18. Ewald, *Who Killed Joe McCarthy?*, 162.

19. Seaton to Stevens, Jan. 8, 1954, FASP, Eyes Only, B4; Ewald, *Who Killed Joe McCarthy?*, 163–65.

20. J. Adams, *Without Precedent*, 106.

21. Hagerty diary, Jan. 13, 1954, JHP, B1 (1), DDEPL.

22. DDE, News Conference, Jan. 13, 1954, *PPP*; "Now the Tests," *The New York Times*, Jan. 17, 1954.

23. Shanley diary, Jan. 14, 1954, BSP, VI (3), 1389; W. H. Lawrence, "Brownell Bars Ouster Details," *The New York Times*, Jan. 22, 1954.

24. DDE to Brownell, Jan. 12, 1954, *DDEP*, no. 658; the two quotes are from no. 658 footnotes, cited as Apr. 9, 1954, AWF/A, and Apr. 12; W. H. Lawrence, "Brownell Bars Ouster Details," *The New York Times*, Jan. 22, 1954.

25. DDE, State of the Union Address, Jan. 7, 1954, *PPP*.

26. Stevens to McCarthy, Jan. 14, 1954, FASP, Eyes Only, B4, Stevens' Calls; Ewald, *Who Killed Joe McCarthy?*, 165–66.

27. J. Adams, *Without Precedent*, 110–11.

28. DDE diary, Jan. 18, 1954, *DDEP*, no. 669.

29. J. Adams, Feb. 12, 1954, Memorandum for the Record, Jan. 19–21, FASP, Eyes Only, B5, Misc. Materials; Ewald, *Who Killed Joe McCarthy?*, 166–67; J. Adams, *Without Precedent*, 110–12.

30. Lodge to DDE, Jan. 20, 1954, HCLP, Lodge-Eisenhower Correspondence, 1950–55, microfilm, reel 28.

31. Shanley diary, Jan. 20, 1954, BSP, B2, V. 1 (3), 1396–97.

32. John G. Adams, Feb. 12, 1954, Memorandum for the Record of Jan. 19–21, nts, FAS Eyes Only, B5, Misc. Materials, EL; Sherman Adams, *First-Hand Report: The Inside Story of the Eisenhower Administration* (London: Hutchinson, 1961), 123; John Adams reported Seaton was planning to see the White House on executive privilege in J. Adams to Rogers, Jan. 7, 1954, FAS Eyes Only, B4, EL.

33. Brownell, *Advising Ike*, 257–58.

34. Ibid., 258; J. Adams, memorandum, Feb. 12, 1954, FASP, Eyes Only, B5, Misc. Materials; S. Adams, *First-Hand Report*, 124; Brownell, interview with Fred. I Greenstein, Nov. 18, 1981, courtesy of John P. Burke, University of Vermont.

35. S. Adams, *First-Hand Report*, 123–25; Ewald, *Who Killed Joe McCarthy?*, 167–72; J. Adams, *Without Precedent*, 110–12; Roy Cohn's first attempts to get the White House to intervene on behalf of David Schine are reported in chap. 3.

36. Brownell, *Advising Ike*, 258.

37. Lodge to Brownell, July 12, 1974, HCLP, microfilm, Lodge 11, Reel 2, MHS; Lodge, *As It Was*, 137; Brownell, interview with Fred. I Greenstein, Nov. 18, 1981. Throughout this story, key Eisenhower

subordinates frequently employed euphemisms to refer to the president, e.g., "the executive branch," "the executive mansion," and the old fallback, "the White House."

CHAPTER 7: "NOT FIT TO WEAR THAT UNIFORM"

1. "McCarthy Holds His Hat," *The New York Times*, Jan. 22, 1954.

2. Roy Cohn, *McCarthy* (New York: New American Library, 1968), 117.

3. John G. Adams, Memorandum for Record, Feb. 12, 1954, FASP, Eyes Only, B4, Chronology of Efforts; this memorandum summarizes the January 21 meeting in Brownell's office and subsequent events. On May 12, 1954, in the midst of the televised Army-McCarthy hearings, Adams let slip about the January 21 meeting, whereupon McCarthy insisted on subpoenaing the participants. That led to Eisenhower's historic invocation of executive privilege on May 17, 1954; see William Bragg Ewald, Jr., *Who Killed Joe McCarthy?* (New York: Simon & Schuster, 1984), 171–72; Herbert Brownell, Jr., *Advising Ike: The Memoirs of Attorney General Herbert Brownell* (Lawrence: University Press of Kansas, 1993), 257–58; John G. Adams, *Without Precedent: The Story of the Death of McCarthyism* (New York: Norton, 1983), 113.

4. W. H. Lawrence, "M'Carthy Yields on Subpoena Test," *The New York Times*, Jan. 23, 1954; Ewald, *Who Killed Joe McCarthy?*, 172.

5. Cohn, *McCarthy*, 113–14; Sidney Zion, *The Autobiography of Roy Cohn* (Secaucus, NJ: Lyle Stuart, 1988), 114–15.

6. John G. Adams, Memorandum for Record, Jan. 23, 1954, FASP, Eyes Only, B4, Chronology Efforts; J. Adams, *Without Precedent*, 113–15; Ewald, *Who Killed Joe McCarthy?*, 172–75; Cohn, *McCarthy*, 116–17; Zion, *The Autobiography of Roy Cohn*, 117.

7. W. H. Lawrence, "3 Bolters Won Back to McCarthy Panel," *The New York Times*, Jan. 26, 1954; Lawrence, "M'Carthy Yields in Democrat Bolt," *The New York Times*, Jan. 15, 1954; Lawrence, "M'Carthy Concessions Laid to Combination of Factors," *The New York Times*, Jan. 31, 1954; J. Adams, Memorandum for Record, Jan. 23, 1954, FASP, Eyes Only, B4, Chronology Efforts.

8. DDE, News Conference, Jan. 27, 1954, *PPP*.

9. DDE, News Conference, Feb. 3, 1954 *PPP.*

10. Cabinet Meeting, Feb. 5, 1954, WHOSS, Minnich Series, B1, President (2); Hagerty diary, Feb. 5, 1954, JHP, B1 (1).

11. J. Adams, *Without Precedent,* 117.

12. William Conklin, "M'Carthy Seeking Trial of a Major," *The New York Times,* Jan. 31, 1954; J. Adams, *Without Precedent,* 117–18; Ewald, *Who Killed Joe McCarthy?,* 189.

13. J. Adams, *Without Precedent,* 118–19; Ewald, *Who Killed Joe McCarthy?,* 189.

14. "Stevens Plans Inquiry," *The New York Times,* Feb. 3, 1954.

15. Stevens to J. Adams, Feb. 4, 1954, FASP, Eyes Only, B4, Lucas (2).

16. "M'Carthy Plans Tour," *The New York Times,* Feb. 2, 1954; "M'Carthy Itinerary Set," *The New York Times,* Feb. 4, 1954; W. H. Lawrence, "M'Carthy a Big Gun in the Republican Arsenal," *The New York Times,* Feb. 7, 1954; Dwight D. Eisenhower, *The White House Years: Mandate for Change* (Garden City, NY: Doubleday, 1963), 277.

17. Nixon-Gannon Interview, Day 3, tape no. 3, University of Georgia Archives; "'20 Years of Treason' Charged," *The New York Times,* Feb. 6, 1954; "Hall Backs McCarthy," *The New York Times,* Feb. 8, 1954.

18. William S. White, "Democrats Urge Eisenhower Halt 'Fear Deal' Talk," *The New York Times,* Feb. 9, 1954; White, "White House Says G. O. P. Told 'Facts,'" *The New York Times,* Feb. 10, 1954.

19. Lodge to DDE, Feb. 9, 1954, HCLP, Lodge-Eisenhower Correspondence, 1950–55, Reel 28.

20. News Conference, Feb. 10, 1954, *PPP;* James Reston, "President Advises Party to Temper Political Attacks," *The New York Times,* Feb. 11, 1954.

21. Hagerty diary, Feb. 10, 1954, JHP, B1 (1); Lodge to DDE, Feb. 12, 1954, HCLP, Lodge–Eisenhower Correspondence, 1950–55, Reel 28; "M'Carthy Asserts He Won't Change," *The New York Times,* Feb. 11, 1954.

22. "Senator Criticizes President," *The New York Times,* Feb. 11, 1954; John G. J. Adams, Memorandum for Struve Hensel, March 18, 1954, FASP, Eyes Only, recalling telephone conversations with George Sokolsky on Feb. 5, 12, and 16; J. Adams, *Without Precedent,* 122.

23. No transcript of this meeting is available, but the importance

Eisenhower placed on it is demonstrated by the detailed account in his memoirs; Eisenhower, *Mandate for Change*, 391–92; Ewald, *Who Killed Joe McCarthy?*, 190.

24. "A Week of Debate: Attacks Continue," *The New York Times*, Feb. 14, 1954.

25. James Reston, "Washington," *The New York Times*, Feb. 14, 1954.

26. Hagerty diary, Feb. 15, 1954, JHP, B1 (1); DDE diary, Feb. 8, 1954, *DDEP*, no. 718; Legislative Meeting, Feb. 8, 1954, WHOSS, Minnich Series, B1, Misc. I.

27. "Schine's Treatment at Fort Dix Studied," *The New York Times*, Feb. 2, 1954; "M'Carthy Ex-Aide Called Army 'Pet,'" *The New York Times*, Jan. 30, 1954.

28. J. Adams to Rogers, Feb. 3, 1954, FASP, Eyes Only, B6 (2); Ewald, *Who Killed Joe McCarthy?*, 175–76, 187.

29. J. Adams to Sherman Adams, Feb. 16, 1954, FASP, Eyes Only, B5, JD.

30. J. Adams, *Without Precedent*, 122–23; Joseph W. Alsop, *I've Seen the Best of It* (Mount Jackson, VA: Axios Press, 1992), 396. According to Joe Alsop, the Alsop brothers were "in constant touch" with Henry Cabot Lodge, who agreed with them that McCarthy was out to destroy the president.

31. DDE, News Conference, Feb. 17, 1954, *PPP.*

32. Confidential memorandum, Gerald D. Morgan to Cutler, Feb. 15, 1954, transmitting Young's suggested policy for release of the information regarding the 2200 dismissals, Morgan Files, B7, Security Program (1), DDEPL; "29 of 430 Ousted Called Disloyal," *The New York Times*, Feb. 19, 1954; Hagerty diary, Feb. 15, 1954, JHP, B1 (1).

33. J. Adams, *Without Precedent*, 121–25; "McCarthy vs. the Army," *The New York Times*, Feb. 24, 1954; J. Adams to Stevens, Feb. 16, 1954, FASP, Eyes Only, B4, Lucas; J. Adams and Sokolsky phone conversation, Feb. 16, 1954, FASP, Eyes Only, B4, Chronology of Efforts; Ewald, *Who Killed Joe McCarthy?*, 190–92.

34. J. Adams, *Without Precedent*, 124–26; Ewald, *Who Killed Joe McCarthy?*, 192.

35. Stevens to McCarthy, Feb. 16, 1954, CF/OF, B317, OF-99-U, Army-McCarthy hearings; Eisenhower, *Mandate for Change*, 391–92; Ewald, *Who Killed Joe McCarthy?*, 190.

36. J. Adams call to Robert Stevens, Feb. 18, 1954, FASP, Eyes Only, B4, Lucas (2); Ewald, *Who Killed Joe McCarthy?*, 193; J. Adams, *Without Precedent*, 126–27.

37. J. Adams, Memorandum for the Secretary, March 5, 1954, FASP, Eyes Only, B6, Work Notes and Memos; J. Adams, *Without Precedent*, 125–26.

38. Charles E. Potter, *Days of Shame* (New York: Coward-McCann, 1965), 66–69; Zwicker obituary, Lee A. Daniels, *The New York Times*, Aug. 12, 1991; Arlington National Cemetery website.

39. Ewald, *Who Killed Joe McCarthy?*, 193–94.

40. Hearing Transcript, "Communist Infiltration in the Army," Feb. 18, 1954, Permanent Subcommittee on Investigations of the Government Operations Committee, US Senate online; Ewald, *Who Killed Joe McCarthy?*, 194, J. Adams, *Without Precedent*, 126–27; S. Adams, *First-Hand Report*, 126; Irwin F. Gellman, *The President and the Apprentice: Eisenhower and Nixon, 1952–1961* (New Haven: Yale University Press, 2015), 104–5.

CHAPTER 8: SAVING ROBERT STEVENS

1. *The Washington Post*, Feb. 19, 1954, Gruenther Records, B6, McCarthy news clippings, DDEPL.

2. John G. Adams, *Without Precedent: The Story of the Death of McCarthyism* (New York: Norton, 1983), 128; William Bragg Ewald, Jr., *Who Killed Joe McCarthy?* (New York: Simon & Schuster, 1984), 195.

3. Stevens to Zwicker, Feb. 19, 1954, FASP, Eyes Only, B4, Lucas (2); Ewald, *Who Killed Joe McCarthy?*, 195–96.

4. J. Adams, Memorandum for the Record, Feb. 23, 1954, FASP, Eyes Only, B6; J. Adams, *Without Precedent*, 128–29; Ewald, *Who Killed Joe McCarthy?*, 195–99.

5. In November, Eisenhower had consulted Brownell on the issue of his communist associations in Germany, DDE to Brownell, Jr., Nov. 4, 1953, Administration Series, DDEPL; also *DDEP*, no. 516; Joseph W. Alsop with Adam Platt, *I've Seen the Best of It* (Mount Jackson, VA: Axious Press, Reprint, 2009), 396–97; Robert W. Merry, *Taking on the World: Joseph and Stewart Alsop—Guardians of the American Century* (New York: Viking Press, 1996), 273.

6. "Text of Stevens Letter," *The New York Times*, Feb. 19, 1954; "Army Rebuffs McCarthy," *The New York Times*, Feb. 20, 1954; Zwicker Statement on Hearing, approx. Feb. 20, 1954; Leverett Saltonstall Papers, McCarthy off-site, B205 (24), MHS.

7. Stevens to McCarthy, Feb. 20, 1954, FASP, Eyes Only, B6, Work Notes and Memos (3) and Phone Notes, B9, Secretary of the Army (16); Ewald, *Who Killed Joe McCarthy?*, 199–200; J. Adams, *Without Precedent*, 129.

8. Phone Log, Secretary of the Army, Feb. 20, 1954, FASP, Eyes Only, B9 (16); Stevens and Reston call, Feb. 20, 1954, FASP, Eyes Only, B5; James Reston, "Officers Ordered to Defy M'Carthy and Not Testify," *The New York Times*, Feb. 21, 1954; Ewald, *Who Killed Joe McCarthy?*, 200–3.

9. Stevens to Kyes, Feb. 20, 1954, FASP, Eyes Only, B5, Rhodes; Ewald, *Who Killed Joe McCarthy?*, 203–5; J. Adams, *Without Precedent*, 131.

10. Statement by Secretary of the Army, Feb. 21, 1954, CF/OF, B317, OF-99-U; also in Sherman Adams Papers, B10 (5), McCarthy Hearings—Memoranda C, Dartmouth College.

11. Stevens to Hadley, Feb. 21, 1954, Phone Notes, Secretary of the Army, FASP, Eyes Only, B9 (17); Ewald, *Who Killed Joe McCarthy?*, 206; J. Adams, *Without Precedent*, 131; unpublished MS, Karl Mundt Papers, Dakota State College, Madison, SD.

12. "Text of Statements on Peress Case," *The New York Times*, Feb. 22, 1954; W. H. Lawrence, "Stevens Accepts Public Showdown Against M'Carthy," *The New York Times*, Feb. 22, 1954.

13. Potter to J. Adams, Feb. 22, 1954, Phone Notes, Secretary of the Army, FASP, Eyes Only, B9 (17); "Zwicker Denounces McCarthy's Tactics," *The New York Times*, Feb. 23, 1954; the directive Zwicker cited was based on Section 4 of Public Law 84, passed by the 82nd Congress and signed by President Truman.

14. Anthony Leviero, "President Aloof in Peress Dispute," *The New York Times*, Feb. 23, 1954.

15. "Transcript of Zwicker Testimony," *The New York Times*, Feb. 23, 1954; Phone Notes, Secretary of the Army, Feb. 23, 1954, FASP, Eyes Only, B9 (17).

16. J. Adams, *Without Precedent*, 132–33.

17. Phone Notes, Secretary of the Army, Feb. 23, 1954, FASP, Eyes Only, B9 (17); Ewald, *Who Killed Joe McCarthy?*, 208.

18. Lodge to the President, Feb. 23, 1954, HCLP, Lodge-Eisenhower Correspondence, 1950–55, Reel 28; Dwight D. Eisenhower, *The White House Years: Mandate for Change* (Garden City, NY: Doubleday, 1963), 391–92; Ewald, *Who Killed Joe McCarthy?*, 190.

19. Ewald, *Who Killed Joe McCarthy?*, 209–11; Hagerty diary, Feb. 24, 1954, JHP, B1.

20. Unpublished MS, Karl Mundt Papers, Dakota State College, Madison, SD; J. Adams, *Without Precedent*, 134–35; Ewald, *Who Killed Joe McCarthy?*, 210–11, 214.

21. Sherman Adams, *First-Hand Report: The Inside Story of the Eisenhower Administration* (London: Hutchinson, 1961), 126; Fred I. Greenstein, *The Hidden-Hand Presidency: Eisenhower as Leader* (Baltimore: Johns Hopkins, 1982); Greenstein erroneously dates the Chicken Lunch as February 23; Ewald, *Who Killed Joe McCarthy?*, 211.

22. Ewald, *Who Killed Joe McCarthy?*, 212–13; J. Adams, *Without Precedent*, 135; S. Adams, *First-Hand Report*, 127.

23. Lodge to the President, Feb. 23, 1954, HCLP, Lodge-Eisenhower Correspondence, 1950–55, Reel 28; Lodge mentioned the call from Eisenhower in his subsequent call to Stevens, but no transcript was found for the Eisenhower-Lodge conversation.

24. Lodge to Stevens, Feb. 24, 1954, FASP, Eyes Only, B4, Lucas (2); Jack Lucas, the call transcriber, probably deleted a pithy Lodge expletive in "a good . . . thing;" Ewald, *Who Killed Joe McCarthy?*, 214–15; S. Adams, *First-Hand Report*, 126–27.

25. Stevens to Mundt, Feb. 24, 1954, FASP, Eyes Only, B4, Stevens' Calls; Ewald, *Who Killed Joe McCarthy?*, 215.

26. Phone Notes, Secretary of the Army, Feb. 24, 1954, FASP, Eyes Only, B9 (17); Stevens to Zwicker, Feb. 24, 1954, FASP, Eyes Only, B4, Lucas (2).

27. Seaton to Stevens, Feb. 24, 1954, FASP, Eyes Only, B4, Lucas (2); Ewald, *Who Killed Joe McCarthy?*, 215–16.

28. Senator Mundt continued to believe that if the army secretary had kept the agreement, the subsequent confrontation and hearings could have been avoided; unpublished MS, Mundt Papers,

Dakota State College, Madison, SD; Hagerty diary, Feb. 24, 1954, JHP, B1.

29. Arthur Hadley, *Heads or Tails: A Life of Random Luck and Risky Choices* (New York: Glitterati, 2007), 125–26.

30. W. H. Lawrence, "Stevens Bows to M'Carthy at Administration Behest," *The New York Times*, Feb. 25, 1954; Arthur Krock, "In the Nation," *The New York Times*, Feb. 25, 1954; Ewald, *Who Killed Joe McCarthy?*, 217–18.

31. "Outcome 'Shocks' Stevens," *The New York Times*, Feb. 25, 1954; J. Adams, *Without Precedent*, 139.

32. Hagerty diary, Feb. 25, 1954, JHP, B1.

33. Stevens to Dirksen, FASP, Eyes Only, B4, Stevens' calls; Ewald, *Who Killed Joe McCarthy?*, 218.

34. Richard M. Nixon, *RN: The Memoirs of Richard Nixon* (New York: Grosset & Dunlap, 1978), 142; W. H. Lawrence, "A Day of Parleys," *The New York Times*, Feb. 26, 1954; Hagerty diary, Feb. 25, 1954, JHP, B1; Greenstein, *The Hidden-Hand Presidency*, 186.

35. Hagerty diary, Feb. 25, 1954, JHP, B1.

36. Phone Notes, Secretary of the Army, Feb. 25, 1954, FASP, Eyes Only, B9 (17); J. Adams, *Without Precedent*, 204; President's App. Schedule, Feb. 25, 1954, Miller Center online; S. Adams, *First-Hand Report*, 127.

37. Clay to Stevens, Feb. 25, 1954, FASP, Eyes Only, Lucas, B4 (2).

38. Clay to DDE, Feb. 25, 1954, DDE diary, Phone Calls, B5 (2), DDEPL; Ewald, *Who Killed Joe McCarthy?*, 220–21; Greenstein, *The Hidden-Hand Presidency*, 185–86.

39. Ewald, *Who Killed Joe McCarthy?*, 221, 229; J. Adams, *Without Precedent*, 140.

40. J. Adams, *Without Precedent*, 204; Nixon, *RN*, 142.

41. Shanley diary, BSP, B2, V1 (4), 1453–54; J. Adams, *Without Precedent*, 139.

42. Hagerty diary, Feb. 25, 1954, JHP, B1; W. H. Lawrence, "A Day of Parleys," *The New York Times*, Feb. 26, 1954; S. Adams, *First-Hand Report*, 127–28; Ewald, *Who Killed Joe McCarthy?*, 222; Greenstein, *The Hidden-Hand Presidency*, 186.

43. Statement by the Secretary, Feb. 25, 1954, Sherman Adams Papers, B5 (10) McCarthy Hearings—Memoranda C, Dartmouth College;

an earlier draft can be found in FASP, Eyes Only, McCarthy, B4 (4); W. H. Lawrence, "A Day of Parleys," *The New York Times*, Feb. 26, 1954; Ewald, *Who Killed Joe McCarthy?*, 222; J. Adams, *Without Precedent*, 139; Greenstein, *The Hidden-Hand Presidency*, 186; Irwin F. Gellman, *The President and the Apprentice: Eisenhower and Nixon, 1952–1961* (New Haven: Yale University Press, 2015), 105–7.

CHAPTER 9: EISENHOWER IN COMMAND

1. Ann Whitman, notes in DDE diary, Feb. 26, 1954, *DDEP*, no. 741; William Bragg Ewald, Jr., *Who Killed Joe McCarthy?* (New York: Simon & Schuster, 1984), 222.

2. Hagerty diary, Feb. 26, 1954, JHP, B1; W. H. Lawrence, "A Day of Parleys," *The New York Times*, Feb. 26, 1954; James Reston, "Stevens Case Stuns Capital," *The New York Times*, Feb. 26, 1954.

3. Years later, the day after he issued the order to send troops into Little Rock, Arkansas, to enforce a federal court order for school desegregation, Ann Whitman recorded that Ike "played 18 holes of golf and practiced putting, chipping and driving for almost two additional hours," DDE diary, Sept. 25, 1957, Schedules, Sept. 1957, B27, DDEPL; John G. Adams, *Without Precedent: The Story of the Death of McCarthyism* (New York: Norton, 1983), 204.

4. Arthur Krock, interview with Nixon, Feb. 26, 1954, Black Book Interviews, SGMML; Ewald, *Who Killed Joe McCarthy?*, 223; Fred Greenstein con firms the importance of the Krock interview, Fred I. Greenstein, *The Hidden-Hand Presidency: Eisenhower as Leader* (Baltimore: Johns Hopkins, 1982), 187.

5. Stevens to Clay, Feb. 26, 1954, FASP, Eyes Only, B4, Lucas (2).

6. DDE to Milton Eisenhower, Sept. 12, 1955, *DDEP*, no. 1583.

7. J. Adams, *Without Precedent*, 142.

8. DDE diary, April 1, 1953, *DDEP*, no. 118; Dwight D. Eisenhower, *The White House Years: Mandate for Change* (Garden City, NY: Doubleday, 1963), 278–85.

9. DDE diary, Feb. 26, 1954, *DDEP*, no. 741; the complexity of the Bricker Amendment fight cannot be adequately addressed in this book; see Duane Tannanbaum, *The Bricker Amendment Controversy: A*

Test of Eisenhower's Political Leadership (Ithaca, NY: Cornell University Press, 1988), 166–74.

10. Tannanbaum, *The Bricker Amendment Controversy*, 175–90; Ewald, *Who Killed Joe McCarthy?*, 224.

11. Lodge to the President, Feb. 23, 1954, HCLP, Lodge-Eisenhower Correspondence, 1950–55, Reel 28.

12. "Walking with the Devil," *The Washington Post*, Feb. 26, 1954.

13. W. H. Lawrence, "Both Parties Act to Curb M'Carthy," *The New York Times*, Feb. 27, 1954.

14. "President Presses Senators to Curb Role of M'Carthy," *The New York Times*, Feb 28, 1954; Conklin, "McCarthy Doubts President 'Wants to Curb My Powers,'" *The New York Times*, March 1, 1954.

15. Richard M. Nixon, *RN: The Memoirs of Richard Nixon* (New York: Grosset & Dunlap, 1978), 149; Ewald, *Who Killed Joe McCarthy?*, 238; Ewald's succinct summary of Eisenhower's method for handling adversaries is in William Bragg Ewald, Jr., *Eisenhower the President: Crucial Days, 1951–60* (Englewood Cliffs, NJ: Prentice–Hall, 1981), 32.

16. Legislative Meeting, March 1, 1954, DDE diary, B4, Staff Notes, DDEPL; a similar version is in—WHOSS, Minnich Series, B1, Misc.-C (3); The "did not even tell me" line is from WHOSS, Legislative Meetings, B2, March 1, 1954, Folder L-11, Minnich Series; Greenstein, *The Hidden-Hand Presidency*, 187–88; Shanley diary, BSP, B2, V1 (4), 1469–71; Sherman Adams, *First-Hand Report: The Inside Story of the Eisenhower Administration* (London: Hutchinson, 1961), 128.

17. Nixon, *RN*, 143.

18. President's Appt. Schedule, Feb. 28, 1954, Miller Center online.

19. Stevens to Hensel, March 1, 1954, FASP, Eyes Only, B4, Lucas (2).

20. "Peress Says Hoodlums Stoned His Home," *The New York Times*, March 1, 1954.

21. Arthur Krock, Nixon interview, Feb. 26, 1954, Black Book Interviews, SGMML; Krock, "Senate to Investigate Investigating Methods," *The New York Times*, Feb. 28, 1954; Roy Cohn, *McCarthy* (New York: New American Library, 1968), 120–21; Cohn erroneously lists the date of the Krock column as February 27.

22. Knowles, "Five Congressmen Shot in House," *The New York Times*,

March 2, 1954; DDE to Rayburn, March 1, 1954, DDE diary, B5 Phone Calls, Jan–May 1954 (2), DDEPL; "Eisenhower Target for Fanatics Also," *The New York Times*, March 2, 1954.

23. Anne O'Hare McCormick, "Abroad," *The New York Times*, March 3, 1954.

24. Walter Lippman, "Today and Tomorrow: Terrorists and Spies," *New York Herald Tribune*, n.d but approx. March 2 or 3, 1954, in Gruenther Records, B6, McCarthy News Clippings (3), DDEPL.

25. "Atom Blast Opens Test in Pacific," *The New York Times*, March 2, 1954; "The Bravo Test," http://www.atomicarchive.com.

26. "M'Leod Authority Is Cut by Dulles" and "Mr. M'Leod's Demotion," *The New York Times*, March 2, 1954; "Drafts Letter to Dulles," *The New York Times*, March 3, 1954.

27. Robert Kieve diary, March 2, 1954, provided to the author by Robert Kieve.

28. "Chairman of G. O. P. Rebukes M'Carthy on Stevens Fight," *The New York Times*, March 3, 1954.

29. Lodge notes about meeting with Eisenhower and memorandum, March 2, 1954, HCLP, Lodge-Eisenhower Correspondence, 1950–55, Reel 28.

30. DDE to Rogers, DDE diary, March 2, 1954, B5, Phone Calls (2), DDEPL; Ewald, *Who Killed Joe McCarthy?*, 239.

31. A. M. Sperber, *Murrow: His Life and Times* (New York: Fordham University Press, 1999), 429–30.

32. James Reston, "Other Cheek Is Struck," *The New York Times*, March 4, 1954

33. DDE, News Conference, March 3, 1954, *PPP*; Greenstein, *The Hidden-Hand Presidency*, 189–91; S. Adams, *First-Hand Report*, 128–29; Irwin F. Gellman, *The President and the Apprentice: Eisenhower and Nixon, 1952–1961* (New Haven: Yale University Press, 2015), 109.

34. William Ewald shared Edwards's account of rushing to McCarthy headquarters and unsuccessfully trying to talk McCarthy out of making a hot response. As he put it, "the American people had seen the kick in the groin, and they would not forget it." To Edwards, that was "the day McCarthy died." Ewald, *Who Killed Joe McCarthy?*, 242.

35. "Texts of Statements by President and Senator McCarthy's Reply," *The New York Times*, March 4, 1954; Greenstein, *The Hidden-Hand Presidency*, 191–92.

36. Reston, "Other Cheek Is Struck," *The New York Times*, March 4, 1954; W. H. Lawrence, "President Chides M'Carthy," *The New York Times*, March 4, 1954

37. "Turning the Other Cheek," *The Washington Post*, March 4, 1954, in Gruenther Records, B6, McCarthy News Clippings (3), DDEPL.

38. Herblock, *The Washington Post*, March 4, 1954, reprinted in *Herblock's Here and Now* (New York: Simon & Schuster, 1955), 114; Ewald, *Who Killed Joe McCarthy?*, 243.

39. "The Chips Go Down," *Washington Star*, March 4, 1954, in Gruenther Records, B6, McCarthy News Clippings (3), DDEPL.

40. Hagerty diary, March 4, 1954, JHP, B1.

41. John Crider to Sherman Adams, March 5, 1954, Adams Papers, B10, McCarthy Controversy (3), Dartmouth College.

42. DDE to Cabinet, March 5, 1954, *DDEP*, no. 757; Cabinet Meeting, March 5, 1954, Cabinet Series, Minnich version, B3, DDEPL; Ewald, *Who Killed Joe McCarthy?*, 244; Fred Greenstein noted all that Eisenhower had done the previous week to set the stage for confronting McCarthy, but he found the March 5 cabinet meeting remarkable in that Ike "barely mentioned the divisive McCarthy issue" but used "preventive medicine"; Greenstein, *The Hidden-Hand Presidency*, 193–94.

43. Lodge to DDE, March 6, 1954, HCLP, Lodge-Eisenhower Correspondence, 1950–55, Reel 28.

44. John Popham, "Stevenson Backs Army's Red Fight," *The New York Times*, March 6, 1954.

45. Text of Stevenson Address, *The New York Times*, March 7, 1954; Ewald, *Who Killed Joe McCarthy?*, 246; Gellman, *The President and the Apprentice*, 110.

46. Hagerty diary, March 4 and 6, 1954, JHP, B1.

47. "Eisenhower Pleased by New Song," *The New York Times*, March 7, 1954; Donovan would eventually write the first sanctioned biography of Eisenhower prior to the 1956 campaign: Robert J. Donovan, *Eisenhower: The Inside Story* (New York: Harper, 1956).

48. "Eisenhower Took Lead in Applauding Stevens," *The New York Times*, March 9, 1954; Ewald, *Who Killed Joe McCarthy?*, 245–46.

CHAPTER 10: A POLITICAL D-DAY

1. John Popham, "Stevenson Says President Yields to M'Carthyism," *The New York Times*, March 7, 1954; Arthur Krock, "G. O. P. Seeks to Avert M'Carthy Showdown," *The New York Times*, March 7, 1954.

2. James Reston, "Washington: The President Plays the Waiting Game," *The New York Times*, March 7, 1954.

3. A. M. Sperber, *Murrow: His Life and Times* (New York: Fordham University Press, 1999), 430–33.

4. "McCarthy Seeking Air Time to Reply," *The New York Times*, March 8, 1954; Richard M. Nixon, *RN: The Memoirs of Richard Nixon* (New York: Grosset & Dunlap, 1978), 144; William Bragg Ewald, Jr., *Who Killed Joe McCarthy?* (New York: Simon & Schuster, 1984), 246–47; Fred I. Greenstein, *The Hidden-Hand Presidency: Eisenhower as Leader* (Baltimore: Johns Hopkins, 1982), 194; Irwin F. Gellman, *The President and the Apprentice: Eisenhower and Nixon, 1952–1961* (New Haven: Yale University Press, 2015), 111.

5. Hagerty diary, March 8, 1954, JHP, B1; DDE diary, March 8, 1954, B5, Phone Calls (2), DDEPL; Ewald, *Who Killed Joe McCarthy?*, 246–247; Nixon, *RN*, 144.

6. Hagerty diary, March 8, 1954, JHP, B1; Ewald, *Who Killed Joe McCarthy?*, 247; the typed version of the Hagerty diary entry reads that Ike was "dead set *against* stopping McCarthy," clearly a typing error, given the context. Ewald appropriately rewrote it as "dead set [on] stopping McCarthy."

7. Hagerty diary, March 8, 1954, JHP, B1; DDE diary, March 8, 1954, B5, Phone Calls (2), DDEPL; Ewald, *Who Killed Joe McCarthy?*, 246–47; Nixon, *RN*, 144; the Hagerty-Shanley-Eisenhower encounter almost certainly took place in the late afternoon.

8. Streibert to McCarthy, March 8, 1954, Sherman Adams Papers, B10, McCarthy Controversy (3), Dartmouth; Ewald, *Who Killed Joe McCarthy?*, 247.

9. Lodge to DDE, March 6, 1954, and DDE to Lodge, "eyes only,"

March 8, 1954, HCLP, Lodge-Eisenhower Correspondence, 1950–55, Reel 28; also *DDEP*, no. 759; Eisenhower eventually did the logical thing, offering the job as White House political strategist to Lodge, but Lodge declined, arguing that he could not get along with the "top men" on the White House staff; Lodge to DDE, March 22, 1954, and DDE to Lodge, March 24, 1954, HCLP, Lodge-Eisenhower Correspondence, 1950–55, Reel 28.

10. Symington to Stevens, March 8, 1954, FASP, Eyes Only, B4, Stevens' Calls; Ewald, *Who Killed Joe McCarthy?*, 248–49.

11. Hagerty diary, March 9, 1954, JHP, B1, DDEPL; Ewald, *Who Killed Joe McCarthy?*, 249–50; John G. Adams, *Without Precedent: The Story of the Death of McCarthyism* (New York: Norton, 1983), 143; according to Ewald, Struve Hensel later told him that he believed that Seaton had prodded Charlie Wilson to call Potter and ask for the letter. John Adams incorrectly concluded that the letter had been sent on March 10, but Potter apparently had a copy when he and other Republicans met with McCarthy.

12. W. H. Lawrence, "Nixon to Answer Stevenson on Air," *The New York Times*, March 9, 1954; "Senator Plans a Fight," *The New York Times*, March 9, 1954.

13. DDE to Helms, March 9, 1954, *DDEP*, no. 762; Ewald, *Who Killed Joe McCarthy?*, 251.

14. Ewald, *Who Killed Joe McCarthy?*, 250–51.

15. Flanders speech on Senate Floor, Monday, March 9, 1954, Congressional Record, 2nd session, 83rd Congress; Ralph E. Flanders, *Senator from Vermont* (Boston: Little, Brown, 1961), 255–56; Ewald, *Who Killed Joe McCarthy?*, 250; W. H. Lawrence, "M'Carthy Strives 'to Shatter'" G.O.P, *The New York Times*, March 10, 1954.

16. Hagerty diary, March 9, 1954, JHP, B1, Ewald, *Who Killed Joe McCarthy?*, 250.

17. DDE to Flanders, "Personal," March 9, 1954, and Wire Service Report, March 10, 1954, both in CF/OF, B317, OF-99-R, McCarthy; Ewald, *Who Killed Joe McCarthy?*, 250.

18. Script, *See It Now*, March 9, 1954, www.lib.berkeley.edu/MRC/murrowmccarthy.html; Sperber, *Murrow*, 436–39.

19. Sperber, *Murrow*, 434.

20. Hagerty diary, June 7, 1954, JHP, B1, June 1954; Lodge to DDE, Feb. 23, HCLP, Lodge-Eisenhower Correspondence, 1950–55, Reel 28; Lodge call to Stevens, Feb. 24, 1954, FASP, Eyes Only, B4, Lucas (2).

21. Hagerty diary, March 10, 1954, JHP, B1.

22. DDE, News Conference, March 10, 1954, *PPP*; Greenstein, *The Hidden-Hand Presidency*, 194–96.

23. Hagerty diary, March 10, 1954, JHP, B1, Jan. 1–April 6, 1954; Greenstein, *The Hidden-Hand Presidency*, 196; Hensel to Stevens, March 10, 1954, FASP, Eyes Only, B9, Phone Notes, Secretary of the Army (18); also in FASP, B5, Pike; Seaton to Stevens, FASP, Eyes Only, B4, Lucas (2).

24. W. H. Lawrence, "M'Carthy, Wilson in Accord on Reds," *The New York Times*, March 11, 1954; Ewald, *Who Killed Joe McCarthy?*, 252–53.

25. Roy Cohn, *McCarthy* (New York: New American Library, 1968), 124; Sidney Zion, *The Autobiography of Roy Cohn* (Secaucus, NJ: Lyle Stuart, 1988), 121.

26. Hagerty diary, March 10, 1954, JHP, B1; Ewald, *Who Killed Joe McCarthy?*, 253.

27. Cohn, *McCarthy*, 124; Zion, *The Autobiography of Roy Cohn*, 121.

28. Gellman, *The President and the Apprentice*, 112.

29. "McCarthy Aide Ordered to Guard Duty at Kilmer," *The New York Times*, March 11, 1954.

30. Anthony Leviero, "President Implies M'Carthy Is Peril to Unity of G. O. P.," "Straws in the Wind," and "Highlights of News Parley," *The New York Times*, March 11, 1954. "M'Carthy Gives Hug to Critical Senator," *The New York Times*, March 11, 1954.

31. J. Adams to Stevens, March 11, 1954, FASP, Eyes Only, B4, Lucas (2); Ewald, *Who Killed Joe McCarthy?*, 253–54.

32. McCarthy to Seaton, March 11, 1954, FASP, Eyes Only, B4, McCarthy (2); Ewald, *Who Killed Joe McCarthy?*, 254–55.

33. Stevens to Lehrbas, March 11, 1954, FASP, Eyes Only, B4, Lucas (2), and B9, Phone Notes, Secretary of the Army (18); Ewald, *Who Killed Joe McCarthy?*, 255–56.

34. Stevens to Seaton, March 11, 1954, FASP, Eyes Only, B4, Lucas (2), and B9, Phone Notes, Secretary of the Army (18); Ewald, *Who Killed Joe McCarthy?*, 256.

35. Seaton to Stevens, March 11, 1954, FASP, Eyes Only, B9, Phone Notes, Secretary of the Army (18); White House (unnamed contact) to Stevens, FASP, Eyes Only, B9, Phone Notes, Secretary of the Army (18); Ewald, *Who Killed Joe McCarthy?*, 256.

36. Stevens to Hensel, March 11, 1954, FASP, Eyes Only, B4, Lucas (2), and B9, Phone Notes, Secretary of the Army (18).

37. Hagerty diary, March 11, 1954, JHP, B1 (2); Ewald, *Who Killed Joe McCarthy?*, 256.

38. Greenstein, *The Hidden-Hand Presidency*, 198; Greenstein did not have access to Fred Seaton's "Eyes Only" collection of documents; Dwight D. Eisenhower, *The White House Years: Mandate for Change* (Garden City, NY: Doubleday, 1963), 396.

39. Schedule for Delivery (not so labeled), March 11, 1954, FASP, Eyes Only, B4, McCarthy (4). John Adams recalled incorrectly that the report was delivered by midafternoon, confirming that Seaton, not Adams, was in charge of distribution. The army counsel recalled that his office was "overrun with reporters seeking copies of this precious document," which he was able to share. Adams said to a colleague, now that the report was out, that "when it's all over, I'll be lying flat on the floor;" J. Adams, *Without Precedent*, 143.

40. The attendees at the dinner are listed in the President's Appt. Schedule for March 11, 1954, Miller Center online Dwight D. Eisenhower Appointment Schedule.

CHAPTER 11: "A WAR OF MANEUVER"

1. Hagerty diary, March 12, 1954, JHP, B1 (2).

2. "Senator Attacks," *The New York Times*, March 12, 1954; "Text of Army Report Charging Threats," *The New York Times*, March 12, 1954; "Stevens a Target," *The New York Times*, March 12, 1954.

3. "Schine Is Getting Rugged Training," *The New York Times*, March 12, 1954.

4. Knowland to DDE & Kyes to Knowland, DDE diary, March 12, 1954, B5, Phone Calls (2).

5. Hagerty diary, March 12, 1954, JHP, B1 (2).

6. Stevens to Hensel, 2 calls, March 12, 1954, FASP, Eyes Only, B4,

Lucas (2); Wire Service Report, March 12, 1954, FASP, Eyes Only, B4, McCarthy (6); W. H. Lawrence, "M'Carthy Charges Army 'Blackmail,'" *The New York Times*, March 13, 1954.

7. William Bragg Ewald, Jr., *Who Killed Joe McCarthy?* (New York: Simon & Schuster, 1984), 369–70.

8. Thomas C. Reeves, *The Life and Times of Joe McCarthy* (New York: Stein & Day, 1982), 576; "Text of Memoranda Issued by McCarthy," *The New York Times*, March 13, 1954; Ewald, *Who Killed Joe McCarthy?*, 262–68, provides a detailed summary of the content of all eleven memoranda.

9. Wire service report, March 12, 1954, FASP, Eyes Only, B4, Lucas (2).

10. Stevens to Hensel, March 13, 1954, FASP, Eyes Only, B5, Rhodes.

11. Stevens, telegram to McCarthy, March 13, 1954, Sherman Adams Papers, B10, McCarthy Hearings—Memoranda (5), Dartmouth; "Text of Stevens-McCarthy Exchange" and "Stevens in Attack," *The New York Times*, March 14, 1954.

12. Hagerty diary, March 10, 1954, JHP, B1 (2); DDE to Robinson, Mar. 12, 1954, *DDEP*, no. 773.

13. Richard M. Nixon, *RN: The Memoirs of Richard Nixon* (New York: Grosset & Dunlap, 1978), 145–46; Irwin F. Gellman, *The President and the Apprentice: Eisenhower and Nixon, 1952–1961* (New Haven: Yale University Press, 2015), 113–15.

14. "Text of Nixon Reply to Stevenson" and W. H. Lawrence, "Nixon Says 'Questionable Methods' and 'Reckless Talk,'" *The New York Times*, March 14, 1954.

15. "McCarthy Says He'll Get Rough," "M'Carthy Gets Right to Murrow TV Time," and "Murrow Time Offer for M'Carthy Alone," *The New York Times*, March 14–15, 1954; James Reston, "Washington," *The New York Times*, March 14, 1954; W. H. Lawrence, "M'Carthy on Defensive," *The New York Times*, March 14, 1954; "Some Moving Fingers Write," *The New York Times*, March 14, 1954.

16. Roy Cohn, *McCarthy* (New York: New American Library, 1968), 128–29; Clayton Knowles, "Cohn Again Denies He Asked Favors," *The New York Times*, March 15, 1954.

17. "Random Notes from Washington," *The New York Times*, March 15, 1954; Adams to Hensel, FASP, Eyes Only, B5, Rebuttal to McCarthy.

18. Stevens to Hensel, March 15, 1954, FASP, Eyes Only, B4, Lucas (2).

19. Ewald, *Who Killed Joe McCarthy?*, 283.

20. Stevens to Hensel, March 15, 1954, FASP, Eyes Only, B4, Lucas (2); John G. Adams, *Without Precedent: The Story of the Death of McCarthyism* (New York: Norton, 1983), 152.

21. W. H. Lawrence, "M'Carthy Refuses to Speed Inquiry," *The New York Times*, March 16, 1954; J. Adams, *Without Precedent*, 153; "The Senate Inquiry," *The New York Times*, March 17, 1954.

22. W. H. Lawrence, "Mundt Will Direct Senate Unit Study," *The New York Times*, March 17, 1954; Ewald, *Who Killed Joe McCarthy?*, 284; Cohn, *McCarthy*, 131–32.

23. Hagerty diary, May 11–12, 1954, during the Army-McCarthy hearings, JHP, B1; Ewald, *Who Killed Joe McCarthy?*, 284.

24. W. H. Lawrence, "Mundt Will Direct Senate Unit Study," *The New York Times*, March 17, 1954; Streibert to McCarthy, March 8, 1954, Sherman Adams Papers, B10, McCarthy Controversy (3), Dartmouth; Hagerty diary, March 14, 1954, JHP, B1 (2); "M'Carthy Books Barred," *The New York Times*, March 17, 1954.

25. "2 Draft Delays for Cohn Recited," *The New York Times*, March 20, 1954.

26. News Conference, March 17, 1954, *PPP*; C. P. Trussell, "President Voices Faith in Stevens," *The New York Times*, March 18, 1954.

27. Joseph Alsop, "McCarthy-Cohn-Schine Tale Was Half-Told," *The Washington Post*, March 15, 1954; Stevens to Hensel, March 15, 1954, FASP, Eyes Only, B4, Lucas (2).

28. J. Adams, *Without Precedent*, 147, 204.

29. Symington to Seaton, March 17, 1954, FASP, Eyes Only, B4, McCarthy (2).

30. "Random Notes from Washington," *The New York Times*, March 22, 1954.

31. Jackson Log, March 20, 1954, CDJP, B68 (2); Jackson lists this conversation as taking place on Wednesday," but it was actually Thursday, March 18; DDE diary, March 18, 1954, B5, Phone Calls (2), DDEPL.

32. Jackson Log, March 20, 1954, CDJP, B68 (2); DDE diary, March 20, 1954, B5, Phone Calls (2).

33. "Wants Senator Step Down," *The New York Times*, March 23, 1954; W. H. Lawrence, "M'Carthy Battles to Retain Power to Cross-Examine," *The New York Times,* March 23, 1954; "The M'Carthy Inquiry," *The New York Times*, March 24, 1954.

34. Hagerty diary, March 24, 1954, JHP, B1 (2); Jackson log, March 24, 1954, CDJP, B68 (2); Hagerty's typed original entry quotes Eisenhower as saying that "the leadership *can* duck that responsibility," but the context makes it clear that he intended to write "cannot." Hagerty's tiny handwriting was difficult to read, perhaps resulting in a transcriber's error.

35. DDE, News Conference, March 24, 1954, *PPP*; W. H. Lawrence, "President Opposes M'Carthy as Judge in His Own Dispute," and Anthony Leviero, "President to Keep F.B.I. Files Secret," *The New York Times*, March 25, 1954.

36. Hazlett to DDE, March 25, 1954, Name Series, B18, Hazlett 1954 (2), DDEPL.

37. Milton Eisenhower to DDE, n.d. (approx. Apr. 1, 1954), DDE diary, B6 (3), DDEPL.

38. Hagerty diary, Feb. 24, 1954, JHP, B1.

39. Hagerty diary, March 25, 1954, JHP, B1 (2); W. H. Lawrence, "All, Including McCarthy, Deny 'a Settlement by Resignations,'" *The New York Times*, March 26, 1954; "Mundt Supports M'Carthy Stand," *The New York Times*, March 28, 1954; "The Nation," *The New York Times*, March 28, 1954.

40. Roscoe Drummond, "A New 'Mess' in Washington?," *New York Herald Tribune*, March 26, 1954, in ACW diary, B1 (1), DDEPL; "Hall Says M'Carthy 'Has Done Harm,'" *The New York Times*, March 27, 1954.

41. C. P. Trussell, "Senate's Inquiry on M'Carthy Bogs," *The New York Times*, March 20, 1954; Trussell, "Bar Head Rejects post of Counsel," *The New York Times*, March 23, 1954; Trussell, "M'Carthy Inquiry Bogged on Counsel," *The New York Times*, March 30, 1954; William R. Conklin, "M'Carthy Seeking to Push Inquiries," *The New York Times*, March 31, 1954.

42. Warren Olney III to Hensel, Apr. 7, 1954, FASP, Eyes Only, B4; "'Barefaced Lies,' Hensel Declares," *The New York Times*, Apr. 21, 1954.

43. Dewey to JFD, March 31, 1954, and JFD to Brownell, Apr. 1, 1954, JFDP, Tel. Call Series, B2 (2).
44. Ewald, *Who Killed Joe McCarthy?*, 297–302.

CHAPTER 12: COUNTDOWN

1. William Bragg Ewald, Jr., *Who Killed Joe McCarthy?* (New York: Simon & Schuster, 1984), 300; Roy Cohn, *McCarthy* (New York: New American Library, 1968), 132.
2. Ewald, *Who Killed Joe McCarthy?*, 298–302.
3. Brownell, letter to Duane W. Krohnke, Aug. 13, 1986, provided to the author by Krohnke, Apr. 18, 2013; handwritten note, n.d., Sherman Adams Papers, B10 (5), McCarthy Hearings—Memoranda, C, Dartmouth.
4. Fred Fisher, memorandum, dictated June 10, 1954, provided to the author by Duane Krohnke, Apr. 18, 2013; Fisher gave a copy to Mr. Krohnke in 1983 when he visited the Hale & Dorr Law Firm, Boston; David M. Oshinsky used a portion of the Fisher narrative in *A Conspiracy So Immense: The World of Joe McCarthy* (New York: Oxford University Press, 2005), 457–58; Ewald, *Who Killed Joe McCarthy?*, 301.
5. C. P. Trussell, "Man Who Praised McCarthy Chosen Counsel" and "Sears, New Counsel for Inquiry, Backed McCarthy in 1952 Race," *The New York Times*, April 2, 1954; "McCarthy's Wife Named in Debate Role," *The Washington Post*, Apr. 6, 1954; Statement by Sec. of Defense, Apr. 2, 1954, Sherman Adams Papers, B10 (5), McCarthy Hearings—Memoranda, Darthouth College; C. P. Trussell, "Inquiry Counsel Named by Army," *The New York Times*, April 3, 1954; "Mundt Envisages Case for Perjury" and Foster, Article I—No Title, *The New York Times*, Apr. 5, 1954.
6. Fisher memorandum, May 20, 1963; Hagerty diary, April 2, 1954, JHP, B1(2); Ewald, *Who Killed Joe McCarthy?*, 301–2.
7. "M'Carthy Arrives at the Crossroad," *The New York Times*, Apr. 4, 1954; *The Gallup Poll: Public Opinion 1935–1971*, ed. William P. Hansen and Fred L. Israel, vol. 2, *1949–1958* (New York: Random House, 1972); "Schine Rejected," *The New York Times*, Apr. 3, 1954.

8. Hagerty diary, March 27, 1954, JHP, B1 (2); DDE to Brownell, March 23, 1954, ACW diary, B1 (2), DDEPL; Lester Markel, in "Report from 'Foggy Bottom,'" *The New York Times Magazine*, March 28, 1954, identified "two great fears: the fear of depression and the fear of communism."

9. Hagerty diary, April 2, 1954, JHP, B1; DDE, notes for speech, DDE diary, April 3, 1954, B6, (3), DDEPL.

10. Legislative Supplementary Notes, Apr. 5, 1954, DDE diary Series, B4, Staff Notes, DDEPL; Hagerty diary, Apr. 5, 1954, JHP, B1 (2); Shanley diary, BSP, B2, VI (5), 1500–01.

11. "Television in Review," Apr. 6, 1954, ACW diary, B2 (3), DDEPL.

12. Eisenhower Radio and TV Address, Apr. 5, 1954, *PPP*.

13. Hagerty diary, Apr. 6, 1954, JHP, B1 (2); DDE diary, Apr. 6, 1954, B5, Phone Calls (2), DDEPL.

14. Peter Kihss, "H-Bomb Held Back," *The New York Times*, Apr. 7, 1954; A. M. Sperber, *Murrow: His Life and Times* (New York: Fordham University Press, 1999), 448–53.

15. DDE, News Conference, Apr. 7, 1954, *PPP*; Elie Abel, "Eisenhower Sees No Need to Build a Larger H-bomb," and "Eisenhower Declares Murrow Is His Friend," *The New York Times*, Apr. 7, 1954; Sperber, *Murrow*, 453; Hagerty diary, Apr. 7, 1954, JHP, B1 (2).

16. "Drama Explodes Where Jenkins Is," *The New York Times*, Apr. 11, 1954; W. H. Lawrence, "Tennessean Gets Post of Counsel," *The New York Times*, Apr. 8, 1954; Ewald, *Who Killed Joe McCarthy?*, 303–4.

17. Hagerty diary, Apr. 8, 1954, JHP, B1 (2).

18. Brownell, *Report to the Nation*, "The Fight Against Communism," broadcast Apr. 9, 1954, Gerald D. Morgan Papers, B2 (Communism—Legislation), DDEPL; Hagerty diary, Apr. 8, 1954, JHP, B1 (2); "The Communist Conspiracy," *The New York Times*, Apr. 10, 1954.

19. Hagerty diary, Apr. 8 and 9, 1954, JHP, B1 (2).

20. Hagerty diary, Apr. 9 and 10, 1954, JHP, B1 (2); "McCarthy on H-Bomb," *The New York Times*, Apr. 10, 1954.

21. Hagerty diary, Apr. 11, 1954, JHP, B1 (2).

22. Hagerty diary, Apr. 13, 1954, JHP, B1; "Dr. Oppeneimer Suspended," *The New York Times*, Apr. 13, 1954.

23. Hagerty diary, Apr. 13, 1954, JHP, B1.

24. "Oppenheimer Action Late, M'Carthy Says," *The New York Times*, Apr. 14, 1954.

25. "M'Carthy Queried on Political Aims," *The New York Times*, Apr. 10, 1954.

26. W. H. Lawrence, "M'Carthy Gains Delay in Inquiry," *The New York Times*, Apr. 10, 1954; "Mundt Will Limit M'Carthy Inquiry," *The New York Times*, Apr. 11, 1954.

27. W. H. Lawrence, "Mundt Requests Inquiry Previews," *The New York Times*, Apr. 13, 1954; "Mundt Envisages Case for Perjury" and Foster, Article I—No Title, *The New York Times*, Apr. 5, 1954.

28. "The 'Ground Rules'" and W. H. Lawrence, "Army Bolsters Its Charges," *The New York Times*, Apr. 15, 1954; "Text of Army Bill of Particulars," *The New York Times*, Apr. 16, 1954; Ewald, *Who Killed Joe McCarthy?*, 307–8.

29. Welch to Stevens, Apr. 16, 1954, Phone Notes, Secretary of the Army (21), FASP, Eyes Only, B9; W. H. Lawrence, "M'Carthy to Shun Inquiry" and "McCarthy Accuses Symington," *The New York Times*, Apr. 16, 1954.

30. The report on Cohn's letter is found at the end of "Text of Army Bill of Particulars," *The New York Times*, Apr. 16, 1954.

31. "M'Carthy Pressed by Mundt to Quit Inquiry Entirely," *The New York Times*, Apr. 17, 1954; "McCarthy Is Vague," *The New York Times*, Apr. 17, 1954; Ewald, *Who Killed Joe McCarthy?*, 309.

32. "Mundt to Meet McCarthy Today," *The New York Times*, Apr. 19, 1954; "McCarthy Reported Willing to Limit His Inquiry Role," *The New York Times*, Apr. 20, 1954.

33. "Texts of McCarthy 46-Point Charges and Hensel Reply," *The New York Times*, Apr. 21, 1954; "M'Carthy in Reply Says Defense Aide Profited in War," *The New York Times*, Apr. 21, 1954; Ewald, *Who Killed Joe McCarthy?*, 309–10.

34. Hensel Statement, Apr. 20, 1954; George J. Gould to JEH, Apr. 21, 1954; Memorandum, Office of the Assistant Secretary of Defense, possibly to Sherman Adams, Adams Papers, all in B10 (5), McCarthy Hearings—Memoranda, Dartmouth; " 'Barefaced Lies,' Hensel Declares," *The New York Times*, Apr. 21, 1954.

35. Shanley diary, Apr. 21, 1954, BSP, B2, VI (5) 1514; Hensel to Welch, Apr. 21, 1954, Phone Notes, Secretary of the Army (21), FASP, Eyes Only, B9; Ewald, *Who Killed Joe McCarthy?*, 312; George Gallup, "Majority Supports Stevens," *The Washington Post*, Apr. 21, 1954.

36. "McCarthy-Army Hearing Rules," *The New York Times*, Apr. 21, 1954.

37. John G. Adams, *Without Precedent: The Story of the Death of McCarthyism* (New York: Norton, 1983), 161–62; Ewald, *Who Killed Joe McCarthy?*, 313–16, provides additional detail on the scene, the dress of the principals, and so on.

CHAPTER 13: THE EISENHOWER-MCCARTHY HEARINGS

1. Thomas C. Reeves, *The Life and Times of Joe McCarthy* (New York: Stein & Day, 1982), 596; "Hearing Room Is like Circus," *The New York Times*, Apr. 23, 1954.

2. Karl E. Mundt, unpublished manuscript, p. 11, Dakota State College, Madison, SD.

3. Sidney Zion, *The Autobiography of Roy Cohn* (Secaucus, NJ: Lyle Stuart, 1988), 127.

4. John G. Adams, *Without Precedent: The Story of the Death of McCarthyism* (New York: Norton, 1983), 206.

5. Ibid., 162–63; Hearings (Army-McCarthy) Before the Special Subcommittee on Investigations of the Committee on Government Operations, 83rd Congress, pt. 1, Apr. 22, 1954, 27–30.

6. James Reston, "McCarthy Changes Plan," *The New York Times*, Apr. 23, 1954; David M. Oshinsky, *A Conspiracy So Immense: The World of Joe McCarthy* (New York: Oxford University Press, 1983, 2005), 418; Army-McCarthy Hearings Transcript, Subcommittee on Investigations, pt. 1, Apr. 22, 1954, 31.

7. Colegrove, "For a Moment Bob Stevens Was the U. S. Army," probably April 23, 1954, *New York Herald Tribune*, Gruenther Records, B6, McCarthy News Clippings (2), DDEPL; The Gruenther copy bears the stamped date of April 21, inaccurate since that was the day prior to the first day of hearings; J. Adams, *Without Precedent*, 164; Army-McCarthy Hearings Transcript, Subcommittee on Investigations, pt. 1, Apr. 22, 1954, 81–82.

8. W. H. Lawrence, "Stevens Swears M'Carthy Falsified," *The New York Times*, Apr. 23, 1954; Reeves, *The Life and Times of Joe McCarthy*, 598; Stevens Testimony, Army-McCarthy Hearings Transcript, Subcommittee on Investigations, pt. 1, Apr. 22, 1954, 79–83, 89–98.

9. Joseph and Stewart Alsop, "The Seventh Principal," *The Washington Post*, Apr. 26, 1954; President's Appointment Schedule, April 22, 1954, Miller Center online.

10. DDE, Speech to American Newspaper Publishers Association, Apr. 22, 1954, *PPP.*

11. DDE to Hazlett, Apr. 27, 1954, *DDEP*, no. 848.

12. Walter Lippmann, "The President and the Press," *The Washington Post*, April 26, 1954.

13. DDE, President's Remarks at Lincoln's Birthplace, Apr. 23, 1954, *PPP.*

14. W. H. Lawrence, "Senate Inquiry Subpoenas All Data on Monitored Calls," *The New York Times*, Apr. 24, 1954; John Chadwick, "Mundt Signs Subpenas for Phone Data," *The Washington Post*, Apr. 25, 1954; Reeves, *The Life and Times of Joe McCarthy*, 598.

15. JFD to DDE, DDE diary, Apr. 23, 1954, B6 (1), DDEPL; DDE to JFD, April 23, 1954, *DDEP*, no. 839; Hagerty diary, Apr. 24–25, 1954, JHP, B1.

16. Hagerty diary, Apr. 26, 1954, JHP, B1.

17. Seaton to Sherman Adams, Adams Papers, B10 (5), Army-McCarthy McCarthy Hearings, Memoranda, Dartmouth; Brownell to Sherman Adams, May 3, 1954, Morgan Papers, B15, Investigations— Congressional (3), DDEPL.

18. J. Adams, *Without Precedent*, 179; W. H. Lawrence, "Army Charges a 'Doctored' Picture," *The New York Times*, Apr. 28, 1954; Reeves, *The Life and Times of Joe McCarthy*, 600–3.

19. J. Adams, *Without Precedent*, 178–81; Oshinsky, *A Conspiracy So Immense*, 426–27; Reeves, *The Life and Times of Joe McCarthy*, 600–3.

20. Shuster, "That Calm 'Man Named Welch,'" *The New York Times*, May 3, 1954; Army-McCarthy Hearings, Subcommittee on Investigations, pt. 14, Apr. 30, 1954, 543; Reeves, *The Life and Times of Joe McCarthy*, 603; Ewald, account of entire doctored photograph episode, in *Who Killed Joe McCarthy?* (New York: Simon & Schuster, 1984), 325–31.

21. Handwritten note, FASP, Eyes Only, B4, McCarthy (3).

22. Ewald, *Who Killed Joe McCarthy?*, 337; Reeves, *The Life and Times of Joe McCarthy*, 608–12.

23. W. H. Lawrence, "M'Carthy on Stand," *The New York Times*, May 6, 1954; J. Adams, *Without Precedent*, 181.

24. Ewald, *Who Killed Joe McCarthy?*, 339; Reeves, *The Life and Times of Joe McCarthy*, 612; W. H. Lawrence, "Secret FBI Paper Used by M'Carthy," *The New York Times*, May 5, 1954.

25. Arthur Krock, "In the Nation," *The New York Times*, May 4, 1954.

26. Closed-Door Hearing, Thursday, May 6, 1954, 245, U.S. Senate, Special Subcommittee on Investigations of the Committee on Government Operations, Washington, DC, US Senate website.

27. Ewald, *Who Killed Joe McCarthy?*, 341–43; Oshinsky, *A Conspiracy So Immense*, 436–38.

28. Hagerty diary, Apr. 29, 1954, JHP, B1; "Ike Unaware of McCarthy on 'Stump,'" *The New York Times*, Apr. 30, 1954.

29. "McCarthy Dispute Irks the President," *The New York Times*, Apr. 30, 1954; "Army–McCarthy Hearing Stirs Scorn of President," *The Washington Post*, Apr. 30, 1954; DDE, News Conference, Apr. 29, 1954, *PPP*.

30. "White House Aide Denies Move to Halt Hearings," *The New York Times*, May 1, 1954.

31. J. Adams, *Without Precedent*, 172.

32. Herbert Brownell, Jr., *Advising Ike: The Memoirs of Attorney General Herbert Brownell* (Lawrence: University Press of Kansas, 1993), 260.

33. Charles E. Potter, *Days of Shame* (New York: Coward-McCann, 1965), 182; DDE to Bullis, May 6, 1954, *DDEP*, no. 862; Ewald, *Who Killed Joe McCarthy?*, 343.

34. Reeves, *The Life and Times of Joe McCarthy*, 605, details a proposal Senator Potter claims he made to Eisenhower for ending the hearings on May 3; however, the accuracy of Potter's claims in his memoirs is open to question, especially his assertion that Ike wanted "an immediate end to the hearings." Ewald, *Who Killed Joe McCarthy?*, 343–44, assumes erroneously that Welch originated the proposal to limit testimony to the two principals, Stevens and McCarthy, and that Robert Stevens vetoed the deal. The evidence suggests otherwise

and that Welch had simply adopted an initially courteous tone re-
garding the Dirksen proposal. See Roy Cohn, *McCarthy* (New York:
New American Library, 1968), 155; Murray Marder, "GOP Move to
End Quiz Is Blocked," *The Washington Post*, May 5, 1954.

35. Army-McCarthy Hearings, pts. 17 and 19, May 4–5, 1954, 655–58,
    716; the entire effort to truncate the hearings, May 3–5, is tran-
    scribed in pts. 15–20.

36. DDE, News Conference, May 5, 1954, *PPP*; Anthony Leviero, "Ei-
    senhower Backs Stevens," *The New York Times*, May 6, 1954.

37. DDE to Brownell, May 5, 1954, DDE diary, B5, Phone Calls (1),
    DDEPL.

38. Dwight D. Eisenhower, *The White House Years: Mandate for Change*
    (Garden City, NY: Doubleday, 1963), 341, 356, 373, 340–75; Ron-
    ald H. Spector, *Advice and Support: The Early Years, 1941–1960* (New
    York: Free Press, 1985), noted that Eisenhower set out six conditions
    that would have to be met "before the President would agree to
    ask Congress for authority to commit American forces," 212; W. H.
    Lawrence, "Challenges Rule," *The New York Times*, May 7, 1954.

39. Cohn, *McCarthy*, 155–57; Reeves, *The Life and Times of Joe McCarthy*,
    613–15, blends Cohn's account into Dirksen's third attempt to end
    the hearings on May 11; John Morris, "Inquiry Colleagues Oppose
    Dirksen Plan," *The New York Times*, May 9, 1954; Jack Bell and Mil-
    ton Kelly, "Democrats Frown on Plan to Shut Probe Door," *The
    Washington Post*, May 9, 1954; Clayton Knowles, "M'Clellan Warns
    G.O.P.," *The New York Times*, May 10, 1954.

40. Hagerty diary, May 10, 1954, JHP, B1.

41. Dirksen Motion and Army's Position on Proposal, FASP, Eyes Only,
    B4, McCarthy (2); Cohn, *McCarthy*, 157; Army-McCarthy Hearings
    Transcript, Subcommittee on Investigations, pt. 26, May 11, 1954,
    971.

42. Hagerty diary, May 11, 1954, JHP, B1; W. H. Lawrence, "2 Plans to
    Speed M'Carthy Hearing," *The New York Times*, May 11, 1954; Fos-
    ter, "Plan to Cut Probe Short Hailed by McCarthy," *The Washington
    Post*, May 10, 1954.

43. Mundt's commitment to vote "no" if the army objected to the
    Dirksen proposal is in the Army-McCarthy Hearings Transcript,

Subcommittee on Investigations, pt. 26, May 11, 1954, 979; the remainder of the debate is detailed in the subsequent pages of pts. 26 and 27, ending with the vote on 998.

44. Hagerty diary, May 11, 1954, JHP, B1; W. H. Lawrence, "Veto by Stevens," *The New York Times*, May 12, 1954; Murray Marder, "Stevens Veto Nips Plan," *The Washington Post*, May 12, 1954.

45. Cohn, *McCarthy*, 159.

46. Hagerty diary, May 12, 1954, JHP, B1; Ewald, *Who Killed Joe McCarthy?*, 345.

47. Account by Professor Ann Lousin, John Marshall Law School, Chicago, IL, based on phone conversation with the author, confirmed by e-mail May 26, 2013.

CHAPTER 14: PROTECTING THE PRESIDENT

1. Joseph and Stewart Alsop, "Political Silver Lining," *The Washington Post*, May 12, 1954.

2. DDE, News Conference, May 12, 1954, *PPP*; Clayton Knowles, "President Decries Party Aspersions," *The New York Times*, May 13, 1954; Anthony Leviero, "Eisenhower Firm," *The New York Times*, May 13, 1954.

3. Lodge to DDE, "Eyes Only," May 7, 1954, HCLP, Lodge-Eisenhower Corres., reel 28; DDE to Lodge, May 10, 1954, *DDEP*, no. 866.

4. Lodge to Brownell, July 12, 1974, Lodge 11, reel 2, HCLP; Henry Cabot Lodge, Jr., *As It Was* (New York: Norton, 1976), 137.

5. Warren Unna, "Adams Role on Stand," *The Washington Post*, May 13, 1954; John G. Adams, *Without Precedent: The Story of the Death of McCarthyism* (New York: Norton, 1983), 190, 210–13.

6. J. Adams, *Without Precedent*, 195.

7. Ibid., 190–96; Thomas C. Reeves, *The Life and Times of Joe McCarthy* (New York: Stein & Day, 1982), 617.

8. Hagerty diary, May 13, 1954, JHP, B1.

9. DDE to Wilson, DDE diary, May 13, 1954, *DDEP*, no. 874; "Wilson Reaches Tokyo." *The New York Times*, March 14, 1954; the longer, more formal version of this letter was hand-delivered to Wilson on

May 17, the day the president issued an executive order forbidding testimony by his advisers, *DDEP*, no. 879.

10. Anderson to Stevens, May 13, 1954, FASP, Eyes Only, B4, McCarthy.

11. Hagerty diary, May 14, 1954, JHP, B1.

12. J. Adams, *Without Precedent*, 196, 210–13.

13. Murray Marder, "Administration Gag on Adams," *The Washington Post*, May 15, 1954; W. H. Lawrence, "Executive Branch Silences Adams," *The New York Times*, May 15, 1954.

14. Army-McCarthy Hearings Transcript, Subcommittee on Investigations, May 14, 1954, pt. 32, 1169; Reeves, *The Life and Times of Joe McCarthy*, 617.

15. J. Adams, *Without Precedent*, 196–97.

16. Lawrence, "Executive Branch Silences Adams."

17. J. Adams, *Without Precedent*, 196–97.

18. Hagerty diary, May 14, 1954, JHP, B1.

19. Hagerty diary, May 15, 1954, JHP, B1; Lawrence, "Executive Branch Silences Adams."

20. Walter Lippmann, "Today and Tomorrow: The Big Brawl," *The Washington Post*, May 16, 1954; Arthur Krock, "Senate's Caucus Room Stage for High Drama," *The New York Times*, May 16, 1954.

21. Herbert Foster, "Ike Expected to Bar Aides' Testimony," *The Washington Post*, May 16, 1954; John Morris, "Mundt Supports Silence by Army," *The New York Times*, May 16, 1954.

22. Brownell, memorandum, May 17, 1954, Gerald D. Morgan Papers, B15, Investigations—Congressional (3), DDEPL; Hagerty diary, May 17, 1954, JHP, B1.

23. J. Adams, *Without Precedent*, 200.

24. Murray Marder, "Ike Silences Army," *The Washington Post*, May 18, 1954; W. H. Lawrence, "Senator Is Irate," *The New York Times*, May 18, 1954.

25. DDE to the Secretary of Defense, May 17, 1954, *DDEP*, no. 879; Administrative Series, B25, McCarthy Letters, DDEPL; Fred I. Greenstein, *The Hidden-Hand Presidency: Eisenhower as Leader* (Baltimore: Johns Hopkins, 1982), 205; J. Adams, *Without Precedent*, 201; Reeves, *The Life and Times of Joe McCarthy*, 617; Irwin F. Gellman, *The President and the Apprentice: Eisenhower and Nixon, 1952–1961*

(New Haven: Yale University Press, 2015), 118; Adams's presentation of the president's letter and the attorney general's memorandum is found in the Army-McCarthy Hearings Transcript, Subcommittee on Investigations, May 17, pts. 34–35, beginning on 1248.

26. Karl E. Mundt, unpublished manuscript, 11, Dakota State College, Madison, SD.

27. Sidney Zion, *The Autobiography of Roy Cohn* (Secaucus, NJ: Lyle Stuart, 1988), 138–39.

28. W. H. Lawrence, "Senator Is Irate," *The New York Times*, May 18, 1954.

29. J. Adams, *Without Precedent*, 201–2; Marder, "Ike Silences Army."

30. Roy Cohn, *McCarthy* (New York: New American Library, 1968), 176–77; Sherman Adams, *First-Hand Report: The Inside Story of the Eisenhower Administration* (London: Hutchinson, 1961), 130–31.

31. Marder. "Ike Silences Army." W. H. Lawrence, "Two Senators Ask M'Carthy Hearing Resume," *The New York Times*, May 19, 1954.

32. Murray Marder, "Search Begun to End Impasse," *The Washington Post*, May 19, 1954.

33. Hagerty diary, May 18, 1954, JHP, B1.

34. DDE, Address on Freedom Celebration Day, May 18, 1954, *PPP*; Edward Folliard, "Ike Shows He Is Still for Stevens," *The Washington Post*, May 19, 1954; Knowles, "Eisenhower Backs Stevens," *The New York Times*, May 19, 1954; Hagerty diary, May 18, 1954, JHP, B1.

35. DDE, News Conference, May 19, 1954, *PPP*.

36. Hagerty diary, May 19, 1954, JHP, B1.

37. Statement by Secretary of the Army, Robert T. Stevens, May 19, 1954, Sherman Adams Papers, B10 (5), McCarthy Hearings—Memoranda, C. Dartmouth; Anthony Leviero, "Let Chips Fall," *The New York Times*, May 20, 1954; Reeves, *The Life and Times of Joe McCarthy*, 618.

38. Hagerty diary, May 19, 1954, JHP, B1.

39. "Mundt Says Army Quiz Will Reopen on Monday," *The Washington Post*, May 20, 1954; Leviero, "Let Chips Fall."

40. *The Gallup Poll, Public Opinion 1935–1971*, ed. William P. Hansen and Fred L. Israel, vol. 2, *1949–1958* (New York: Random House, 1972); Hagerty diary, May 20, 1954, JHP, B1; Reeves, *The Life and Times of Joe McCarthy*, 619.

41. Hagerty, May 20–21, 1954, JHP, B1.

42. W. H. Lawrence, "M'Carthy Gears Plan," and Richard Johnston, "M'Carthy Asserts He Will Testify," *The New York Times*, May 23, 1954.

43. Interview with Nixon, Feb. 26, 1954, Arthur Krock Black Book Interviews, SGMML; William Bragg Ewald, Jr., *Who Killed Joe McCarthy?* (New York: Simon & Schuster, 1984), 223; Greenstein, *The Hidden-Hand Presidency*, 187, says the interview was on Feb. 25 (an error) but states that his interviews with Lodge, Brownell, and Sherman Adams in the 1980s confirmed that "Eisenhower was well aware of the Cohn-Schine abuses and was countenancing the strategy of using them as the vehicle for attacking McCarthy"; Arthur Krock, "Eisenhower 'No' in Line," *The New York Times*, May 23, 1954.

44. W. H. Lawrence, "M'Carthy Alleges Army's Evidence Is Contradictory," *The New York Times*, May 25, 1954; Murray Marder, "Senator Accuses Army Secretary," *The Washington Post*, May 25, 1954; J. Adams, *Without Precedent*, 206–7.

45. Walter Lippmann, "Disorderly Government," *The Washington Post*, June 3, 1954.

46. J. Adams, *Without Precedent*, 206–8.

CHAPTER 15: "NO SENSE OF DECENCY?"

1. Murray Marder, "Senator Accuses Army Secretary of Either Perjury or 'Bad Memory,'" *The Washington Post*, May 25, 1954; W. H. Lawrence, "M'Carthy Alleges Army's Evidence Is Contradictory," *The New York Times*, May 25, 1954; Lawrence, "M'Carthy Inquiry Dismisses Cases," *The New York Times*, May 27, 1954; Marder, "Probe Votes Not to Act," *The Washington Post*, May 27, 1954; Hagerty diary, May 26, 1954, JHP, B1; Thomas C. Reeves, *The Life and Times of Joe McCarthy* (New York: Stein & Day, 1982), 621–23.

2. Hagerty diary, May 27, 1954, JHP, B1.

3. Hagerty diary, May 27–28, 1954, JHP, B1; "Dirksen Denies Whitewash," *The Washington Post*, May 28, 1954; "Under the Carpet," *The Washington Post*, May 28, 1954.

4. Murray Marder, "U. S. Employees Told Their Oath to Nation Tops Bans on Secrets," *The Washington Post*, May 28, 1954; Reeves, *The Life and Times of Joe McCarthy*, 623.

5. Hagerty diary, May 28, 1954, JHP, B1, DDEPL; Herbert Brownell, Jr., *Advising Ike: The Memoirs of Attorney General Herbert Brownell* (Lawrence: University Press of Kansas, 1993), 260; Statement by the Attorney General, May 28, 1954, DDE diary, B7, PDEPL, May 1954.

6. Hagerty diary, May 28, 1954, JHP, B1.

7. W. H. Lawrence, "Charges Threats," *The New York Times*, May 28, 1954.

8. W. H. Lawrence, "Senators Seek to Determine Just What Work Schine Did," *The New York Times*, May 29, 1954; Joseph Loftus, "Senator Retorts," *The New York Times*, May 29, 1954; Reeves, *The Life and Times of Joe McCarthy*, 624; Hagerty diary, May 28, 1954, JHP, B1.

9. ACW diary, May 29, 1954, B2 (1), DDEPL.

10. Roscoe Drummond, "McCarthy Issue," *The Washington Post*, May 31, 1954.

11. Hagerty diary, May 30–31, 1954, JHP, B1.

12. DDE, President's Address, Columbia University Bicentennial Dinner, May 31, 1954, PPP; Edward Folliard, "Decries 'Thirst for Personal Power,'" *The Washington Post*, June 1, 1954; Grutzner, "Eisenhower Warns U.S. of Demagogues," *The New York Times*, June 1, 1954.

13. Hagerty diary, May 31, 1954, JHP, B1.

14. Hagerty diary, May 28, 1954, JHP, B1.

15. Robert Albright, "M'Carthy Hit as Menace," *The Washington Post*, June 2, 1954; William S. White, "Flanders Likens M'Carthy, Hitler," *The New York Times*, June 2, 1954; Reeves, *The Life and Times of Joe McCarthy*, 624–25; Irwin F. Gellman, *The President and the Apprentice: Eisenhower and Nixon, 1952–1961* (New Haven: Yale University Press, 2015), 119–20.

16. Roy Cohn, *McCarthy* (New York: New American Library, 1968), 244–45; the author interviewed a veteran journalist active during the period and asked him what "hold" he thought Roy Cohn had on McCarthy, that the senator had not dismissed him. The journalist quickly responded, "We thought McCarthy was gay. We could not publish it but that is what we thought."

17. DDE, News Conference, June 2, 1954, PPP; "President Glares Down Question," *The New York Times*, June 3, 1954.

18. Seaton to McCarthy, June 3, 1954, FASP, Eyes Only, B4, McCarthy

(1); "U.S. Bars Secrecy, Text of Seaton Letter to McCarthy," *The New York Times*, June 4, 1954.

19. Memorandum by Sherman Adams, June 4, 1954, FASP, Eyes Only, B4, McCarthy (1); Anderson to Stevens, May 13, 1954, FASP, Eyes Only, B4, McCarthy.

20. "Texts of Telephone Calls," *The New York Times* and *The Washington Post*, June 6, 1954; "Senator Dared Stevens," *The New York Times*, June 6, 1954.

21. W. H. Lawrence, "M'Carthy Bids Symington Quit," *The New York Times*, June 5, 1954; Richard Johnston, "McCarthy Accuses Symington of 'Plot,'" *The Washington Post*, June 6, 1954; Murray Marder, "Democrat Warns Against 'Anarchy,'" *The Washington Post*, June 8, 1954.

22. Murray Marder. "McCarthy Is Told to See Psychiatrist," *The Washington Post*, June 9, 1954; W. H. Lawrence, "Democrats Fight Plan to Cut Short M'Carthy Inquiry," *The New York Times*, June 9, 1954; "McCarthy Called Genius," *The Washington Post*, June 9, 1954.

23. Fred Fisher Memorandum, dictated June 10, 1954, provided to the author by Duane Krohnke; J. Adams, *Without Precedent*, 227; Reeves, *The Life and Times of Joe McCarthy*, 628–29.

24. The entire Welch-McCarthy confrontation is transcribed in the Army-McCarthy Hearings, Subcommittee on Investigations, June 9, 1954, pt. 59, 2424–30; W. H. Lawrence, "Exchange Bitter," *The New York Times*, June 10, 1954; Murray Marder, "Senator Is Flayed," *The Washington Post*, June 10, 1954; Reeves, *The Life and Times of Joe McCarthy*, 628–32.

25. "Calls Fisher a 'Fine Kid,'" *The New York Times*, June 10, 1954; "M'Carthy Speaks," *The New York Times*, June 10, 1954.

26. J. Adams, *Without Precedent*, 226–29.

27. "McCarthy Takes Stand," *The Washington Post*, June 10, 1954; J. Adams, *Without Precedent*, 231–33; Hagerty diary, June 7, 8, 10, 1954, JHP, B1; DDE, News Conference, June 10, 1954, *PPP*.

28. DDE, Address to District Chairs, National Citizens for Eisenhower Congressional Committee, June 10, 1954, *PPP*; Hagerty diary, June 9, 1954, JHP, B1.

29. Ralph E. Flanders, *Senator from Vermont* (Boston: Little, Brown, 1961), 260; Reeves, *The Life and Times of Joe McCarthy*, 633.

30. Army-McCarthy Hearings, Subcommittee on Investigations, June 11, 1954, pt. 62, 2588–91; Karl Mundt, "Highlights of the Army-McCarthy Hearings," unpublished manuscript, chap. 5, Dakota State College, Madison, SD; Cohn, *McCarthy*, 246; Robert Albright, "Motion Is Filed in Senate," *The Washington Post*, June 12, 1954; C. P. Trussell, "Flanders Moves in Senate," *The New York Times*, June 12, 1954.

31. "Flanders Sets Deadline," *The Washington Post*, June 14, 1954; Knowles, "Flanders Slates Early Showdown," *The New York Times*, June 14, 1954; Egan, "Flanders' Motion to Curb M'Carthy Hit by Knowland," *The New York Times*, June 13, 1954; "Flanders' Move to 'Bump' McCarthy," *The Washington Post*, June 13, 1954; DDE to Brownell, ACW diary, June 15, 1954, B2 (2).

32. "Flanders' Home Given Police Guard," *The Washington Post*, June 15, 1954.

33. W. H. Lawrence, "M'Carthy Hearing May Finish Today," *The New York Times*, June 16, 1954; Murray Marder, "Army-McCarthy Hearings Near Conclusion," *The Washington Post*, June 16, 1954; Marder, "Senator Draws Rebuke," *The Washington Post*, June 17, 1954.

34. Murray Marder, "Record Declared Saturated with Perjury," *The Washington Post*, June 18, 1954; W. H. Lawrence, "M'Carthy Hearings End on 36th Day," *The New York Times*, June 18, 1954; "Schine Ordered to Report Today," *The Washington Post*, June 18, 1954; Reeves, *The Life and Times of Joe McCarthy*, 634–37.

35. J. Adams, *Without Precedent*, 232–37.

36. "Army Vindicated, Stevens Asserts," *The New York Times*, June 19, 1954.

37. Roscoe Drummond, "Highly Publicized Distractions," *New York Herald Tribune*, June 14, 1954.

38. Robert Stevens, conversation with Ann Lousin, e-mail account to the author, May 25, 2013; Joseph Alsop, "McCarthy Crackdown Ordered," *The Washington Post*, June 20, 1954.

39. Fred I. Greenstein, *The Hidden-Hand Presidency: Eisenhower as Leader* (Baltimore: John Hopkins University Press, 1982).

40. DDE, News Conference, June 16, 1954, *PPP*; "President Dodges 2 Questions," *The Washington Post*, June 17, 1954.

41. Hagerty diary, June 16, 1954, JHP, B1.

42. "Welch Sees Eisenhower," *The New York Times*, June 19, 1954; Hagerty diary, June 18, 1954, JHP, B1; Reeves, *The Life and Times of Joe McCarthy*, 636.

EPILOGUE

1. Ralph E. Flanders, *Senator from Vermont* (Boston: Little, Brown, 1961), 260; Karl Mundt, "Highlights of the Army-McCarthy Hearings," unpublished manuscript, chap. 5, 1–2, Dakota State University, Madison, SD; Thomas C. Reeves, *The Life and Times of Joe McCarthy* (New York: Stein & Day, 1982), 377–416, 633, 641–44; James Cross Giblin, *The Rise and Fall of Senator Joe McCarthy* (New York: Clarion Books, 2009), 131–41, 344.

2. Reeves, *The Life and Times of Joe McCarthy*, 645–46; Arthur V. Watkins, *Enough Rope* (Englewood Cliffs, NJ: Prentice-Hall, 1969) 3; Giblin, *The Rise and Fall of Senator Joe McCarthy*, 347.

3. DDE, News Conference, Aug. 4, 1954, *PPP*.

4. Reeves, *The Life and Times of Joe McCarthy*, 645–46, 648–49; Watkins, *Enough Rope*, ix.

5. "Nixon Ascribes Loss to Split over Reds," *The New York Times*, Nov. 9, 1954; Gallup Polls, *The New York Times*, Nov. 6 and 7, 1954.

6. "Text of McCarthy Speech," *The New York Times*, Nov. 11, 1954; Murray Marder, "Lawmaker Labels Investigative Body 'Hand-Maiden' of Communist Party," *The Washington Post*, Nov. 10, 1954; Watkins, *Enough Rope*, 132–33; Reeves, *The Life and Times of Joe McCarthy*, 656–57.

7. Watkins, *Enough Rope*, 129; Murray Marder, "McCarthy Warned on New 'Abuse' of Senators," *The Washington Post*, Nov. 11, 1954.

8. Reeves, *The Life and Times of Joe McCarthy*, 658.

9. Ibid., 644, 660–61; David M. Oshinsky, *A Conspiracy So Immense: The World of Joe McCarthy* (Oxford University Press, 2005), 488.

10. "Text of McCarthy Speech," *The Washington Post*, Nov. 30, 1954.

11. "Pleas on Censure Taken to Capitol," *The New York Times*, Dec. 2, 1954; Anthony Leviero, "Final Move Today," *The New York Times*, Dec. 2, 1954.

12. "The Censure Proposals," *The New York Times*, Dec. 2, 1954; Anthony Leviero, "Final Move Today," *The New York Times*, Dec. 2, 1954.

13. "McCarthy Asserts People Are Not Fooled," and "McCarthy Unit Resumes Public Inquiry Tuesday," *The New York Times*, Dec. 2, 1954.

14. William S. White, "Leader Votes 'No,'" *The New York Times*, Dec. 2, 1954; Anthony Leviero, "Final Move Today"; Hagerty diary, Dec. 1, 1954, JHP, B1a.

15. President's Appt. Schedule for Dec. 2, 1954, Miller Center, Dwight D. Eisenhower Appointment Schedule.

16. DDE, News Conference, Dec. 2, 1954, *PPP*; William S. White, "Eisenhower Warns G. O. P. Right Wing," *The New York Times*, Dec. 3, 1954.

17. Watkins, *Enough Rope*, 149–51; "Text of Final Resolution," *The New York Times*, Dec. 3, 1954; Anthony Leviero, " 'Censure' in Title Stricken by Nixon," *The New York Times*, Dec. 4, 1954; Anthony Leviero, "Republicans Split," *The New York Times*, Dec. 3, 1954; the breakdown of the vote, senator by senator, is found in the *Washington Sunday Star*, Dec. 5, 1954.

18. Hagerty diary, Dec. 3–4, 1954, JHP, B1a; ACW diary, Dec. 4, 1954, B3 (5), DDEPL; John Chadwick, "Ike Praises Watkins for Splendid Job," *The Washington Post*, Dec. 5, 1954.

19. Anthony Leviero, "M'Carthy Breaks with Eisenhower," and "Text of McCarthy Statement," *The New York Times*, Dec. 8, 1954.

20. John Adams, *Without Precedent: The Story of the Death of McCarthyism* (New York: Norton, 1983), 249.

21. Legislative Leaders Meeting, June 21, 1955, WHOSS, Minnich Series, B1, Msc.-Mc; William S. White, "Knowland Shuns M'Carthy Attack," *The New York Times*, June 17, 1955; White, "Senate, 77–4, Balks McCarthy on Big 4," *The New York Times*, June 23, 1955.

22. J. Adams, *Without Precedent*, 258–59.

23. T. C. Reeves, *The Life and Times of Joe McCarthy*, 671.

24. The article was published in *Reader's Digest* in April 1969, after Eisenhower's death on March 28; the author is indebted to Timothy Rives, the deputy director of the Dwight D. Eisenhower Presidential Library and Museum, for sharing the article draft from the Ben Hibbs Papers.

INDEX